Global Capital, Political Institutions, ͏ ͏ ͏ ͏ ͏ ͏ ͏ in Developed Welfare States

This book argues that the dramatic post-1970 rise in international capital mobility has not, as many claim, systematically contributed to the retrenchment of developed welfare states. Nor has globalization directly reduced the revenue-raising capacities of governments and undercut the political institutions that support the welfare state. Rather, institutional features of the polity and the welfare state determine the extent to which the economic and political pressures associated with globalization produce welfare state retrenchment. In systems characterized by inclusive electoral institutions, social corporatist interest representation and policy making, centralized political authority, and universal and social insurance–based program structures, pro–welfare state interests are relatively favored. In nations characterized by majoritarian electoral institutions, pluralist interest representation and policy making, decentralization of policy-making authority, and liberal program structure, the economic and political pressures attendant on globalization are translated into rollbacks of social protection. Consequently, globalization has had the least impact on the large welfare states of Northern Europe and the most effect on the already small welfare states of Anglo nations.

Duane Swank is associate professor of political science at Marquette University. He specializes in the international and comparative political economy of advanced capitalist democracies, comparative public policy, and European politics. His articles have appeared in such journals as the *American Journal of Political Science*, *American Political Science Review*, *Comparative Political Studies*, *European Journal of Political Research*, and *Political Studies*, as well as numerous edited volumes.

Cambridge Studies in Comparative Politics

General Editor

Margaret Levi   *University of Washington, Seattle*

Associate Editors

Robert H. Bates   *Harvard University*
Peter Hall   *Harvard University*
Stephen Hanson   *University of Washington, Seattle*
Peter Lange   *Duke University*
Helen Milner   *Columbia University*
Frances Rosenbluth   *Yale University*
Susan Stokes   *University of Chicago*
Sidney Tarrow   *Cornell University*

Other Books in the Series

Continued on the page following the index.

Global Capital, Political Institutions, and Policy Change in Developed Welfare States

DUANE SWANK

Marquette University

CAMBRIDGE
UNIVERSITY PRESS

CAMBRIDGE UNIVERSITY PRESS
Cambridge, New York, Melbourne, Madrid, Cape Town, Singapore, São Paulo

Cambridge University Press
40 West 20th Street, New York, NY 10011-4211, USA

www.cambridge.org
Information on this title: www.cambridge.org/9780521806688

First published 2002
Reprinted 2004, 2005

Printed in the United States of America

A catalog record for this publication is available from the British Library.

Library of Congress Cataloging in Publication Data

Swank, Duane.
Global capital, political institutions, and policy change in developed welfare states /
Duane Swank.
p. cm. – (Cambridge studies in comparative politics)
Includes bibliographical references and index.
ISBN 0-521-80668-2 – ISBN 0-521-00144-7 (pb.)
1. Welfare state. 2. Capital movements. 3. Globalization. 4. Comparative
government. I. Title. II. Series.
JC479. S9 2001
330.12′6–dc21   2001025914

ISBN-13   978-0-521-80668-8 hardback
ISBN-10   0-521-80668-2 hardback

ISBN-13   978-0-521-00144-1 paperback
ISBN-10   0-521-00144-7 paperback

For Melanie, my wife,
and in the memory of my parents,
Howard and Eva

Contents

Contents

List of Figures and Tables

Preface

This book finds its origins in my early 1990s work on the political economy of redistribution in the developed capitalist democracies. I have accumulated many debts since then and they ought now to be gratefully acknowledged. First, I wish to express my appreciation to the German Marshall Fund of the United States for providing a GMF Research Fellowship that made possible invaluable research, travel, and writing time during 1996 and 1997. In addition, the Marquette University Committee on Research provided generous financial support in the form of regular and summer faculty fellowships during 1996 and 1997. Second, I would like to thank the many individuals who provided helpful comments on my arguments and analyses. In particular, Keith Banting, Hans-Georg Betz, Markus Crepaz, Bernhard Ebbinghaus, John Freeman, Miriam Golden, Peter Hall, Torben Iversen, Desmond King, Anders Lindbom, Andrew Martin, Cathie Jo Martin, Kathleen McNamara, John Myles, Jonas Pontusson, Michael Shalev, and Sven Steinmo provided especially helpful suggestions and criticisms at one or more junctures (as have many other colleagues at the forums listed below). I am especially grateful to Francis Castles, Geoffrey Garrett, Paul Pierson, Dennis Quinn, John Stephens, and Michael Wallerstein for extensive discussions or written comments on material in the book. I have also learned a good deal about the political economy of advanced industrial societies by reading their work. Third, I wish to thank Lewis Bateman, Political Science Editor at Cambridge University Press, for sage advice and support of this manuscript, and to Cambridge's anonymous readers for very helpful comments on the first draft.

Most importantly, I would like to express my gratitude to Alexander Hicks of Emory University for countless conversations, critical comments, and occasional prodding with regard to the project. I have benefited immensely over the years from my collaboration with Alex on a number of papers on the welfare state, and Alex's Northwestern University graduate seminars in the early 1980s provided the original impetus for my study of comparative political economy.

In addition, I would like to express my sincere thanks to Christa-Barbara Wilson at the German Information Center in New York and to Agnes Gerlach of Inter Nationes in Bonn for invaluable assistance in organizing interviews with a broad array of German national policy makers, political party leaders and staff, and representatives of trade union and employer associations. For release of unpublished data utilized in this book, grateful acknowledgment is due Marco Doudeijns and Willem Adema of the Social Policy Division of the Organization for Economic Cooperation and Development in Paris, as well as Professors Miriam Golden, Michael Wallerstein, and Peter Lange (for early versions of their labor and industrial relations data set) and Dennis Quinn (for international financial liberalization data). Finally, I would also like to thank my graduate research assistants at Marquette University, especially Dengmeng Chen, Craig Goodman, Klaus Hertweck, Mariano "Paco" Iso, William Muck, and William Nichols, for exceptional research support during the past few years.

Early drafts of portions of the manuscript have been presented at conferences and colloquia. The papers and forums are: "Globalization, Political Institutions, and European Welfare States: The Corporatist Conservative Cases," presented at the 2000 Annual Meeting of the American Political Science Association, August 31–September 3, Washington, DC; "Globalization, Democracy, and the Welfare State: Why Political Institutions Are So Important in Shaping the Domestic Impact of Internationalization," presented to the Research Group on the Political Economy of European Integration, Center for International Affairs, Harvard University, November 6, 1998; "Globalization, Political Institutions, and European Welfare States," presented at the 11th Annual Conference of Europeanists, February 27–March 1, 1998, Baltimore; "Global Markets, Democratic Institutions, and the Public Economy in Advanced Market Economies," presented at the Conference on Internationalization and Democracy, University of Vienna, December 14–15, 1997, and Center for European Studies, Harvard University, March 6, 1998; "Internationalization, Political Institutions, and the Welfare State," and "Social Democratic Welfare States in the Global Economy: Scandinavia in Comparative Perspective," both presented at the 1997 Annual Meeting of the American Political Science Association, September, Washington, DC; "Funding the Welfare State: Globalization and the Taxation of Business in Advanced Market Economies," paper presented at the 1996 Annual Meeting of the American Political Science Association, September, San Francisco, the Workshop on Change and Continuity in Contemporary Capitalism, Duke University/University of North Carolina at Chapel Hill, May, 1997, and the Institute of Policy Research, Northwestern University, October, 1996, Evanston, IL; "Politics, Taxes, and the Structural Dependence of the State in a Global Economy," paper presented at the 1996 Annual Meetings of the Midwest Political Science Association, April, Chicago.

Sections of Chapters 2, 3, and 7 originally appeared as Political Economy of European Integration Working Paper 1.66, University of California Center for German and European Studies–Harvard Center for International Affairs. Portions of the analysis of the Nordic social democratic welfare states in Chapter 4 have been published in "Social Democratic Welfare States in the Global Economy: Scandinavia in Comparative Perspective," in Robert Geyer, Christine Ingebritsen, and Jonathon Moses, eds., *Globalization, Europeanization, and the End of Scandinavian Social Democracy?* (London and New York: Macmillan/St. Martin's, 2000), and are reprinted here with permission of Palgrave Publishers. I thank the editors of that volume for many insightful comments on my analysis of globalization and the Nordic welfare states. My initial arguments about globalization and taxation, elaborated in Chapter 7, were originally offered in "Funding the Welfare State: Globalization and the Taxation of Business in Advanced Market Economies," *Political Studies* 46 (No. 4, 1998), pp. 671–92; all of the empirical analysis of taxation in this volume is new. Excerpts from the original article are reprinted here with the permission of Blackwell Publishers. I thank the editor and anonymous referees for helpful suggestions on that work. Finally, after completion of the draft and empirical analysis of this volume, I have extended this volume's argument, first, to the relationships between internationalization and domestic welfare state pressures, political institutions, and social policy change and updated and broadened the analysis of a few of the basic empirical models to 1995 in "Political Institutions and Welfare State Restructuring: The Impact of Institutions on Social Policy Change in Developed Democracies," in Paul Pierson, ed., *The New Politics of the Welfare State* (New York: Oxford University Press, 2001). Excerpts from that article are reprinted here with permission of Oxford University Press. Second, I have extended portions of the volume's argument to the relationships between globalization, political institutions, and the scope of the public economy in "Mobile Capital, Democratic Institutions, and the Public Economy," *Journal of Comparative Policy Analysis* (August, 2001). Excerpts from that article are reprinted here with permission of Kluwer Academic Publishers.

1

Introduction

At first glance, the welfare states of the rich democracies appear to be alive and well. Governments in these nations devoted an average of 24 percent of national economic product to social protection in 1995; in 1980, the comparable figure was 20 percent.[1] Indeed, most observers of social welfare policy agree with Paul Pierson (1994, 1996) that the systems of social protection created during the first half of the twentieth century, and dramatically expanded during the third quarter of the century, have not been dismantled during the current era. At the same time, it is equally clear that the welfare states of advanced capitalist democracies have come under serious pressure. During the 1980s and 1990s, conservative governments in Britain, the United States, and the other Anglo democracies have reduced the generosity of benefits, tightened program eligibility, implemented cost controls in service delivery, and encouraged privatization of some social insurance and many social services. Neoliberal policy changes have not been confined to these right-of-center governments; Swedish, German, and other Western European governments of all ideological complexions have on occasion reduced pension and other social insurance benefits, limited benefit indexation, and restricted eligibility for unemployment compensation and social assistance. They have also imposed budget caps, user co-payments, and other cost-control measures for health and social services. Moreover, these efforts to restrain the

---

[1] Data pertain to the 1980 and 1995 18-nation averages for total social welfare expenditure (OECD definition) as percentages of Gross Domestic Product. The nations are: Australia, Austria, Belgium, Canada, Denmark, Finland, France, Germany, Ireland, Italy, Japan, the Netherlands, New Zealand, Norway, Sweden, Switzerland, the United Kingdom, and the United States. See Chapter 3 and Appendixes for full documentation and sources.

welfare state have occurred at a time of rising need for social protection (Clayton and Pontusson, 1998).

A widely discussed explanation of these changes in social welfare policy – and an argument with substantial implications for the viability of democratic institutions generally – is that globalization, especially the dramatic post-1960s rise in the international mobility of capital, forces all elected governments to roll back the welfare state.[2] In fact, contemporary neoliberal economists (e.g., McKenzie and Lee [1991]), Marxian analysts (e.g., Gill and Law [1988]; Ross and Trachte [1990]), international relations theorists (e.g. Cerny [1996]; Strange [1996]), and popular analysts (e.g., Greider [1997]) have all argued that the ability of international firms and financial institutions to shift assets across national borders forces incumbent governments (regardless of ideology or constituency) to reduce social welfare expenditures and to make social policy more market-conforming. This is purportedly the case because, in the presence of international capital mobility, governments must encourage internationally mobile firms to remain in the domestic economy, induce foreign enterprises to invest, and allay international financial market fears of high taxes, inflationary pressures, and economic inefficiency associated with moderate to large welfare states.

Scholars have also suggested that international capital mobility may weaken the welfare state through largely indirect mechanisms. Internationalization may force policy makers to reduce taxation of mobile assets and shift tax burdens to relatively less mobile factors; this may undercut redistribution as well as reduce the revenue-raising capacity of the state (e.g., McKenzie and Lee [1991]; Steinmo [1993]). Capital mobility may also undermine social corporatist institutions that support the welfare state (e.g., Kurzer [1993]; Mishra [1993]) and weaken or eliminate important elements of economic policy that promote the low unemployment necessary for maintenance of generous social protection (Huber and Stephens, 1998). The heart of the thesis is essentially an argument about "dimin-

---

[2] Numerous explanations for policy change in contemporary welfare states exist. Synoptic overviews of new welfare state pressures typically emphasize the adverse effects of post-1973 economic stagnation and rising unemployment, burgeoning public sector deficits, and demographic shifts (e.g., the "crisis of aging"); they also include the ascendence of neo-conservative critiques of the welfare state and the weakening of trade union movements and social democratic parties (Esping-Andersen, 1996b; George and Taylor-Gooby, 1996; Rhodes, 1997; van Kersbergen, 2000). In addition, some observers argue that the transition from a Fordist to post-Fordist economy mandates a change to more efficiency-oriented welfare states (Jessop, 1996; Burrows and Loader, 1994).

ished democracy," or the declining capacity of democratic institutions to sustain public policies that depart from market-conforming principles in a world of global asset mobility.

The purpose of this book is twofold. First, I wish to subject the "theory of diminished democracy" to systematic empirical analysis; despite the emergence of theoretical and substantive critiques of the globalization thesis, there is still a paucity of rigorous empirical assessments of the theory. Second, I hope to develop and assess an alternative theory of how globalization has shaped contemporary welfare state change. My alternative argument brings political interests and institutions center-stage to argue that democratic processes and national institutions are fundamentally important to determining how internationalization affects domestic policy change. In the remainder of this introduction, I offer a brief synopsis of the globalization thesis, an outline of my theoretical argument, and an overview of my methodological approach. I conclude with a preview of subsequent chapters of the book.

Global Capital, Democratic Institutions, and the Welfare State: A Theoretical Overview

As I detail in Chapter 2, international movements of capital and the potential for such movements have increased dramatically in the post-1960s era. Total inflows and outflows of direct foreign investment in the developed democracies increased from a decade total of U.S. $390 billion in the 1970s to $474 billion in 1995 alone (United Nations Centre for Transnational Corporations 1996). Total borrowing on international capital markets by actors in the developed democracies was $732 billion in 1995 and only $4.3 billion in 1970 (OECD 1996). By the mid-1990s, the monetary value of annual turnover in bonds and equities between foreigners and residents has been estimated at 135 percent of GDP in the United States, 160 percent in Germany, and 1000 percent in the United Kingdom (Economist 1995). Reductions in some forms of interest rate differentials across countries and markets, as well as removal of legal restrictions on financial movements, have also proceeded rapidly. Today, few formal impediments to transnational capital flows exist in the large majority of advanced capitalist democracies.[3] What are the consequences of these dramatic increases in international capital mobility for welfare states?

---

[3] Trade openness, in terms of relative GDP shares of imports and exports, has also increased significantly. It has increased much more slowly than capital openness, however. For that

As indicated above, a large chorus of commentators has argued that capital mobility effectively enhances the power of increasingly mobile business enterprises over governments that seek to pursue relatively generous social protection and the tax burdens needed to finance it. Generally, the impact of rises in capital mobility on the autonomy of domestic policy makers to pursue their preferred social policies may be channeled through three mechanisms. The first and most commonly discussed linkage rests on the "economic logic" of international capital mobility; the second and third mechanisms effectively involve politics, and together they constitute the "political logic" of globalization. In brief, the economic logic argues that international capital mobility constrains the social policies of democratically elected governments through the operation of markets: in a world of high or near perfect capital mobility, mobile asset holders pursue the most profitable rate of return on investment and governments compete to retain and attract that investment. Thus, for example, analysts commonly cite the outflows of foreign direct investment in 1980s Sweden and 1990s Germany as sources of retrenchment pressures on these generous welfare states.

Politically, international capital mobility may constrain the social welfare policies of democratically elected governments through the routines of conventional politics; the credible threat of exit may enhance the conventional political resources of mobile asset holders and their interest associations. As I discuss in subsequent chapters, transnationally mobile business and employers' associations frequently lobby governments for rollbacks in welfare spending and tax burdens by citing adverse welfare state effects on profits, investment, and employment and the advantages of foreign investment environments. Second, international capital mobility may matter because neoliberal arguments for reforms of the welfare state are enhanced by appeals for policy changes that improve international competitiveness and business climate. As I demonstrate below, center-right governments often invoke the economic logic of globalization when

and other reasons discussed more fully in Chapter 2, I provide a much less thorough analysis of the welfare state impacts of trade in the present study. In addition, I do not offer a systematic study of impacts of the European Union. Part of the impact of Europeanization is captured by general analyses of international capital mobility and financial integration. Given the complexity of additional EU effects on the welfare state (e.g., such as those mediated through direct EU legislation, regulations, and decisions), however, I defer comprehensive analysis until later work. That said, in the case of both trade and Europeanization, I do provide some analysis of major hypotheses in subsequent chapters.

attempting to justify neoliberal welfare reforms. Finally, in several versions of the globalization thesis, these economic and political pressures, individually or in interaction, are thought to be most dramatically felt in relatively costly welfare states and those whose program structures depart substantially from market-conforming principles. Thus, the Nordic social democratic welfare states and the generous social insurance systems of continental Europe may be especially vulnerable to internationally induced pressures for "social dumping" or a "run to the bottom."

As an alternative to the globalization thesis, I advance the argument that the actual domestic policy impacts of international capital mobility are complex and variable, and are fundamentally and systematically shaped by national political institutions. In short, it is my contention that international capital mobility has actually had quite uneven impacts on domestic policy across democratic nations; the direction and magnitude of these effects are a function of the polity's systems of collective group and electoral interest representation and structure of decision-making authority, as well as the institutional structures of the welfare state. As the arguments and analysis of the subsequent chapters demonstrate, *the political institutions and programmatic structures of the larger welfare states of Western Europe are precisely those most likely to blunt the pressures of internationalization; the political institutions and programmatic structures of (relatively small) liberal welfare states are those most likely to facilitate some retrenchment in the presence of economic and political pressures generated by globalization. As a result, we are not likely to see substantial convergence around a market-conforming model of minimal public social protection.*

With regard to specific features of national institutions, the polity's system of collective interest representation – especially the degree to which the polity is social corporatist (as opposed to pluralist) – and the system of electoral representation – especially the degree to which it entails inclusive institutions such as proportional representation and multiparty legislatures and cabinets (as opposed to majoritarian institutions) – should matter. So, too, should the extent to which the political system consists of institutions that disperse decision-making authority (federalism, separation of powers) as apposed to those that concentrate policy-making power. Finally, welfare state institutions, themselves, should matter. Universalistic program structures (i.e., comprehensive population coverage with relatively high benefit equality) and occupationally based systems of generous social insurance (i.e., the "corporatist conservative" structure) have significantly different implications for the politics of welfare state retrenchment than do liberal program structures (i.e., disproportionate reliance on means testing and private insurance).

To expand, national political institutions, as the "new institutionalism" literature stresses, privilege some actors, strategies, and outcomes over others (e.g., Shepsle [1989]; Hall and Taylor [1996]). Perhaps most fundamentally, *political institutions determine the forms and quality of representation of domestic interests that are affected by the internationalization of markets.* Specifically, political institutions provide (or restrict) opportunities for representation for those that are adversely affected by globalization and for those ideologically opposed to – or materially harmed by – the common neoliberal responses to globalization. Institutional structures that promote encompassing interest representation of pro-welfare state interests – and, thus, provide veto points over policy change and other opportunities for interest articulation (short of formal veto power) – dampen the pressures for neoliberal reform attendant on globalization. Social corporatist (as opposed to pluralist) systems of collective interest representation and inclusive electoral institutions should be especially important to maximizing the representation of pro–welfare state interests in the face of economic and political pressures flowing from internationalization. So, too, are the administrative structures in the occupationally based welfare states of continental Europe. Extensive participation in the administration and routine social insurance policy making by labor, employers, and other constituency groups offers substantial opportunities for interest articulation not found in centralized state-administered programs. Fragmentation of decision-making authority (e.g., federalism, separation of powers) inherently creates veto points (and other representational opportunities) that are potentially useful to pro–welfare state interests.

As I illustrate in Chapter 2, however, and as a central feature of the theoretical argument of this volume, *political institutions not only have a "first-order" or relatively immediate effect of privileging particular interests (through representation as well as structuring strategic choices, interactions, and outcomes), they have "second-order" effects, or impacts that evolve over the long term of democratic political practice: institutions significantly shape the relative political capacities of collective actors and they promote a prevailing cluster of values, norms, and behaviors that condition the policy-making process.* For instance, as I detail in Chapter 2, historically embedded institutional structures of decentralization of power systematically create weak welfare programmatic alliances, fragment pro-welfare groups and parties, and suppress the formation of pro-welfare national political coalitions; they also reinforce norms of conflict and competition as well as antistatism.

More systematically, *national political institutions influence directly and indirectly the relative political strength of traditional welfare state constituencies* as well the relative strength of supporting and opposing coalitions of social groups and classes. Specifically, institutions affect the relative weight of conventional political capacities of pro-welfare state interests. By political capacities, I mean the size and unity of programmatic alliances, collective actors, and national coalitions; the ability of these interests to pursue coherent national strategies of establishment and maintenance of social protection; and the political resources of collective actors – organization, funding, and access. For instance, while systems of fragmented policy-making authority tend to weaken the political capacities of pro–welfare state interests, social corporatist interest representation and inclusive electoral institutions tend to strongly enhance them (e.g., votes, seats, and cabinet participation of social democratic and communitarian Christian Democratic parties). Universal and occupationally based systems of social protection tend to create cohesive national electoral coalitions of working- and middle-class constituencies who jointly benefit from generous social protection of these welfare states. Liberal program structures (e.g., significant means-tested programs and private insurance) will tend to fragment populations along social class lines.

In addition, as recent work by Putnam (1993), Rothstein (1998) and Visser and Hemerijck (1997) makes clear, national institutions have fundamentally important structural effects on prevailing cultural orientations that shape the national policy process. Specifically, *political institutions foster distinct clusters of norms, values, and subsequent behaviors that fundamentally structure the policy process and make particular policy outcomes much more likely* than others. That is, political institutions foster or impede certain constellations of norms and values important to social welfare policy change: some institutions (e.g., social corporatism, inclusive electoral institutions, universalistic program structures) tend to promote cooperation and consensus as well as support for (and confidence in) the efficacy and fairness of the welfare state. In this context, rapid and substantial welfare state retrenchment becomes inherently less likely. Other national institutional structures (the disproportionately means-tested structure of liberal welfare states) tend to promote competition, conflict, and distrust among constituency groups as well as to foster antistatist and/or pro-market orientations; in these contexts, retrenchment and neoliberal restructuring may be more readily forthcoming.

In sum, my argument is that political institutions determine the degree to which the economic and political logics of globalization contribute to welfare state retrenchment. Rises in capital mobility will be weakly or largely unrelated to welfare state retrenchment in polities where social corporatism, inclusive electoral institutions, and concentration of policy-making authority are strong and where welfare state institutions are characterized by extensive universalism or occupationally based social insurance. In polities characterized by pluralist interest representation, exclusive electoral institutions (e.g., majoritarian electoral systems), and historically embedded systems of fragmented authority, as well as liberal welfare state structures, internationalization will produce appreciable welfare state retrenchment.

The Methodological Approach: Combining Quantitative and Qualitative Analysis

In Chapter 2, I elaborate theory and derive specific propositions from the globalization thesis. I also develop a set of propositions from my alternative theory about how national institutional structures shape the domestic policy impacts of internationalization. To address these propositions, I employ both quantitative and qualitative analysis of the relationships between capital mobility, national political institutions, and welfare state change. I initially utilize pooled time-series analysis of data gathered from 15 developed capitalist democracies between 1965 and 1993. Pooled time-series, or "panel," analysis offers a powerful technique for employing both spatial and temporal variation in the phenomena of interest to systematically evaluate theoretical propositions about causal relationships; it also provides an especially useful instrument for evaluating hypotheses involving factors such as internationalization that significantly vary across time, and factors such as political institutions whose variation is primarily spatial (Hicks 1994).

I initially examine the direct welfare state effects of several dimensions of international capital mobility, and the ways in which national institutions mediate those impacts. As I discuss in Chapters 2 and 3, there are a variety of theoretical, conceptual, and technical reasons for employing multiple indications of international capital mobility. I focus on five core dimensions in the quantitative analysis: total transnational flows of capital;

flows of foreign direct investment; borrowing on international capital markets; liberalization of national controls on capital movements; and covered interest rate differentials. I also provide a summary assessment of hypotheses about the general welfare state effects of increasing trade openness; I do this by utilizing measures of aggregate trade flows and of trade between the developed capitalist democracies and developing (i.e., "low-wage") political economies.

I initially use one encompassing measure of social welfare effort; this makes feasible a concise analysis of the direct welfare state effects of multiple dimensions of international capital mobility and the policy effects of these multiple dimensions across several diverse institutional settings. While these initial tests provide a baseline evaluation of the study's central hypotheses, methodological and substantive considerations suggest refinements. Thus, I examine, in the presence of controls for structural and cyclical welfare determinants, the effects of global capital on several major dimensions of the welfare state: cash income maintenance, the social wage (i.e., income replacement for the average unemployed production worker), government health effort, and the public-private ratio of health spending. To further refine the analysis, I assess the impacts of internationalization on individual dimensions of the welfare state across the entire sample of countries and for subsets of nations according to welfare state type (universal, conservative, liberal). To compensate for weaknesses in any one statistical estimation technique for panel models (e.g., see Greene [2000]; Judge et al. [1985]; Stimson [1985]), I employ several estimators.

With respect to the measurement of national institutions, I use newly available data on cross-national and time-varying properties of political institutions. For instance, I employ recently collected data on 1950 to 1992 attributes of labor and industrial relations systems in the developed democracies in assessing hypotheses about social corporatism (Wallerstein, Golden, and Lange, 1997; see Chapters 2 and 3 and the Appendix for a full discussion of all data and measures). In deriving indicators of institutional properties of electoral systems and the structure of decision-making authority within the polity, I also utilize cross-nationally and temporally varying indicators of electoral and party systems, as well as constitutional structures. As a result, this study improves on past analyses of national political institutions and domestic policies that have usually relied on temporally invariant indicators of institutional dimensions.

This quantitative assessment of theoretical questions is in effect what Ragin (1987) calls "variable-oriented analysis," or the use of quantitative indicators of attributes of social systems to provide probabilistic assessments of causal propositions. While one can derive estimates from the quantitative models of the effects of causal factors (e.g., international capital mobility) on the phenomenon of interest (social welfare protection) in specific cases (i.e., nations), these estimates and the important inferences we derive from them are only as good as our conceptualization, measurement, data sources, and statistical estimation techniques. Moreover, despite the power of "large-N" quantitative tests of hypotheses to contribute to theoretical knowledge (e.g., by assessing the generalizability of propositions), the analysis often leaves many questions concerning causal sequences, actors' motivations and the interpretation of events by political agents, and how nation-specific contexts modify causal effects.

To further assess the central theoretical propositions of the study, I also utilize case-study analysis of internationalization, political institutions, and welfare state change in a sample of larger welfare states.[4] As noted, explicit in much of globalization theory is the notion that international financial integration is particularly consequential for larger welfare states that significantly depart from market-conforming precepts. In this view, the social democratic welfare states of the Nordic countries and the generous occupationally based social insurance systems of continental Europe are under especially strong pressures to reduce costs and restructure along market-conforming lines. On the other hand, my alternative theoretical argument highlights institutional features of these welfare states (e.g., universalism and its political correlates) that may buffer them from the economic and political pressures flowing from globalization. Social democratic and occupationally based welfare states tend to have moderate-to-strong social corporatism and inclusive electoral institutions; to a less conforming degree, they rank low on dispersion of policy-making authority. Thus, contra globalization theory, my argument highlights features of these welfare states and their broader political and institutional contexts that should make them less susceptible to the economic and political forces attendant on internationalization. In sum, these developed welfare states are theoreti-

---

[4] The strengths and weaknesses of statistical analysis of quantitative indicators across a large range of relevant cases and the comparative case-study method have been widely debated. For an elaboration of the issues discussed here, and a variety of additional considerations in designing comparative political analysis, see the seminal work by Ragin (1987), as well as contributions to the 1995 *American Political Science Review* symposium and the influential work of King, Keohane, and Verba (1994).

cally the most important cases for understanding how globalization affects the domestic policy autonomy of governments in democratic polities.

I select seven specific countries for intensive case-study analysis. These include Denmark, Finland, Norway, and Sweden, effectively the universe of nations that most closely approximate the universalistic or social democratic welfare state model. I also select France, Germany, and Italy, which represent a majority of the nations with welfare states that approximate the corporatist conservative model of occupationally based social insurance. Several other nations could have been included – most notably, Austria, Belgium, and the Netherlands; however, these and others (e.g., Switzerland) are excluded from intensive case analysis for a variety of reasons.[5] Because the focal cases constitute a large and representative sample of the welfare states of interest and because material on excluded nations is included in general comparative analysis, case selection itself should not bias conclusions about the welfare impacts of globalization.

With regard to smaller, more market-conforming welfare states, the systems of social protection of the Anglo democracies generally adhere to the liberal or "residual" welfare state model (although see Chapter 2 on the heterogeneity of this group). These welfare states tend to be strongly pluralist and have majoritarian electoral institutions; the majority are also systems of dispersed policy-making authority. In subsequent chapters, they are used as a baseline for comparison in both quantitative and qualitative analysis. In addition, given that my theoretical predictions suggest globalization should be associated with some retrenchment in precisely these welfare states, I offer succinct case studies of internationalization,

---

[5] Cases were selected in order to balance three goals. First, it is desirable to assess central theoretical propositions in as many cases as possible to overcome the limits on generalizability inherent in "small-N" case analysis. Thus, as many universal and corporatist conservative welfare states as feasible were included. Second, with regard to feasibility, limits on resources, expertise, and length suggested some truncation of the list of nations selected for intensive case-study analysis. Third, to eliminate a variety of additional complexities in the analysis, I tended to exclude cases that did not relatively strongly conform to the broad programmatic attributes of universalistic or corporatist conservative welfare states, or cases where the welfare state and economic institutions and policy mixes that surround them were "atypical." For instance, the Dutch welfare state has strong elements of universalism, but some characteristics of the occupationally based program structure and a political context of Christian Democratic–led governments typical of the corporatist conservative nations (e.g., van Kersbergen and Becker [1988]; Cox [1993]). Austria's welfare state generally conforms to the corporatist conservative model, but has broad political economic institutions (e.g., a strong social democratic party and social corporatist institutions) that resemble the Nordic countries (Huber and Stephens, 1998).

institutions, and social policy change in liberal welfare states. For reasons outlined above, however, intensive case analysis is focused on the generous social democratic and corporatist conservative welfare states.

For each of the intensive case studies, I provide a chronological narrative of major changes in social welfare policy and their political economic contexts for years from the late 1970s to mid-1990s. Analytically, I address three central questions. First, I explore the degree to which rises in international capital mobility (and in less finely grained analysis, trade openness) can be linked to specific neoliberal welfare state reforms. Second, following theory to be developed in Chapter 2, I assess to what degree the influence of internationalization on welfare state reform is contingent on specific conditions such as government fiscal crisis. Finally, I provide an analysis of the degree to which national political institutions and welfare state structures themselves have blunted or otherwise shaped the impact of internationalization.[6] Overall, the case-study analysis provides a second body of empirical evidence that contributes to ultimate conclusions about the welfare state effects of globalization and the extent to which democratic institutions, themselves, shape these impacts.

The Organizational Structure of Analysis

In Chapter 2, I examine in detail the international capital mobility thesis. I initially provide an overview of the scope and character of internationalization of markets. Next, I offer an elaboration of the theory of diminished democracy and variations. I also succinctly review recent critiques of the globalization theses, such as the claim that the postwar political economic structures of "embedded liberalism," or the combination of international liberalism and significant domestic state intervention and social protection, continue to have relevance to the contemporary period. Finally, I devote the bulk of this chapter to the development of my argument that democratic politics and national political institutions determine the direction and magnitude of impacts of internationalization on the welfare state. I conclude the chapter with an actual empirical analysis of dimensions of national institutions.

---

[6] As a summary exercise, I also assess for each welfare state the degree to which 1970s–90s policy changes have actually produced a restructuring of the welfare state in the direction of the more residual, market-conforming welfare model and, if so, the relative weight of internationalization in that cumulative process.

In Chapters 3 through 7, I present the core empirical analysis of the central questions of this study. Chapter 3 provides the bulk of the quantitative analysis of the central assertions derived from the globalization thesis and my alternative argument. In Chapters 4 and 5, I offer a largely qualitative analysis of globalization and social welfare policy change in the large social democratic and corporatist conservative welfare states. In Chapter 4, I offer a case-oriented analysis of social policy reform in the Nordic political economies – Denmark, Finland, Norway, and Sweden. In Chapter 5, I replicate this intensive case-study analysis for predominately corporatist conservative welfare states, focusing principally on France, Germany, and Italy. In Chapter 6, I provide a much more succinct analysis of internationalization and welfare state reform in the Anglo democracies, focusing on case studies of Britain and the United States and summary analysis of Australia, Canada, and New Zealand.

In Chapter 7, I address the arguments that international capital mobility may contribute to the retrenchment of the welfare state through its impacts on the funding basis of the welfare state, on the strength of particular political institutions that support the welfare state – most notably social corporatism, and on the efficacy of macroeconomic policy to control unemployment and promote economic growth (and hence to prevent fiscal stresses that may lead to retrenchment). I extend arguments I have offered elsewhere about internationalization and tax policy (Swank 1998) and provide new evidence on international capital mobility's effects on tax burdens on capital, labor, and consumption, as well as on the tax share of GDP. In the case of the linkage between internationalization and social corporatism, I review the arguments, weigh the best recent evidence, and offer some new empirical analysis. Finally, I provide a succinct assessment – relying on the best recent treatments of the topic, as well as analytic summaries of my case study evidence – of the view that the decline in the efficacy of monetary, exchange rate, and related policies associated with rises in international capital mobility forces governments, through a deterioration in economic performance (most notably, escalating unemployment rates), to cut benefits, tighten eligibility, and otherwise restrain soaring welfare state costs.

In Chapter 8, I conclude with a summary and integration of findings from the quantitative and case-study analysis presented in the book. I also situate my arguments about the centrality of democratic institutions in shaping contemporary welfare state trajectories within recent welfare state theory. In this context, I illustrate the relationship of my theory with "power resources" theory and the emergent theory of welfare state retrenchment most closely associated with the work of Paul Pierson; I also offer conclusions on what I believe to be the essential components of an adequate theory of the welfare state in the contemporary era. Finally, I discuss implications of my findings for the future of the national systems of social protection in advanced capitalist democracies and for the autonomy of the nation-state in a world of global markets.

2

Globalization, Democracy, and the Welfare State

In this chapter, I examine the international capital mobility thesis, namely, that notable post-1970 rises in transnational capital mobility have significantly diminished the capacity of democratically elected governments to pursue social welfare policies that depart from market-conforming principles. I initially provide an overview of the internationalization of markets, focusing especially on trends in the liberalization of capital controls, international capital flows, and financial market integration. Next, I offer an exegesis of the theory of diminished democracy, outlining the economic and political logics that link capital mobility to retrenchment and neoliberal restructuring of the welfare state. I also confront the theory with the counterclaim that, in reality, the postwar structure of embedded liberalism, or the combination of international liberalism with substantial state intervention and social compensation, continues to have relevance to the contemporary period. Finally, I devote the bulk of the chapter to the development of my alternative argument that the institutional structure of the polity and welfare state – national systems of group and electoral interest representation, the organization of policy-making authority within the polity, and programmatic structures of welfare states – determine the direction and magnitude of the social policy impacts of internationalization. I conclude with an empirical analysis of focal dimensions of national institutions, an exercise that sets the stage for the empirical assessments of theory in subsequent chapters.

International Capital Mobility: An Overview

Facilitated by national policy change, technological innovations, new financial institutions, and market forces, international flows of capital and

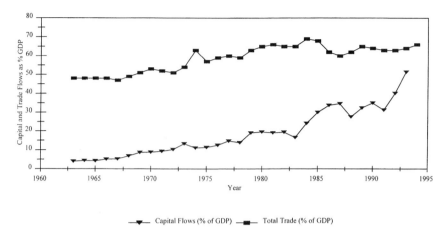

Figure 2.1 Capital and Trade Flows Annual Average – Advanced Democracies

the potential for such movements have increased notably since the early 1970s.[1] Figure 2.1 offers an overview of capital movements in the developed democracies by displaying annual 18-country averages of total inflows and outflows of capital (foreign direct investment [hereafter FDI], portfolio investment, and bank lending) expressed as a percentage of Gross Domestic Product (hereafter GDP).[2] To highlight the relatively rapid

[1] The causes of the internationalization of finance have been analyzed extensively. Some observers emphasize that dramatic technological changes in information processing, communications, and transportation have reduced transaction costs and otherwise made the expansion of international markets feasible (e.g., Carnoy et al. [1991]; McKenzie and Lee [1991]; Williams [1993]). Still others stress the importance of 1970s supply shocks, rising budget and trade imbalances, and instability in the world monetary system (e.g., see the survey of IMF [1991]). In addition, scholars have highlighted the importance of the deregulation of financial markets and, in turn, the role of political interests, actors, and institutions in shaping this process (e.g., Helleiner [1994]; Sobel [1994]; Quinn and Inclan [1997]; Goodman and Pauly [1993]). For a synoptic survey, see Cohen (1996); on the history of the international financial system see Eichengreen (1996), Schwartz (1994a), and Thompson (1997).

[2] The 18 nations included here are Australia, Austria, Belgium, Canada, Denmark, Finland, France, Germany, Ireland, Italy, Japan, the Netherlands, New Zealand, Norway, Sweden, Switzerland, the United Kingdom, and the United States. The measure of covered interest rate differentials discussed below excludes Finland, Ireland, New Zealand, and Switzerland because of missing data. Ireland, New Zealand, and Switzerland, as well as small developed democracies (e.g., Iceland, Luxembourg), are excluded in much of the subsequent analysis because of the unavailability of data on one or more key dimensions. See the Appendix and relevant sections below on measurement and sources of data.

16

growth of capital flows, the figure also displays annual average trade openness, or the annual average of total imports and exports of goods and services as a percentage of GDP. As the figure suggests, total transnational flows of capital have increased notably. During the 1950s and 1960s Bretton Woods–era of trade liberalization and relatively closed capital markets, total flows of capital averaged roughly five percent of GDP in the advanced capitalist democracies; by the end of the 1970s, total capital movements hovered at 20 percent of GDP. By the mid-1990s, transborder movements of capital exceeded on average 50 percent of GDP. Imports and exports of goods and services have increased relative to GDP, but growth in trade openness has been much slower than expansion of capital mobility; average trade openness in the advanced market economies expanded from roughly 48 percent of GDP in the mid-1960s to approximately 65 percent in the mid-1990s; trends for other measures of trade such as flows between North and South exhibit even less growth.[3]

While these data are instructive, reliance on total capital flows alone to measure capital mobility can be deceptive. First, there are major differences in the actors, temporal dynamics, and domestic economic and political implications of different forms of capital mobility. For example, rising levels of FDI largely reflect the activities of global corporations and manifest increases in transborder mergers, acquisitions, and establishment of new production facilities. On the other hand, the rise in borrowing on international capital markets entails increased exposure to the preferences and actions of nonresident lenders – institutional investors, fund managers, and banks. Second, severe fiscal and macroeconomic imbalances and instabilities may produce periods of relatively substantial capital flows when the

---

[3] Often highlighted as a source of manufacturing wage decline and unemployment in the OECD, and as part of the general process of factor price convergence, the developing country share (for non–oil exporting countries) of total imports in the typical developed democracy actually dropped from roughly 23 to 17 percent between the mid-1960s and mid-1990s; total trade flows between the average OECD nation and (non–oil exporting) developing economies relative to GDP have also declined slightly over the long-term; in the mid-1960s these flows amounted to 8.3 percent of GDP (1963–6 average), while in the early 1990s they averaged 7.4 percent (average for 1990–3). On the other hand, it is important to point out that trade with developing countries may have social policy impacts: increases in the export of manufactured goods to the North (e.g., components) from developing countries has changed the composition of trade (Wood, 1994). Possible employment impacts associated with changes in trade composition, generalized concerns over manufacturing competitiveness (real and politically constructed), and other factors have implications for the welfare state (also see A. Martin [1996]).

Figure 2.2 International Capital Flows: Direct Investment and Capital Market Borrowing

"real" levels of capital mobility and financial integration are moderate. Conversely, aggregate flows may be limited at near perfect capital mobility if capital is relatively efficiently allocated. To remedy these problems, I use multiple indicators in empirical analysis: several measures of actual capital flows, a measure of the liberalization of capital controls, and interest rate–based measures of financial integration.

Figure 2.2 displays trends in two major components of capital flows discussed above: FDI and borrowing on international capital markets. As the figure reveals, annual inflows and outflows of FDI in the typical developed democracy hovered at roughly 1 percent of GDP for much of the 1960s and 1970s. However, reflecting in part the post-1980 wave of mergers, acquisitions, and strategic alliances by multinational corporations (e.g., IMF [1991]; OECD [1992a]), FDI grew from the 1 percent level to roughly 3 percent of GDP in the average developed nation in the early 1990s. A similar pattern can be observed for borrowing in international capital markets. Financial flows pursuant to issuance of international bonds, equity, and related financial instruments typically equaled about 1 percent of GDP in the pre-1970 era. In the 1970s and 1980s, markets for foreign bonds and equities as well as international banking institutions developed rapidly; total borrowing for the typical developed nation exceeded 5 percent of GDP by the mid-1990s.

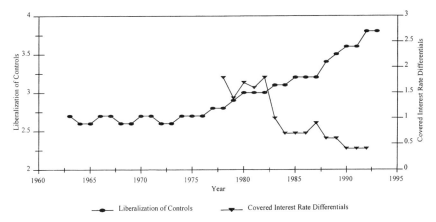

Figure 2.3 International Financial Markets: Liberalization and Convergence

Figure 2.3 presents two additional measures of international capital mobility: the degree of liberalization of national capital controls, or the formal-legal potential for such flows, and covered interest rate differentials, or the difference between domestic and "off-shore" interest rates for assets denominated in a country's currency adjusted for the forward premium on that country's currency.[4] The first measure consists of an interval–level index where 0.0 indicates complete formal control of capital movements and 4.0 denotes complete freedom of movement. As the figure reveals, liberalization of capital controls accelerates in the 1970s (e.g., with removal of key controls in Britain, Japan, and the United States) and continues in the 1980s and 1990s (almost everywhere else). By the mid-1990s, the large majority of developed nations had removed most formal barriers to capital movements. The same general conclusion holds for a broader

---

[4] As in the case of capital flows, these two measures of capital mobility are imperfect. The index of formal-legal restrictions on capital does not capture the impact of informal and illegal capital flows that develop from technological, market, and institutional innovations. In fact, some have argued capital controls may be "obsolete" (e.g., Goodman and Pauly [1993]). In addition, Willett and Ahn (1998) have argued that, while departures from near-zero covered interest differentials typically indicate that financial integration is low, the interaction of arbitrage and speculative activity impairs the ability of this measure to accurately gauge the actual degree of financial integration at near-zero covered interest differentials. That is, "real" capital mobility can be either relatively high or low when covered interest differentials are near zero.

indicator of both controls on capital movements and on payments for goods and services (Quinn and Inclan, 1997). The second indicator – covered interest differentials – indexes the integration of a domestic market with world markets, or the absence of substantial barriers to capital movements between domestic and "off-shore" markets (e.g., Eurobond markets). Net of the currency premium, there appears to be substantial convergence between domestic and world markets as (absolute values) of covered interest differentials moved toward 0.00 in the average advanced democracy from the late 1970s onward. While a number of important arguments about capital *im*mobility exist (see below), the patterns presented in Figure 2.3 further reinforce the notion that, from the perspective of the developed democracies, international capital mobility had increased considerably by the mid-1990s. What are the consequences for the welfare state?

The Impacts of International Capital Mobility: Diminished Democracy?

It is commonplace to link the dramatic increase in international capital mobility with reductions in social protection and redistribution. Both classic political economists, such as Adam Smith (1976 [1776]), as well as modern scholars, such as Bates and Lien (1985), have argued that increasingly mobile capital poses substantial economic and political problems for governments that seek to raise revenues and pursue policies adverse to the economic interests and ideological orientations of (mobile) business. So, too, have contemporary neoliberal economists such as McKenzie and Lee (1991), Marxian analysts such as Gill and Law (1988) and Ross and Trachte (1990), international relations theorists such as Cerny (1996) and Strange (1996), and popular analysts such as Greider (1997). These observers, and a large chorus of similarly situated commentators, use nearly identical reasoning to argue that the globalization of capital markets has effectively increased the power of capital over governments that seek to expand or maintain relatively high levels of social protection and taxation. Generally, the impact of rises in capital mobility on the autonomy of democratically elected governments to pursue their preferred social policies may be transmitted by three mechanisms. The first linkage rests on the "economic logic" of international capital mobility, while the second and third mechanisms comprise the "political logic" of the globalization. Specifically:

1. International capital mobility may constrain the social welfare policies of democratically elected governments through the operation of markets where mobile asset holders pursue the most profitable rate of return on investment and governments compete to retain and attract investment.

2. International capital mobility may constrain the social welfare policies of democratically elected governments through the routines of democratic politics where mobile asset holders enjoy enhanced conventional political resources as a result of the "exit option."

3. International capital mobility may constrain the social welfare policies of democratically elected governments through the ascendance of neoliberal economic orthodoxy where the arguments for neoliberal reforms – retrenchment and efficiency-oriented restructuring – of the welfare state reinforce, and are reinforced by, appeals for policies that improve international competitiveness and business climate.

The Economic Logic of International Capital Mobility

Implicit in much of the topical writing by social scientists of all disciplinary and ideological perspectives is the notion that governments are structurally constrained by internationally mobile capital. The economic logic of "structural dependence" is grounded on the proposition that governments in democratic capitalist nations are dependent on the willingness of the owners of productive assets to invest (see Lindblom [1977] and Block [1977] for seminal statements, and Przeworski and Wallerstein [1988] and Swank [1992] for critical assessments).[5] Proponents of the thesis argue or assume that (a) economic performance – output, jobs, price stability, and income – is significantly determined by the willingness of the owners of capital to continue to invest in productive activities; (b) strong economic performance is usually necessary for the continued popular approval and reelection of incumbent policy makers and for extraction of the essential

---

[5] The notion that business possesses structural power in democratic capitalist systems is associated with neopluralist and some neo-Marxist schools of political theory. Block's seminal statement critically builds on a series of works by Offe, Poulantzas, and other neo-Marxian state theorists. Carnoy (1984) offers an excellent critical synthesis of structuralist theory, juxtaposing it with instrumentalist theorists who view the power of capital as deriving from its ability to directly control the state. Yet, as illustrated below, neoliberal economists and commentators who emphasize efficiency-equity tradeoffs and the way globalization disciplines profligate governments also implicitly make a structural power argument.

21

revenues that support government personnel and programs; and (c) if governments significantly extend the scope of social provision and taxation, they potentially undercut the confidence of business in a profitable rate of return on investment and, by doing so, reduce growth. According to the logic of the thesis, governments – whether they wish to maximize reelection prospects, the long-term interests of particular social aggregates (e.g., blue-collar workers, pensioners), or the aggregate public interest – will necessarily regularly provide investment incentives in the face of low rates of investment and be loath to pursue policies significantly detrimental to business confidence.[6]

With respect to social welfare provision, relatively high levels (or extensions) of the social wage that raise the floor of collective bargaining, generous social insurance payments that may diminish work effort (e.g., absenteeism), and generally high levels of social protection that necessitate large tax burdens on capital or on high income–earners will be difficult policies to develop and sustain given the inherent risks to governments of diminished investment or disinvestment. In addition, much of the work on structural dependence assumes or explicitly argues that, on balance, business not only has a substantive interest in moderate-to-low levels of social welfare spending but has a clear ideological preference for a generally small, market-conforming welfare state. At the same time, it is important to note that most scholars who work in this tradition acknowledge that some forms of government spending and regulation can bolster business confidence. Basic infrastructure investment and education as well as cyclical demand stimulus may be salutary for private investment. All else being equal, however, a moderate-to-high level of social welfare spending, and the taxes needed to finance it, are thought to be detrimental to business investment in most structural dependence theory and in much of the contemporary writing about the domestic policy consequences of globalization.[7]

Extending this logic to the case of substantial international capital mobility, theory suggests that governments of all ideological and pro-

---

[6] Much of the work on "domestic structural dependence" calls into question any simple reading of the "privileged position of business" thesis. (On the United States, see Quinn and Shapiro [1991]; Vogel [1989]; Williams and Collins [1993]; on Europe, see Wickham-Jones [1995]; Pontusson [1992]; and on the advanced democracies as a whole, see Przeworski and Wallerstein [1988], and Swank [1992]).

[7] For introductions to the literature on the welfare state interests and preferences of business, see Martin (1995, 2000), Mares (1997), Swank and Martin (forthcoming), and Swenson (1991, 1998).

grammatic complexions not only have to consider the domestic requisites of business confidence – of actual and anticipated profitability – but in a world of few impediments to international capital movements, they also have to consider international investment climates, the relevant policies of other nations, and policy assessments of internationally mobile asset holders and markets. The strategic interaction of governments and transnationally mobile business and finance becomes a prisoner's dilemma for national policy makers. In the face of inherent impediments to international policy coordination (Herring and Litan, 1995; Kapstein, 1994; Webb, 1995), governments have incentives to engage in competition for investment through the process of social dumping, or reductions in social costs that retard efforts to retain or attract internationally mobile capital. While theorists recognize that governmentally provided public goods, such as infrastructure and education (as well as potential private market benefits of social policies), may partially offset the deleterious effects of high social costs, most conclude that widespread competition to retain and attract investment will place significant downward pressure on welfare states (e.g., Aspinwall [1996]). In the most extreme case, such competition is thought to lead to a bidding war where social welfare transfers, social services, and the tax burdens that support them are progressively lowered to a "lowest common denominator," or as Jessop (1996) puts it, a "Schumpetarian workfare state." Such a welfare state tends to be residualist, increasingly organized along the lines of minimum means-tested benefits, reliance on private insurance, work and efficiency principles, and relatively low (and distributionally neutral) tax burdens. When and where social welfare programs are maintained at modest levels of generosity, programs and their extensions can only be justified as social investment programs that enhance human capital (e.g., training programs) or otherwise contribute to economic growth (e.g., Drache [1996]; Taylor-Gooby [1997]). The heart of the thesis – what has been called the structural dependence (of the state) on internationally mobile capital – is essentially an argument about diminished democracy, or the declining capacity of democratic institutions to produce policies that depart from market-conforming principles in a world of global asset mobility.

The Political Logic of International Capital Mobility: Interests and Ideas

Structural dependence arguments stress the domestic policy impacts of the actions of individual economic actors pursuing profits and minimizing risks within markets. Yet, the conscious political action of large enterprises with mobile assets, as well as the interest associations that represent them, may also produce substantial domestic policy consequences. In his seminal exposition of the "privileged position of business" thesis, Lindblom (1977) argued that the control over asset allocation in market-oriented capitalist economies also bolsters the conventional political resources of business; that is, the control of investment enhances the political influence that stems from organizational, financial, and access resources of firms and their collective representatives. With respect to internationally mobile enterprises, Adam Smith (1976 [1776]), Bates and Lien (1985), and others have suggested that rises in capital mobility have historically advantaged mobile asset holders in conventional political arenas.

At minimum, authoritative policy makers within the state have consistently given substantial weight to the explicit policy preferences of mobile capital in formulating policies and designing institutions (Bates and Lien, 1985). At most, mobile enterprises and business interest associations representing them are able to consistently and credibly use the "exit option" as leverage in legislative, centralized bargaining, and executive branch policy-making forums, enhancing the conventional political resources that are commonly brought to bear in efforts to shape policy (e.g., Block [1987]; Kurzer [1993]; Schmidt [1995]). For instance, internationally mobile enterprises may criticize the home-country social costs, regulatory interventions, and tax burdens as they openly discuss relocation of production and administrative facilities abroad. In fact, Thomas (1997) argues that the degree of capital mobility is the most important determinant of the relative power of the state, labor, and business enterprises to shape policy outcomes: increases in capital mobility make the threat of disinvestment more credible, reduce the costs of actual movement of production facilities, and otherwise advantage mobile capital in bargaining situations. Overall, the conventional political resources of business enterprises and interest associations – funding capacity, organization, and access – may well be systematically augmented by the credible threat of international exit.

Also, the impact of international capital mobility on domestic policies in recent decades may in part be channeled through the increasing acceptance of neoliberal macroeconomic orthodoxy. Specifically, the widespread ascendance of neoliberal macroeconomic ideas, which call for rollbacks in government intervention and highlight market distortions of social welfare programs and redistributive taxation, provides a supportive theoretical framework for appeals for market-oriented reforms in social and tax policies to enhance trade competitiveness and business climate; arguments about the adverse impacts of moderate-to-high levels of social welfare provision and taxation on a nation's international economic performance lend further weight to neoliberal claims of general welfare state inefficiencies and calls for market-oriented reforms.[8] In fact, in his synoptic survey of economic policy change in the Nordic countries in the 1980s and 1990s, Mjøset (1996) argues that, with the exception of Sweden, pressures from internationalization on domestic policy reform have been primarily channeled by the acceptance of neoliberal macroeconomic ideas. Other scholars (e.g., Singh [1997]; Evans [1997]) have stressed that a neoliberal policy "regime," displacing the post–World War Two framework of substantial international liberalization and state intervention and social protection (see below on "embedded liberalism"), has become the predominant ideology throughout the developed democracies and has made difficult the maintenance of many state strategies for economic management and social protection.

Finally, it is important to emphasize that internationalization, political forces, and ideas may interact in complex ways. Peter Hall (1993) has illustrated an important pattern in his insightful analysis of the rise of monetarism in Britain. Hall argues that the incorporation of monetarist principles in British economic policy in the late 1970s and 1980s began to occur when much of the British government's macroeconomic policy community was still largely Keynesian; the official ascendance of monetarism was primarily fueled by the electoral victories of the Conservative Party. Colin Hay (1998) has made a similar point with regard to political actors and domestic and international neoliberalism. In his critical assessment of the acceptance by British Labour of the "logic of no alternative" (i.e., the necessity of neoliberal policy reform in response to globalization), Hay argues that 1970s and 1980s political action by the new right heavily influenced the ascendence of neoliberal economic doctrine and "the political deployment" of the globalization thesis. In a similar fashion, Mishra (1996) suggests that parties of the Left are significantly deterred from proposing progressive policy, and governments of the Center and Right aided in rationalizing social welfare retrenchment by the prevalence of globalization rhetoric. Scholars such as Helleiner (1994) and Singh (1997) argue

---

[8] On economic performance crises, the decline of Keynesian welfare state policies, and the rise of neoliberalism, see Bruno and Sachs (1985), Crafts and Toniolo (1996), Scharpf (1991), and Tsai (1989).

that the ascendance of the new neoliberal policy regime was significantly influenced by the political action of a "neoliberal coalition" of internationally mobile enterprises, international organizations such as the World Bank and International Monetary Fund, and government central bankers and finance ministers. In sum, pressures on the welfare state from the political logic of globalization may significantly augment the social policy pressures from the economic logic of globalization.

The Indirect Effects of Globalization

In addition to the relatively direct welfare state impacts of international capital mobility, internationalization may contribute to rollbacks in social protection and otherwise constrain democratically elected governments in their pursuit of social policy goals through several indirect mechanisms. Specifically, internationalization may matter because of its impacts on the funding basis of the welfare state, the strength of particular political institutions that support the welfare state, and the efficacy of macroeconomic policy. With regard to taxation, work on internationalization and domestic policy autonomy has commonly highlighted the impact of international capital mobility on the revenue-raising capacity of the state. From the literature of classic political economy to modern social science, scholars have suggested that revenue-dependent governments have generally imposed lower tax rates on mobile assets and, as noted, incorporated the preferences of these asset holders into policies and even institutions. Steinmo (1993, 1994) and McKenzie and Lee (1991), among other contemporary observers, have argued that increases in capital mobility have effectively led governments to reduce tax burdens on corporate profits and high income–earners, substantially reducing tax-based income redistribution and the general revenue-raising capacities of the state. Some economists have concurred: in theoretical models of taxation in small economies with fully mobile capital, the optimal rate of tax on income from capital is thought to be zero; shortfalls of revenue are offset by shifting the tax burden to relatively less mobile factors such as labor and land (e.g., Gordon [1986]; Razin and Sadka [1991]; Gordon and Mackie-Mason [1995]).

Second, Kurzer (1993), Mishra (1993), Moses (1994, 2000), and others have argued that capital's exit option weakens unions and social corporatist institutions. As I demonstrate below, social corporatism is not only an important direct influence on social welfare effort, it is one of a core set of democratic institutional mechanisms that blunts pressures for neoliberal reform stemming from internationalization. The globalization thesis suggests that international capital mobility shifts power from labor to capital and diminishes the gains to business from engaging in tripartite forums (e.g., wage restraint). Coupled with domestic structural change (e.g., the move to flexible specialization), internationalization may engender decentralization of collective bargaining and generally weaken unions. Thus, capital mobility may indirectly affect the welfare state through its hypothesized negative impact on union power and social corporatism.

Third, scholars have argued that because of the decline in the efficacy of monetary and exchange rate policy associated with rises in international capital mobility, governments face a deterioration in economic performance that, in turn, forces (particularly larger) welfare states to cut benefits and tighten eligibility (e.g., Huber and Stephens [1998]; Martin [1996]). This is most pronounced in the case of sustained rises in unemployment where unemployment-induced changes in social spending create a "fiscal crisis" for the larger welfare states. In addition, Martin (1996) notes that some of the literature suggests internationalization itself – through increased mobility of production and the changing trade composition between North and South (see Note 3) may directly increase unemployment in the developed democracies and, in turn, augur welfare retrenchment. In other words, capital mobility may have spillover effects: It leads to welfare retrenchment because it leads to the loss of economic policy efficacy and performance effects.

I systematically consider these arguments about the indirect impacts of internationalization on the welfare state in Chapter 7. There, I provide a relatively comprehensive analysis of the impact of globalization on government revenue-raising capabilities. I also provide an explication of theory, review of the evidence, and some new analysis about whether or not capital mobility contributes to the weakening of corporatism. Finally, I consider the linkages between globalization, macroeconomic policy and performance, and the welfare state. I discuss recent theory and extant evidence, as well as the pertinent findings from my case analyses in Chapters 4 and 5.

The Role of Trade Openness.   It is also important to point out that some of the work on globalization and the welfare state highlights trade openness as a source of pressure for policy change (e.g., Drache [1996]; Pfaller, Gough, and Therborn [1991]). In this familiar argument, policy makers in increasingly open economies may encounter pressures for reduced (social security and other) tax burdens on domestic producers in order to lower labor costs and promote price competitiveness of exports; increases in trade openness may push governments to reduce social outlays in order to lessen market distortions (e.g., reduce perceived work disincentives) and roll back the "reservation wage," or the social welfare–determined floor under collective bargaining. Moreover, cuts in social spending may be viewed as a primary mechanism to reduce public sector debt and hence interest rates that, in turn, will promote productivity-enhancing investments. As discussed below, the argument that the welfare state harms trade competitiveness is a well-worn justification for reductions in "welfare state costs." Business interest associations and their spokespeople, as well as parties of the Right, have frequently employed this argument in national political debates over welfare state restructuring; this is particularly common in welfare policy debates in "high-wage economies" such as Germany (see Chapter 5).

In subsequent analysis, I examine linear and nonlinear welfare state impacts of aggregate trade flows, trade with developing (i.e., low-wage) economies, and the interaction of trade openness with international capital mobility; I also consider welfare state impacts of trade openness in my case-study analysis. I exclude, however, a full and systematic analysis of the question of trade impacts in the present work. I do so for several reasons. First, a complete analysis of trade impacts that parallels the one for global capital mobility is a complex enterprise and would require a second volume. Second, as Huber and Stephens (1998) forcefully argue, the large welfare states of Northern Europe developed in the context of highly open markets for goods and services; well-developed social welfare protection played an important role in the process of structural adjustment to international competition. Thus, trade openness alone is not likely to be a central mechanism that pressures welfare state retrenchment. In fact, as I discuss below, there is a familiar and large literature that argues for the historical as well as contemporary role of trade openness in promoting or maintaining state intervention and a relatively large welfare state (the theory of embedded liberalism). Finally, as noted, the growth in trade openness has been relatively moderate (when compared to rises in capital mobility). Although the changing composition of North-South trade may have effects (see Note 3), the magnitude of the increases in international financial integration, as well as their potential policy impacts, are arguably much greater than those associated with trade.

The Resilience of the Welfare State?

Despite the prominence of conventional globalization theory, there are a number of arguments that call into question the central propositions of the thesis. After a brief review of some important criticisms, I will focus on one major stream of research that is particularly important for welfare state studies. As to general critiques, numerous questions about the actual extent of capital mobility and international financial integration have been raised. First, historical analyses of interest rate–based measures of market integration (Zevin, 1992) and net capital stock transfers across countries (Epstein and Gintis, 1992) illustrate that the level of international financial integration during the 1870–1914 "gold standard" era was probably greater than integration in the 1980s and 1990s (also see Thompson [1997]; Hirst and Thompson [1996]). Second, while covered interest rate differentials have largely converged in developed economies, there is an absence of deeper forms of financial integration: there are still nontrivial currency premiums (tapping exchange rate variability and expected currency depreciation) for many nations and these keep uncovered and real interest differentials apart (e.g., Frankel [1991]).[9] Moreover, most recent surveys of international financial market integration are quick to point out that there is still a dramatic "home country" bias in nearly all forms of capital investment (e.g., French and Poterba [1991]). In addition, the large majority of direct foreign investment and capital market flows consists of financial movements between developed capitalist democracies and not between developed and developing political economies (e.g., Obstfeld [1995]).

Beyond the limits of capital mobility, scholars have emphasized the persistence of distinct national trajectories of economic performance, domestic economic structures, and "production regimes." For instance, major aspects of macro- and microeconomic performance (e.g., productivity rates) and policy instruments continue to diverge despite a general convergence in some aspects of macroeconomic performance and monetary policies (e.g., contributions to Berger and Dore [1996]). Moreover, recent

---

[9] Convergence of uncovered interest rate differentials entails identical returns from assets denominated in different currencies when expressed in a single currency; convergence in real interest rate differentials involves the same returns across countries when rates are adjusted for inflation. Of course, beginning in 1999, the European Monetary Union has overcome currency-based impediments to financial market convergence for member nations.

theory and research suggests that alternative models for the organization and regulation of advanced capitalist economies (i.e., nationally coordinated, sector-coordinated, and uncoordinated capitalism) have not converged to any substantial degree (Boyer, 1996; Kitschelt, Lange, Marks, and Stephens, 1999; Soskice, 1999; Wade, 1996; c.f., Crouch and Streeck, 1997).[10]

Contemporary Embedded Liberalism. In sharp contrast to conventional globalization theory, some scholars highlight the ways in which international economic openness may actually promote a relatively high level of state intervention and a large welfare state. In well-known work of the late 1970s, both David Cameron (1978) and John Stephens (1979) argue that there are important structural and dynamic linkages between high levels of international economic openness and a large welfare state. Structurally, both Cameron and Stephens emphasize the political consequences of economic concentration that is typical of small, open economies: a highly concentrated industrial sector (i.e., the concentration of production in a small number of relatively large firms in each of a limited number of product areas) facilitates the organization of trade unions, centralized collective bargaining, and electorally consequential leftist parties (c.f., Wallerstein, 1989). These actors and institutions, in turn, foster the development of high levels of social protection and overall government intervention. In terms of dynamics, a large welfare state provides governments in open economies with mechanisms to smooth business cycles and ameliorate insecurity and risk attendant on international economic openness.

From a more consciously international perspective, John Ruggie (1982) argues that a multilateral international regime of embedded liberalism emerged in the post–World War Two era, in which a liberal international

---

[10] The persistence of national models of capitalism is important for the welfare state. As Kitschelt, Lange, Marks, and Stephens (1999) argue (also see Huber and Stephens [2001], and Manow [1998]), nationally coordinated production regimes (e.g., social corporatist systems of labor and industrial relations with statist supply-side policies) are complemented by redistributive welfare states built around universal income maintenance and social service programs; sector-coordinated market economies (e.g., industry-level business enterprise coordination with supportive state regulatory frameworks) tend to have large occupationally based welfare states that feature comprehensive and generous cash social insurance programs. On the other hand, liberal production regimes (e.g., competitive market-based economies with noninterventionist, pluralist polities) tend to have residualist welfare states that heavily rely on means-tested programs and private insurance and services. Thus, the resiliency of different production regimes suggests the absence of intense domestic structural pressures for welfare convergence.

trading order was supported by (cross-nationally varied) domestic political structures of interventionist government (e.g., Keynesian demand management, indicative planning) and social compensation for the insecurity and risks produced by liberal internationalism. Peter Katzenstein (1985) extends these works by analyzing the origins, structure, and consequences of national policy strategies of domestic compensation in the smaller open economies of Northern Europe. Complementing regulatory, active labor market, and related policies, the income maintenance programs of small states are central components of national strategies for adaptation to world markets. Empirical research by the aforementioned authors and others has consistently confirmed a substantively strong and statistically significant relationship between trade openness and the size of the public economy generally, and the welfare state specifically.[11]

In fact, some authors have asserted that the provision of social insurance and domestic compensation in response to internationally generated economic dislocations, insecurities, and risks is still a viable strategy for contemporary governments faced with increasing globalization of markets. Most notable is the work of Geoffrey Garrett (1998a, 1998b) and Dani Rodrik (1996; 1997), who have argued that governments continue to provide ample social compensation to those hurt by greater internationalization and to maintain (if not expand) social insurance against exposure to internationally generated risks. Indeed, Garrett (1998b) and Rodrik (1997) have contended that it may well be desirable to maintain and strengthen embedded liberalism in order to avert the severe social and political upheavals that potentially arise with the turbulence of international markets. Empirically, Garrett and Mitchell (forthcoming) have presented evidence that trade openness, trade volatility, and international financial integration have not substantially reduced income maintenance in the developed democracies. Similar findings have been presented by Rodrik, both for developing countries and the advanced democracies. Unlike Garrett and Mitchell, however, Rodrik's analysis suggests that rises in capital mobility (combined with high trade openness) collectively undercut the ability of governments to finance social compensation and otherwise maintain the joint efficiency and equity gains often associated with embedded liberalism (also see Pauly [1995]; Ruggie [1994]).

---

[11] I review the literature and provide additional evidence in Swank (1988) and Hicks and Swank (1992). For a critical assessment of the linkage between trade openness and the size of the public economy, see Iversen (2001).

A Summary of Principal and Supplementary Hypotheses

The literature on the domestic social policy impacts of international capital mobility leads to three straightforward hypotheses.

Conventional Wisdom: Net of other forces, rises in international capital mobility will be systematically associated with declines in public social welfare provision across the developed democracies.

Run to the Bottom: Increases in capital mobility will generate significantly greater pressures to roll back social protection in larger welfare states.

The latter hypothesis formalizes a basic version of the convergence thesis which, as discussed above, foresees moderate and large welfare states as particularly susceptible to the economic and political pressures generated by rising international capital mobility. As a result, policy makers in these systems may engage in a "run to the bottom" where social policies increasingly embody market-conforming principles. The primary difference between the two hypotheses involves the treatment of past levels of welfare state development. The first hypothesis assumes that after political, social, and economic determinants of welfare state size are taken into account, increases in capital mobility will systematically produce similar downward policy pressures across all of the developed democracies. The latter hypothesis is more complex in that it assumes that even after exogenous sources of welfare state effort are held constant, past welfare state development is important: increases in international capital mobility will place the greatest pressures on national policy makers to reform the welfare state precisely where the welfare state is most extensive and where the mix of social and tax policies is presumably the least attractive to mobile asset holders.

The Compensation Hypothesis: Increases in international capital mobility will be either unrelated or positively related to the magnitude of social protection.

This hypothesis, derived from traditional and contemporary versions of the embedded liberalism thesis, expresses the alternative view about contemporary internationalization: economic dislocations and increased insecurity associated with globalization will, at minimum, reinforce commitments to social insurance and domestic compensation; at most, new demands and social upheaval will generate pressure for expanded domestic compensation.

Contingencies and Conjunctures. In addition, one might formalize an additional set of supplementary hypotheses. Each of these propositions goes beyond the logic of a simple linear relationship between capital mobility and social welfare provision, as well as the notion that welfare states converge toward a more market-conforming model of social protection. Instead, each specifies a complex, often contingent or conjunctural impact of international financial openness on social welfare states.

The Curvilinear Hypothesis: Hicks (1999), drawing on arguments by Rodrik (1997) and others, has argued that international capital mobility may initially generate upward pressures on the welfare state as groups press for insurance against new insecurities and compensation for structural adjustments. At high levels of asset mobility, however, international financial openness may well undercut the ability of the state to fund generous social welfare protections and engender some retrenchment in social welfare effort. Thus, the relationship between capital mobility and social welfare effort is best expressed as nonlinear in form (i.e., as a polynomial) where an initial positive relationship gives way to a negative relationship after capital mobility has reached some threshold.

The Trade and Capital Openness Interaction: Rodrik (1997) has argued that while trade openness is generally associated with upward pressures on social welfare effort, high trade openness coupled with high levels of capital mobility is likely to produce reductions in social protection. This is so because the absence of capital restrictions (and associated movements of mobile assets) erodes the funding base of embedded liberalism in trade dependent economies. One might add that (real and perceived) pressures from international competitiveness at high levels of trade openness, and the economic and political pressures generated by capital mobility at high levels of financial integration, may reinforce each other.

Also, Garrett (1998b) has observed that international capital markets penalize governments that run high budget deficits and this, in turn, has domestic policy consequences. *Domestic Fiscal Imbalance:* With large deficits, markets expect high inflation (and other adverse economic outcomes and future tax increases), bid down the value of the deficit country's currency, and thus create an "interest premium" for governments who borrow to finance substantial deficits. Other mobile asset holders (e.g., global corporations that anticipate adverse consequences of fiscal imbalance) may also put pressure on policy makers in the deficit nation. Thus, one might expect capital mobility to interact with budgetary imbalance, exerting downward pressure on social welfare effort for those governments that tend to run substantial deficits.

Capital Flight: Finally, a substantial amount of attention has been devoted to the policy consequences of speculative capital movements and relatively short-term capital flight, especially in developing political economies (e.g., Kant [1996]; Mahon [1996]; Williamson and Lessard [1987]). The developed democracies have not been immune to adverse capital movements. Accelerating outflows and stagnant inflows of foreign direct investment in 1980s Sweden and in 1990s Germany, as well as adverse short-term flows in a number of other countries (e.g., early 1980s France) have typically generated calls for curbs on public spending and taxing (see Chapters 4 and 5 below). Thus, one might propose that adverse capital movements – "capital flight" – will create downward pressures on the welfare state and the taxes that finance it as governments attempt to demonstrate fiscal prudence and otherwise create favorable conditions for investment. Moreover, such pressures may be intensified at higher levels of capital mobility as governments have fewer policy instruments to mitigate adverse flows. For instance, when liberalization and financial market integration are high and long-standing, government may find it difficult for practical and political reasons to reimpose significant capital controls in the face of capital flight.

Global Capital, Democratic Institutions, and the Welfare State

As an alternative to conventional globalization theory (and embedded liberalism), I would like to advance a set of theoretical propositions about the roles of the institutional features of democratic polities and their welfare states. My argument is that the domestic policy impacts of international capital mobility should vary substantially across specific configurations of national institutions. In the development of theory and in empirical analysis, I emphasize the macropolitical consequences of institutions for the ability of pro–welfare state interests to resist neoliberal reform programs associated with internationalization. I stress the consequences of institutions for representational opportunities, including the presence of formal veto points and other opportunities for pro-welfare state actors to articulate preferences in the policy process (i.e., "leverage points"). I also stress two structural consequences of institutions that are realized in the long-run. First, I argue that both political institutions and welfare state structures have significant and systematic impacts on the political capacities of pro–welfare state interests. Second, I contend that institutional features of the polity and the welfare state promote distinct clusters of values, norms, and behaviors that either favor or disfavor neoliberal reform. As such, while I draw heavily from the "new institutionalism" literatures, I do not attempt to fully theorize and test its many rich hypotheses about the ways institutions structure actors' goals, interactions, and strategic choices in specific institutional contexts (e.g., in a particular type of bicameral legislature) and in discrete cases of policy choice (for reviews and extensions of this literature, see Hall and Taylor [1996]; Scharpf [1997]; Shepsle [1989]; Thelen and Steinmo [1992]).

To expand, national political institutions determine the forms and quality of representation of domestic interests that are affected by the internationalization of markets. That is, institutions provide (or restrict) opportunities for those that are adversely affected by globalization to seek compensatory policies and for those ideologically opposed to – or materially harmed by – the common neoliberal responses to globalization to resist unwanted policy change. As I illustrate below, institutional structures that promote encompassing interest representation of pro–welfare state interests – social corporatism and inclusive electoral institutions, most notably – dampen the pressures for neoliberal reform stemming from the economic and political logics of globalization. These institutional structures create "veto points" against policy change such as the ability of a party in a coalition government to reject policy initiatives (Tsebelis, 1995; 1999) and opportunities for interest articulation that fall short of formal veto power.[12] For instance, regularized (often informal) tripartite concertation between governments and peak associations of labor and employers characteristic of social corporatism affords trade union movements substantial opportunities to shape economic and social policy (but typically confers no formal right to reject policy proposals). These "leverage points," or formal and routine-informal incorporation of collective actors in the policy process, are inherent in some institutional structures of advanced democracies and, together with formal veto points, are highlighted below.

Fragmentation of decision-making authority (e.g., federalism, separation of powers, bicameralism) establishes (institutional) veto points and

---

[12] Tsebelis (1995, 1999) distinguishes between partisan veto players, such as parties in coalition governments, and institutional veto players, such as the majority in a bicameral legislative chamber. Contingent on the ideological or programmatic distance between actors and the coherence of the constituent elements of the actor, the number of veto players lowers the probability of policy change.

other opportunities for representation that are potentially useful to pro-welfare state interests. As I discuss below, however, historically embedded institutional dispersion of power, especially decentralization (e.g., federalism) and its close correlates (e.g., strong bicameralism), also creates relatively weak welfare programmatic alliances, pro-welfare state groups and parties, and national political coalitions; it also promotes norms and values conducive to retrenchment and neoliberal restructuring of the welfare state. In addition, some institutional structures of welfare states provide important opportunities for interest articulation. Most notable is the systematic incorporation of labor, business, and producer and consumer groups in social insurance fund administration and routine policy making in corporatist conservative welfare states.

Political institutions also influence directly and indirectly the relative political strength (weakness) of traditional welfare state constituencies, as well the relative strength (weakness) of supporting and opposing coalitions of social groups and classes. Specifically, institutions affect the relative political capacities of pro–welfare state interests. By political capacities, I mean the size and unity of programmatic alliances, collective actors, and political coalitions; the ability of these interests to pursue coherent national strategies of establishment and maintenance of social protection; and the conventional political resources of collective actors – organization, funding, and access. Moreover, not only do political institutions determine the relative strength of pro–welfare state interests, specific features of institutions enhance the economic and political forces generated by globalization. In other words, to paraphrase a well-worn characterization from Schattschneider, *political institutions are the structural mobilization of bias.*

My argument is not that political institutions are systematically created by political actors or coalitions to maintain or enhance their power. While the political construction of institutions occurs (e.g., Knight [1992]; Hall and Taylor [1996]: 92–4), institutions are also commonly shaped by a variety of complex domestic and international forces at crucial historical junctures (see, for instance, Riker [1964] on the origins of federalism, and Katzenstein [1985] on democratic corporatism). On the other hand, political institutions fundamentally shape the political capacities of actors and coalitions in subsequent periods of democratic development and practice, and they frequently become the locus of political contestation. For instance, social corporatism in Sweden finds its origins as much in the domestic and international crises of the 1920s and 1930s, and in incentives facing Swedish employers, as it does in the exogenous strength of the trade union movement (e.g., Katzenstein [1985]; Swenson, 1998). Social corporatism in Sweden (and other Northern European polities) is crucially important, however, for enhancing the power of labor and for producing egalitarian policy outcomes.

Finally, as recent work by Rothstein (1998) and Visser and Hemerijck (1997) make clear, political institutions foster distinct clusters of norms, values, and subsequent behaviors that fundamentally structure the policy process and make certain policy outcomes much more likely than others. Specifically, political institutions promote or impede certain constellations of norms and values important to social welfare policy change: some institutions foster cooperation and consensus as well as support for (and confidence in) the efficacy and fairness of the welfare state specifically, and the benefits of state intervention generally. In this context, rapid and substantial welfare state retrenchment under pressure of the economic and political logics of globalization becomes inherently less likely. Other national political institutions tend to promote competition and conflict as well as to foster antistatist and/or pro-market orientations; in these contexts, retrenchment and neoliberal restructuring may be more readily forthcoming.

In the following sections, I outline the case that the institutional structure of the polity and programmatic structures of the welfare state are fundamentally important for determining the quality and character of interest representation of pro–welfare state interests, the relative political capacities of these interests, and the broader constellation of supportive norms and values. As a result, these institutions mitigate the pressures on the welfare state that inhere in the economic and political logics of globalization. Before turning to specific institutions, however, one must address the question of what political economic interests are affected by, and will respond to, the economic and political pressures of globalization.

Interests

. . . reduced barriers to trade and investment accentuate the asymmetry between groups that can cross international borders. . . . and those that cannot. In the first category are owners of capital, highly skilled workers, and many professionals, who are free to take their resources where they are most in demand. Unskilled and semi-skilled workers and most middle managers belong in the second category. (Rodrik, 1997: 4)

As Rodrik's synopsis suggests, theory and research on globalization's impacts on the material interests of classes, sectors, and occupational groups highlights transnationally mobile manufacturing and financial enterprises, as well as highly skilled professionals and technical personnel and high-level managers, as "winners" of internationalization (see below for a detailed overview of theories of economic "winners and losers"). Not only are those with mobile assets economic winners, but interests who ideologically oppose moderate-to-high levels of welfare spending and redistribution (and other policies placed under pressure by the economic logic of internationalization) are favored.

In addition, the political logic of globalization highlights the relationships between internationalization and the political power of those actors who, on balance, oppose moderate-to-high levels of social protection and the taxation needed to finance the welfare state. Most important, internationalization enhances the appeal of policy preferences of Right parties and their core constituencies, neoliberal economists, and other proponents of neoliberal orthodoxy; that is, it reinforces neoliberal calls for elimination of welfare state inefficiencies and economically deleterious tax burdens. Internationalization also augments the conventional political resources of mobile business and their interest associations by conferring on them the "exit option." As discussed above, while business often has an interest in (and on occasion promotes) modest levels of social welfare provision, globalization theory assumes or explicitly argues that business will resist moderate-to-high levels of welfare provision that raise the reservation wage, create work disincentives, contribute to fiscal imbalances, and engender high taxes. In sum, the political logic of globalization argues that Right political parties, upper-income voters, neoliberal economists and bureaucrats, increasingly mobile business enterprises and their interest associations are politically (as well as economically) advantaged by internationalization in that their policy preferences are favored and their political power is enhanced.[13]

Globalization theory and my extrapolations from it tell only part of the story, however, and perhaps a small part at that. In fact, in stressing the ways in which internationalization generates strong economic and

---

[13] I thank Kathleen McNamara for suggesting a more explicit and systematic statement about "winners," and the political interests that serve as conduits of globalization pressures.

political pressures for welfare state retrenchment, proponents of globalization theory fail to take into account the broad array of domestic political actors whose material interests, concrete policy preferences, and ideological goals are threatened by internationalization and attendant neoliberal reform programs; they also say little about the roles of political institutions in shaping the relative political power of these pro–welfare state interests to resist neoliberal reform. Most centrally, globalization of markets generates real (and perceived) losses and new economic insecurities for specific classes, occupational strata, and sectors. Second, neoliberal reform programs generated by globalization threaten the material interests or ideological preferences of a distinct (and important) set of domestic interests.

With regard to those who lose or face new insecurities, most observers agree that, at a macroeconomic level, internationalization exposes larger and larger segments of the domestic economy to the "rigors" of international prices and internationally transmitted shocks. As Rodrik's (1997) quote makes clear, however, classes, occupational strata, and sectors are affected in different ways: labor generally, and unskilled and semiskilled workers specifically, may bear the brunt of new insecurities of employment and income. Indeed, a substantial body of literature in the tradition of Hechsher-Ohlin/Stolper-Samuelson models of factor price convergence suggests that the relative prices commanded by semi- and unskilled workers in the developed capitalist economies declines with internationalization (see Frieden and Rogowski [1996] for a review of the literature and theory). Trade, capital mobility, and immigration of workers, as well as specific processes such as the "outsourcing" of production of components to foreign producers, potentially threaten the relative wages and employment of increasingly large numbers of workers. In addition, even if one emphasizes that expanding trade and financial flows are disproportionately concentrated among developed capitalist economies and hence involve significantly less pressure for factor price convergence than North-South flows, increasing internationalization in all likelihood significantly increases the demand elasticity for labor in developed economies, intensifying income and employment insecurities (Slaughter, 1996; Rodrik, 1997). Moreover, as noted, most globalization theory highlights that power in collective bargaining and other political economic forums has shifted from labor to increasingly mobile employers, contributing to labor's difficulties in expanding and protecting income and jobs. As Rodrik (1997), Garrett (1998b), and others have argued, wages and employment of labor generally, and of semi- and unskilled workers particularly, may well be increasingly subject to instability and insecurity attendant on globalization.[14]

Second, the common neoliberal program associated with internationalization mobilizes social aggregates whose material interests are harmed by retrenchment and market-oriented restructuring of the welfare state and interests who may oppose retrenchment on ideological grounds. The first group consists of what might be called "welfare program alliances." These alliances consist of actual program beneficiaries of social insurance and services, welfare program personnel whose policy commitments and jobs are linked to the development and maintenance of the welfare state, and a variety of private-sector suppliers and contractors whose income is directly tied to maintenance of the welfare state. Given the scope of social insurance and service programs in the contemporary welfare state, programmatic alliances commonly extend beyond wage earners in manual positions and encompass segments of the middle class. The second set of interests consists of collective actors – interest groups and parties – whose ideological preferences (and often material interests, in that their members commonly overlap other affected groups) are directly threatened by retrenchment and market-oriented restructuring. Across the advanced democracies, these actors typically consist of trade union movements and labor-based political parties, communitarian Catholic parties and groups, far-left and left-libertarian groups and parties. Finally, as Esping-Andersen (1990), Hicks (1999), and others have shown, relatively enduring national political coalitions of working- and middle-class voters and their interest associations and parties have been crucial in some polities to the development of the welfare state. Beyond programmatic alliances and focal collective actors alone, the economic and political pressures atten-

---

[14] Domestic structural economic change may reinforce the impacts of internationalization. This change, in part, is associated with the expansion of the service sector and knowledge class; it is also associated with the decline of large-scale, geographically concentrated manufacturing of homogenized products and the ascent of specialized, flexible, small-scale, and spatially diffused production of high value-added products. Each of these changes – postindustrial occupational transition and post-Fordist production – contributes to a general climate of economic uncertainty for semi- and unskilled production and clerical personnel in traditional occupations and industries (e.g., Esping-Andersen [1990]; OECD [1995a]). Moreover, focusing on the overarching process of deindustrialization, the new economic uncertainties may extend to many skilled workers and middle-class strata, as well (see Iversen 2001).

dant on internationalization will tend to mobilize these national coalitions in defense of the welfare state.[15]

The central determinant of the ability of pro–welfare state interests to limit the social policy impacts of the economic and political logics of internationalization is the structure of domestic political institutions. As noted, institutional characteristics of the polity and programmatic structures of welfare states are fundamentally important. Some institutions foster relatively powerful pro–welfare state interests and otherwise offer favorable conditions for the defense of the welfare state. On the other hand, some institutional contexts supplement the economic and political pressures generated by globalization by conferring special political advantages on neoliberal political interests and coalitions or by providing especially conducive contexts for neoliberal restructuring. While I emphasize that the most crucial factors in shaping the impacts of internationalization are the ways in which domestic institutions determine the relative power of pro–welfare state interests, I also highlight additional institutional features that favor the forces generated by rising internationalization.

The Polity: Institutions for Interest Representation

Social Corporatist versus Pluralist Systems of Interest Representation. First, the character of the interest group system, especially the degree to which the system is social corporatist, should facilitate the extent to which affected interests can press their claims for preferred policies and resist adverse policy changes in the face of internationalization. Social corporatism provides an institutional mechanism whereby factions of labor affected negatively by different aspects of globalization can articulate preferences and press claims on national policy makers to maintain or expand social protection. Moreover, given the economic interests and ideological

---

[15] The role of the middle class and their interest groups and political parties is often crucial. Some institutional contexts (inclusive electoral institutions and universalistic program structures) foster and reinforce relative durable coalitions of middle- and working-class actors that effectively buffer the welfare state from strong neoliberal retrenchment and restructuring. Second, the interests and political action of highly skilled labor is also somewhat variable. While generally fully ensconced in pro–welfare state coalitions, specific political economic contexts may ally highly skilled workers with neoliberal coalitions. For instance, as I discuss below in the Swedish case study, skilled workers in the export sector – who bear substantial burdens of rising public sector-generated wage increases, inflation, and taxes – have aligned with employers and neoliberal parties to support reductions in public sector budgets.

orientations of labor, as well as labor's relatively powerful position in highly organized systems of interest representation, social corporatism should constitute a general political barrier to substantial and rapid neoliberal policy change.[16] In fact, corporatist institutions, particularly economy-wide bargaining, in which broadly organized and centralized labor movements have regularly exchanged wage restraint for full employment commitments and improvements in social protection, have been important in the development of welfare states in capitalist democracies (Hicks and Swank, 1992; Katzenstein, 1985; Lehmbruch, 1984; Stephens, 1980). Despite new pressures on such institutions (e.g., Kurzer [1993]; Moses [2000]), we should expect that social corporatism should continue to play an important role in representation of interests affected by internationalization.

First, despite the instability and decentralization of Swedish centralized wage-setting institutions, there is a surprising persistence of relatively centralized labor and industrial relation systems in Northern Europe (Wallerstein and Golden, 1997). Second, the more political forms of corporatism involving representation of labor, business, and other interests on national policy-making and advisory boards, commissions, and committees is still robust. Even in Sweden, where business withdrew its representatives from tripartite boards of several state agencies in 1991 (e.g., Pontusson and Swenson [1996]), extensive corporatist intermediation between business, labor, and the state persists in the area of social policy making (Hoefer, 1996). In addition, moderately centralized social corporatist bargaining and exchange in sector-coordinated market economies such as Germany, Belgium, and Italy are supported by a network of business-labor cooperative relationships (e.g., works councils) and broader economic institutions; there is scant evidence that these (or the broader) features of sector-coordinated market economies are breaking down. Finally, as Visser and Hemerijck (1997) have documented for the Dutch case and Rhodes

---

[16] The efficacy of social corporatism in representing interests materially harmed by internationalization of markets might be challenged by emphasizing that the most vulnerable segments of the labor force (e.g., unskilled workers) are "outsiders" in highly organized systems of industrial and labor representation. However, given that social corporatism is grounded on encompassing interest representation (e.g., high union density), typically involves some solidaristic wage bargaining (through centralized wage bargaining), and offers general representation of labor's interests in tripartite policy making, social corporatist systems of interest representation will be notably superior to pluralist systems even though "insider-outsider" problems exist.

(2001) for a variety of European political economies, (re)centralization of bargaining and corporatist social pacts among employers, labor, and the state have been surprisingly common in European polities during the 1980s and 1990s. While "new" corporatist arrangements often involve the intersection of productivity and redistributional issues and coalitions, the continuation of extensive opportunities for representation of labor's interests is clear.

Social corporatism has also played direct and indirect roles in cultivating the political capacities of other pro-welfare state interests. Most important, corporatism has been an important element in the political success and policy strategies of social democratic parties. In fact, in the post–World War Two era, social corporatism can be directly linked with the electoral and parliamentary strength of parties of the Left. Specifically, the relationships across time and space in the advanced democracies between the measure of corporatism developed below and the percentage of votes and seats won by parties of the Left is highly significant (Pearson correlations of .630 and .637, respectively [$N = 435$] for the years 1960–92 in the 15 focal nations). Relatedly, Cameron (1978), Katzenstein (1985), Korpi (1983), Stephens (1980), and others offer theory and provide evidence that the strength of the trade union movement, the development and maintenance of social corporatism institutions, and social democratic party political success are closely and inextricably linked in the historical development of capitalist democracy.[17]

Social corporatism also cultivates a distinct constellation of norms and values that shape actors' behavior and the character of the policy process. As Katzenstein's (1985) seminal work has shown, social corporatism is dependent on, and in operation reinforces, an "ideology of social partnership," in which policy emerges from the cooperative and consensus-oriented routines of repeated interactions among peak associations of labor and business. Similarly, in their insightful analysis of the 1980s reconstitution of corporatism in the Netherlands, Visser and Hemerijck (1997)

---

[17] In addition, Lange and Garrett (1985) and Hicks (1988) have highlighted how social corporatism and Left government interact to mutually support the pursuit of the policies of wage restraint, full employment, and redistribution. Examining the relationships between liberalization of capital markets, macroeconomic policy and performance, Garrett (1998a) has also shown that labor-oriented governments in social corporatist contexts are likely to maintain full employment and other activist policies in the wake of internationalization. I will return to Garrett's argument about the role of the interaction between Left government and social corporatism below.

argue that corporatist exchanges are analogous to networks of engagement (see Putnam [1993]), where norms of reciprocity, trust, and a sense of duty to other social partners are cultivated. Supplementing the economic logic of corporatist institutions (i.e., the "internalization of externalities" that is achieved through encompassing organization of peak associations of functional economic interests), corporatist bargaining – sustained interaction and accommodation among social partners – facilitates the development of accommodation for the public good (also see Milner [1994]). As Visser and Hemerijck (1997: 68) put it:

Through their participation in "networks of civic engagement," actors do feel and can be held responsible for policy outcomes, defined in terms of public goods, like jobs for all, more work for minorities, etc. This entails a significant shift in the definition and interpretation of what is in the group's best interest. . . . The denser the networks of civic engagement, the more likely trust and "public regarding" behavior will be forthcoming.

Expanding on this view, one can argue that cultivation of reciprocity, trust, and public-regarding behavior tends to be reinforced at multiple levels of social corporatist systems: centralized collective bargaining over wages and conditions of work, tripartite policy-making forums (commissions, boards, committees), and decentralized business-labor exchange through works councils and related institutions. Net of other forces, social policy change in such an environment will typically involve slow, marginal, negotiated changes in which all interests are accounted. The aggressive assertion of neoliberal reform programs by business and the relatively quick and substantial retrenchments of the welfare state in response to internationalization are less likely than under pluralist systems of interest representation.

Inclusive versus Exclusive Systems of Electoral Institutions. In addition, different features of formal constitutional structures and associated institutions that facilitate inclusive forms of representation through the electoral and party systems should matter. Important in this regard is recent work by Crepaz and Birchfield (2000), who have argued that neoliberal policy changes associated with globalization should, at minimum, proceed more slowly in consensus democracies. This is so because consensus democracies have institutional mechanisms that guarantee that "losers" in the process of internationalization are represented and that policy change occurs with incorporation of their interests. In related work, Birchfield and Crepaz (1998) have highlighted particular institutional features associated with consensus democracy that are important to those who pursue maintenance of the welfare state and egalitarian ends. Specifically, Birchfield and Crepaz argue that it is the "collective veto points" afforded by proportional representation, and the number of effective legislative parties, in particular, that insures some protection of these interests and egalitarian policy goals.[18]

Generally, PR and multiparty systems are more likely to afford workers and other economic interests harmed or threatened by globalization relatively potent institutional mechanisms to resist adverse policy changes and to pursue compensation; ideological interests opposed to the potential of globalization-induced, market-conforming policy changes (e.g., Social Democratic parties, communitarian Christian Democratic parties) will also be relatively advantaged. The inclusiveness of representation and therefore institutional opportunities for resisting adverse policy change are much weaker in polities with majoritarian electoral systems (e.g., single-member districts with plurality rules) and two-party dominant systems.[19] In fact, the most successful episodes of relatively rapid neoliberal welfare state reforms (e.g., the 1980s United Kingdom and United States) occurred with single-party majority governments elected with minority shares of the national electorates under single-member district-plurality rules. Everything else being equal, exclusive electoral systems minimize the need for accommodation between winners and losers – supporters and opponents – of existing systems of social protection.

The existence of what might be labeled "inclusive electoral institutions" has also historically advantaged those groups and parties that constitute the core ideological support for the welfare state. As to political parties,

---

[18] The nature of "collective veto points," or what Tsebelis (1995) labels partisan veto points, and their impact on the welfare state, needs clarification. PR and multiparty systems (as indexed by the number of effective legislative parties) offers pro–welfare state interests several representational opportunities – both veto points and important leverage points. First, these inclusive electoral institutions tend to produce coalition governments where pro-redistributive parties can act as partisan veto players. Relatedly, these institutions are associated with oversized cabinets (e.g., "grand coalitions") that maximize party and voter representation in government policy making (Lijphart, 1999). Third, keeping in mind that inclusive electoral institutions are strongly associated with seats held by pro–welfare state parties (see below), the strength of pro–welfare state parties in opposition is systematically associated with lower social policy retrenchment by governing center-right parties (Hicks and Swank, 1992).

[19] As Rogowski (1987) and Katzenstein (1985) have argued, PR is the natural electoral system of open economies. PR tends to maximize representation of interests affected by international competition, as well as to contribute to consensus and stability of national policies necessary in open economies (also see Crepaz and Birchfield [2000]).

Esping-Andersen (1990), Hicks and Swank (1984, 1992), Huber, Ragin, and Stephens (1993), and Wilensky (1981) have offered evidence that social democratic parties, most notably through their impacts on universal social protection and government provision of social services, and Christian Democratic parties, most clearly through their impact on the development of generous cash income maintenance programs, have been important in welfare state development. Examining long-term relationships, the correlations between the index of electoral inclusiveness developed below and shares of votes and national legislative seats for Left and Christian Democratic parties are highly significant (Pearson correlations for 1960–92 data [$N = 435$] across the focal nations are .500, .477, .402, .407, respectively).

In addition, inclusive electoral institutions tend to exist in broader constellations of consensus democratic institutions (Lijphart, 1984; 1999) and tend to involve repeated interactions between a multiplicity of social interests within decision-making institutions such as lower chambers of parliaments and coalition governments. As such, norms of cooperation, reciprocity, and consensus-building may be fostered and adopted policies may enjoy significant legitimacy given that a broad range of social interests have been accounted (Crepaz and Birchfield, 2000; Birchfield and Crepaz, 1998). Similar to the case of social corporatism, social policy change in multiparty parliaments and cabinets is likely to involve negotiation and ultimate compromise among multiple partisan actors; relatively rapid and substantial rollbacks in social welfare provision and neoliberal welfare state restructuring are, on balance, unlikely in this context.[20]

The Polity: Organization of Authoritative Decision Making

Beyond the institutions of collective interest and electoral representation, the organization of formal policy-making authority in the political system also influences the opportunity structure and political capacities of pro-welfare state actors as well as the broader cluster of norms and values that shape the policy process. Unlike the collective interest and electoral

---

[20] Rational choice institutionalism has tended to emphasize the adverse consequences of consensus democratic institutions. For instance, negotiated policy change between multiple parties in coalition governments has been blamed for slow responsiveness to economic shocks and for a bias toward high spending and deficits in some democracies, among other economic problems (see Alesina and Roubini [1997, Ch. 9] for a review); however, these familiar arguments about the inferior policy effectiveness and economic performance of consensus institutions have been seriously questioned by Lijphart (1999) and others.

representation systems, however, the dispersion of policy-making authority has multidirectional impacts on the relative power of pro–welfare state actors. In fact, this institutional dimension highlights the importance of considering not only the relatively direct and immediate effects of institutions on the opportunity structure for representation (and associated dynamics of policy making in specific institutional contexts), but also the long-term effects of institutions on political capacities of actors and prevailing policy norms as well.

As to the impact of dispersion on the opportunity structure for interest articulation, the literatures on welfare state development and veto players provide clear hypotheses. Work on the expansion of the welfare state has highlighted the way in which the "dispersion of policy-making authority" has shaped long-term evolution of the welfare state. Specifically, federalism, bicameralism, presidentialism, and the use of referendums constitute potentially important "institutional" veto points that allow conservative interests the opportunity to oppose welfare policy development and slow policy change (e.g., Immergut [1992]; Huber, Ragin, and Stephens [1993]).[21] In the literature, systematic evidence has emerged to support the claim that fragmentation or dispersion of authority limits the expansion of national systems of social welfare protection. For instance, Huber, Ragin, and Stephens (1993) report a strong negative relationship between the presence of constitutional structures that fragment power (i.e., create veto points) and various dimensions of social welfare provision. Castles (1998), Hicks and Swank (1992), and others report evidence of a substantively large negative relationship between decentralization of policy-making power (most notably federalism) and the size of the public economy and welfare effort. Schmidt (1996, 1997) offers evidence that institutional constraints on the central government (e.g., institutional arrangements that fragment and share power) limit the expansion of the public sector and the welfare state. A burgeoning literature in rational choice institutionalism supports findings from the welfare state literature and provides rich and extensive insights into the dynamics of how federalism, bicameralism, and other aspects of the dispersion of power slow policy change and otherwise condition policy making (see, among others, Scharpf [1988] on the "joint decision traps" of federalism, and Tsebelis and Money [1997] on the policy consequences of bicameralism).

---

[21] The logic of institutional veto points, or what Birchfield and Crepaz (1998) label competitive veto points, is fully explored by Tsebelis (1995).

At first glance, fragmentation or dispersion of power, or the presence of institutional veto points, may accord welfare state constituencies and coalitions opportunities to impede or otherwise shape neoliberal policy changes to their best advantage. Everything else being equal – that is, the political capacities of welfare programmatic alliances, collective actors, and coalitions, as well as norms and values that shape the policy process being equal – dispersion of authority through federalism, bicameralism, separation of powers, and related institutional structures affords welfare state interests opportunities to resist – to veto or otherwise systematically influence – neoliberal reforms attendant on globalization. Case-study evidence presented in Chapters 4 through 6 documents important instances of the operation of institutional veto points. As Bonoli (2001) points out, however, the degree to which institutional fragmentation constrains welfare retrenchment hinges largely on the relative power of welfare state constituencies, groups, and coalitions.

In long-lived systems of dispersed authority, welfare program alliances, collective actors, and coalitions will be systematically weak and the norms and values that condition policy making will be conducive to welfare state retrenchment. First, formal fragmentation of policy-making authority has large effects on the political capacities of program alliances, groups, and coalitions that have traditionally supported the welfare state and that provide the contemporary bulwark against significant retrenchment: dispersion of policy-making authority undercuts the size and unity of actors, coherence of strategies, and conventional political resources. This is especially true for decentralization of authority through federalism and its close correlate, strong bicameralism.[22] Specifically, as Noble's (1997: 28–34) survey of the literature suggests, decentralization of policy-making authority has generally mobilized socially heterogeneous forces (e.g., regionally specific cultural groups), undercut progressive and egalitarian political forces at the national level (e.g., trade union movements, cross-class coalitions), and favored local economic and political elites (also see Castles [1998]; Pierson [1995]; Stephens [1980]). In addition, institutional structures that decentralize policy-making responsibility tend to undercut the formation of coherent national policy strategies by groups and parties;

---

[22] As political analysis presented below and the literature on democratic institutions (e.g., Lijphart [1984], [1999]) illustrate, federalism and strong bicameralism – commonly with regional representation in the upper chamber of national legislatures – are closely related.

the organization of parties and groups tends to be concentrated at regional and local levels and politics tends to focus on narrow distributional issues within regional and local jurisdictions (e.g., on Canada, see Banting [1997], and Bradford and Jenson [1992]; on the United States, see Amenta [1998], Piven [1992], Robertson and Judd [1989], and Skocpol [1995]).

In fact, the long-term relationships between institutional fragmentation on the one hand, and the electoral strength of Left parties and social corporatism on the other, are strong. The correlations across time and space (1960–92 for the 15 focal nations) between the index of "dispersion of policy-making authority" developed below (presidentialism, federalism, bicameralism, and use of referendums) and Left parties' votes and seats are $-.608$ and $-.572$ ($N = 435$, $p < .0005$); for dispersion of authority and social corporatism the correlation is $-.580$ ($p < .0005$). In other words, despite the institutional veto points available to pro-redistributive groups and coalitions, substantial theory and evidence suggests that the political capacities of these collective actors will be relatively weak in historically embedded systems of dispersed (and especially decentralized) policy-making authority.

In addition, one might suggest that to the extent that fragmentation of authority is associated with low levels of welfare state development, dispersion and decentralization will create weak welfare state programmatic alliances. First, in the literature on state structures and welfare state development, fragmentation of policy-making authority is associated with weak national bureaucracies, the absence of traditions of state intervention, and low state capacity to initiate and develop national systems of social protection (e.g., Weir and Skocpol [1985]; Skocpol [1995]). Second, I present evidence below that "dispersion of policy-making authority" (and all individual dimensions of fragmentation) is among the largest determinants – in statistical and substantive terms – of those forces that directly shape (negatively) welfare effort across time and space. As such, welfare programmatic alliances – constituencies, welfare program personnel, and suppliers – will be relatively small, politically weak, and hence less capable of resisting retrenchment.

Moreover, the climate for welfare state retrenchment may be enhanced by the prevailing constellation of norms and values in fragmented polities. First, the decentralization of authority itself suggests a political culture of distrust of centralized political power and national state policy intervention. Second, the dispersion of policy-making power – both separation of powers and decentralization – tends to complement and reinforce the competition and conflict of pluralist politics; the atomistic competition of a multiplicity of interests in pluralist theory is reinforced and bolstered by the proliferation of "entry points" in the political process. In addition, decentralization of authority also tends to promote conflict and competition among subnational entities. For instance, federalism accentuates differences between rich and poor regions and, in turn, generates conflicts over the content of policy, fiscal equalization, and the distribution of financial burdens of national expenditure among often fiscally constrained subnational units (see, among others, de Villiers [1994]; Banting [1997]). Finally, substantial decentralization of power may tend to foster competition for employment- and revenue-generating investment among subnational entities in fully integrated national markets and, thus, may tend to advantage business and market-oriented economic orthodoxy in fragmented polities (e.g., Pierson [1995]).[23] Generally, norms of cooperation, reciprocity, and consensus-building, potentially conducive to defense of the welfare state against substantial and rapid cuts, will be weaker in political systems of dispersed authority than in other polities; the norms of conflict, competition, and antistatism will be stronger.

At the same time, it is important to note that the (negative) impact of dispersion of policy-making authority within the polity on the political strength of welfare program alliances, collective actors, and coalitions, as well as on norms and values embedded in the policy process, is historically conditioned. Where dispersion and decentralization of decision-making authority is deeply embedded in historical development of the polity (e.g., Australia, Canada, Switzerland, and the United States), we should expect that the negative effects of fragmentation on welfare state actors will offset, and supercede in the long run, any advantages accorded welfare state interests by institutional veto points. Where dispersion of policy-making

[23] To strongly argue that asset mobility will notably constrain subnational policy makers is to an extent inconsistent with the thesis of this volume. Yet, subnational policy makers in highly decentralized systems operate with few of the policy tools and advantages of national policy makers, are highly dependent on revenue from mobile asset holders (most business people, skilled workers, and professionals), where there are virtually no barriers to asset and income movement, and tend to develop an ethic of promoting the business climate of the subnational entity (e.g., on the United States, for instance, see Robertson and Judd [1989]; on Australia, Wanna [1991]; and on Canada, Banting [1986]; c.f., Noel [1998] for a critical survey of the theoretical and empirical literature). In addition, the literature on "market-preserving federalism," or how the aforementioned properties of federalism in developed democracies promote market efficiency, reinforces these conclusions (see, among others, Weingast [1995]).

authority is relatively recent, as in Belgian federalism, negative welfare state effects of dispersion (e.g., those channeled through dispersion's impacts on the political capacities of welfare state interests) should be relatively minor. The most important case is Germany, where Second and Third Reich statist legacies and corporatist conservative welfare traditions are combined with notable institutional fragmentation of the postwar Federal Republic. Indeed, there is reason to believe that the role of institutional veto points as a mechanism of 1980s and 1990s welfare state defense may, in the German case, outweigh the negative welfare state impacts of dispersion of authority.[24]

Beyond institutional features of the polity, one might argue that the programmatic structures of welfare states themselves, particularly those that affect program alliances, political coalitions, and public opinion and value orientations, should be considered as a separate set of institutional characteristics that condition the effects of external socioeconomic and political pressures for retrenchment. In fact, one can offer substantial theory that universal and corporatist conservative program structure strengthens welfare state actors, while features of liberalism undercut the political defense of the welfare state.

The Institutional Structures of the Welfare State

Pierson (1994, 1996) outlines the general logic of welfare state retrenchment by noting that, unlike the politics of welfare expansion, welfare retrenchment involves taking away concentrated, political popular benefits from organized constituencies for the promise of future, diffuse benefits; institutional characteristics of program structure constrain various retrenchment strategies. Esping-Andersen (1996b, 1996c) also makes a similar point by arguing that institutional legacies of welfare states shape the impact of the variety of social, economic, and political changes on social welfare policy. As Esping-Andersen (1990) argues, contemporary welfare states may be classified as social democratic, conservative corporatist, and liberal (c.f., Castles and Mitchell [1993] on the fourth world

---

[24] For empirical measures of dispersion of authority developed below, the advent of federalism or other institutional changes is coded accordingly for the postwar era. In the quantitative analysis, however, I do not weight measures of dispersion by differential historical legacies. The case-study analysis of Chapters 4 and 5 attempts to introduce these considerations.

51

of welfare capitalism, the "radical" welfare state model). The core programmatic characteristics of these "three worlds of welfare" consist of universalism, occupationally based social insurance, and selectivity. As Rothstein (1998) notes, universal welfare states entail programmatic structures of extensive or full coverage of target populations, egalitarian benefits, and widely accessible social services; liberal or selective welfare states are characterized by disproportionate reliance on means-tested and private benefits. These aspects of programmatic structure have substantial impacts on the representation and the relative political capacities of pro–welfare state interests, as well as the overarching constellations of values, norms, and orientations that facilitate or impede welfare state retrenchment.

A Note on Welfare State Classifications and Nomenclature. A number of individual welfare states depart notably from the prototype of the welfare state regime to which they are commonly assigned. I attempt to systematically acknowledge nuances of individual cases, the prospects for additional welfare state types (e.g., the "radical" welfare state regime, the Southern European variant of the conservative welfare state), and country departures from core features of the principal welfare state types below. I also incorporate subsequent refinements of the attributes of (original) welfare state models such as the relative reliance on publically provided social services and new information on the redistributive impacts of welfare state types. With these considerations in mind, I use Esping-Andersen's classifications as general analytical categories. When discussing general welfare state models and their political economic correlates in Chapters 4 through 6, I use the terms "social democratic," "corporatist conservative," and "liberal." When discussing core programmatic features of welfare states and groups of welfare states that cohere around these features, I use the terms "universalism," "conservatism," and "liberalism."

Opportunity Structures and Welfare State Retrenchment. Institutional features of existing program structures can play significant roles in impeding or facilitating neoliberal reforms proposed in response to the economic and political pressures generated by globalization. While universal and liberal program structures centralize policy formation and implementation in the hands of governmental institutions and bureaucracies, conservative corporatist welfare states decentralize authority to networks of quasi-public administrative bodies comprised of constituency and professional groups as well as labor, business, and government. As such, conservative corporatist welfare states provide notable opportunities – veto points for routine regulatory policies and leverage points for shaping national policy formation – to programmatic alliances and collective actors (see, among others, Clasen and Freeman [1994] on the prototypical case of Germany); such opportunities are, on balance, more restricted in universal and (especially) liberal welfare program structures, where administration and routine policy making are relatively centralized in public agencies.[25]

Political Support for the Welfare State. Institutional features of welfare states may also strengthen (weaken) the political capacities of programmatic alliances, collective actors, and national coalitions. Central to the politics of welfare retrenchment is the extent to which welfare state institutions promote (retard) large, unified constituencies and unify (fragment) the panoply of other interests that may mobilize to resist rollbacks in social protection (e.g., Pierson, 1994). Universal welfare states, most notably, create large cohesive constituency groups organized around relatively generous, universal programs of social welfare provision. While conservative corporatist welfare states can fragment program constituencies on the basis of occupational status, corporatist conservative program structure has generally promoted broad cross-class coalitions of working- and middle-class interests that coalesce around comprehensive and generous social insurance. In the case of liberal welfare states, fragmentation of constituencies and potential coalitions occurs across social class lines where means-testing and a significant private social insurance sector divide lower and upper strata.

To elaborate, universalism generates high levels of mass political support and fosters the development of broad political coalitions that undergird maintenance of the welfare state. Specifically, Moene and Wallerstein (1996) have highlighted the importance of the use of universal versus means-tested benefits in maintaining the support of median voters for national systems of social protection: universalism cultivates median voter political support for the welfare state since these voters face

---

[25] Important exceptions are the union administered (Ghent) system of unemployment insurance present in the universal welfare states of Denmark, Finland, and Sweden, as well as administration of ATP (earnings-related supplementary) pensions in nations such as Denmark. Also, incorporation of the "social partners" in advisory boards and commissions in universal welfare states is relatively common.

relatively high probabilities of benefiting from universally structured social programs; means-tested programs do not generate such support since median voters face low odds of benefiting from means-tested, targeted programs. Supporting this analysis of the rational calculus of beneficiaries, historical analysis of welfare state development (e.g., Esping-Andersen [1990]) suggests national program structures that provide high levels of universal coverage, basic security, and income replacement have effectively fused the interests of working- and middle-class strata in the development and maintenance of the universal welfare state (also see Rothstein [1998]). While some have suggested that the recent growth in tax preferences for upscale groups and private occupational schemes in social democratic welfare states will contribute to growing fissures within the traditional coalition (Ervik and Kuhnle, 1996), the persistence of universalism should significantly blunt the policy impacts of economic and political pressures attendant on capital mobility when compared to liberal welfare systems (see Chapter 4 on the persistence of universalism).

For corporatist conservative welfare states, program fragmentation across multiple occupationally based schemes can lead to opportunities for proponents of retrenchment and neoliberal reform to employ "divide-and-conquer" strategies. Rothstein (1998), however, points out that the same logic employed by Moene and Wallerstein (1996) for the universal welfare state can be adapted to corporatist conservative welfare states: median voters enjoy generous basic and income security with extensive social insurance against market risks and thus will resist retrenchment of the system. Moreover, much of the literature on corporatist conservative welfare states (see Chapter 5 below) commonly highlights the ways in which generous and comprehensive social insurance effectively integrates the working and middle classes in the contemporary social order, fuses their interests behind the maintenance of the social insurance model, and creates high levels of welfare state legitimacy. For instance, in Germany, 1950s increases in the generosity of pensions, and affirmation of the equivalence principle that links social insurance benefits to the standard of living during employment, join with compensatory provisions for lower-income workers and the poor to foster high levels of cross-class political support for the *Sozialstaat*. In the case of liberal welfare states, the fragmentation of interests across means-tested programs, modest contributory public social insurance schemes, and private social protection makes it extremely difficult to forge broad national political coalitions in support of the welfare state.

Politics, Values, and Social Welfare Provision. Institutional structures of welfare states also promote constellations of norms and values that facilitate or retard retrenchment and neoliberal restructuring. Bo Rothstein's (1998) important and insightful study of the universal welfare state of Northern Europe extends the previous analyses of political dynamics of the institutional features of welfare states and highlights the role of the "moral logic of the welfare state" in retrenchment politics. That is, Rothstein's analysis highlights the ways in which program attributes foster and reinforce specific configurations of norms and values. According to Rothstein, support for the welfare state hinges on the "contingent consent" of strategically self-interested and moral citizens. In turn, this consent is dependent on citizens' appraisals of the substantive, procedural, and distributional fairness of the welfare state. After affirming the political logic of the universal welfare state, as discussed above, Rothstein outlines the moral logic of the universal welfare state: a moral basis of equal respect and concern embodied in program structure, broadly targeted universal benefits, carefully adapted delivery organizations, and participatory administrative processes achieve relatively high levels of contingent consent from the citizenry. Solidarity, trust, and confidence in state intervention are promoted. In liberal welfare states, problems related to substantive justice (e.g., conflicts over defining the "deserving poor"), procedural justice (perceptions of bureaucratic aggrandizement and waste), and fairness in the distribution of burdens (e.g., perceptions of constituency fraud) are endemic. A climate of distrust, conflict, and competition among beneficiaries and among beneficiaries and nonbeneficiaries is promoted by liberal program structure. In sum, Rothstein's work suggests that we might expect notably different magnitudes and paces of welfare policy reform across universalistic and liberal welfare states.[26]

A similar "moral logic" can be applied to the corporatist conservative welfare states. As Clasen (1997), Hinrichs (1995), and others have argued in the German case, the social insurance model promotes – and is supported by – a "culture of solidarity," in which citizens possess a high level of trust in the ability of the model to effectively and comprehensively cover

---

[26] Svallfors (1995) presents detailed panel data on attitudes toward social welfare policies in Sweden. Consistent with the theoretical and formal analyses of Moene and Wallerstein and the arguments and evidence of Rothstein (1998), Svallfors documents the continuation of high levels of support for much of the Swedish welfare state with one exception: a clear erosion of support for means-tested programs, most notably social assistance (c.f., Pierson [1994]).

risks, and accept as morally desirable the redistributive and compensatory aspects of the system. Related, in the French case, Béland and Hansen (2000), Spicker (1997), and others have highlighted the importance to the welfare state of the principle of solidarity, a moral precept (rooted in both secular and Catholic social philosophy) that stresses the integrative functions of the welfare state. Expansion and maintenance of comprehensive social insurance and contemporary extensions of compensatory measures (e.g., to combat social exclusion) are often demanded by broad coalitions of voters and justified by party elites (across the ideological spectrum) on the basis of the principle of solidarity. Moreover, as Esping-Andersen (1996c), Clausen and Freeman (1994), and others have noted, legitimacy and political support for the welfare state in occupationally based systems is reinforced by perceptions of strong legal rights to benefits by the broad spectrum of citizens who contribute while in employment. Generally, and similar to universal welfare states, corporatist conservative systems of social protection are likely to be associated with value structures that significantly blunt the neoliberal retrenchment pressures attendant on globalization.

Overall, substantial theory suggests that rollbacks of social protection in response to internationalization will be notably more difficult in universal and corporatist conservative systems than in liberal welfare states: the relative political strength of pro–welfare state coalitions as well as levels of mass political approval and supportive value orientations will constitute a significant barrier to social policy retrenchment. The reverse should be true in liberal programmatic contexts: weaker welfare state constituencies and alliances, lower levels of mass political support, fragmented coalitions, and the prevalence of anti–welfare state value orientations should reinforce the economic and political logics of globalization.

An Overview of Political Institutions Hypotheses

Taken together, these arguments suggest that institutional features of the polity and welfare state will significantly condition welfare policy responses to the economic and political pressures generated by globalization. At the most general level, the variability in institutional structures – and hence the variability in the character of interest representation, the political capacities of welfare state interests, and the norms and values embedded in the policy process – should lead to a heterogeneous set of responses to internationalization over the focal period of the study. Table 2.1 summarizes the

Table 2.1. *Central Theoretical Propositions: The Roles of National Institutions in Shaping the Welfare State Impacts of Internationalization*

Institutional Dimension	Representation of Pro–Welfare State Interests: Programmatic Alliances, Groups, and Coalitions	Political Capacity of Pro–Welfare State Interests: Programmatic Alliances, Groups, and Coalitions	Norms and Values of the National Policy Process That are Conducive for Welfare State Defense
The Polity			
Social Corporatism	**Positive**-Direct representation of interests/partisan leverage points	**Positive**-Direct and indirect effects on political capacities of welfare interests	**Positive**-Promotion of "ideology of social partnership," trust, and collective responsibility
Electoral Inclusiveness	**Positive**-Direct representation of major interests/partisan veto and leverage points	**Positive**-Direct and indirect effects on the political capacities of welfare interests	**Positive**-Promotion of norms of reciprocity and cooperation
Dispersion of Policy-Making Authority	**Positive**-Opportunities for representation through institutional veto and leverage points	**Negative**-Direct and indirect effects on political capacities of welfare interests	**Negative**-Promotion of norms of conflict, competition, and antistatism
The Welfare State			
Universalism	**Neutral**-Limited representation in program structures	**Positive**-Facilitation of the size and coherence of welfare interests	**Positive**-Promotion of solidarity, trust, and confidence
Conservatism	**Positive**-Representation of interests in program structures/partisan leverage points	**Positive**-Fosters cross-class support (potential political division by occupation?)	**Positive**-Cultivates social solidarity and legitimacy (reinforces stratification?)
Liberalism	**Neutral**-limited representation in program structures	**Negative**-Retards size and coherence of welfare state constituencies, actors, coalitions	**Negative**-Promotes norms of competition, distrust, and conflict among welfare interests

key components of the central theoretical argument of this study. For the sake of parsimony, I do not document the logically deductible corollaries about the way alternative institutional contexts (pluralism, exclusive electoral representation, etcetera) provide relatively conducive contexts for neoliberal reforms and intensify aspects of the economic and political forces generated by globalization.

At minimum, if my argument is correct, the association between international capital mobility and welfare state retrenchment should be weak in systems of relatively strong collective interest and electoral representation. Specifically, social corporatism and inclusive electoral institutions should favor those adversely affected by globalization and those opposed to its neoliberal correlates on material or ideological grounds: these institutions enhance the representation and political capacities of pro–welfare state actors as well as promote norms and values in the policy process that are conducive to the defense of the welfare state. At most, we should expect the countervailing demands for protection against heightened market risk to result in maintenance or expansion of some forms of social provision in these institutional contexts.

We should also expect to see variation in policy responses to globalization across centralized polities and systems of dispersed authority: from the perspective of interest representation generally, and the institutional veto points perspective specifically, we should expect more opportunities for welfare state program alliances, groups, and coalitions to blunt policy change in the face of globalization where dispersion of authority is high; from a broader, long-term perspective on the impact of institutions, we would expect to see bias in favor of neoliberal forces, as pro–welfare state constituencies, groups, parties, and coalitions are notably weaker in systems of dispersed authority, and as norms and values that shape policy making promote competition, conflict, and antistatism, as opposed to trust, compromise, and consensus. As noted, the "second-order" or long-term effects of the structure of decision-making authority are most pronounced for decentralization of policy-making power.

Finally, for reasons discussed in the preceding section (and summarized in the table), we should anticipate that international capital mobility has weaker effects on social welfare policy change as we move from lower to higher levels of universalism and conservatism. As we shift from less to more liberalism, resistence to welfare retrenchment should decline and the effects of internationalization should be more pronounced.

Measuring Democratic Political Institutions

Before turning to the analysis of the globalization thesis and my alternative theory about the mediating roles of domestic political and welfare state institutions, it may be useful to provide an overview of variations in democratic institutions in practice. In this section, I derive empirical indicators for each dimension of national institutions discussed above and highlight national differences and similarities within and across institutional dimensions. To develop a measure of social corporatism, I utilize new cross-nationally and temporally varying data on the organization of trade unions and the labor and industrial relations systems in the advanced industrial democracies. Following the lead of Golden and Londregan (1998), I employ correlation and principal components analysis of theoretically relevant dimensions of corporatism. While there is some disagreement on which aspects of labor and business organization and the labor and industrial relations system constitute corporatism, most scholars highlight at least two or three of the following dimensions: union density, interconfederal concentration, confederal power (e.g., control over strike funds, involvement in wage bargaining), and the level of wage bargaining. I use empirical indicators of these four factors to develop an index of social corporatism. The results of the principal components analysis of the four focal dimensions are presented in Table 2.2 (as are the complete descriptions of measurements). Three characteristics of unions and bargaining systems strongly and consistently cohere (i.e., factor loadings in excess of .80): union density, confederal power, and the level of wage bargaining. A weighted standard-score index of these three factors – an index varying annually and cross-nationally and weighted by each component's factor loading – is used as the principal indicator of social corporatism.[27]

While this index of corporatism clearly improves on extant, temporally invariant indicators, a few weaknesses should be mentioned. First, the focal indicator inherently stresses economic features of social corporatist systems of interest representation – labor market organization and collective bargaining – and does not formally tap incorporation of highly organized and centralized groups in the policy process (beyond what

---

[27] As to union concentration, I exclude from the present analysis an exploration of independent effects of concentration, or the degree to which union members are concentrated in one or few national peak associations.

Table 2.2. *Principal Components Analysis for National Political Institutions,*
1964–1992

Social Corporatism	I	II	National Political Institutions	I	II
Union Concentration	.03	−.98	Proportional Representation	−.20	.85
Union Density	−.86	−.18	Effective # of Parties	.15	.82
Confederal Power	−.85	.05	Presidentialism	−.65	.11
Level of Bargaining	−.85	.28	Federalism	−.77	−.44
			Bicameralism	−.73	−.12
			Referendums	−.78	.35

Note: Temporally and Cross-sectionally Varying Component Indicators:

Union Concentration: Herfindahl index of interconfederal concentration, or the probability that any two union members are members of the same national confederation.

Union Density: Percentage of employed wage and salary workers who are members of unions.

Confederal Power: Index of largest confederation's involvement in wage-setting process, power of appointment, veto over wage agreements, veto over strikes, and maintenance of strike funds.

Level of Bargaining: Four-level scale for centralization of wage bargaining where 0 = plant level, 1 = industry level, 2 = sectoral level without sanctions, and 3 = sectoral level with sanctions.

Proportional Representation: Three-level scale (0 = single member district with plurality rules; 1 = quasi-proportional; 2 = proportional) of degree of proportional representation.

Effective Number of Legislative Parties: Laasko and Taagepera–index as presented in Lijphart [1984: 120].

Presidentialism: Two-level scale where 0 = parliamentary and 1 = presidential government.

Federalism: Three-level scale where 0 = no, 1 = weak, and 2 = strong federalism.

Bicameralism: Three-level scale where 0 = no or symbolic second chamber, 1 = weak bicameralism, and 2 = strong bicameralism.

Use of Referendums: Two-level scale where 0 = none or infrequent use and 1 = frequent use.

Source of data: See Appendix A.

centralized bargaining implies). Confirmatory analysis indicates, however, that the focal measure of social corporatism is highly correlated across time and space with measures of the incorporation of peak functional associations in the national policy process. For instance, it is significantly correlated across time and space with Boreham and Compton's (1992) measure of the incorporation of labor in the national policy process ($r = .759$, using 1970–86 time series data from 13 nations). Second, and related, the focal measure arguably underestimates the degree of social corporatism in Germany and France. In the case of Germany, it does not account for extensive informal coordination of bargaining strategies and outcomes in the labor and industrial relations system (e.g., through economy-wide leadership of collective bargaining by the metalworking industry and by economy-wide coordination within employers associations); most measures of corporatism place Germany in a relatively higher position. In the case of France, the focal measure probably underestimates the strength of unions by using only a formal measure of union density (which varies from roughly 20 to 10 percent of wage and salary employees from the 1960s to early 1990s). That is, the measure developed here does not account for the fact that collectively bargained contracts cover approximately 90 percent of workers (Traxler, 1994). Moreover, unions are typically regarded as agents of larger batteries of nonunionized workers; business-labor exchange (e.g., enterprise-level works councils) is relatively extensive. However, the focal measure is highly correlated (i.e., zero-order correlation coefficients of .70 to .90) with commonly used indicators.[28] Finally, like most operational measures of social corporatism, the organizational attributes of business organization are assumed to roughly correspond with those of labor (e.g., Schmitter, 1981); this less-than-systematic treatment of business is arguably a weakness of much of the corporatism literature. However, my theoretical interest in labor power and representation suggests that the present measure is appropriate.

In order to develop indicators of electoral institutions and the organization of policy-making authority, I follow the convention established by Lijphart's (1984, 1999) seminal work on dimensions of democratic political institutions and conduct analyses of the relationships between aspects of formal democratic institutions and their close correlates: the major institutional dimensions highlighted in the literature discussed above are the focus of this analysis. Specifically, using relatively straightforward operationalizations (see Notes to Table 2.2), I employ principal components analysis of cross-nationally and temporally varying measures of the degree of proportionality in the electoral system, the number of effective legislative parties, presidentialism, bicameralism, federalism, and the use

---

[28] See the analytic review of common measures of corporatism by Lijphart and Crepaz (1991). In addition, it is important to point out that the focal measure of social corporation does not distort the character of French interest intermediation too much: there is considerable fragmentation of union organization (i.e., between the main federations of CFDT, FO, and CGT) and employers (i.e., CNPF and CGPME), and substantial decentralization of bargaining (e.g., Wallerstein, Golden, and Lange [1997]). Policy making in practice is characterized by substantial pluralism in the context of statist and corporatist traditions (e.g., G. Freeman, 1994).

of referendums. As Table 2.2 reveals, and as prefigured in the literature, PR and the number effective legislative parties strongly cohere. In addition, presidentialism, federalism, bicameralism, and the use of referendums form a distinct institutional dimension. Thus, weighted standard-score indices of PR and effective legislative parties and of presidentialism, federalism, bicameralism, and referendums are used to measure what I label "inclusive electoral institutions" and "dispersion of policy-making authority," respectively. Given the theoretical significance accorded decentralization of policy-making authority and the fact that the presidential-parliamentary dimension is less strongly related to the underlying dimension of "dispersion," I also compute a weighted index for "decentralization" of policy-making authority that is used in the analysis.

To measure attributes of welfare systems, I rely on Esping-Andersen's (1990, Ch. 3) rankings of welfare state program structure on dimensions of stratification: "socialism," or what might simply be called universalism (i.e., universal coverage with high benefit equality), "conservatism" (i.e., occupationally stratified welfare programs and special public employee plans), and "liberalism" (i.e., means-testing and reliance on private pensions and health insurance). Clearly, "universalism," "conservatism," and "liberalism" provide general indicators of those programmatic attributes of welfare states emphasized above. However, Esping-Andersen's rankings of welfare states on these dimensions of stratification, as well as his placement of countries on a scale of decommodifcation of labor, have been criticized. For instance, Castles and Mitchell (1993) raise measurement questions about the country rankings on both the stratification and decommodification scales, ultimately arguing that Esping-Andersen's "three worlds of welfare" should be modified to include a fourth welfare state type – the "radical" welfare state (typified by Britain and the Antipodes, and based on high equality of benefits, high relative use of income and profit taxes, and moderately successful income redistribution). Despite these methodological concerns, Esping-Andersen's rankings are the most meticulous and comprehensive accounting of the theoretically important program attributes currently available and will be used here.[29]

---

[29] Another potential problem in the indexes of programmatic characteristics of welfare states is the static nature of measurement (i.e., the indexes are based on welfare program attributes circa 1980). However, for those welfare states whose programmatic structure was largely in place by the late 1960s and who experienced no significant structural reforms in the 1970s or 1980s, these measures are sufficient. Notable exceptions include Finland, whose social democratic welfare state was still developing in the 1970s, and Britain, whose

The 1964–92 average scores of the 15 focal nations on the institutional dimensions of social corporatism, inclusive electoral institutions, and dispersion of authority, as well as the three dimensions of welfare state structure, are listed in Table 2.3. Based on the relative rank of each nation, I organize the table according to groups of welfare states (and these categorizations inform disaggregated analysis presented in Chapter 3). The universal welfare state cluster includes Denmark, Finland, the Netherlands, Norway, and Sweden, while the conservative welfare state group consists of Austria, Belgium, France, Germany, and Italy; the liberal welfare state cluster includes Australia, Canada, Japan, the United Kingdom, and the United States. Classifications of the Netherlands, Japan, the United Kingdom, Australia, and Austria merit comment. First, the Dutch welfare state has been regarded as a "passive social democratic welfare state" (e.g., van Kersbergen and Becker [1988]), where Nordic–Social Democratic universalism is blended with elements of the corporatist conservative or Christian Democratic model. For instance, the Dutch welfare state ranks high on universalism (tied for fourth with Finland on Esping-Andersen's scale), but also embodies elements of liberalism, as well as occupationally based welfare (high levels of occupationally based social insurance taxes) and low levels of public social service provision that typify the continental (corporatist conservative) welfare states (see Cox [1993]; van Kersbergen [1995]; and Visser and Hemerijck [1997]). On Japan, recent analysis by Esping-Andersen (1997) highlights the fact that the Japanese welfare state embodies strong elements of both liberalism and conservatism; however, its relative ranking on the two basic indices suggests that, for the present analysis, it should be included with the liberal group.

The United Kingdom is also a problematic case because of notable elements of universalism (e.g., national health service structure); it is ranked in an identical relative position on universalism (4 on a scale of 0–8) and liberalism (6 on a scale of 0–12). However, given that the degree of 1970s means-testing may be underestimated by Esping-Andersen (1990: 78) and that means-testing and privatization increased notably in the 1980s (e.g., Gough et al. [1997]; OECD [1992b]), I place the United Kingdom in the liberal camp. With respect to the Australian welfare state, Australia ranks second only to New Zealand in reliance on means-tested social assistance

welfare state increased reliance on means-testing and otherwise became notably more liberal in the 1980s.

Table 2.3. *National Political and Welfare State Institutions: Annual Country Averages for 1964–1992*

Nation	Social Corporatism	Electoral Representation	Dispersion of Authority	Universalism	Conservatism	Liberalism
Sweden	1.26	.29	-.38	8	0	0
Norway	1.01	.32	-.42	8	4	0
Denmark	.73	.74	-.42	8	2	6
Finland	.65	.85	-.03	6	6	4
The Netherlands	.11	.67	-.19	6	4	8
Austria	.35	-.04	-.19	2	8	4
Belgium	.08	1.31	-.19	4	8	4
France	-.71	-.29	-.03	2	8	8
Germany	-.55	.11	.50	4	8	6
Italy	.19	.41	-.19	0	8	6
United States	-1.01	-1.28	.89	0	0	12
Canada	-.78	-1.15	.04	4	2	12
Japan	-.55	-.46	-.19	2	4	10
Australia	.27	-.57	.27	4	0	10
United Kingdom	-.39	-1.21	-.42	4	0	6

Note: Definitions of measures of institutional dimensions.

Social Corporatism: Weighted standard score index of union density, union peak association power, and level of collective bargaining, annual average, 1964–92.

Electoral Representation: Weighted standard score index of degree of proportional representation and number of effective legislative parties, annual average, 1964–92.

Dispersion of Authority: Weighted standard score index of degree of presidentialism, federalism, bicameralism, and use of referendums, annual average, 1964–92.

Universalism: Esping-Anderson's (1990) score for degree of universalism and benefit equality in social welfare programs, circa 1980.

Conservatism: Esping-Andersen's (1990) score for degree welfare is occupationally stratified and public employees have special programs, circa 1980.

Liberalism: Esping-Andersen's (1990) score for degree welfare state relies on means-testing and degree of private pensions and health care, circa 1980.

Source of data: See Appendix A.

in the 1980–92 era (Gough et al., 1997) and second only to the United States in reliance on private health benefits (see Chapter 6). On the other hand, features of the Australian welfare state produce relatively high social benefit equality with relatively progressive financing (Castles and Mitchell, 1993), and wage-setting institutions supplement public social provisions by enhancing the material well-being of employees in the "wage-earners welfare state" (Castles, 1985). As such, the strong liberal character of much of the formal structure of the social welfare state must be considered in the context of these broader characteristics of the Australian political economy. Finally, with regard to Austria, it is sometimes grouped with the Social Democratic cases, given the strength of its Social Democratic party, social corporatism, and full employment orientation (e.g., Huber and Stephens [1998]). Based on attributes of welfare states alone, however, the Austrian case is solidly ensconced in the corporatist conservative camp (see Chapter 5).

With respect to political institutions, one can see that these clusters of welfare states are also differentiated, at least in part, by their relative positions on the three focal dimensions of democratic institutions. Universal welfare states are characterized by relatively strong social corporatist systems of interest representation. In fact, Sweden, Norway, Denmark, and Finland score very high on 1964–92 annual averages for the index of social corporatism; the Netherlands is also above average in the degree of social corporatism, ranking seventh on the scale. Universal welfare states are also characterized by moderately strong electoral inclusiveness; all five cases rank above average on 1964–92 mean levels of inclusive electoral representation. In addition, the universal welfare states are typified by concentrated political authority (with the exception of Finnish presidentialism). Overall, these five cases – the Nordic countries and the Netherlands – highlight how the institutional dimensions themselves tend to cohere: the universal welfare states are characterized by encompassing collective interest and electoral representation within the context of concentrated political power.[30]

On the other hand, liberal welfare states are typically pluralist (with the exception of the labor-based corporatism of post-1982 Australia) and have relatively exclusive electoral institutions; the overall position on dispersion

---

[30] As discussed in Chapter 4, there is a substantial amount of devolution of administrative and policy-making power in the Nordic social democratic welfare states within the context of concentrated political authority at the national level.

of authority is somewhat mixed, although the group includes three relatively fragmented polities (Australia, Canada, and the United States). Conservative welfare states tend to have average levels of social corporatism (although Austria is moderately high and France moderately low), moderately high electoral inclusiveness (although France is slightly below average), and (with exceptions) below average dispersion of policy-making authority. In sum, one can argue that institutional attributes of corporatist conservative and liberal welfare states also tend to cohere: Austria, Belgium, France, Germany, and Italy tend to combine occupationally based welfare states with average-to-high levels of encompassing representation of interests and moderate levels of concentration of policy-making power within the polity. Liberal welfare states tend to blend selective welfare state structure (means-testing and private-public schisms) with pluralist interest group representation and exclusive electoral representation; the majority are above average in dispersion of authority within the polity.

I now turn to the empirical assessment of the questions of this study. In Chapter 3, I provide a quantitative analysis of the impacts of international capital mobility on the welfare state and the degree to which national political institutions shape the magnitude and direction of these effects. In Chapters 4 through 6, I utilize largely qualitative methodology to evaluate the role of internationalization in shaping the timing and character of social welfare policy change in individual welfare states. Chapter 7 assesses the indirect welfare state impacts of globalization.

3

Global Capital, Political Institutions, and Contemporary Welfare State Development: Quantitative Analysis

In this chapter, I present a quantitative analysis of the central questions of this study. I initially provide a brief overview of the structure and recent development of the contemporary welfare state in advanced capitalist democracies. This exercise, significantly augmented in the country studies of subsequent chapters, brings into concrete relief the changing fortunes of the welfare state across the latter years of welfare expansion and the contemporary era of retrenchment initiatives and restructuring. Subsequently, I discuss my methodological approach to the quantitative analysis of internationalization and social policy change, addressing measurement issues, econometric model development, and statistical estimation techniques. In the main body of the chapter, I present assessments of the direct welfare state effects of international capital mobility, the impacts of internationalization on the dynamics of welfare state convergence and divergence, and the contingent and conjunctural policy effects of capital mobility (following the supplementary hypotheses outlined in the preceding chapter).

I also provide a series of analyses of the ways in which national institutions shape the domestic policy consequences of internationalization. I evaluate my arguments about the foundational role of democratic institutions by examining how capital mobility affects total social welfare effort in different institutional contexts across the entire sample of years and countries (i.e., 1965–93 in 15 developed democracies). To deepen the analysis, I then analyze the direct welfare state impacts of international capital mobility on three key dimensions of social welfare protection – income maintenance, the social wage, and government provision of health care – for the entire sample and within three clusters of welfare states defined by programmatic attributes (and, indirectly, by political institutional contexts). As suggested in Chapter 2, these clusters are defined by universal, conservative, and liberal program characteristics. I conclude with preliminary assessments of the strength of conventional and alternative theories about the welfare state consequences of globalization and the domestic policy autonomy of democratic governments.

The Structure and Recent Development of Advanced Social Welfare States

In the contemporary era, the rich democracies devote substantial shares of national resources to social welfare provision: welfare expenditures for income maintenance, health care, and social services have, in fact, significantly ameliorated the material deprivations of old age, disability, sickness, unemployment, and child-rearing for the majority of citizens in advanced democratic societies (see country studies for evidence on welfare outcomes). As illustrated in Table 3.1, the typical developed democracy allocated roughly one-quarter of national economic product (24.4 percent) for social welfare provision in the early to mid-1990s. Cash transfers for income maintenance accounted for the bulk of total social welfare outlays: cash disbursements for old-age and disability pensions, unemployment compensation, sickness and health benefits, family allowances, and social assistance averaged 18.4 percent of GDP in the typical rich democracy in the years 1990–4. An average production worker who found himself unemployed in the 1991–5 period could count on a "social wage" of public insurance and assistance benefits equal to 44 percent of gross earnings for the first year of unemployment; income replacement rates for old-age and disability pensions and sick pay are commonly more generous.[1] Government spending for health care, largely in the form of in-kind benefits and direct government provision of hospital, physician, and related care, equaled on average 6.3 percent of GDP. As Table 3.1 indicates, this publically financed expenditure accounted on average for three-quarters of total health care spending during the years 1990–3. Outlays

---

[1] Comprehensive data across time and countries for income replacement rates for pensions and other forms of social insurance are not yet available; the OECD "social wage" data utilized here is by far the most encompassing for assessing income replacement across time and countries. For representative data in other areas of social insurance in subsamples of years and countries for which they are available, see Hagen (1992) and Ploug and Kvist (1996); Whiteford (1995) reviews or references several extant studies that rely on income replacement rates and provides an analysis of the problems with such data.

Table 3.1. Structure and Change in the Social Welfare State, 1960–1995

Social Policy Dimension[a]	Level 1960–4	Level 1980–4	Change[b] 1960/4–80/4	Level 1990–3/5	Change[b] 1980/4–90/4
Total Social Welfare	11.6	21.6	.48 (4.1)	24.4	.25 (1.2)
Income Maintenance					
Cash Transfers	8.7	16.9	.39 (4.5)	18.4	.18 (1.1)
Social Wage	25.0	40.0	.71 (2.8)	44.0	.36 (.9)
Public Health Spending	2.8	5.8	.14 (5.0)	6.3	.04 (.7)
Public Health as % Total	64.5	76.8	.58 (1.1)	75.5	–.12 (–.1)
Nonhealth Social Services	—	1.3	—	1.6	.02 (.2)
Active Labor Market Outlays	—	—	—	1.0	—

[a] Data in the table represent period averages for the 15 focal nations of this study. For the level in the 1990s, data end variously in 1993, 1994, and 1995, as noted below. The countries are: Australia, Austria, Belgium, Canada, Denmark, Finland, France, Germany, Italy, Japan, the Netherlands, Norway, Sweden, the United Kingdom, and the United States.

[b] Change is equal to the annual average absolute change in the social policy dimension from 1960–4 to 1980–4 means, or from 1980–4 to 1990–93/5 means. (The annual percentage change for a given social policy dimension for these periods is displayed in parentheses.)

Variable Definitions:

Total Social Welfare: total government expenditure for social welfare programs (OECD definition) as a percentage of GDP (to 1993).

Cash Income Maintenance: cash payments for old-age and disability assistance, sickness and health benefits, unemployment compensation, family allowances, and social assistance as a percentage of GDP (to 1994).

Social Wage: percentage of average production worker's gross income replaced by unemployment compensation, unemployment assistance, and various entitled social welfare benefits during first year of unemployment (to 1995).

Public Health Spending: government spending on health programs as a percentage of GDP (to 1993).

Public Health as % of Total Health: government health expenditure as a percentage of total health spending (to 1993).

Social Services: Spending on public social services for the elderly, disabled, families and children as a percentage of GDP.

Active Labor Market Spending: Expenditure on job training, placement, relocation, and related programs as a percentage of GDP (to 1993).

Source of data: See Appendix A.

for direct public provision for nonhealth social services for the elderly, disabled, families, and children averaged 1.6 percent of GDP in the early 1990s.

Table 3.1 also provides a systematic comparison of the rates of change in these dimensions of social welfare effort between the latter years of welfare expansion (i.e., the 1960s and 1970s) and the current period of welfare retrenchment initiatives and restructuring. Specifically, the third column of Table 3.1 provides the annual average absolute change in focal dimensions of social welfare protection between the early 1960s (i.e., 1960–4) and the early 1980s (i.e., 1980–4); the table also displays (in parentheses) the annual average percentage rate of growth in each area of social protection. During the 1960s and 1970s, policy makers in most welfare states increased benefit generosity and coverage, as well as lowered qualifying criteria for relatively mature income security programs established in prior decades; many nations also established and expanded direct government provision of social services. In addition, governments in a minority of welfare states, especially those regarded as welfare state "laggards," initiated basic income security and insurance programs in areas where national government social protection had been minimal. Thus, for example, Canada established comprehensive social insurance for hospital and physician care (1957, 1968), the United States legislated health insurance programs for the poor and aged (1964, 1965), and Japan initiated national family allowances (1971).[2] Together, these policy changes produced relatively substantial absolute (and percentage) annual changes in social welfare provision. As the table indicates, absolute growth in total social welfare effort averaged .48 percent of GDP per year between the early 1960s and early 1980s, as total social welfare expenditure grew from 11.6 to 21.6 percent of GDP. Comparable changes (in percentage terms) occurred in the areas of income maintenance and health care spending. While the percentage rate of change was slower for the social wage and for the government share of health care outlays, the 20-year growth in these areas was also notable: the social wage expanded from 25 to 40

---

[2] The literature on the "completion" and "expansion" of the welfare state in the post–World War Two era is vast. For descriptive treatments of late 1940s to early 1980s programmatic development of the welfare state, see Flora (1988), M. Gordon (1988), and Köhler and Zacher (1982). For representative empirical analyses of the forces that shaped welfare expansion, see Esping-Andersen (1990), Hicks and Swank (1984, 1992), Myles (1989), Huber, Ragin, and Stephens (1993), and Pampel and Williamson (1989), as well as the literature cited in these works.

percent of gross wages while the public share of total health expenditure rose from 64.5 to 76.8 percent.

The picture for the evolution of social welfare effort in the 1980s and 1990s is different: in the late 1970s and early 1980s, policy makers in many developed welfare states proposed (and often enacted) cost controls and, on occasion, modest rollbacks in benefits and eligibility. From the early 1980s onward, policy makers commonly proposed (and often enacted) cuts in benefit levels and restrictions in program eligibility in social insurance, increased the use of targeting in social protection (e.g., means or income tests), and emphasized greater reliance on private insurance against market risks. In the areas of health and social services, governments have implemented market-oriented mechanisms for greater efficiency in service delivery, privatized some social services, often imposed budget freezes, and increased user charges for publically provided services.[3] As I document and analyze in subsequent chapters, the incidence of these "market-oriented" reforms has been widespread, although the depth has varied significantly across time and countries. For instance, cost controls, moderate rollbacks in benefits, and efficiency-oriented reforms in services were enacted in the late 1970s and (especially) early 1980s in several liberal and corporatist conservative welfare states; comparable welfare reforms did not occur until the early 1990s in Sweden and Finland.

Concomitant with neoliberal reforms, governments have extended social protection moderately in a limited number of areas. Most extensions have addressed the demands that stem from high levels of general and long-term unemployment, industrial restructuring, problems of balancing the demands of work and family, and needs attendant on relatively new pools of dependent citizens (e.g., the growing population proportion of "frail elderly"). For instance, labor shedding in the context of industrial restructuring and rises in unemployment attendant on economic downturns have been followed by new resources for active labor market programs, expansions of early retirement pensions, and related social supports in a majority of West European polities in the 1980s and early 1990s. In France, policy makers enacted in 1988 the *revenu minimum d'insertion* (minimum insertion income, or RMI), a new social assistance program

---

[3] For details on the examples of neoliberal reforms, as well as extensions of social protection, see the extensive material in Chapters 4 through 6. Useful and relatively comprehensive overviews of substantive policy changes in the 1980s and 1990s can be found in contributions to Clasen (1997), George and Taylor-Gooby (1996), Ploug and Kvist (1994, 1996), and Esping-Andersen (1996a).

designed to provide basic income support (and supports for social and labor-market reintegration) to socially excluded groups (e.g., the long-term unemployed). German policy makers created in 1994 long-term care insurance for the elderly. Extensions of family leave and child care assistance and services have occurred in the 1980s and 1990s in many rich democracies.

The consequences for social welfare effort of the interaction of variable but widespread neoliberal reforms and limited welfare expansions, as well as the automatically activated programmatic entitlements (generated by rising needs for extant benefits), are displayed in Table 3.1. Reflecting the neoliberal direction, scope, and depth of programmatic reforms, average annual (absolute and percentage) changes in all of the focal dimensions of welfare provision are notably lower than those during the 1960s and 1970s; in the case of some areas of social welfare, there is virtually no growth. The annual percentage rate of change in total social welfare and income maintenance outlays relative to economic product was approximately 1 percent (as apposed to 4 percent or more in the 1960s and 1970s); the social wage expanded only modestly between the early 1980s and 1990s (at a growth rate of .9 percent per year). The annual average percentage increase in government health care spending dropped from 5 to .7 percent per year and the percentage of total health care outlays accounted for by public programs dropped slightly (from 76.8 to 75.5 percent) in the typical advanced democracy.[4]

Generally, the data of Table 3.1 confirm recent academic thinking about the structure and size of the welfare state in developed capitalist democracies. On the one hand, it is clearly the case that by most measures of social welfare spending, programmatic characteristics (e.g., social insurance replacement rates), and public-private mixes, the welfare states of advanced democracies have not been dismantled or dramatically retrenched. On the other hand, the data also show that there appears to be a clear "growth to limits" in contemporary social policy development. Moreoever, in many areas of social protection there is slow growth or

---

[4] Analyses of secular trends in the magnitude of cross-national variability in levels of social protection (using measures of dispersion such as the coefficient of variation) reveal modest declines in the extent of cross-national differences among welfare states in both the period of welfare state expansion and the contemporary era of welfare state restructuring and retrenchment. Comparing the 1990s to the 1960s, welfare states are much larger, are growing more slowly or not at all, and, despite the persistence of substantial differences, are generally more similar in levels of social protection.

stability; in some, there is modest decline.[5] As I detail in country studies, more finely grained data on programmatic change actually reveals moderately significant retrenchment in specific areas of social protection in some nations. After a brief consideration of empirical indicators of welfare effort, I provide a comprehensive quantitative assessment of the determinants of 1960s to 1990s social welfare policy. I account for the effects of rising need and demand on the welfare state and the general economic and political influences on social welfare effort. Most centrally, I systematically explore the roles of internationalization and national institutions in shaping contemporary patterns of social welfare development in the developed capitalist democracies.

A Note on Empirical Indicators

Descriptive indicators of social welfare effort presented in Table 3.1, as well as those utilized below in systematic quantitative analysis, disproportionately rely on final social welfare expenditure data. These measures of social welfare effort have been criticized as being a blunt tool for systematically capturing elements of social policy (e.g., Esping-Andersen [1990]). However, there are a number of considerations that justify their use in the quantitative portion of the present inquiry. First, for some areas of social welfare policy, such as publically provided social services and public-private shares of social insurance or service provision, final expenditure–based measures are relatively precise indicators of cross-national and temporal variations in the underlying dimension of welfare effort. Second, measures such as total social welfare outlays, or total income maintenance relative to national income, are highly correlated with more theoretically and substantively important outcomes, such as income redistribution (see Korpi and Palme [1998] for recent evidence). In fact, with proper need, income, and business cycle controls, such measures provide useful (albeit imprecise) summary indicators of benefit generosity and eligibility standards over extended periods of time and sets of countries.

[5] After completion of the analysis for this study, the OECD made available updates of the Social Expenditure Data Base through 1995; analysis of that data and supplementary data (e.g., from OECD Health Data [1998]) reveal that the trends documented here hold through 1995. Moreover, it is important to note that efforts to standardize or otherwise account for rising needs (e.g., poverty, unemployment, and so forth) reveal similar rates of change in social protection indicators (albeit smaller expansions and more frequent declines) to those discussed here (Clayton and Pontusson, 1998).

In addition, with the exception of the data utilized here, systematic cross-national and temporal data (i.e., for the 1960s to mid-1990s for most developed democracies) on programmatic measures of benefit levels, eligibility criteria, and other aspects of social policy are simply not yet available. Generally, one may confirm results of quantitative analysis of social welfare outlays with analyses of more precise indicators of policy change, and I do that here by systematic inclusion of analysis of the "social wage." I also do so in the individual country studies, where I present analysis of the forces that shape additional (quantitatively measured) features of welfare states, such as changes in the relative use of means-tested social assistance and patterns of overall levels of income replacement (e.g., for pensions, sickness) between two points in time (i.e., typically 1980 and a point in the mid-1990s). In addition, quantitative analysis of welfare outlays may be checked against (and extended by) the results of case studies of globalization and the timing and character of programmatic social welfare reforms presented in Chapters 4–6.

The Quantitative Analysis of Globalization, Political Institutions, and Welfare Effort

While descriptive data on period and annual changes in levels of welfare effort are instructive, they are not especially useful in disentangling the effects of international and domestic political economic forces on welfare state restructuring. To generate systematic evidence about the general social welfare effects of globalization and to assess my alternative arguments about the roles of domestic political institutions in conditioning these effects, I offer quantitative analysis of the social welfare impacts of international capital mobility, where central hypotheses are evaluated in the context of a general model of social welfare provision. In subsequent chapters, I enrich the analysis by qualitatively examining the timing, character, and international and domestic contexts of welfare policy change for the most developed welfare states from the late 1970s to mid-1990s.

The Methodological Approach to Quantitative Analysis

I initially examine the direct effects of international capital mobility on an aggregate measure of welfare state size: total social welfare expenditures as a share of GDP. The use of one encompassing measure of social welfare effort makes feasible a concise analysis of the direct welfare state effects of multiple dimensions of international capital mobility and the policy effects of these multiple dimensions across several diverse institutional settings. While these initial tests provide a baseline evaluation of the study's central hypotheses, methodological and substantive considerations suggest a series of refinements and more nuanced analyses of the welfare effects of international capital mobility. Thus, I examine, in the presence of controls for structural and cyclical determinants of welfare effort, the effects of global capital on income transfers (as shares of national income), the social wage (total income replacement for the average unemployed production worker), and public health effort (government health spending as a share of GDP). I also report (although less systematically) the effects of capital mobility on the public health share of total health spending. For models of the social wage – the most direct measure of statutory welfare entitlement used in the present analysis – I also analyze interactions between capital mobility and national political institutions; this step should provide a check on results about the roles of national political institutions in shaping the welfare impacts of internationalization that emerge from models of total social welfare effort. I conduct the analysis of individual dimensions of the welfare state across the entire sample of countries and for subsets of nations according to welfare state type (universal, conservative, liberal). (All variable operationalizations are given in Table 3.2 below, and data sources for focal indicators are given in Appendix A.)

As to welfare state types, I construct my groupings on the basis of Esping-Andersen's (1990) ranking of the programmatic attributes of universalism (degree of universal coverage and benefit equality), conservatism (degree of occupational stratification and existence of separate public employee benefit plans), and liberalism (degree of means-testing and private insurance). The details of the measurement of these dimensions, their patterned relationships with institutional features of the polity, and a discussion of problems and qualifications is given in Chapter 2 under the heading "Measuring Democratic Political Institutions." Evaluation of the impacts of international capital mobility on individual dimensions of the welfare state within distinct clusters of nations augments and checks findings from the "full sample" analysis on the role of institutions in shaping the impacts of internationalization discussed above. According to theory outlined in Chapter 2, I expect various dimensions of capital mobility to have small positive or no effects on social policy change in universal and conservative welfare states; I expect to find that rises in international capital mobility are associated with welfare state

Table 3.2. *Principal Variable Definitions*

Social Welfare Effort	
Total Social Welfare	Total government expenditure for social welfare programs as a percentage of GDP.
Cash Transfers	Cash payments for old age, disability, injury, sickness, unemployment, and social assistance as a percentage of GDP.
Social Wage	Percentage of average production worker's gross income replaced by unemployment compensation, unemployment assistance, and various entitled social welfare during first year of unemployment.
Public Health	Government spending on health programs as a percentage of GDP.
Public Health Share	Government health expenditure as a percentage of total health spending.
International Capital Mobility	
Total Capital Flows	Average (lags 1, 2, and 3 years) of total capital inflows and outflows as a percentage of GDP, where capital consists of direct, portfolio, and bank finance (as defined in IMF, *Balance of Payments Statistics*).
Direct Investment	Average (lags 1, 2, and 3 years) of inflows and outflows of direct investment as a percentage of GDP.
Capital Markets	Average (lags 1, 2, and 3 years) of borrowing on international capital markets (e.g., bonds, equities, bank borrowing) as a percentage of GDP.
Capital Market Liberalization	Index (0.00 to 4.00 at increments of .5) of the absence of national restrictions on the cross-border movement of payments and receipts of capital.
Covered Interest Rate Differentials	Absolute value of covered interest rate parities: world market rate of interest on financial instruments denominated in a nation's currency minus the domestic rate adjusted for the forward premium on a nation's currency.
Political Institutions	
Social Corporatism	Weighted standard score index of union density, confederal power, and level of wage bargaining. Union density is measured as union membership (excluding retired, self-employed, and unemployed) as a percentage of wage and salary workers; confederal power is an unweighted standard score index of power of appointment, veto over wage agreements, veto over strikes, control of strike funds, and involvement in wage setting of largest union confederation; and level of wage bargaining is a 1–4 scale of centralization of wage bargaining in the economy (also see Table 2.2).

Table 3.2 *(continued)*

Inclusive Electoral Institutions	Weighted standard score index of degree of proportional representation (0, 1, 2 scale) and effective number of legislative parties (computed using the Laasko and Taagepera index as presented in Lijphart [1984, p. 120]) (also see Table 2.2).
Dispersion of Authority	Weighted standard score index of presidentialism (0, 1 scale), federalism (0, 1, 2 scale), bicameralism (0, 1, 2 scale), and use of referendums (0, 1 scale) (also see Table 2.2).
Decentralization of Authority	Weighted standard score index federalism (0, 1, 2 scale), bicameralism (0, 1, 2 scale), and use of referendums (0, 1 scale) (also see Table 2.2).
The General Model	
Trade	Real imports plus real exports as a percentage of real GDP.
Economic Development	Per capita GDP in constant (1985) international prices (1,000s of dollars)
Old	The percentage of the population 65 years of age or older.
Unemployment	The percentage of the civilian labor force unemployed.
Inflation	Year-to-year percentage changes in the Consumer Price Index.
Growth	Percentage change in real GDP.
Left	Annual percentage of Left party cabinet portfolios.
Christian Democrat	Annual percentage of Christian Democratic party cabinet portfolios.

Source of data: See Appendix A.

retrenchment in liberal welfare state settings. The simple version of globalization theory predicts that after accounting for other exogenous sources of social welfare effort, rises in capital mobility will contribute to welfare state retrenchment everywhere; the more nuanced version predicts that internationalization will place particularly strong pressures on large welfare states (e.g., typically those in the universal and conservative clusters). As such, conventional theory and my alternative argument make diametrically opposed predictions about the welfare state consequences of globalization.

Measurement and Model Development. I examine effects of several relevant aspects of international capital mobility and, thus, as noted, compensate for weaknesses in individual indicators. I include in the analysis the major dimensions and indicators of international capital mobility utilized in Chapter 2 to highlight rises in transnational capital mobility and financial integration. I examine the policy effects of total inflows and outflows of capital and two components of capital flows highlighted in the literature: total inflows and outflows of foreign direct investment (FDI) and a nation's total borrowing on international capital markets. Each of these measures is standardized by a nation's GDP and, to smooth occasionally volatile annual movements (see below on capital flight), is operationalized as a three-year moving average (lags 1–3). As discussed, the disaggregation of total capital flows facilitates a more refined analysis of the multidimensionality of the potential domestic policy effects of capital mobility (given different actors, temporal dynamics, and implications for domestic policy across types of capital). To capture the policy effects of the *potential* for international capital mobility, I examine the impacts of the aforementioned measure of liberalization of capital markets; this index effectively taps the formal-legal environment for capital mobility. As a supplement, I also employ a broader index of the liberalization of financial flows: an index of the degree of liberalization of restrictions on capital and on payments for goods and services (see Quinn [1997]; Quinn and Inclan [1997]). This broader measure of the liberalization of cross-border financial transactions offers a relatively encompassing measure of formal international financial openness. In addition, I examine the policy impacts of overall integration of domestic and world financial markets by using the interest rate–based measure discussed above: covered interest rate differentials (operationalized as absolute values of differentials). As suggested by conventional theory, rises in flows and liberalization should be negatively associated with measures of social welfare provision; declines in interest rate differentials should be accompanied by declines in social welfare effort (and, therefore, according to globalization theory, one should observe a positive relationship between rate differentials and social welfare effort).

To augment these measurements and tests of the direct welfare effects of capital mobility, I explicitly examine the role of capital mobility in promoting convergence of welfare states toward a market-conforming model of social protection. Following hypotheses developed in Chapter 2, I examine whether rises in capital mobility tend to facilitate a "run to the bottom," where rises in capital mobility produce increasingly intense pressures for retrenchment as one moves from smaller to larger welfare states. Relatedly, I examine the hypothesis (see above) that increases in global capital mobility affect primarily the larger welfare states, whose expenditure levels and financial burdens exceed the average levels of social provision in the developed democratic capitalist systems. These hypotheses are examined, respectively, by estimating the welfare state consequences of the interaction of capital mobility and the past level of welfare effort, and of capital mobility and past welfare effort, where the measure of past effort is scored 0.00 for welfare states falling below the average level of welfare provision (and otherwise calculated as social welfare effort in a specific country and year minus the cross-national annual mean of welfare effort in the focal year). The mechanics of interaction analysis are discussed below.

As to tests of the supplementary hypotheses discussed in Chapter 2, I proceed as follows. To facilitate manageability and parsimony, I use the core indicator of capital control liberalization as the measure of capital mobility; it also serves as a central control variable when considering other aspects of internationalization (e.g., "capital flight"). I first evaluate the argument that international capital mobility may be associated with expansions of the welfare state and then – after a threshold has been reached – associated with retrenchments of the welfare state. I do so by using a standard polynomial specification $(\ldots + \beta_1 * \text{capital liberalization} - \beta_2 * \text{capital liberalization}^2)$: β_1 is expected to be positive, reflecting welfare state expansion with initial rises in internationalization; β_2 is expected to be negative, reflecting growing pressures of globalization on domestic policy makers at higher levels of international capital mobility. I next examine the proposition that high levels of trade and capital openness combine to create downward pressures on the welfare state. The primary test of this hypothesis is given by the interaction term for trade openness and capital liberalization. In addition, I explore the proposition developed above that capital mobility's effects are most pronounced in environments of domestic fiscal stress. To test this hypothesis, I use an interaction between the government budget balance and capital liberalization, expecting to find that capital mobility exerts greater downward pressure on the welfare state as fiscal stress increases. Finally, I assess the idea that adverse movements of capital (e.g., capital flight) promotes welfare state retrenchment. While many indicators of "capital flight" exist (e.g., Williamson and Lessard [1987]), I assess the direct welfare state effects of inflows minus outflows of foreign direct investment (FDI). As Kant (1996) has shown, measures based on FDI are highly correlated with various alternative measures of short-term capital flight and financial crisis. Moreover, as noted in Chapter 2, net FDI provides a substantively important summary indicator, in that this dimension of capital flows has been the focus of policy-maker attention in several developed democracies. However, I also evaluated the capital flight hypothesis by using additional measures of capital flight and note these results below.[6]

To ascertain direct effects of democratic institutions and to offer ready tests of the extent democratic institutions shape the social policy consequences of international capital mobility (through tests of the effects of interactions between institutional dimensions and capital mobility), I include in all empirical models empirical indicators of institutional structures developed in Chapter 2. Again, these indicators consist of indexes of systems of collective interest and electoral representation – social corporatism and inclusive electoral institutions – as well as a measure of the "dispersion of national policy-making authority." In subsequent models, I test individually for the roles of welfare state (programmatic) structure – universalism, conservatism, and liberalism – in shaping the direction and depth of the impacts of international capital mobility.

The General Model of Social Welfare Provision. To evaluate focal hypotheses, it is essential to account for the variety of significant determinants of social welfare effort. As discussed above, the openness of the domestic economy to international trade has figured prominently in analysis of welfare state expansion; hypothesized (negative) welfare state effects of trade openness have also played a role in contemporary globalization theory. Thus, I control for the overall level of trade openness in general models of social welfare provision. I also report the results of analysis of the welfare state effects of alternative measures of trade pressures, such as the magnitude of merchandise trade with low-wage nations. In addition, I follow a large body of theory and research and incorporate the level of economic development (i.e., per capital GDP in international

---

[6] Numerous measures, many concentrating on net movements of short-term capital, have been developed (see Lessard and Williamson [1987]; Williamson and Lessard [1987]). Recently, Kant (1996) has illustrated that the most commonly used measures are strongly associated with FDI inflows; Frankel and Rose (1996) also illustrate that FDI inflows significantly lower the probability of financial crises. Substantively, FDI inflows and net FDI flows are arguably particularly relevant to the study at hand. For instance, substantial attention has been devoted to perceived declines in FDI inflows and increases in FDI outflows within several advanced democracies in the 1980s and 1990s, and these perceived adverse changes in direct investment are often cited as evidence of a poor business climate and, consequently, of the need to reform tax, welfare, and regulatory policies.

prices) in the general model of social welfare effort. In welfare state theory, rises in the level of economic development are commonly thought to transfer welfare state functions from market to state, increase altruism among an increasingly affluent mass public, and bolster the revenue base for funding the welfare state (e.g., Hicks and Swank [1992]; Pampel and Williamson [1989]; Wilensky [1975]). Related, scholars have commonly asserted that the objective needs, entitlement pressures, and political mobilization of the elderly population shape temporal and crossnational variations in social welfare effort (e.g., Hicks and Swank [1992]; Huber, Ragin, and Stephens [1993]; Pampel and Williamson [1989]; Wilensky [1975]). Thus, I incorporate the share of the population 65-and-over in the general model.

Beyond these forces, business cycle dynamics are often highlighted as central sources of variations in social welfare provision. Automatic entitlement pressures, political demands, and discretionary policy responses associated with unemployment are often hypothesized to be important determinants of social welfare effort (e.g., Hicks and Swank [1992]; Huber, Ragin, and Stephens [1993]; Pampel and Williamson [1989]); similar forces emanate from variations in short-term economic growth rates. Specifically, net of the general level of unemployment, recessions activate income-tested program outlays, foster early retirement, call forth discretionary fiscal stimuli, and otherwise engender pressures for amelioration of economic deprivation. Finally, the general rate of inflation is a potentially important influence on social welfare provision. High rates of inflation generate demands for increments to social benefits, activate cost-of-living indexation, and, when and where non-indexed progressive taxation forms an important source of welfare state funding, engender rises in the revenue base of the welfare state through bracket creep (e.g., Hicks and Swank [1992]; Pampel and Williamson [1989]).

Political factors also play a large role in welfare state theory. Juxtaposed to the economic structures and dynamics and sociopolitical correlates of industrial capitalism, partisan forces, especially the alternation in government of ideologically distinct parties, are commonly highlighted as important determinants of variation in social welfare provision.[7]

---

[7] Beyond those political forces already discussed, welfare state theory also stresses the way in which political competition in developed democratic polities shapes social welfare policy. Two factors stand out: the degree of competitiveness of the party system and the electoral business cycle. Specifically, high levels of party competition are hypothesized to promote the expansion of popular income maintenance programs; preelection vote seeking by

Paralleling the research stream on partisan government effects on macro-economic policies and outcomes (e.g., Alesina and Rubini [1997]; Hibbs [1987a], [1987b]), scholars have devoted substantial attention to the direct welfare state effects of alternations in government control by Left, Christian Democratic, and Right parties. While some theoretical and empirical work has stressed Left party government incumbency (e.g., Cameron [1978]; Stephens [1980]) or the presence of a unified party of the Right (e.g., Castles [1982]; Castles and McKinlay [1979]), a substantial amount of research on welfare policy determination in developed capitalist democracies has emphasized the positive welfare state impacts of both Left and Christian Democratic party government control (e.g., Hicks and Swank [1984]; Swank [1988], Huber, Ragin, and Stephens [1993]). In addition, scholars have highlighted the differential welfare effects of Left and Christian Democratic party government: Left governments have played particularly strong roles in developing universalistic transfers and expanding public social services, while Christian Democratic governments have expanded (largely occupationally based) cash transfer systems (e.g., Esping-Andersen [1990, 1996b, 1996c]; Huber, Ragin, and Stephens [1993]; Huber and Stephens [1996]). Thus, I account for Left and Christian Democratic party government control in subsequent analysis.

Here, it is important to reiterate that my argument about the foundational role of democratic political institutions consciously incorporates partisan control of government by Left and Christian Democratic parties. To review, my argument stresses the ways in which configurations of national democratic institutions structure representation of pro–welfare state interests; shape directly and indirectly the political capacities of pro–welfare state constituencies, groups, parties, and coalitions (i.e., size and unity, coherence of strategy, conventional resources); and influence the character of norms and values embedded in the policy process. As I argue in Chapter 2, one linkage between political institutions, political capacities, and welfare policy runs through the political power of pro–welfare state parties. That is, the institutional structures of social corporatism and inclusive electoral institutions increase the votes, seats, and government participation of Left and Christian Democratic parties. And,

incumbents is also hypothesized to engender extensions of popular welfare programs (see, among others, the literature and evidence in Hicks and Swank [1992]). In models presented below, the electoral cycle and the degree of party competition have no consistent and systematic social policy impacts and hence are not incorporated in the general model.

as research has shown, votes and seats of opposition Left and Christian Democratic parties matter to welfare state development, as does Left and Christian Democratic government incumbency (Hicks and Swank, 1992). There are, however, two justifications for a separate assessment of partisan control of government. First, a substantial amount of work highlights partisan government incumbency as the central political determinant of social policy outcomes. Second, and relatedly, a strict interpretation of partisan theory suggests that party government is the main conduit of the influence of the focal political institutional factors. For example, the social policy effects of social corporatism, the strength of the union movement, and the electoral appeal and cohesion of redistributive parties and movements more generally, may be primarily channeled through Left party incumbency; inclusive electoral institutions may matter only to the extent that they foster Left and Christian Democratic governance. Thus, incorporation of partisan government in the general model allows a more complete assessment of my general theory; evidence of strong direct and mediating roles for political institutions, in the presence of controls for direct policy effects of partisan government, bolsters confidence in the more general consequences of democratic political institutions.

In sum, the empirical models of social welfare provision presented below incorporate principal empirical indicators for factors highlighted in the general model, as well as for international capital mobility and domestic political institutions. While there is some variation among the models of different dimensions of social welfare provision (e.g., the size of the elderly population is assumed to be irrelevant to the social wage), most models include (one-year) lagged levels of trade openness (imports plus exports of goods and services as a percent of GDP), the level of economic development (per capita GDP in international prices), and the size of the elderly population (the proportion of the population 65 years or older). Models also include (one-year) lagged economic growth, unemployment, and inflation rates. Finally, the general models incorporate Left and Christian Democratic party control of government (i.e., the percent of cabinet portfolios held by each party group).[8]

---

[8] For most basic models reported in the book, I used ten-year averages of the percentage of cabinet portfolios held by parties of the Left and Christian Democracy. I use this general specification because, while many partisan policies have immediate effects on spending and statutory entitlements (i.e., within the upcoming fiscal year), others are scheduled for implementation in future years or take several years to have major effects on social welfare outlays or other aspects of policy outcomes. In some models, such as those for the social wage,

Statistical Estimation. To estimate the direct policy effects of international capital mobility and to test propositions about the roles of domestic political institutions in mediating these effects, I utilize empirical models of annual 1965–93 total social spending in the 15 focal nations. It is important to note that available data on total social welfare spending across the developed democracies for a long time-span is highly imperfect. The major sources of such data contain major breaks in the spending series.[9] Thus, to correctly test the book's central propositions, I control for eight significant series breaks through the use of dummy variables (i.e., 0 for country years before and outside of the country series break, 1.00 for country years following the break). I end the analysis in 1993 for several reasons. When the principal work for this volume was completed, the OECD's Social Welfare Expenditure Data Base, a major source of data utilized in this study, extended only to 1993. Moreover, the newly released time-series cross-section data on the components of labor and industrial relations systems, crucial to the construction of measures of social corporatism, extended only to 1993; this time limitation on data availability also extended to several other variables.

I estimate the empirical models by Ordinary Least Squares (OLS) regression with corrections for first-order autoregressive errors, panel correct standard errors (i.e., standard errors computed with heteroskedastic-consistent variance-covariance matrices for panel data), and unit dummies (see Beck and Katz [1995]). Given that inclusion of a full set of unit dummy variables produced high (even prohibitive) levels of multicollinearity for some institutional variables – R^2-deletes exceeding .90 in some cases – a conventional fixed effects model is not used; country dummies to adjust for potentially significant unit effects (and thus obviate potential biased estimation) are included when t-statistics for country dummies exceeded 1.00. However, a number of alternative estimators of pooled–time series cross-sectional models exist (e.g., Judge et al. [1985]) and I use several of these to provide a check against accepting findings that

I use a short-term lag for partisan effects. In supplementary analyses, I explored various (re)specifications of these variables (e.g., short-term and long-term lags, cumulative years in office, and so forth). Generally, these alternative specifications are consistent with results discussed below for the focal measures of partisan control of government.

[9] Both major sources of such data – the International Labour Organization's *Cost of Social Security* and the OECD's Social Expenditure Data Set contain major breaks in the spending series. Because of the wider range of coverage (e.g., more social service categories) and longer time coverages (1993 rather than 1989 as the series' end point), I chose the OECD series.

are artifacts of method. Specifically, to address potential bias from omitted country and time effects, a complete fixed effects model is used where time dummies in addition to all unit-country dummies are included. Second, a lagged endogenous variable (i.e., the lagged level of welfare effort), an alternative to a first-order autoregressive parameter (Beck and Katz, 1996), is added to the full fixed effects model. Finally, a "generalized error correction" model is used where the change in social welfare spending is regressed on lagged levels in welfare spending, the change and level of a specific international capital mobility variable, and controls; the change and level variables for international capital mobility are interacted with institutional variables to (re)test specific hypotheses about the role of institutions in shaping the domestic impacts of internationalization (see below).[10] I report the results obtained from these alternative estimators in Appendix B and discuss them below. (Note: Readers who wish to acquire an appreciation of the overall pattern of quantitative findings may skip the discussion of the individual findings and move to the concluding section of this chapter, "What We Know: Summing Up the Results of the Quantitative Analysis.")

A Note on Interaction Analysis. Given that central hypotheses about globalization and welfare state convergence and the role of political institutions in mediating the effects of international capital mobility employ interactions, it may be helpful to discuss the interpretation of findings generated by this technique. Briefly, the interaction of, let's say, X_1 (e.g., past welfare effort) and X_2 (e.g., global capital flows), when the explanandum is Y (e.g., social welfare effort), will tell us whether the effect of X_2 (global capital) on Y (social welfare) varies with levels of X_1 (past welfare effort), or vice versa. The significance test for the interaction simply tells us whether differences in the effect of X_2 (global capital) on Y (welfare effort) across levels of X_1 (past welfare effort) are significantly different from zero. The coefficient for interaction term itself, when multiplied by a value of X_1 (past welfare effort) and added to the regression coefficient of X_2 (global capital), becomes the slope for the effect of X_2 (global capital) at that level of X_1 (past effort). Moreover, standard errors necessary for testing

[10] Generalized error correction models are quite useful in providing an additional check on robustness of significant findings. For instance, they are useful for assessing spuriousness of significant effects in the presence of nonstationary variables and they allow researchers to differentiate between structural and dynamic effects. For a discussion these dynamic models for pooled time-series analysis, see Beck and Katz (1996).

the significance of the effects of X_2 at some level of X_1 are easily derived (see Friedrich [1982]). Thus, using the present example from the convergence hypotheses, we can derive specific effects of international capital flows on welfare effort across levels of past welfare effort (and test the significance of these effects), as well as evaluate whether or not these effects differ from one another. (For examples on how interactions can evaluate theoretical propositions about the nonlinear and contingent effects of a focal variable, see Lange and Garrett [1985] and Hicks and Swank [1992]).

Results of the Econometric Analysis

The findings from the statistical estimation of the baseline models of aggregate social welfare effort are presented in Table 3.3. The table presents tests for direct (linear) welfare effects of the five focal dimensions of international capital mobility, the three central dimensions of national democratic institutions, and the factors comprising the general model. In addition, I present the results for two tests of the hypothesis that rises in international capital mobility foster welfare state convergence. One test evaluates the notion that there has been a "run to the bottom," or that internationalization has engendered a movement toward the lowest common denominator of residual market-conforming social policies. The other test examines a modified version of this hypothesis, in which larger welfare states are hypothesized to be especially vulnerable to globalization-induced retrenchment pressures. As noted, the models for the first four measures of capital mobility are estimated with 1965–93 data for the 15 focal nations; for the final equation, which estimates the effect of covered interest rate differentials, data unavailability constrains model estimation to the 1979–93 period and 14 nations.

As the table reveals, conventional wisdom is not supported. That is, there is no evidence that rises in international capital mobility are systematically associated – net of other forces shaping social welfare effort – with retrenchments of social welfare provision. To the contrary, two dimensions of international capital mobility – borrowing on international capital markets and liberalization of capital controls – are actually positively and significantly related to total welfare spending. Total financial flows, direct foreign investment, and interest rate differentials are unrelated to social welfare provision across the entire sample. Moreover, I also examined the social welfare impacts of a variety of alternative measures of international capital mobility. These include total capital movements,

Quantitative Analysis

Table 3.3. *Global Capital, National Institutions, and Social Welfare Effort, 1965–1993*

	I	II	III	IV	V
Global Capital					
Capital Liberalization	.5790* (.1892)	—	—	—	—
Total Capital Flows	—	.0086 (.0071)	—	—	—
Direct Investment	—	—	.0208 (.1174)	—	—
Capital Markets	—	—	—	.1404* (.0803)	—
Interest Rate Differentials	—	—	—	—	−.0549 (.0771)
National Political Institutions					
Social Corporatism	.8820* (.3614)	.7500* (.3600)	.7453* (.3691)	.7046* (.3659)	1.8288* (.4991)
Inclusive Electoral Institutions	1.3001* (.3251)	1.3093* (.3198)	1.2962* (.3100)	1.3665* (.3189)	1.9513* (.4197)
Dispersion of Authority	−4.8053* (.7393)	−4.3309* (.7723)	−4.4579* (.7726)	−4.1294* (.7678)	−2.7371* (.8672)
General Model					
Old_{t-1}	.8075* (.1143)	.8900* (.1220)	.8828* (.1229)	.8602* (.1229)	1.0153* (.1338)
$Unemployment_{t-1}$	.3794* (.0585)	.3806* (.0540)	.3886* (.0537)	.3886* (.0528)	.4176* (.0555)
$Inflation_{t-1}$	.0404* (.0212)	.0383* (.0213)	.0379* (.0215)	.0408* (.0216)	.0592* (.0348)
$Growth_{t-1}$	−.1284* (.0219)	−.1277* (.0217)	−.1291* (.0218)	−.1279* (.0223)	−.0906* (.0363)
$Affluence_{t-1}$	.8060* (.0969)	.8136* (.1029)	.8356* (.1023)	.7919* (.1012)	.6228* (.1312)
Left Government	−.0038 (.0078)	−.0064 (.0084)	−.0048 (.0082)	−.0038 (.0079)	.0012 (.0082)
Christian Democratic Government	.0066 (.0132)	.0045 (.0142)	.0059 (.0141)	.0062 (.0137)	−.0040 (.0166)
$Trade_{t-1}$	.0253* (.0130)	.0254* (.0131)	.0246* (.0132)	.0246* (.0131)	.0291* (.0161)
A Run to the Bottom?					
Past Welfare State Effort$_{(t-1)}$	.8130* (.0401)	.8602* (.0324)	.8677* (.0322)	.8340* (.0334)	.7062* (.0643)

(continued)

Table 3.3 *(continued)*

	I	II	III	IV	V
Global Capital Factor of	.2545	−.0063	.0146	−.3394*	−.2191
Equation (see first panel above)	(.2054)	(.0178)	(.1552)	(.1198)	(.3045)
Past Welfare Effort* Global	.0128	.0005	.0042	.0141*	.0048
Capital Factor	(.0119)	(.0006)	(.0064)	(.0051)	(.0125)
A Convergence of Large Welfare States to the Mean?					
Gap in Welfare Effort (Welfare	1.0151*	1.0349*	.9828*	1.0045*	.9948*
Effort minus Mean Effort)	(.1242)	(.0523)	(.0500)	(.0500)	(.0843)
Global Capital Factor of	.2604*	.0057	−.0787	−.1167*	.0335
Equation (see first panel above)	(.1278)	(.0069)	(.0866)	(.0598)	(.0719)
Gap*Global Capital Factor	.0081	.0007	.0338*	.0193*	−.0104
	(.0376)	(.0015)	(.0163)	(.0098)	(.0150)
intercept	−6.4900	−5.8940	−6.0090	−5.4900	−5.3190
standard error of the estimate	.9120	.9080	.9090	.9190	.8990
mean of the dependent variable	19.6570	19.6570	19.6570	19.6570	22.4910
Buse R^2	.8610	.7920	.7910	.8150	.9140

Note: Each model is estimated with 1965–93 data (or 1979–93 data for the Interest Rate Differentials model of column 5) by Ordinary Least Squares; equations are first-order autoregressive. The table reports OLS unstandardized regression coefficients and panel correct standard errors. For discussion of this econometric technique, see Beck and Katz (1995). Each set of interactions is entered in separate versions of the five equations. All models include nation-specific dichotomous variables (if $t > 1.00$) to account for unmodeled country effects and dichotomous variables to control for series breaks in the dependent variable.
* Significant at the .05 level or below.

foreign direct investment, and capital market borrowing standardized by gross domestic investment and the broader measure of liberalization of restrictions on financial flows. These supplementary tests confirm that capital mobility is either unrelated to social welfare effort or, in the case of a minority of dimensions, is positively related to social welfare provision.

With respect to these positive welfare effects, the results are consistent with arguments made by Garrett (1998b) and Rodrik (1996), or what Garrett and Mitchell (forthcoming) call the compensation hypothesis: globalization generates pressures for insurance against new risks, compensation for losses, and policies that generally bolster social cohesion. It is also important to point out, however, that the substantive magnitude of the welfare effects of liberalization and international capital markets is quite small. For instance, a shift of 1.5 in the index of liberalization of capital markets (say a shift from 2.5 to 4.0, which is typical of the developed democracies during the sample period) is associated with an increase in social welfare outlays equivalent to slightly less than 1 percent of GDP. Thus, at this stage of analysis, the only clear conclusion is that internationalization has not resulted in large, systematic rollbacks of social welfare effort.

With respect to the direct social welfare impacts of domestic institutions, each dimension has systematic, substantively large, and statistically significant impacts on total social welfare effort. Social corporatism has a large positive direct welfare effect in all five variations of the basic model. Consistent with theory, "inclusive electoral institutions" is directly and positively associated with social protection is each equation, as well. Finally, "dispersion of policy-making authority" has a large negative effect on the magnitude of social welfare effort; net of other forces, the difference in social welfare spending (as a share of national product) between countries at approximately one standard deviation above the index mean of "dispersion" (e.g., the United States) and those at one-half standard deviation below the index mean (e.g., Norway and Denmark) is about 7 percent of GDP (i.e., the column I coefficient for dispersion of −4.8053* 1.5). Similar (albeit slightly larger) effects are found for the index of "decentralization," in which presidential-parliamentarism is not included in computations; all of the individual dimensions of dispersion (e.g., presidentialism, federalism) have significant and negative direct effects on welfare effort (results not reported in Table 3.3). In addition, the direct welfare effects of democratic political institutions do not wane or disappear in the post-1979 era of internationalization of markets and neoliberal macroeconomic orthodoxy. All three dimensions of national political institutions have significant and substantively large impacts on social welfare provision in the 1979–93 model of Column V, Table 3.3. Moreover, tests of period effects of political institutions (derived from 1965–93 equations with post-1979 dummy variable-institutions interactions) show that the substantive magnitude of the effects of social corporatism and inclusive electoral institutions are actually significantly larger in the post-1979 era than in the earlier period. If anything, *cross-national variations in democratic political institutions become more (not less) important in structuring domestic policy choices as we move into the contemporary era of global markets.*

As to the other forces shaping social welfare effort, the size of the aged population, unemployment, inflation, and the level of affluence are all positively and significantly associated with total social welfare outlays;

the economic growth rate is negatively and significantly related to social welfare effort indicating that, as expected, downturns in economic activity themselves invoke automatic and discretionary increases in social welfare provision. In addition, congruent with the classic arguments of Cameron (1978) and Katzenstein (1985), as well as the embedded liberalism and compensation theses – but inconsistent with the conventional globalization hypotheses – the social policy effects of overall trade openness for the entire sample covering 1965–93 (equations 1–4) and for the 1979–93 period (equation 5) are positive and significant; the substantive magnitude of the trade effect on social protection is, however, very small. Finally, I estimated the (linear and nonlinear) social welfare policy effects of a variety of alternative dimensions of trade openness, such as the extent of merchandise trade with developing nations. The results from these analyses confirm that trade openness is either unrelated or positively and significantly related to the magnitude of social welfare effort.

Finally, in the presence of controls for national institutions, the relatively short-term direct social welfare impacts of both Left and Christian Democratic governments are statistically insignificant in the basic models of Table 3.3. It is important to note, however, that in the presence of unit dummies and institutional variables, levels of multicollinearity for partisan variables are high. In fact, if one deletes unit dummies, allowing institutional, partisan, and other variables to absorb cross-national variance, government control by Christian Democratic parties is positively and significantly related to total social protection (e.g., Christian Democratic Government in the column 1 equation is .0532 with a t-statistic of 4.568); Left government is also significant in some specifications of the basic model. Moreover, I report below several additional partisan effects in disaggregated analysis of income maintenance, the social wage, and health provision. Generally, though, configurations of national political institutions (which shape features of the relative capacities of partisan and other actors) have the most consistent and substantively largest direct effects on variations in total social welfare effort.

A Run to the Bottom?

As discussed above, a common argument is that, net of other forces, rises in international capital mobility will put substantial pressure on moderately and very large welfare states to reform policies – to cut income replacement ratios, tighten eligibility standards, and otherwise enact market-oriented reforms to achieve efficiency and reduce costs. That is, internationalization of capital markets will place the greatest pressures on larger welfare states to move toward the residual, market-conforming model of social protection. Here, I first report the interactions between the focal dimensions of international capital mobility and the past size of the welfare state. (This set of interactions and the subsequent one reported in the table are estimated independently in two separate stages of analysis conducted after the estimation of the basic models.) As the table reveals, there is no evidence that international capital mobility has produced, net of other forces, rollbacks in social protection in the larger welfare states relative to smaller welfare states as the convergence hypothesis predicts. In fact, the four coefficients for the interactions involving liberalization and the three types of capital flows are incorrectly signed (columns I–IV). Moreover, the interaction between past size of the welfare state and borrowing on international capital markets (column IV) is also statistically significant.[11]

In addition, I explored the question of whether or not the welfare state effects of international capital mobility have occurred primarily in large welfare states (i.e., where welfare state size is above the mean level of social welfare provision). Similar to the first test, there is no evidence that internationalization has produced convergence of large welfare states toward the average level of social protection. Specifically, all of the coefficients for the interactions are incorrectly signed and those for FDI and international capital market borrowing are significant and in the positive direction. These findings indicate that, at least for some dimensions of capital flows, rises in international capital mobility are associated with small extensions of social welfare effort in large welfare states. (The political foundations of these findings are elaborated in the course of tests of the ways in which specific political institutions condition the impact of internationalization on domestic policy choices.)

---

[11] Using the mechanics of interactions discussed above, it easy to derive the specific impacts of rises in exposure to world capital markets in small (welfare spending is 10 percent of GDP), moderate (20 percent of GDP), and large (30 percent of GDP) welfare states. In moderate and large welfare states, the welfare impact of rises in borrowing on international capital markets is insignificant; in small welfare states (e.g., pre-1980s Australia, Japan, the United States) it is negative (i.e., assuming 10 percent of GDP, $\beta = -.1988$, t-statistic $= -2.71$). Again, this pattern of social policy effects is the exact opposite of that predicted by globalization theory.

Supplementary Hypotheses

I present the results of tests of four supplementary hypotheses about the domestic policy consequences of international capital mobility in Table 3.4. As summarized in Chapter 2, these involve the "curvilinear" hypothesis, the trade-capital openness hypothesis, the domestic fiscal stress-capital mobility hypothesis, and the "capital flight" hypothesis. As the table suggests, there is no evidence to support the curvilinear hypothesis, or the idea that rises in international capital openness initially produce increases in social protection but eventually create downward pressures on the welfare state: the column I model reveals that the elements of the polynomial specification are insignificant. In addition, the findings reported in column II indicate that high levels of trade and capital openness do not interact to generate systematic retrenchment pressures on the welfare state. Moving to the fourth column of the table, the hypothesis that adverse capital movements, or "capital flight," produces rollbacks of social welfare provision is also rejected: the model of column IV displays an insignificant (and incorrectly signed) relationship between inflows minus outflows of foreign direct investment (FDI) and social welfare effort. A variety of additional tests for direct linear effects of FDI inflows, net short-term flows (e.g., net portfolio and bank lending), and related measures of short-term capital flight, also produced null results. Finally, the four alternative measures of capital mobility utilized above were substituted for capital liberalization and the findings with respect to the three supplemental hypotheses were identical.[12]

The results are, however, more supportive of the notion that domestic fiscal stress and international capital mobility interact to place pressure on the welfare state. In the model presented in column III of Table 3.4, the interaction between international capital mobility and budget imbalances is statistically significant and correctly signed. Using the mechanics of interactions (as outlined above), it is relatively easy to show that the effect

---

[12] In the individual country analyses of Chapters 4 through 6, I encounter episodes where short-term adverse capital movements have generated at least some political and economic pressures on national policy makers to shift tax and spending policies. The cases include early 1980s France, 1980s Sweden, and 1990s Germany. However, while "capital flight," or perceptions of it, proved important in policy debates, and in some cases reforms, the nature of capital movements and the political economic contexts varied notably across episodes. Thus, like the econometric results, country experiences suggest little in the way of systematic and strong welfare effects of capital flight.

Table 3.4. *Global Capital and the Welfare State, 1965–1993: Tests of Supplemental Hypotheses*

	I	II	III	IV
Global Capital Specification	Nonlinear	Trade * Capital Openness	Mobile Capital * Fiscal Stress	"Capital Flight"
Capital Liberalization	.7463	.6795*	.7314*	.5674*
	(.8837)	(.3946)	(.2007)	(.1891)
Capital Liberalization^2	−.0292	—	—	—
	(.1484)			
Trade Openness	—	.0319^a	—	—
		(.0215)		
Trade Openness* Capital Liberalization	—	−.0018	—	—
		(.0067)		
Public Sector Fiscal Deficit/Surplus	—	—	−.5295*	—
			(.0640)	
Deficit/Surplus* Capital Liberalization	—	—	.1186*	—
			(.0434)	
Net Foreign Direct Investment (FDI) Inflows minus Outflows	—	—	—	−.2756
				(.1724)
National Political Institutions				
Social Corporatism	.8929*	.8996*	.9153*	.9650*
	(.3622)	(.3638)	(.3525)	(.3663)
Inclusive Electoral Institutions	1.3642*	1.3644*	1.4928*	1.3915*
	(.3240)	(.3244)	(.3173)	(.3254)
Dispersion of Authority	−4.5810*	−4.6949*	−4.5327*	−4.3177*
	(.7216)	(.7933)	(.6940)	(.7358)
General Model				
Old$_{t-1}$	.7980*	.7884*	.8097*	.7773*
	(.1127)	(.1164)	(.1068)	(.1138)
Unemployment$_{t-1}$	.3761*	.3764*	.2984*	.3782*
	(.0520)	(.0522)	(.0538)	(.0527)
Inflation$_{t-1}$	.0413*	.0415*	.0330	.0382*
	(.0212)	(.0213)	(.0201)	(.0216)
Growth$_{t-1}$	−.1294*	−.1291*	−.1297*	−.1299*
	(.0220)	(.0220)	(.0218)	(.0221)
Affluence$_{t-1}$	.8021*	.8107*	.7758*	.7747*
	(.0949)	(.0977)	(.0904)	(.0952)
Left Government	−.0038	−.0038	−.0022	−.0044
	(.0077)	(.0077)	(.0076)	(.0078)
Christian Democratic Government	.0063	.0060	.0109	.0053
	(.0130)	(.0131)	(.0126)	(.0131)
Trade$_{t-1}$	.0274*	—	.0268*	.0301*
	(.0127)		(.0122)	(.0130)
intercept	−6.6094	−6.6497	−6.1939	−5.8877
standard error of the estimate	.9224	.9212	.9059	.9170
mean of the dependent variable	19.6540	19.6540	19.6540	19.6540
Buse R^2	.8232	.8217	.8385	.8200

Note: Each model is estimated with 1965–93 data by Ordinary Least Squares (OLS); equations are first-order autoregressive. The table reports OLS unstandardized regression coefficients and panel correct standard errors. For discussion of this econometric technique, see Beck and Katz (1995). All models include nation-specific dichotomous variables (if $t > 1.00$) to account for unmodeled country effects and dichotomous variables to control for series breaks in the dependent variable.
* Significant at the .05 level. ^{a} Significant at the .10 level.

of capital market liberalization is positive (although substantively small) and significant (β = .7314; t = 2.0) when budgets are in balance (Deficit/Surplus = 0.00). When budget deficits average in the range of five percent of GDP, however, rises in international capital mobility are unrelated to social welfare effort; when budgets reach and exceed roughly 10 percent of GDP (e.g., for several years in Belgium and Italy since the early 1980s, and in Sweden in the early 1990s), the effect of capital mobility becomes negative (e.g., –.46 when deficits account for 10 percent of GDP) and statistically significant. Moreover, when one substitutes borrowing on international capital markets – perhaps the most relevant dimension with respect to the fiscal crisis–internationalization interaction – the findings are duplicated. This set of results suggests that rises in international capital openness, or exposure to international capital markets, does not exert significant downward pressure on the welfare state at moderate levels of budget imbalance; when budget deficits don't exist, some expansion of social protection is possible even in the context of international capital mobility. When budget deficits become high, however, capital mobility engenders cuts in social welfare effort. As noted above, international capital markets and mobile asset holders may well expect higher inflation, higher taxes, and other adverse outcomes in the wake of severe fiscal imbalance and, in turn, bid down the value of currency; currency depreciation itself will create a substantial interest rate premium for the focal nation (Garrett, 1998b). In such a political economic environment, policy makers may well turn to retrenchment of social welfare spending.[13]

---

[13] Two points are in order. First, the idea that international capital markets do not necessarily pressure policy makers in large welfare states when budgets are in balance or of moderate magnitude is generally consistent with Mosley's (1998) findings about the preferences and behavior of international capital market actors. In this research, Mosley relies on extensive interview data to observe that international capital markets are not particularly concerned with a large public sector, per se; they are primarily focused on the "big numbers" of fiscal and economic instability – the budget deficit and inflation rate, most notably. In Mosley's interviews, however, international capital markets typically prefer budget balances to approach or fall below 3 percent of GDP. My estimates of when international markets exert clear pressure on the welfare state (i.e. deficits circa 10 percent of GDP) allow welfare policy makers much more latitude.

Second, in new analysis of 1979–95 domestic fiscal and internationalization pressures on the welfare state – work that consciously extends the theory and empirical analysis of the present inquiry (Swank 2001) – I find a nearly identical interaction between the level of public debt and capital mobility. Capital mobility does not negatively and significantly influence levels of welfare spending until public debt reaches 100 percent of GDP (e.g., Belgium in the 1980s and Italy in the 1990s).

Democratic Institutions and the Mediated Impacts of Globalization

Table 3.5 reports the results of analysis of the roles of institutional features of the polity in shaping the domestic policy impacts of capital mobility. The first panel of the table reports the interactions between the five dimensions of capital mobility and political institutions; the following four sections report estimates of the social welfare effects of a particular dimension of capital mobility at specific levels of social corporatism, inclusive electoral institutions, and dispersion of decision-making authority, as well as decentralization of authority. (I report the analysis of the mediating roles of institutional structures of welfare states in the following section.) As the first row of the table indicates, the social welfare impacts of all three measures of capital flows – total flows, FDI, and capital market borrowing – and liberalization of capital markets are conditioned by social corporatism.[14] In each case, the interaction is significant and positive. The substantive meanings of these interactions are illustrated in the second section of Table 3.5: for instance, estimated welfare state effects of all three measures of capital flows are negative where social corporatism is low (i.e., corporatism index values of roughly –1.00, as in the United States), insignificantly related to social welfare provision at average levels of corporatism (index levels of 0.0), and positively related to social protection at high levels of social corporatism (i.e., index values of roughly 1.00, as in the Nordic countries).

To briefly review the computation of these effects, the impact of a feature of capital mobility – say FDI – on social welfare effort where social corporatism in low – say the United States (index score of –1.01, as given in Table 2.3) – is given by the slope of FDI (.0205, not reported) plus the coefficient for the interaction (.5102) multiplied by the value of corporatism (–1.01). Thus, the welfare impact of FDI in pluralist polities is .0205 + (.5102* – 1.10), or –.4948, as reported in the table. Using the

---

[14] It is unclear why there is no significant interaction between international financial integration (as measured by covered interest differentials) and national institutions in the 1979–93 period. One explanation is that this dimension of international capital mobility is less relevant than others; another potential explanation is that fewer degrees of freedom make it more difficult to find statistically significant effects. In addition, it is useful to recall Willett and Ahn's (1998) finding that this measure is somewhat flawed in its power to measure financial integration when covered interest differentials are 0.00. It is also important to note that while institutions do not generally mediate (otherwise insignificant) effects of covered interest differentials on aggregate social welfare effort in the 1979–93 period, this measure does exhibit significance in some of the analyses reported below.

95

Table 3.5. *The Impact of International Capital Mobility on Social Welfare Effort across Democratic Institutional Contexts, 1965–1993*

	Capital Liberalization	Capital Flows	Direct Investment	Capital Markets	Interest Rate Diffs
Effects on Social Welfare					
Social Corporatism*	.8112*	.0695*	.5102*	.3840*	ns
Column Variable	(.2496)	(.0162)	(.1569)	(.0997)	
Inclusive Electoral	.3645*	.0164*	.2265*	.4247*	ns
Institutions* Column	(.2100)	(.0062)	(.0851)	(.0836)	
Dispersion of Authority*	ns	−.0642*	−.5722*	−.3769*	ns
Column		(.0241)	(.3222)	(.2333)	
Decentralization of Authority*	−1.8834*	−.0490*	−.8641*	−.6996*	ns
Column	(.4659)	(.0180)	(.2865)	(.1735)	
By Institutional Context Social Corporatism					
Low (United States)	−.3339[a]	−.0796*	−.4948*	−.4660*	—
	(.2234)	(.0203)	(.1674)	(.1032)	
Average (Belgium)	.4853*	ns	ns	ns	—
	.2211				
High (Norway)	1.3046*	.0609*	.5307*	.3097*	—
	(.2200)	(.0151)	(.2188)	(.1559)	
Inclusive Electoral Institutions					
Low (United Kingdom)	ns	−.0194*	−.3271*	−.4397*	—
		(.0101)	(.1342)	(.1118)	
Average (Austria)	.6458*	ns	ns	ns	—
	(.2017)				
High (Finland)	.9556*	.0146*	ns	.4352*	—
	(.3296)	(.0083)		(.1154)	
Dispersion of Authority					
Low (Denmark)	—	.0313*	ns	.2100*	—
		(.0126)		(.1052)	
Average (Austria)	—	ns	ns	ns	—
High (United States)	—	−.0527*	−.6039*	ns	—
		(.0212)	(.3491)		
Decentralization of Authority					
Low (Norway)	.8159*	.0336*	.2724*	.2815*	ns
	(.2316)	(.0124)	(.1518)	(.1004)	
Average (Japan)	.4038*	.0120*	ns	ns	—
	(.1850)	(.0073)			
High (United States)	ns	−.0262*	−.7818*	−.5720*	—
		(.0141)	(.2665)	(.1566)	

Note: Interactions are estimated in the focal equations of Table 3.3. Estimation is by OLS with AR1 autoregressive parameters and panel correct standard errors. Direct effects of Table 3.3 factors remain virtually unchanged in terms of significance levels and substantive effects and, hence, full table results are not reported. Tables are available from the author.

* Significant at the .05 level.
[a] Significant at the .10 level.

information in the variance-covariance matrix for the equation (see Freidrich [1982]), one can derive a standard error for the significance of FDI in pluralist contexts of .1674 and, in turn, a t-statistic of -2.96 for the coefficient ($-.4948/.1674$). Although the table does not report the coefficients for individual capital mobility variables in the presence of interactions, one can derive them by using the institutional index values of Table 2.3 for the countries designated in Table 3.5 and the value of the interaction (e.g., $[.5102* - 1.01] + X = -.4948$; thus $X = .0205$).

A similar pattern of results emerges for countries that have inclusive electoral institutions: all three measures of capital flows and capital liberalization significantly and positively interact with "electoral inclusiveness." Examining the third section of the table, one can see that, net of other forces, the different dimensions of capital flows and liberalization of capital markets are either unrelated or negatively related to social welfare spending at low or average levels of "electoral inclusiveness" (roughly -1.00 or 0.00 scores on the inclusiveness index, respectively); where inclusive electoral institutions are strong (e.g., index scores of 1.00 or more, as in Belgium), all three measures of capital flows are positively and significantly related to social protection (although the magnitude of these effects is small).

The findings for the level of dispersion of decision-making authority within the polity parallel those for social corporatism and electoral inclusiveness, although, for this institutional dimension, the results are the reverse. That is, as the third row of the table indicates, the welfare effects of capital flows and liberalization are negative at higher levels of dispersion of policy-making authority. The penultimate section of the table displays estimates for the effects of international capital mobility at low (roughly a -1.00 index value), average (0.0), and high (1.00) levels of dispersion of authority. At low levels (e.g., Denmark), all three indicators of flows and liberalization have positive effects on the welfare state; at average levels (e.g., Austria), the effects are largely insignificant. In polities where dispersion of authority is extensive (e.g., the United States), however, capital flows and liberalization are negatively associated with welfare provision. Similar but even stronger mediating roles are reported for decentralization of policy-making authority. I report these parallel findings for the mediating role of decentralization in the final section of the table (and the last row of the first panel of interactions).

Again, the role of decentralization (and more broadly dispersion) of policy-making authority is important and complex. From an institutional veto points perspective alone, vertical and horizontal dispersion of policy-making authority establishes a range of institutional veto points (and similar leverage points for interest articulation) for both proponents and opponents of social policy change. Not all "veto players" are created equal, however, and the second-order, long-term structural effects of institutions are significant. As I have argued, historically embedded systems of dispersed authority disadvantage pro–welfare state constituencies, groups, parties, and coalitions through a variety of mechanisms. They also generally promote pluralist norms of conflict and competition, as well as pro-market orientations. Although retrenchment-minded governments in countries such as Canada and the United States certainly faced institutional impediments to social program cuts, the structure and relative weakness of pro–welfare state political interests and prevailing values in these polities – factors we can directly link to dispersion of authority itself – are strongly conducive to rollbacks of welfare effort.

As I argued in Chapter 2, the theoretical foundations linking fragmentation of authority to weak political capacities and to an adverse set of prevailing norms and values for pro–welfare state interests is particularly pronounced for decentralization (i.e., federalism and its correlate, strong bicameralism). Although separation of powers is negatively associated with the strength of welfare programmatic coalitions (through its negative impact on the development of welfare state effort) and is complementary to the competition and conflict norms of pluralist politics, decentralization of authority is more systematically linked to the political capacities of pro–welfare state interests and the prevailing norms and values of the policy process. In fact, an examination the individual roles of separation of powers, federalism, and bicameralism in mediating the welfare impacts of internationalization confirms theoretical expectations: estimation of the interactions of separation of powers with liberalization and the three forms of capital flows produces two insignificant coefficients and two substantially tiny positive coefficients; however, estimation of the (eight) interactions between federalism and bicameralism on the one hand, and the four capital mobility variables on the other, produces eight negative and significant coefficients. Thus, the dimension of decentralization, as conceptualized and measured here, is the most important aspect of the structure of policy-making authority for conditioning the impact of internationalization.

Analyses of the roles of welfare state program structures in shaping the social policy effects of capital mobility are presented in Table 3.6. The first

Table 3.6. *The Impact of International Capital Mobility on Social Welfare Effort across Welfare State Institutional Contexts, 1965–1993*

	Capital Liberalization	Capital Flows	Direct Investment	Capital Markets	Interest Rate Diffs
Effects on Social Welfare					
Universalism* Column	.2188*	.0223*	.2486*	.0866*	ns
Variable	(.0784)	(.0063)	(.0318)	(.0318)	
Conservatism* Column	ns	ns	ns	.0869*	ns
				(.0231)	
Liberalism* Column	−.1376*	−.0073*	−.0911*	−.0548*	.0293[a]
	(.0513)	(.0020)	(.0311)	(.0147)	(.0201)
By Institutional Context Universalism					
Low (United States)	−.4206[a]	−.0838*	−1.1618*	−.5294*	—
	(.3292)	(.0259)	(.2539)	(.2220)	
Average (Germany)	.4546*	ns	ns	ns	—
	(.1733)				
High (Sweden)	1.3298*	.0944*	.8272*	.2639*	—
	(.3855)	(.0262)	(.2551)	(.1134)	
Conservatism					
Low (Australia)	—	—	—	ns	—
Average (Netherlands)	—	—	—	.2680*	—
				(.0926)	
High (Austria)	—	—	—	.6127*	—
				(.1593)	
Liberalism					
Low (Sweden)	1.4183*	.0536*	.5323*	.3726*	−.1748[a]
	(.3920)	(.0165)	(.2324)	(.1194)	(.1091)
Average (Italy)	.5926*	ns	ns	ns	ns
	(.1871)				
High (Canada)	ns	−.0340*	−.5607*	−.2852*	ns
		(.0107)	(.2043)	(.1125)	

Note: Interactions are estimated in the focal equations of Table 3.3. Estimation is by OLS with AR1 autoregressive parameters and panel correct standard errors. Direct effects of Table 3.3 factors remain universally unchanged in terms of significance levels and substantive effects and, hence, full table results are not reported. Tables are available from the author.
* Significant at the .05 level.
[a] Significant at the .10 level.

section of the table presents the coefficients (standard errors and significance levels) of the interactions between dimensions of capital mobility and welfare state institutions, while the remaining sections illustrate the substantive effects of international capital mobility at low, average, and high levels of "universalism," "conservatism," and "liberalism." As Table 3.6 suggests, there is a systematic pattern of mediation of the effects of international capital flows and capital market liberalization by welfare state programmatic structures. All three measures of capital flows and liberalization of capital controls positively interact with universalism, or the level of universal coverage and benefit equality (see Table 2.3 for country scores on universalism, conservatism, and liberalism). Examining the second section of the table, one can see that all three dimensions of capital flows and liberalization are negatively associated with total welfare spending where universalism is low (e.g., the United Sates) and positively with social welfare provision where it is high (e.g., Norway). While an inconsistent set of capital mobility effects obtains for countries at average levels of universalism, the overall pattern for welfare effects of four of the five facets of international capital mobility is pronounced and consistent with theoretical arguments presented above. In sum, universalism significantly mutes the retrenchment pressures stemming from globalization.

Unlike the case for the universal welfare state, and contra theoretical predictions above, the degree of occupationally based social insurance does not appear to be an important factor in mediating international pressures on the welfare state. Only one interaction is significant: the interplay of borrowing on capital markets and conservatism. While the coefficient for the interaction is correctly signed and estimated effects at different levels of conservatism are consistent with theory, there is little evidence to support a conclusion that the amount of occupational stratification is systematically important in shaping the domestic policy impacts of internationalization. It might be the case, however, that the precise degree of "conservative structure" is not the best measure to use in assessing the mediating role of institutional features of the corporatist conservative model; the most important factor may be whether or not the institutional structure of a welfare state is comprised of the main features of the social insurance model. Thus, as an alternative test, I substituted in the general model of social welfare effort a dichotomous variable coded 1.00 for predominately corporatist conservative welfare states (Austria, Belgium, France, Germany, and Italy) and 0.00 otherwise. Controlling for factors in the baseline model and for universal program structure (to better isolate the role of conservative program structure), I assessed the policy effect of the interaction between the presence of the social insurance model and the five dimensions of international capital. While the interactions involving capital controls and interest rate differentials were insignificant, those between total capital flows and borrowing on international capital markets on the one hand, and the presence of the corporatist conservative model on the other, were positive and highly significant; the interaction involving direct investment flows was positive, but fell just short of significance at conventional levels. Overall, these results suggest we can not rule out the relevance of the patterns of interest representation, political support, and values associated with a corporatist conservative structure for maintenance of the welfare state. In fact, I will present additional quantitative analysis below, and qualitative evidence in Chapter 5, that highlights the political features of this model as a buffer against neoliberal reforms.

Turning to the last set of interactions, the degree to which a welfare state is "liberal" – disproportionate reliance on means-tested programs and private pensions and health insurance – seems to provide an especially conducive institutional context for rollbacks of social protection. As the last row of the first section of Table 3.6 illustrates, welfare state effects of all three types of capital flows and liberalization of capital controls are shaped by "liberalism;" there is a marginally significant interaction between interest rate differentials and liberalism, as well. Where liberalism is low (e.g., Sweden), international capital effects on social policy tend to be positive or inconsequential; where liberalism is high (e.g., Canada), global capital mobility is associated with rollbacks in social welfare provision. As noted above, there are substantial theoretical reasons to believe that liberal welfare states provide few institutional mechanisms to retard retrenchment: liberal program structures provide few opportunities for constituency representation; tend to weaken pro-welfare constituencies, coalitions, and mass support; and promote value orientations that make welfare states highly susceptible to retrenchment.

Finally, I also addressed the possibility that the roles of welfare state structures in mediating the effects of internationalization may simply reflect other political forces. For instance, since universalism is significantly correlated with social corporatism, the interactions between international capital mobility and universalism may disappear after accounting for the mediating roles of corporatist institutions. However, results in models that include both corporatist and welfare structure interactions with international capital mobility indicate that *social corporatism and welfare state structures play important and independent roles in mediating the pressures of internationalization*: capital mobility effects vary simultaneously across levels of universalism (or liberalism) and social corporatism.

Alternative Statistical Approaches. I also estimated all of the empirical models of social welfare provision discussed to this point by the three alternative statistical approaches outlined above. I present results in Appendix B, Table 1. For each core finding, two of the three alternative estimators give the same result on the focal relationship (or the absence of a relationship between capital mobility and social protection); in the large majority of cases, all three alternative estimators produce the same result as that reported above. In addition, it is instructive to highlight that the findings from the generalized error correction models suggest that the interactions between international capital mobility and political institutional dimensions may be structural and long-term in character. That is, in each case, the interaction between the level (but not the year-to-year change) of international capital mobility on the one hand, and the dimensions of national political institutions on the other, is significant. For instance, rises in the level of international capital mobility are associated, net of other forces, with declines in social welfare provision in pluralist, electorally exclusive, and fragmented polities, as well as in liberal welfare states.

These findings, to the extent we wish to privilege this econometric specification, suggest that policy makers to do not necessarily respond immediately to variations in the magnitude of year-to-year changes in international capital mobility. The results, however, are consistent with the view that rises in capital mobility and attendant changes in economic incentives surrounding social policy choice, increases in the prevalence and weight of neoliberal arguments for welfare state retrenchment, and shifts in the balance of power toward increasingly mobile business directly contribute to a long-term program of welfare state retrenchment in liberal institutional contexts and in pluralistic, electorally exclusive, and fragmented polities. These pressures do not lead to long-term rollbacks in welfare states where universalism predominates program structure and where social corporatism, electoral inclusiveness, and centralization characterize the polity. In the latter group, rises in the level of capital mobility are unrelated to the long-term evolution of social protection or are associated with small increments in welfare effort. The exact nature of the relationship between internationalization and social policy change, and the role of national institutions in shaping that relationship, is further developed in the additional quantitative analysis below and in the case analysis that follows in Chapters 4 through 6.

Disaggregating the Analysis

In this section, I present the results of analysis of the impact of internationalization on income transfers (as a percentage of national income), the social wage (share of gross income replaced by social welfare programs for the average production worker), and public health spending (as a percent of GDP) in all of the developed democracies and in universal, conservative, and liberal welfare states.[15] I attempt to foster comparability across welfare dimensions and welfare state clusters by estimating the same general model of social welfare effort in all cases. Only where a variable is theoretically or substantively irrelevant (i.e., the elderly for the social wage, Christian Democratic government in liberal welfare states) do I exclude it. As to national political institutions, I report below the direct welfare influences of institutional factors only for the "all nations" analysis. I do this because of the absence of institutional variation and the presence of a pattern of insignificant welfare effects of institutional dimensions within welfare state clusters.[16]

Globalization and Income Maintenance. Table 3.7 displays the results of the analysis of how capital mobility, political institutions, and general model factors have shaped cash income maintenance programs in the contemporary welfare state. The reader should note that the impact of the five individual dimensions of capital mobility are estimated in five separate equations and the reported social welfare impacts of political institutions

---

[15] I also refer to analyses of the share of total health expenditure accounted for by public programs. However, since results of analysis of the impact of internationalization on public health share are nearly identical to those for public health spending (as a percentage of GDP), I do not systematically report these empirical findings.

[16] Within the three welfare state clusters, the three institutional variables have correct signs and approach statistical significance in the large majority of cases. The most notable case is for liberal welfare states where dispersion of policy-making authority varies substantially across Australia, Canada, Japan, the United Kingdom, and the United States. Here, the direct welfare state effect of dispersion of authority is negative and is significant at the .10 level ($\beta = -1.7031$; $t = -1.56$). Again, however, there is simply not enough variation in dimensions of political institutions within welfare state clusters to systematically and adequately test within-cluster effects of institutional variables.

Table 3.7. *Global Capital, National Institutions, and Income Maintenance, 1965–1993*

	I	III	IV	V
Global Capital	All Nations	Universal Welfare States	Conservative Welfare States	Liberal Welfare States
Capital Liberalization	.4138*	.7117	.3067	−.0273
	(.2070)	(.4440)	(.3654)	(.2295)
Total Capital Flows	.0058	.0655*	.0173	−.0099[a]
	(.0115)	(.0357)	(.0162)	(.0069)
Direct Investment	.0138	.6714*	.0030	−.3179*
	(.1597)	(.2367)	(.2466)	(.1265)
Capital Markets	.1462*	.1501	.6470*	−.2854*
	(.0820)	(.1036)	(.2729)	(.0736)
Interest Rate Differentials	−.1496*	.0534	−.0881	−.2582
	(.0855)	(.1186)	(.1430)	(.1627)
National Political Institutions				
Social Corporatism	.8248*	—	—	—
	(.3927)			
Inclusive Electoral	.5870*	—	—	—
Institutions	(.3336)			
Dispersion of Authority	−4.0088*	—	—	—
	(.9304)			
General Model				
Old_{t-1}	.7284*	1.5289*	−.2282	.6606*
	(.1382)	(.4612)	(.2792)	(.3213)
$Unemployment_{t-1}$	.4120*	.4734*	.5866*	.3294*
	(.0596)	(.0920)	(.1083)	(.0621)
$Inflation_{t-1}$	.0308	−.0358	.1134*	.0272
	(.0226)	(.0477)	(.0416)	(.0248)
$Growth_{t-1}$	−.1293*	−.2504*	−.1257*	−.1220*
	(.0234)	(.0571)	(.0364)	(.0321)
$Affluence_{t-1}$	.7484*	.4408	1.0001*	.4841*
	(.1242)	(.2917)	(.2123)	(.1760)
Left Government	.0104[a]	−.0059	.0302*	.0127*
	(.0081)	(.0101)	(.0143)	(.0057)
Christian Democratic	.0277*	—	.0071	—
Government	(.0114)		(.0220)	
$Trade_{t-1}$	−.0103	.0137	−.0215	.0385
	(.0153)	(.0269)	(.0291)	(.0256)
Intercept	−6.2984	−11.5740	4.5170	−5.7840
Standard Error of the Estimate	.9603	1.1398	1.0482	.6570
Mean of the Dependent Variable	17.1130	19.5580	20.3530	11.4270
Buse R^2	.6397	.8433	.7955	.8594

104

Notes to Table 3.7 *(continued)*

Note: Each model is estimated with 1965–93 data (or 1979–93 data for the Interest Rate Differentials models) by Ordinary Least Squares; equations are first-order autoregressive. The table reports OLS unstandardized regression coefficients and panel correct standard errors. For discussion of this econometric technique, see Beck and Katz (1995). All models include nation-specific dichotomous variables (if $t > 1.00$) to account for unmodeled country effects and dichotomous variables to control for series breaks in the dependent variable. The table reports the full model results of the equation that includes liberalization of capital controls; the effects of the three capital flows and interest rate differential measures are estimated in four additional equations for each set of countries. Effects of institutions and general model factors are virtually unchanged across these and the liberalization equation and thus these additional models are not reported.
* Significant at the .05 level or below.
Universal welfare states include Denmark, Finland, the Netherlands, Norway, and Sweden; Conservative welfare states include Austria, Belgium, France, Germany, and Italy; Liberal welfare states include Australia, Canada, Japan, the United Kingdom, and the United States.

and general model factors are taken from the equation that estimates the welfare impact of liberalization of capital controls.[17] While conventional theory predicts that rises in international capital mobility should be associated with a reduction in income maintenance across all democracies and within the welfare state clusters, my alternative argument suggests that we should see a distinct pattern of institutional mediation: international capital mobility should be unrelated or positively associated with cash income transfers in universal and conservative institutional contexts and it should be negatively associated with income maintenance in the liberal cluster. In addition, the disaggregated analysis, by focusing on individual dimensions of social protection and by examining determinants of social welfare provision within individual clusters of welfare states, should shed light on the accuracy of conclusions reached in the preceding analysis.

Turning to column I of Table 3.7, welfare state impacts of international capital mobility, political institutions, and general model forces on income maintenance parallel those for total social welfare effort. While cash income maintenance for the elderly, disabled, sick, the unemployed, and other "dependent" groups does account for roughly three-quarters of total social welfare benefits in the 1990s (see Table 3.1), it also excludes direct government provision of health and other social services, as well as active

---

[17] The direct linear effects of political institutions and general model factors (and the overall model statistics) are virtually identical for all five estimating equations. Thus, only the complete model results are reported for one measure of capital mobility – capital market liberalization – in each of the four analysis: "all nations," universal, conservative, and liberal welfare state groups.

labor market policy; a near identical pattern of findings is therefore not necessarily guaranteed. With respect to the welfare impacts of capital mobility across all of the developed democracies, there is once again no evidence to support conventional wisdom that internationalization systematically leads to neoliberal domestic policy consequences. In fact, three of the five dimensions of global capital – capital liberalization, capital market borrowing, and interest rate differentials – are actually significantly and positively related to income maintenance spending. (Note that declines in interest rate differentials indicate more financial market integration and should call forth declines in welfare provision; Table 3.7 actually shows that a decline in interest rate differentials – more capital mobility – is related to more income maintenance protection.) The other two dimensions of international capital movements – total flows and FDI – are unrelated to income maintenance. Taken together, the findings offer modest support for the compensation hypothesis. The impact of capital mobility on cash income maintenance is substantively small, however. For instance, the average 1965–93 change for a nation on the (0–4) index of capital market liberalization is 1.5; thus, net of other factors, the increase in income maintenance associated with this change is roughly .62 percent of national income (.4138, the coefficient for liberalization, multiplied by 1.5).

With regard to the question of whether international capital mobility effects cash income transfers in all three welfare state institutional contexts, Table 3.7 provides some relatively clear evidence. Examining the capital mobility impacts on cash transfers in universal and corporatist conservative welfare state contexts, none of the possible ten relationships between the five dimensions of international capital markets and cash income maintenance is consistent with conventional globalization theory. Seven of the ten possible relationships are statistically insignificant and three are positive and significant. In liberal welfare states, however, four of the five possible relationships between capital mobility and income maintenance are negative and three of these are statistically significant (two at the .05 level and one at the .10 level).

In sum, this stage of the disaggregated analysis lends support to the conclusions from the baseline analysis of total social welfare effort: the welfare effects of international capital mobility appear to be largely contingent on domestic institutional contexts. In addition, a qualification seems in order. The finding that international capital mobility does not systematically promote welfare state retrenchment in corporatist conservative welfare states (but does in liberal welfare states) is consistent with the original theoretical prediction that corporatist conservative structure would blunt the effects of internationalization. The present evidence also confirms the results for the alternative analysis: the presence of the social insurance model (but not the index measuring the degree of occupational stratification) plays a modest role in mediating the social policy impacts of internationalization.

As to the direct welfare effects of other forces, domestic political institutions – social corporatism, inclusive electoral institutions, and dispersion of policy-making authority – have substantively large and statistically significant effects on income maintenance across the developed democracies. Indeed, the impacts of variations in national political institutions on cash income transfers are among the largest effects in the overall model. As to trade openness, results suggest that for the entire sample of countries and years, and for the individual welfare state clusters, trade openness is not significantly related to income maintenance. Given the theory that links openness with domestic compensation (or the rival hypothesis posited by the globalization thesis), this finding is unexpected. However, for aggregate trade openness or alternative measures, such as the relative magnitude of trade with low wage nations, there are no systematic relationships between trade and income maintenance in the present analysis. As to the impacts of socioeconomic structures and dynamics, the analysis for the total set of nations and years and within welfare state clusters points to the general relevance of the size of the aged population, unemployment and growth rates, and the level of economic affluence; the substantive effects of these factors are relatively large and variables are significant in three or all four sets of analysis.

As to the effects of partisan control of government (and note Christian Democratic government is excluded from universal and liberal welfare state models), Christian Democratic government has a substantively large and statistically significant effect on income maintenance in the "all nations" analysis. Everything else being equal, the difference in income maintenance (as a percent of national income) between no Christian Democratic government (cabinet portfolios equals 0.00) and constant rule by Christian Democratic parties (portfolio share is 100) during the prior ten years is a substantively large 2.77. The comparable impact of Left party government across all countries and years is 1.0 percent of national income. The impact of Left government within two of the three welfare state types is more pronounced, however. Comparing partisan differences within conservative and liberal welfare states, Left government has substantively large and statistically significant effects on cash income maintenance. Generally, this evidence underscores the role of party government in directly shaping social welfare provision, a role that was obscured in the prior analysis of total social welfare.[18]

International Capital, National Institutions, and the Social Wage. Table 3.8 displays the results of the analysis of the impact of international capital mobility on the social wage, or the proportion of the average production worker's gross income replaced in the first year of unemployment. I consider the social wage impacts of capital mobility across all nations and years and within universal, conservative, and liberal welfare states. Again, conventional globalization theory posits a negative relationship between rises in capital mobility and social protection. My alternative argument stresses the contingency of globalization effects: international capital mobility should be unrelated to the social wage (or exhibit small positive effects) in universal and conservative welfare states; it should be negatively associated with the social wage in the liberal welfare states. Finally, given that the social wage is the most proximate source of statutory welfare entitlement to be considered in quantitative analysis, I extend the examination of the social wage to include a systematic evaluation of whether or not institutions of interest representation, the organization of policy-making authority, and welfare state programmatic attributes systematically condition the social wage impacts of internationalization.

The first panel in column I of Table 3.8 displays the social wage effects of international capital mobility across all nations and time points. As the table indicates, there is no support for the conventional globalization thesis. Net of other forces, variations in international capital flows and

---

[18] Two points are in order. First, the pattern of welfare state effects of Christian Democracy (principally the large positive effects in the "all nations" analysis) highlights the important expansionary role of Christian Democratic governments in continental welfare states (versus non–Christian Democratic governments elsewhere) in developing large cash transfer-based systems of social protection. Second, the large Christian Democratic government effect and the smaller Left party effects on income maintenance emerge in the presence of institutional and country unit controls; the difference between these analyses where "parties matter," and the analysis of total social welfare effort where parties appear to matter little in the presence of institutions and country effects, may well be the narrower focus of the present analysis. Subsequent analyses of social wage and public health spending, for instance, also reveal limited party effects in the presence of controls for country effects.

Table 3.8. *Global Capital, National Institutions, and the Social Wage, 1965–1993*

	I	III	IV	V
Global Capital	All Nations	Universal Welfare States	Conservative Welfare States	Liberal Welfare States
Capital Liberalization	.0178	.0127	.0039	−.0453*
	(.0143)	(.0305)	(.0195)	(.0178)
Total Capital Flows	.0001	−.0017	.0005	−.0003
	(.0004)	(.0022)	(.0006)	(.0003)
Direct Investment	−.0069	−.0170	−.0134[a]	−.0227*
	(.0062)	(.0121)	(.0076)	(.0083)
Capital Markets	.0029	.0078	.0123	−.0141*
	(.0055)	(.0068)	(.0100)	(.0057)
Interest Rate Differentials	−.0101*	−.0049	.0004	−.0066
	(.0049)	(.0055)	(.0004)	(.0081)
National Political Institutions				
Social Corporatism	.0101	—	—	—
	(.0231)			
Inclusive Electoral Institutions	−.0299	—	—	—
	(.0195)			
Dispersion of Authority	−.0978*	—	—	—
	(.0498)			
General Model				
Unemployment$_{t-1}$	.0044	.0012	−.0039	.0084*
	(.0033)	(.0068)	(.0046)	(.0031)
Inflation$_{t-1}$	.0025	.0043	−.0025	.0041*
	(.0017)	(.0043)	(.0021)	(.0018)
Growth$_{t-1}$	.0001	−.0036	−.0034	−.0023
	(.0002)	(.0055)	(.0025)	(.0030)
Affluence$_{t-1}$	.0191*	.0513*	.0099*	.0061
	(.0044)	(.0081)	(.0055)	(.0041)
Left Government	−.0001	−.0003	.0002	.0003*
	(.0002)	(.0002)	(.0004)	(.0001)
Christian Democratic Government	−.0001	—	−.1001	—
	(.0003)		(.0004)	
Trade$_{t-1}$	.0002	.0015	.0013	−.0005
	(.0008)	(.0015)	(.0011)	(.0019)
intercept	−.1236	−.1354	−.0491	.2419
standard error of the estimate	.0622	.0815	.0415	.0522
mean of the dependent variable	.3759	.5142	.3202	.2934
Buse R^2	.4637	.5928	.7951	.7243

(*continued*)

liberalization of capital markets are unrelated to variations in the social wage. The only significant relationship to emerge involves interest rate differentials and the social wage. The direction of the relationship is wrong, however: declines in interest rate differentials (more financial market integration) are associated with (substantively small) increases in the social wage. With regard to the predictions generated by my alternative theory, the first panel in columns II through IV displays some relatively clear evidence. Specifically, of the 10 possible relationships between the five dimensions of capital mobility and the social wage in universal and conservative welfare state contexts, nine are statistically insignificant. The one (marginally) significant relationship involves a substantively small association between rises in FDI and declines in the social wage in conservative welfare states. However, when we turn to the social wage impacts of capital mobility in liberal welfare states, four of five relationships are negative and three of these statistically significant. That is, rises in the international mobility of capital are systematically associated, net of other forces, with declines in the social wage in the predominately liberal welfare states of Australia, Canada, Japan, the United Kingdom, and the United States. Several of these effects are moderate in size. For instance, given a mean of .29 (or 29 percent) for the social wage in liberal welfare states (see equation statistics in the last panel of Table 3.8), an increase from 3 to 4 on the index of capital market liberalization is associated with a decline of .045 (or 4.5 percent) in the social wage. In sum, the social wage analysis confirms – even strengthens – the conclusions drawn from the analysis of

Notes to Table 3.8 *(continued)*

Note: Each model is estimated with 1965–93 data (or 1979–93 data for the Interest Rate Differentials models) by Ordinary Least Squares; equations are first-order autoregressive. The table reports OLS unstandardized regression coefficients and panel correct standard errors. For discussion of this econometric technique, see Beck and Katz (1995). All models include nation-specific dichotomous variables (if $t > 1.00$) to account for unmodeled country effects and dichotomous variables to control for series breaks in the dependent variable. The table reports the full model results of the equation that includes liberalization of capital controls; the effects of the three capital flows and interest rate differential measures are estimated in four additional equations for each set of countries. Effects of institutions and general model factors are virtually unchanged across these and the liberalization equation and thus these additional models are not reported.
* Significant at the .05 level or below.
Universal welfare states include Denmark, Finland, the Netherlands, Norway, and Sweden; Conservative welfare states include Austria, Belgium, France, Germany, and Italy; Liberal welfare states include Australia, Canada, Japan, the United Kingdom, and the United States.

globalization and income maintenance and aggregate social welfare effort: the impact of capital mobility on welfare provision is dependent on the national political institutions in place in the countries and time frames of interest.

As to the direct social wage effects of political institutions, trade openness, party government, and socioeconomic factors, Table 3.8 indicates that the direct effects of political institutions and general model forces on the social wage are limited. As to institutions, the dispersion of policymaking authority has a significantly and substantively large effect on the social wage, but social corporatism and electoral inclusiveness do not. Supplemental tests did reveal that social corporatism significantly influences the social wage in the post-1979 era of welfare state retrenchment and restructuring. With respect to impacts of general model forces, the level of economic affluence is the only factor to have consistent and significant effects across the different analyses (three of the four basic models). Effects of business cycle dynamics – unemployment, inflation, and growth rates – are sporadic. The impact of variations in the general level of trade openness on the social wage is systematically inconsequential (as are alternative measures of trade flows and competitiveness). In addition, there is no effect of alternations in government of ideologically distinct parties in the "full sample" analysis, or in the analysis of the social wage within universal and conservative welfare states. There is, however, a significant positive impact of Left government on the social wage in liberal welfare states. Specifically, the social wage impact of a majority Left government (100 percent of cabinet portfolios held by the Left) is, net of other forces, .03 (or 3 percent) when the mean level of the social wage is .29 (or 29 percent) of gross income of the average production worker.

As noted, I also examined the social wage impact of the interaction of the five dimensions of capital mobility with the six basic political institutional factors highlighted in theory. That is, using the column-I model of Table 3.8, I replicated the analysis that was undertaken for total social welfare effort using a precise measure of statutory social protection. The results are presented in Table 3.8A. The findings strongly confirm – virtually duplicate – the results of the earlier analysis of total social welfare effort. With respect to the social wage impacts of capital mobility across pluralist and corporatist systems of interest representation, the findings presented in the first row of the table indicate that there is a strong positive interaction between each of the five dimensions of international capital mobility and social corporatism: where social corporatism is strong, the

Table 3.8A. *The Impact of International Capital Mobility on the Social Wage across Institutional Contexts, 1965–1993*

	Capital Liberalization	Capital Flows	Direct Investment	Capital Markets	Interest Rate Diffs
Effects on Social Welfare					
Social Corporatism*	.0631*	.0042*	.0304*	.0258*	−.0120*
Capital Mobility Factor	(.0211)	(.0013)	(.0152)	(.0071)	(.0068)
Electoral Inclusiveness	.0357*	.0006*	.0055^a	.0143*	.0172*
*Capital Mobility Factor	(.0137)	(.0003)	(.0042)	(.0056)	(.0075)
Dispersion of Authority	−.0211	−.0027*	−.0197	−.0219^a	.0207^a
*Capital Mobility Factor	(.0388)	(.0016)	(.0202)	(.0139)	(.0160)
Universalism* Capital	.0073^a	.0010*	.0077^a	.0060*	−.0004
Mobility Factor	(.0049)	(.0004)	(.0052)	(.0020)	(.0012)
Conservatism* Capital	.0023	.0001	−.0003	.0005	−.0021
Mobility Factor	(.0038)	(.0001)	(.0016)	(.0017)	(.0016)
Liberalism* Capital	−.0104*	−.0004*	−.0048*	−.0043*	.0044*
Mobility Factor	(.0050)	(.0001)	(.0028)	(.0011)	(.0012)

Note: Interactions are estimated in the equation of column I of Table 3.8. Estimation is by OLS with AR1 autoregressive parameters and panel correct standard errors. Direct effects of Table 3.8 factors remain universally unchanged in terms of significance levels and substantive effects and, hence, full table results are not reported. Tables are available from the author.
* Significant at the .05 level.
^{a} Significant at the .10 level.

social wage consequences of increases in capital mobility is insignificant or positive; where interest representation is pluralist, the social wage effects of internationalization are negative. A similar pattern is obtained for inclusive electoral institutions: the three measures of international capital flows, as well as liberalization of capital markets, have increasingly positively (negative) impacts on the social wage as we move to more (less) inclusive electoral institutions.[19]

[19] The only inconsistent finding for the 30 possible interactions between dimensions of capital mobility and national institutions pertains to the fifth measure of capital mobility – interest rate differentials – and inclusive electoral institutions. Here, the positive interaction suggests that declines in interest rate differentials tend to be associated with cuts in the social wage as we move toward more inclusive electoral institutions. In fact, using the information from the full estimating equations and computational procedures for interaction analysis outlined above, it is easy to show that at high levels of electoral

With regard to dispersion of authority and welfare program structures, results strongly parallel those for total social welfare effort. In the case of each dimension of international capital mobility, more capital mobility is associated with rollbacks in the social wage in systems of dispersed authority and in liberal welfare state contexts. Separate tests for the decentralization of authority, highlighted in theory and previous analysis, produced results identical to those for overall fragmentation of policy-making power. With respect to universalism, four of the five dimensions of internationalization interact with universal programmatic structure in shaping the social wage: where universalism is strong (e.g., the Nordic countries) international capital flows and liberalization tend to have no or small positive impacts; where universalism is weak (North America), rises in flows and liberalization are associated with retrenchments in the social wage.[20] In sum, the pattern of results for the social wage clearly supports my theory of the institutional contingency of the domestic policy effects of internationalization and leads to rejection of the hypotheses derived from conventional globalization theory.

Globalization and Public Provision of Health Care. Patterns of expansion and contraction and of convergence and divergence in the public provision of health care in the 1980s and 1990s loosely conform to the conventional globalization hypothesis. In the case of both government health spending (as a percentage of GDP) and the public share of total health outlays, relatively constant or modestly declining levels of public provision were observed through the mid-1990s; these trends were accompanied by modest convergence across the developed democracies. The analysis presented in Table 3.9 (as well as a directly analogous assessment

inclusiveness, there is no relationship between interest rate differentials and the social wage; at average levels, there is a small negative relationship and at low levels (exclusive electoral institutions) there is a larger negative relationship between interest rate differentials and the social wage. This single inconsistent finding can not be explained by the conventional globalization thesis or my alternative theory.

[20] Only one institutional dimension highlighted in theory – the degree of occupationally-based welfare program structure – fails to play a consistent role in shaping the direction and magnitude of the welfare effects of global capital markets. There is no interaction between international capital mobility and the degree of conservative welfare state attributes (occupationally based social insurance and privileged public sector plans) in shaping variations in the social wage. However, again, the findings from the disaggregated analysis that rises in capital mobility had no systematic social policy effects within the corporatist conservative welfare subgroup and the interactions between dimensions of international capital mobility and the presence of the social insurance model do provide support for initial theory.

Table 3.9. *Global Capital, National Institutions, and Public Health, 1965–1993*

	I	III	IV	V
Global Capital	All Nations	Universal Welfare States	Conservative Welfare States	Liberal Welfare States
Capital Liberalization	−.0148	−.1243	.0306	−.0704
	(.0577)	(.1254)	(.0859)	(.0896)
Total Capital Flows	.0004	−.0202[a]	.0045*	−.0020
	(.0022)	(.0107)	(.0025)	(.0030)
Direct Investment	−.0116	−.0401	.0679*	−.0690[a]
	(.0340)	(.0721)	(.0404)	(.0516)
Capital Markets	−.0142	−.0261	.0587	−.0582*
	(.0247)	(.0342)	(.0664)	(.0344)
Interest Rate Differentials	.0465*	.0285	.1025*	−.0882[a]
	(.0214)	(.0362)	(.0356)	(.0478)
National Political Institutions				
Social Corporatism	.1612*	—	—	—
	(.0995)			
Inclusive Electoral Institutions	.1037	—	—	—
	(.0847)			
Dispersion of Authority	−1.9133*	—	—	—
	(.2798)			
General Model				
Old_{t-1}	.0001	.3192*	.0290	−.0490
	(.0342)	(.1235)	(.0901)	(.1285)
$Unemployment_{t-1}$	.0353*	−.0440[a]	.0731*	.0859*
	(.0157)	(.0247)	(.0283)	(.0220)
$Inflation_{t-1}$	.0101	.0055	.0074	.0160*
	(.0063)	(.0130)	(.0109)	(.0077)
$Growth_{t-1}$	−.0365*	−.0500*	−.0246*	−.0354*
	(.0064)	(.0147)	(.0095)	(.0101)
$Affluence_{t-1}$	.3740*	.2731*	.3438*	.3324*
	(.0302)	(.0766)	(.0647)	(.0684)
Left Government	.0008	.0005	.0009	.0021*
	(.0008)	(.0010)	(.0012)	(.0010)
Christian Democratic Government	−.0004	—	−.0004	—
	(.0019)		(.0022)	
$Trade_{t-1}$	.0078*	.0107	.0081	.0116
	(.0030)	(.0071)	(.0059)	(.0086)
intercept	.1217	−1.2110	.7062	−.9775
standard error of the estimate	.2668	.3171	.2408	.2306
mean of the dependent variable	5.3468	6.0757	5.404	4.5603
Buse R^2	.6379	.6705	.7555	.7024

of the impact of capital mobility on public health share) addresses the question of whether there are actually systematic relationships between globalization and subsequent health policy change.

As the first panel of column I in Table 3.9 reveals, there is little evidence that, net of other forces, international capital mobility plays much of a role in retrenchment of health care in the public sector. Four of the five dimensions of international capital mobility are unrelated to health care outlays; only declines in covered interest rate differentials are associated with lower government spending for health programs. Turning to the first panel of results in columns II through IV, conventional globalization theory is once again rejected by tests for the welfare effects of internationalization within welfare state groups. In universal welfare states, four of the five relationships between internationalization and health care are insignificant (with a marginally significant negative relationship between total capital flows and health care). In the conservative welfare states of Austria, Belgium, France, Germany, and Italy, three of the five relationships between global capital and health care are significant, but two of these three are actually positive; this suggests that as total international capital flows and FDI increase, public provision of health care is slightly expanded (note the small substantive magnitude of these effects). In the liberal welfare state contexts, however, four of the five relationships between capital mobility and public health care are negative, and two of these are clearly statistically significant; rises in FDI and borrowing on

Notes to Table 3.9 *(continued)*

Note: Each model is estimated with 1965–93 data (or 1979–93 data for the Interest Rate Differentials models) by Ordinary Least Squares; equations are first-order autoregressive. The table reports OLS unstandardized regression coefficients and panel correct standard errors. For discussion of this econometric technique, see Beck and Katz (1995). All models include nation-specific dichotomous variables (if $t > 1.00$) to account for unmodeled country effects and dichotomous variables to control for series breaks in the dependent variable. The table reports the full model results of the equation that includes liberalization of capital controls; the effects of the three capital flows and interest rate differential measures are estimated in four additional equations for each set of countries. Effects of institutions and general model factors are virtually unchanged across these and the liberalization equation and thus these additional models are not reported.
* Significant at the .05 level or below.
Universal welfare states include Denmark, Finland, the Netherlands, Norway, and Sweden; Conservative welfare states include Austria, Belgium, France, Germany, and Italy; Liberal welfare states include Australia, Canada, Japan, the United Kingdom, and the United States.

international capital markets, net of other forces, are associated with declines in government provision of health care.

With respect to the government share of total health outlays (results not reported in tabular form), all factors in the empirical model of health policy exhibit the same policy effects as they do for government health spending as a percentage of GDP. In fact, the pattern observed across welfare state types for the impact of internationalization on the public health share is even more pronounced: in universal and conservative welfare state contexts, six of the ten possible relationships between capital mobility and public health share are insignificant (and the other relationships consist of a mix of positive and negative effects). In liberal welfare states, rises in all forms of capital movements and liberalization of capital markets are negatively associated with the total health share accounted for by government programs; three of these four negative relationships are clearly significant at the .05 level. In other words, the analysis of the determinants of the public provision of health care – as in the case of analyses of other dimensions of social welfare provision – suggests that international capital mobility generates downward pressures on the welfare state, primarily in liberal welfare state contexts.

With respect to the direct impact of political institutions, trade, party government, and socioeconomic factors, Table 3.9 presents evidence that highlights the roles of many of these factors in shaping public provision of health care. With respect to the direct effect of variations in political institutions on government health spending, results from the "all nations" analysis highlights two central findings: net of other forces, government health spending is significantly higher in social corporatist contexts and significantly lower in systems of dispersed authority. In fact, the impact of dispersion of policy-making authority within the polity is substantively very large ($\beta = -1.9133$). With respect to economic structure and dynamics, variations in unemployment and growth rates (but not general inflation rates), as well as the level of economic affluence, are all important determinants of public resource commitments to health care provision. Economic downturns appear to generate substantial pressure on health budgets (see the coefficients for growth and unemployment) and the level of economic affluence systematically undergirds the public resource base to fund health care. Party government is primarily important in liberal welfare states where Left governments have substantively small yet significant effects on the public provision of health care. Finally, trade openness is relevant: consistent with the embedded liberalism thesis (but not conventional globalization theory), the aggregate level of trade openness is positively associated with government provision of health care across the entire sample of countries and years; the positive effect of trade openness falls just short of statistical significance in each of the three welfare state types. In sum, the findings with regard to health policy conform to the results observed for other dimensions of social welfare provision. There is little evidence for the conventional view about the negative welfare state impacts of globalization; there is, however, moderately strong evidence to underscore important direct and mediating roles of national political and welfare state institutions in shaping social policy trajectories in the contemporary era.

What We Know: Summing up the Quantitative Analysis

In Table 3.10, I present a summary of the principal findings about the role of globalization in shaping the contemporary trajectory of developed welfare states. I also present a summary of findings about the impacts of national political institutions in directly influencing the size and character of the welfare state and in shaping the direction and magnitude of the welfare effects of international capital mobility. The table also summarizes the direct welfare state impacts of trade openness, party government, and socioeconomic structure and dynamics. For the policy effects of the five dimensions of international capital mobility, I designate as a "positive" or "negative" effect those cases where a majority (three or more) of the dimensions have directionally similar and statistically significant impacts; where two or fewer facets of international capital mobility are significant, I designate this situation as one of "no effect."

With regard to the direct effects of internationalization, the preceding analysis offers little evidence for the conventional view that rises in capital mobility are systematically related to retrenchments, rollbacks, and neoliberal restructuring of the contemporary welfare state. Nor do the findings support the idea that globalization creates the most serious challenges for relatively larger welfare states; there is virtually no evidence of a globalization-induced "run to the bottom" or "run to a middle ground" of more market-conforming social policy. As I have documented – and as Chapters 4 and 5 bring into concrete relief – many large welfare states adopted neoliberal policy reforms and otherwise moved social policy in a market-conforming direction; all welfare states have experienced some neoliberal reforms. There is, however, scant evidence in the present

Table 3.10. *A Summary of Findings*

Panel A: Direct Effects of Hypothesized Determinants on Dimensions of Social Welfare Protection

Principal Explanatory Factor	Total Social Welfare Effort	Cash Income Maintenance	The Social Wage	Public Provision of Health Care
International Capital Mobility	no effect	positive effect	no effect	no effect
Social Corporatism	positive effect	positive effect	positive effect[a]	positive effect
Inclusive Electoral Institutions	positive effect	positive effect	no effect	no effect
Dispersion of Authority	negative effect	negative effect	negative effect	negative effect
Trade	positive effect	no effect	no effect	positive effect
Left and ChrDem Government	positive effect[b]	positive effect	no effect[c]	no effect[c]
Business Cycle Dynamics[d]	positive effect	positive effect	no effect	positive effect
Level of Economic Affluence	positive effect	positive effect	positive effect	positive effect
Aging	positive effect	positive effect	not applicable	no effect

[a] Social corporatism has a significant impact on the social wage in the post-1979 era only.
[b] The effects of parties are taken from the model specification that deletes unit effects.
[c] The effect of Left party government is significant in liberal welfare states.
[d] The general pattern of effects for unemployment, growth, and inflation rates.

Panel B: The Mediation of the Social Welfare Effects of International Capital Mobility by Levels of National Institutions: The Nature of the Mediation

Mediation of Capital Mobility By:	Total Social Welfare	The Social Wage
Social Corporatism	positive	positive
Inclusive Electoral Institutions	positive	positive
Dispersion of Authority	negative	negative
Universalism	positive	positive
Conservatism	no mediation[a]	no mediation[a]
Liberalism	negative	negative

[a] This summary ("no mediation") pertains to findings from the analysis involving the degree of occupational stratification. As noted in the text, alternative procedures for estimating the effects of international capital mobility on social policy change in corporatist conservative welfare states suggest that the features of the social insurance model may indeed mediate the effects of internationalization.

Table 3.10 *(continued)*

Panel C: Disaggregating the Analysis: Impacts of International Capital Mobility in Welfare State Clusters

Welfare State Type:	Cash Income Maintenance	The Social Wage	Public Provision of Health Care
Universalist Welfare States	no effect	no effect	no effect
Conservative Welfare States	no effect	no effect	no effect
Liberal Welfare States	negative effect	negative effect	negative effect[a]

[a] In the case of public health spending, the five dimensions of international capital mobility register four negative effects, but only two of these are clearly significant; three of the four negative effects of internationalization on public health share are significant and thus the sum of the analysis for health is denoted as negative effect.

analysis that international capital mobility or, for that matter, trade openness, has much if anything to do in a direct and systematic way with these policy changes. The principal piece of evidence that supports a general role for globalization concerns the internationally generated pressures national policy makers face under conditions of notable fiscal imbalance (e.g., budget deficits approaching and exceeding 10 percent of GDP); it is in this context – where national policy makers experience increasingly large interest rate premiums and other adverse conditions that international capital markets impose (also see Garrett [1998b]) – that higher levels of international capital mobility have a negative impact on the welfare state.

Standing in contrast to the sharp rejection of conventional globalization theory, the findings support the view that social welfare effects of notable post-1970 rises in international capital are largely shaped by national political and welfare state institutions. The economic and political pressures generated by globalization appear to operate, as conventional theory would suggest, in the context of pluralist systems of interest representation, exclusive electoral institutions, and polities of fragmented (especially decentralized) policy-making authority. They also appear to operate in accordance with conventional theory where welfare states are structured according to liberal programmatic principles. Where universalism in welfare state structure is strong, or where the social insurance model is present, and in political institutional contexts of moderate-to-strong social corporatism, inclusive electoral institutions, and centralized policy-making authority, the conventionally hypothesized globalization dynamics are absent. Internationalization has no systematic impact on social welfare policy change, or it is related to small positive increments in social protection in these institutional contexts.

In addition, national political institutions – most notably the character of the systems of collective and electoral interest representation and the organization of policy-making authority in the polity – directly shape social welfare provision. Social corporatism has substantively large and positive significant impacts on each dimension of social welfare provision. The dispersion of policy-making authority exhibits similarly generalized and large effects, although in the case of dispersion the welfare impact is negative. With regard to electoral institutions, inclusiveness has moderately large and significant positive effects on total social welfare effort and income maintenance. Taken together, these direct institutional influences on the contemporary trajectory of the welfare state explain a substantial amount of the temporal and cross-national differences in the developed welfare states. Examining the direct and indirect roles of political institutions together, one can conclude that democracy matters a great deal to the magnitude and direction of change of contemporary social welfare policy.

As to the influence of trade openness, party government, and socioeconomic structures and dynamics – forces that motivate much theory and research about the welfare state – Table 3.10 (Panel A) offers a succinct summary of the relevant findings presented in this chapter. The findings on the welfare state effects of trade openness largely support the theory of embedded liberalism: trade openness is positively associated with total social welfare effort and the public provision of health care. There is, however, no evidence to support a conventional globalization thesis: aggregate trade openness and other dimensions of trade, such as the volume of imports and exports between developed capitalist democracies and "low-wage economies," are not associated with welfare retrenchment.[21] With respect to partisan control of government, the preceding analysis offers some new evidence. In the case of total social welfare effort and cash income maintenance, Left governments and, especially,

---

[21] One must keep in mind, however, that to fully test the arguments about the welfare state impacts of trade openness, it is necessary to examine the policy effects of more precise measures of factor price convergence (Rogowski, 1998), levels and changes in relative unit labor costs, and the changing composition of North-South trade (Wood, 1994). I will also broadly address the question of the social policy impacts of trade openness in the case-study analysis in subsequent chapters and hence provide additional evidence.

Christian Democratic governments have moderately strong impacts on the magnitude of social welfare provision across all democracies. Left government is also consequential for the social wage and the public provision of health care in liberal welfare states. Finally, the preceding analysis has underscored the role of business cycle dynamics, aging, and the level of affluence in shaping variations in social welfare protection. In most areas of social welfare policy and in most contexts, economic growth and unemployment rates exercise substantively important and significant effects on social welfare provision; the level of affluence is positively related to the magnitude of social welfare effort everywhere. The effects of aging are most clearly pronounced in the case of total social welfare effort and in cash income maintenance, where age-related entitlement and political pressures on pensions are most closely felt. I also consider the long-term effects of aging and unemployment (i.e., as impetuses to retrenchment) in Chapters 4 through 6, below.

I now turn to the qualitative stage of the empirical analysis. As noted, Chapters 4 and 5 consist of an analysis of the impact of globalization on the timing and character of social policy change in the large and encompassing welfare states of Northern and Central Europe, contexts in which the globalization thesis predicts the effects of capital mobility will be especially acute and in which I argue democratic political mechanisms for defense of the welfare state will be particularly strong. Chapter 6 utilizes succinct case-study analysis to assess the impact of globalization on policy change in liberal welfare states, systems where predictions from conventional theory and my alternative argument (and Chapter 3 findings) also diverge.

4

Big Welfare States in Global Markets: Internationalization and Welfare State Reform in the Nordic Social Democracies

In this chapter and the next, I offer a largely qualitative analysis of globalization and the timing and character of social welfare policy change in the large social democratic and corporatist conservative welfare states. In the present chapter, I offer a case-oriented analysis of social policy reform in the Nordic political economies – Denmark, Finland, Norway, and Sweden. In comparative perspective, the Nordic welfare states are the most developed among the rich democracies, representing Esping-Andersen's (1990) social democratic welfare state regime and closely approximating what Titmuss (1974) has called the "institutional welfare state." The Nordic welfare states are characterized by comprehensive, universal, and egalitarian income maintenance programs, as well as relatively high levels of universally and publically provided social services (e.g., Esping-Andersen [1990; 1996b]; Huber and Stephens [1996]). Traditionally, the Nordic welfare states have been supported by redistributive general taxation and strong work orientations (i.e., in program structure and in economic policy) and they have produced the highest levels of income and gender equality within the advanced market-oriented democracies (see analysis below).

I proceed with the case-oriented analysis of the Nordic welfare states as follows. First, I provide a comparative overview of the structure of the welfare state and recent social policy change. I then examine absolute and relative levels and trends in capital mobility. Next, I explore the character and timing of social policy change – retrenchments, restructurings, and extensions of social protection – in individual welfare states from the late 1970s through the mid-1990s. I combine information on rises in international capital mobility with material from primary and secondary sources on the content, economic and political contexts, and causes of social policy

122

changes to construct a body of case-study evidence on the social policy impacts of capital mobility. For the analysis, I construct a somewhat more detailed picture of social welfare reform in the Swedish case (than I do for Denmark, Finland, and Norway) because of the centrality of the Swedish welfare state in the Scandinavian and comparative political economy literatures. Overall, this case-oriented analysis should significantly augment the findings from the quantitative analysis.

To highlight expectations, the simplest version of conventional globalization theory predicts that we should observe retrenchment and neoliberal restructuring subsequent to rises in capital mobility across the large majority of welfare states and that these policy changes should be relatively easy to link to internationalization. The more complex version suggests that the larger welfare states should be most susceptible to the economic and political logics of globalization. That is, we should expect to see clear evidence of internationalization-induced retrenchment and some neoliberal restructuring in the Nordic social democratic welfare states. On the other hand, my alternative formulation predicts that welfare states structured along the lines of universalism and nested in a broader configuration of inclusive electoral institutions, social corporatism, and centralized political authority – as the Nordic welfare states are – should be relatively less susceptible to the economic and political logics of international capital mobility. (See the analysis of interrelationships among institutional dimensions in Chapter 2.)

The Nordic Welfare States: Characteristics, Continuities, and Change

In many ways, the Nordic welfare states form a distinct cluster within Europe and the advanced democracies as a whole.[1] These welfare states are generally characterized by comprehensive protections against the range of socioeconomic risks in advanced capitalist societies and virtually universal coverage of populations at risk (e.g., the elderly, disabled, sick). They also provide such comprehensive and universal coverage at relatively generous levels of support, covering both basic security (i.e., relatively high minimum levels of basic benefits) and income protection (i.e., relatively

---

[1] For overviews of the Nordic model, see contributions to Greve (1996) and Hansen et al. (1993), as well as Esping-Andersen (1990), Stephens (1996), and the relevant literature cited below.

high replacement rates for earnings-related benefits). Moreover, state finance and administration of relatively integrated public programs of social protection have been the norm; quasi-private and state-regulated occupational welfare schemes have been relatively small.

Comprehensive, universal, and generous income maintenance programs are coupled with a strong emphasis on work. Active labor market policies provide relatively large budgets for training, placement, relocation, and related employment services and there are relatively strong work incentives embedded within the income maintenance system (e.g., limits on the duration of unemployment benefits). Until recently, with the exception of Denmark, demand management and supply-side policies have prioritized full employment.[2] These economic policies have been supported by corporatist institutions, particularly economy-wide bargaining, in which labor has regularly exchanged wage restraint for full employment commitments and improvements in social protection (e.g., Lehmbruch [1984]; Katzenstein [1985]). Wage restraint, along with selective currency devaluations, have been particularly important to Nordic economic strategies for maintaining growth and employment in core export-oriented industries during the 1970s and 1980s (e.g., Mjøset [1987, 1996]; Moses [2000]; Huber and Stephens [1998]).[3]

In addition, Nordic welfare states are distinct with regard to social services. Unlike the relatively large Christian Democratic welfare states, governments in the Nordic political economies (most notably at subnational levels of government) provide a broad array of social services to the elderly, disabled, families, children, and disadvantaged groups. Indeed, Esping-

---

[2] With the exception of (pre-1980s) Finland, Scandinavian governments have regularly employed (moderate) Keynesian demand management interventions during recessions. Nordic governments have also utilized tax-based incentives (e.g., credits, allowances, investment reserves) for productive investment (e.g., Swank [1992, 1998]) and extensive control of banking and credit, particularly in Norway and Finland (e.g., Stephens [1996]). However, fiscal balance has been emphasized within the Nordic model. For instance, a central element of the Rehn-Meidner model of Sweden was the use of restrictive fiscal policy to hold down profits (and hence wages) in successful enterprises in order to facilitate solidaristic wage bargaining and other goals (e.g., Pontusson [1992a]).

[3] For a review of similarities and differences in contemporary Scandinavian macroeconomic policies and approaches to the problem of full employment, see Mjøset (1987, 1996); for a thorough analysis of the widely debated Rehn-Meidner model of the Swedish political economy, see Pontusson (1992a); and for discussions of the interaction of social welfare and employment policies in the Nordic countries, and the importance of full employment to Nordic welfare states, see Esping-Andersen (1990, 1996b), Huber and Stephens (1998), and Stephens (1996).

Andersen (1996b) has recently argued that the most distinctive feature of the contemporary Scandinavian welfare state is the expansion of government spending on social services, including employment services, and the associated high level of employment, particularly of women, in health, education, and welfare sectors. Relatedly, the Nordic social democratic welfare states generally conform to an "individual model" of social welfare provision (as opposed to the "breadwinner model"), where social policy tends to emphasize relatively equal treatment of men and women as contributors and beneficiaries of social benefits (e.g., Bussemaker and van Kersbergen [1996]; Sainsbury [1996]). They also devote a relatively large share of national resources to public funding of health care, provided disproportionately through government and nonprofit providers (OECD 1993a).

Table 4.1 provides (in comparative perspective) a synopsis of social program structure and spending in the Nordic welfare states. Using the nonrecessionary 1985–9 period as a base, total social expenditure averaged 26 percent of GDP in Nordic countries versus 22.3 percent of GDP in the advanced democracies as a whole. Cash transfers in the Nordic welfare states averaged 15.4 percent of GDP in the late 1980s and 14.4 percent of GDP for the entire sample of developed democracies. However, in comparing total social spending and cash transfers in the Nordic countries to corporatist conservative welfare states, it should be clear that total and cash outlays for social provision in Scandinavia are, on average, not that distinct from the relatively generous "Bismarckian welfare states." A more distinct picture of the Nordic model emerges when one focuses on income replacement rates and social service, public health, and active labor market program expenditures. Focusing on the "social wage," or the percentage of income replaced by social supports for the average unemployed production worker, Nordic countries generally provide much higher income replacement than other rich democracies (although a notable exception is the Netherlands). Data on replacement rates (and coverage rates) for pensions, sickness, disability, work injury, and other types of market withdrawal, often averaging 90 percent of income, reveal similar patterns (e.g., Hagen [1992], M. Gordon [1988], and Ploug and Kvist [1996]). Relatively moderate levels of cash benefits within this context of comprehensive, universal, and generous income maintenance entitlements is largely a function of the aforementioned emphasis on full employment.

Subsequent portions of Table 4.1 (Parts B and C) underscore the point that public provision of general social services, health care, and

Table 4.1. *The Nordic Social Democratic Welfare State in Comparative Perspective, 1980–1995*

Part A

	Total Social Protection[a]			Social Wage[b]			Cash Benefits[c]		
	1980–4	1985–9	1990–3	1980–4	1985–9	1990–5	1980–4	1985–9	1990–3
Nordic-Social Dem									
Denmark	27.0	25.8	28.0	.70	.61	.59	16.2	15.4	17.3
Finland	19.4	22.8	30.1	.27	.53	.59	11.9	14.6	19.8
Norway	21.3	25.2	30.5	.43	.62	.62	12.6	14.6	17.8
Sweden	29.8	30.0	33.1	.76	.84	.81	16.0	17.2	19.8
Average	24.4	26.1	30.4	.54	.65	.65	14.2	15.4	18.7
Corp Conservative	24.1	24.5	25.2	.34	.35	.35	17.4	17.5	17.6
Anglo-Liberal	16.3	15.8	17.8	.30	.30	.30	9.8	9.6	11.7
Average-All Nations	21.8	22.3	24.5	.40	.44	.44	14.1	14.4	16.1

Part B

	Social Services[d]			Public Health[e]			Labor Market Policies[f]		
	1980–4	1985–9	1990–3	1980–4	1985–9	1990–5	1980–4	1985–9	1990–3
Nordic-Social Dem									
Denmark	4.7	4.5	4.5	5.7	5.3	5.4	—	1.2	1.6
Finland	1.8	2.2	2.8	5.3	5.8	7.0	—	1.1	1.5
Norway	1.8	3.4	4.9	6.5	6.9	7.5	—	.6	1.1
Sweden	4.2	4.2	5.3	8.7	7.8	7.0	—	1.8	2.6
Average	3.2	3.6	4.4	6.6	6.4	6.7	—	1.2	1.7
Corp Conservative	.6	.6	.6	6.1	6.2	6.7	—	1.0	1.0
Anglo-Liberal	.4	.4	.6	5.2	5.4	6.1	—	.5	.5
Average-All Nations	1.3	1.4	1.6	6.0	6.0	6.5	—	.8	1.0

[a] Total social welfare expenditures (OECD definition) as a percentage of gross domestic product. (See Appendix for all data sources.)
[b] "Social Wage:" proportion of gross income for the unemployed average production worker replaced by unemployment insurance and compensation, social assistance, and various entitled welfare schemes.
[c] Cash Benefits: total cash transfers for the elderly, disabled, survivors, families, the unemployed, and poor as a percent of gross domestic product.
[d] Social Services: expenditure for government social services for the elderly, disabled, children, and families as a percentage of gross domestic product.
[e] Government health care expenditures as a percentage of gross domestic product.
[f] Active labor market program (e.g., training, placement) expenditures as a percentage of gross domestic product.

126

Part C

	Public Health Share[g]			Total Taxation[b]			Social Insurance Share[i]		
	1980–4	1985–9	1990–3	1980–4	1985–9	1990–5	1980–4	1985–9	1990–3
Nordic-Social Dem									
Denmark	85.0	84.2	84.4	45.9	50.7	49.8	2.9	3.2	3.0
Finland	79.3	79.4	80.1	38.0	42.0	46.2	18.7	19.0	24.0
Norway	97.9	96.4	94.2	47.2	47.8	45.9	21.3	23.8	25.0
Sweden	91.8	89.7	86.5	49.9	54.0	52.4	27.8	26.1	28.8
Average	88.5	87.4	85.8	45.3	48.6	48.6	17.7	18.0	20.4
Corp Conservative	78.7	78.0	78.1	40.3	41.4	42.9	35.4	36.1	36.5
Anglo-Liberal	67.3	67.2	66.7	32.3	33.0	32.6	13.9	15.2	16.1
Average-All Nations	78.2	77.6	77.0	39.1	40.6	41.0	25.1	25.7	26.0

Part D

	Poverty Reduction[j]			Inequality-Income/Gender[k]			
	Pre-TR	Post-TR	% Ch	Pre-TR	Post-TR	% Ch	Gender
Nordic-Social Dem							
Denmark	—	—	—	—	—	—	.594
Finland	—	—	—	—	—	—	.652
Norway	30.6	5.3	83	.385	.285	26	.600
Sweden	36.5	5.6	85	.417	.241	42	.652
Average	33.6	5.4	84	.401	.263	34	.624
Corporatist Conservative	33.7	7.4	78	.439	.297	29	.391
Anglo-Liberal	27.5	12.0	56	.405	.331	18	.554
Average-All Nations	30.6	9.2	68	.412	.300	25	.513

[g] Government health outlays as a percentage of total public and private health outlays.

[b] Total taxation as a percentage of gross domestic product.

[i] Social insurance contributions as a percentage of total taxation.

[j] Percentage of families below the poverty line (defined as 50% of adjusted median income) before and after the effects of income transfers.

[k] GINI index of pre- and post-transfer income inequality for the early 1980s; gender inequality is an index of (1) ratio of female to male labor force participation; (2) ratio of male to female unemployment rates; (3) ratio of female to male industrial wages; and (4) female percentage of political economic elites.

employment services is more developed in the Nordic model than in other welfare states. Again, focusing on the benchmark years of 1985–9, the table suggests this is most pronounced in the case of social services; the Nordic average of 3.6 percent of GDP is three times the overall average for the advanced democracies. The Nordic average for public health expenditure is also higher than other nations although, until recently, this has been a function of the large public health sectors in Norway and (especially) Sweden. As the first section of Part C, Table 4.1, illustrates, the Nordic model entails the predominance of public funding of health care in the late 1980s: 87 percent of health care spending was made by the public sector. An additional distinctive feature of the Nordic model involves labor market programs: with the exception of Norway, active labor market programs in Scandinavia have channeled more national resources to employment services (1.2 percent of GDP in the 1985–9 period) than the average advanced democracy (.8 percent of GDP). The same conclusion holds if one examines Active Labor Market Policy (ALMP) outlays per unemployed worker: the average outlay per unemployed worker (in 1985 U.S. dollars) in the Nordic countries was $15,632 while the same figure was $3,184 and $1,712 in the corporatist conservative and Anglo welfare states, respectively.

The social democratic welfare states are also distinct in their strategies for funding social protection. First, Nordic welfare states employ relatively high levels of taxation on consumption, labor income, and capital income (see Chapter 7 for details on taxation). As Table 4.1 (Part C) suggests, total tax shares of national income are higher in all Nordic countries than the average corporatist conservative or Anglo political economy in the late 1980s; Sweden stands out among the Scandinavian nations as having the highest total tax burdens. The most distinct feature of financing arrangements of the Nordic welfare states is the reliance on general taxation (as opposed to social insurance contributions) to fund social provision: only 18 percent of all taxes in the late 1980s were collected in the form of employer and employee social insurance contributions (although see below on recent policy change).

Utilizing recent data (e.g., Mitchell [1991]; OECD [1995b]), Part D, Table 4.1, reports the comparative impact of social transfers on poverty rates and income inequality (for Norway and Sweden only), as well as a general measure of gender inequality that indexes female (versus male) labor force participation, unemployment, wages, and high-strata employment. The latter dimension of socioeconomic inequality is influenced by the welfare state in that social policy shapes the structure of labor markets through impacts on relative female labor force participation and unemployment rates and affects wage dispersion through the reservation wage, the facilitation of centralized wage bargaining, and other mechanisms (e.g., Esping-Andersen [1990]). As the table makes clear, social welfare transfers of the Nordic welfare states have a substantial impact: the percentage reduction of family poverty rates and income inequality (measured by the familiar GINI index) is 84 and 34 percent, respectively. While the occupationally based conservative welfare states also perform well in the alleviation of poverty and the narrowing of income distributions (78 and 29 percent reductions, respectively), the Nordic nations surpass the Bismarckian welfare states and, most notably, the Anglo-liberal welfare states. In addition, the index of gender equality for the Nordic nations suggests that the programmatic structure of the social democratic welfare state promotes socioeconomic gains for women. For instance, high levels of public social service provision facilitate high levels of female labor force participation through day care and family services and through employment; an "individualistic" (as opposed to breadwinner) orientation in social insurance programs alleviates female dependency (also see Sainsbury [1996; contributions to Sainsbury 1994]).

Patterns of Welfare State Change in the Nordic Cases

As I detail below, some neoliberal reforms of social policy can be observed in varying degrees in the Nordic welfare states. Referring to trends across the 1980–4, 1985–9, and 1990–3/5 periods (Table 4.1), one can observe some specific evidence of efforts to control welfare state expansion, if not retrenchment. The "social wage" has fallen in Denmark across all periods and, from the late 1980s to 1990s, it fell modestly in Sweden, as well. On average, the social wage has remained constant between the mid-1980s and mid-1990s in the Nordic nations as a whole. Public health expenditure has grown little between the early 1980s and mid-1990s (and declined across the 1980s), despite continuing health care cost pressures; in Denmark and, particularly, in Sweden, public health spending has declined in relation to GDP. As country studies below will illustrate, there has been a general movement toward restricted eligibility and modestly lower benefits in social insurance and a greater emphasis on cost control and efficiency in social services. Keeping in mind the expenditure effects of the particularly severe economic downturn in the early 1990s in Finland and Sweden, total social welfare expenditure rose little between the early 1980s and 1990s in Denmark and only modestly in Sweden. The expenditure effects of 1970s and 1980s expansive social policy reforms and a notably severe early 1990s economic crisis account for substantial growth in Finnish social outlays. With regard to welfare state funding, overall tax levels and effective tax rates have stabilized and the progressivity of income taxation has been reduced (see Chapter 7). In addition, there appears to be a modest increase in reliance on social security contributions. While few observers argue that the Nordic model has been dismantled, most agree there have been non-trivial cuts in some areas of social protection and in social services, as well as greater emphases on linking benefits to work. I now turn to the question of whether or not these social welfare policy changes can be linked directly to the notable post-1970 increase in international capital mobility.

International Capital Mobility in the Nordic Cases

As discussed in Chapter 2, international movements of capital, and the potential for such movements, have increased dramatically in the last 15 to 20 years. Key features of this growth in the Nordic political economies (in comparison to the rich democracies as a whole) are illustrated in Figures 4.1 and 4.2. Figure 4.1 displays the 18-nation (see Chapter 2) and Nordic annual averages for the absence of restrictions on payments and receipts of capital. Data on the degree of liberalization suggests that the Nordic political economies generally lagged the developed capitalist democracies as a whole in formal-legal potential for international capital mobility for much of the focal period.[4] While liberalization in both the Nordic countries and the rich democracies in aggregate increased during the 1970s and early 1980s, Scandinavian capital markets remained more closed until an acceleration of deregulation in the mid- to late 1980s. Indeed, central elements of Nordic economic policy, particularly control of credit, presumed some restriction of international capital movements (e.g., Mjøset [1987, 1996]; Huber and Stephens [1998]; Schwartz [1994b]); moreover, because of ideological and constituent interests, social democratic governments have generally been less willing to liberalize (Quinn and Inclan, 1997).

---

[4] It is important to note, following Mjøset (1996), that Swedish multinational enterprises had regularly received exemptions from capital controls for a variety of financial transactions. Also, as the data in Figure 4.2 illustrate, actual capital flows in the Nordic countries actually differ little from the advanced democracies on average for much of the focal period.

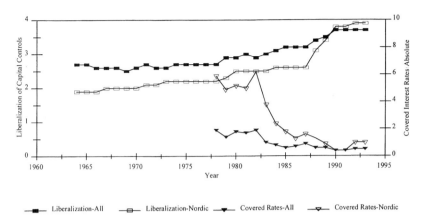

Figure 4.1   Financial Market Integration and Liberalization: All versus Nordic Nations

The figure also displays comparable trends in the Nordic countries and in the advanced democracies as a whole for a somewhat broader measure of international financial integration – the average of (the absolute value of) covered interest rate differentials (see Chapter 2). Figure 4.1 suggests that the capital markets of the Nordic nations were substantially less integrated with world markets than the whole of the developed democracies until the early and mid-1980s.[5] Given the role of banking and credit policies in economic policy, this is not surprising; interest rates in Nordic countries often fell above or below world rates (net of the country premium) as such rates were used to direct investment domestically. In the early to mid-1980s, however, a neoliberal shift in economic policies occurred (see case analysis for details) and capital markets in the Nordic countries became much more integrated with international markets. By the late 1980s, capital liberalization and overall integration with world financial markets in the Nordic nations closely resembled the rest of the advanced democratic world.

Figure 4.2 displays the trends in total cross-border capital flows and foreign direct investment (FDI). Unlike liberalization and covered

---

[5] An identical picture emerges when using available 1974–92 data for all of Scandinavia (except Finland) and a subset of the complete group of nations (with 1974 being the first year such data are available for more than a handful of nations).

131

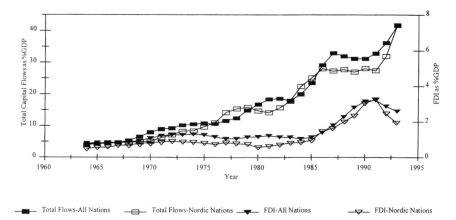

Figure 4.2 Total Capital Flows and FDI: All Democracies and the Nordic Nations

interest rate differentials, the level and pattern of change in actual capital flows in the Nordic nations generally follows the overall average for the rich democracies in aggregate. During the Bretton Woods–era of trade liberalization and relatively closed capital markets (i.e., 1950s and 1960s), inward and outward flows of direct and portfolio investment and bank lending averaged roughly five percent of GDP in both the Nordic nations and the advanced democracies generally. By the mid-1980s, however, the volume of capital flows equaled approximately 20 percent of GDP in both sets of nations; by the mid-1990s, the monetary value of financial flows exceeded 45 percent of GDP in both the Nordic countries and the typical rich democracy. With regard to FDI, flows in the Nordic countries were modestly lower than flows in the typical developed democracy through the early 1980s; however, average FDI movements in both sets of political economies generally moved together. The Nordic nations, as in the developed democracies as a whole, experienced accelerating FDI from the mid-1980s to early 1990s (and a decline with the early 1990s economic downturn).

With regard to similarities and differences across the Nordic political economies, increases in capital mobility in all four focal countries generally occurred at the same time and were of similar magnitudes. There is, however, some variability across countries. Sweden's more internationally oriented firms made substantial direct investments in the EC during the 1980s, particularly after passage of the Single Europe Act (e.g., Pontusson [1992a]). Denmark's capital markets have generally been more integrated with the rest of Europe while capital in Norway and Finland has traditionally been more inwardly oriented and structurally intertwined with relatively large state sectors (e.g., Huber and Stephens [1998]). What is the social welfare impact of internationalization in the four Nordic cases?

Globalization and Social Policy Change in Sweden

From the mid-1970s through the early 1980s, Sweden, like most rich democracies, faced substantial pressures to control social expenditure.[6] At this time, the immediate stress in Sweden (and elsewhere) stemmed from a burgeoning public sector deficit (averaging roughly 5 percent of GDP between 1980 and 1982) and inflation (which exceeded 10 percent in 1980 and 1981); while unemployment remained low (averaging 1.9 percent annually between 1974–9), productivity growth had lagged notably in the 1970s in the Nordic countries (averaging .5 percent per year from 1974 to 1979).[7] After the 1976 election loss of the Social Democratic Party (SAP), some significant reductions in the scope and generosity of the Swedish welfare state might have been anticipated; however, no significant reductions or rollbacks of social protection were forthcoming between 1976 and 1979. In fact, most observers agree that the Swedish "bourgeois" government (i.e., Center-Right government in the Swedish context) faced a number of political constraints on policy change, including the continued high levels of popular support for the welfare state, the prospect of a quick SAP election triumph if neoliberal policies were rapidly adopted, and the broader context of trade union strength and social corporatist support for the welfare state (e.g., Gould [1996]; Rothstein [1998]; Stephens [1996]).

---

[6] For the four Nordic case studies, I rely heavily on the following sources for information: *Social Security in Europe*, published by the Danish National Institute for Social Research (particularly, Ploug and Kvist [1994, 1996]), Ploug (1998), Marklund (1988), and Stephens (1996); for Sweden, the work of Arthur Gould (1993, 1996) and Ståhlberg (1997); for Denmark, research by Jørgen Goul Andersen (1997), Kvist (1997), and Villadsen (1996); for Finland, the work of Jäntti, Kangas, and Ritakallio (1996) and Andersson, Kosonen, and Vartiainen (1993); and, for Norway, the work of van Wormer (1994) and Ervik and Kuhnle (1996) was particularly helpful.

[7] Indicators and sources for all data discussed in this and subsequent sections are given in Appendix A.

In the context of the early 1980s economic downturn, however, the bourgeois government undertook several measures to control spending in the 1980–2 period and proposed more substantial retrenchment for 1983. Specifically, the government reduced the part-time pension benefit from 65 to 50 percent of income, increased user fees for some forms of medical care and housing, instituted new controls on national transfers to local authorities for social services, and initiated some (cost-saving) changes to the formula for indexation of many social benefits. Most significantly, the Center-Right government proposed changes in sick pay by initiating two waiting days and reducing benefits from 90 to 80 percent of income. These changes, due to take effect in 1983, were never implemented by the new SAP government elected in 1982.

During the period 1982–91, the governing Social Democrats simultaneously engaged in modest expansions of some social programs and rights and initiated policy changes to control welfare state costs. These changes occurred against three overlapping backdrops. First, impetus for policy changes came from a variety of domestic socioeconomic factors and programmatic cost pressures, namely, concerns over expansion of an already large elderly population, rising demands on sickness and early retirement programs, accelerating cost pressures on already expensive health care, and long-term performance and attendant fiscal problems.[8] Second, social policy reforms were also made against the backdrop of a shift in economic policy orientation, changes in economic policy instruments, and alterations in domestic and international economic structure and performance.[9] Upon entering office, SAP consciously advocated a "third road" in economic policy that would be charted on a middle ground between French Socialist reflationary policy and Thatcherite neoliberalism. Initially, the chief element in this program was a 16-percent devaluation of the Swedish kroner, a continuation of the policy of selective devaluations practiced by the 1976–82 bourgeois governments and a policy that was supported by union wage restraint. In addition, SAP entered government in the context

[8] For instance, Ståhlberg (1997) notes that paid sick days per worker increased from 20 to 26 between 1980 and 1988 and that the early retirement pension program added 50,000 pensioners per year in the 1980s.

[9] I rely heavily in this section on work by Pontusson (1992a, 1992b), Moene and Wallerstein (1993), Mjøset (1987, 1996), Moses (1994, 2000), Ryner (1997), and Notermans (1993). Unless otherwise noted, I draw facts and interpretations from these sources. On interpreting the causes of the 1980s shift in Scandinavian economic policy, see Moses (2000), Notermans (1993), and Forsyth and Notermans (1997).

of a (partial) ascent of neoliberal economic orthodoxy in Sweden. In the late 1970s and early 1980s, the Swedish Employers Association (hereafter SAF) had funded numerous think-tank studies and reports that called for a neoliberal reorientation of Swedish economic policy and restructuring of the public sector and the welfare state. Moreover, neoliberal economists had gained some leverage in the new SAP government, as well, especially in the form of a circle of economists around the Finance Minister Kjell-Olof Feldt. Although there was substantial opposition to a new neoliberal policy regime by Swedish Confederation of Trade Unions (LO) economists, officials in the social ministries, and many policy makers within SAP, Swedish economic policy had shifted moderately in a neoliberal direction by the mid-1980s.

Generally, SAP economic policy in the 1983–9 period consisted of self-described "norms-based economic policy," where the relative priorities of price stability, external balance, and economic growth increased in importance. By 1985, the government actually abandoned devaluation for a fixed–exchange rate regime, increased central bank autonomy, and, most important for the issues at hand, a substantially increased openness of the economy to international financial flows. This shift occurred as Swedish transnational enterprises accelerated outward direct investment (especially in the European Community economies).[10] Indeed, as Finance Minister Feldt (as cited in Ryner [1997]) noted in 1991, international capital mobility and the transactions of Swedish multinationals had increased to the point where capital controls were nearly impossible to maintain. In addition, as Ryner's (1997) analysis makes clear, the Central Bank and Finance Ministry's policy of deregulation of credit and international financial transactions was aimed at increasing the pressure (through interest rates) on private domestic actors and on the social ministries and public budget makers. Excessive wage and price increases and expansionary budgets would be met with higher interest rates necessary to defend the now-fixed kroner in a context of high capital mobility (an adverse development for these domestic actors). As Moses (2000) argues in his analysis of Swedish and Norwegian economic policy change in the 1980s, one of the central roles of international capital mobility has been to tighten the budget

---

[10] While commentators often note that the rise in outward FDI in 1980s Sweden had adverse impacts on domestic job creation and investment, others minimize these negative economic effects (e.g., Glyn [1995]; Lindbeck et al. [1994]; Weiss [1998]). For instance, Weiss, citing Glyn's analysis, notes that the acceleration of outward FDI in Sweden corresponded to a rebound in domestic investment and rising capital stock.

constraint on social welfare expenditure. In the wake of the reorientation of economic policy, economic growth, export earnings, and profits in the exposed sector of the economy grew. Employment was relatively strong and the public sector deficit moved to balance by 1987. Inflation, which had averaged 10.8 percent in the 1980–3 period fell to 4.2 percent for 1986 and 1987.

With regard to the third backdrop for social policy change, social corporatist wage-setting institutions decentralized and employers and unions experienced some fragmentation. In 1983, centralized economy-wide bargaining between SAF and LO broke down. Specifically, motivated by the desire for more flexibility in wage negotiations and influenced by changing economic and political contexts, the Engineering Employers' Association (VF) persuaded the Metalworkers Union (Metall) to engage in independent bargaining, effectively decentralizing wage setting. In subsequent years, unions and employers periodically returned to economy-wide negotiations (with supplemental industry-wide bargaining), although the dominant trend has been decentralization. Symbolizing this change, SAF disbanded its central bargaining unit in 1990 and withdrew representatives for some corporatist boards of state agencies in 1991. In addition, conflicts between private sector blue-collar unions and white-collar unions, especially those in the public sector, have undercut union cohesion to an extent and, in turn, influenced the politics of social welfare policy reform. As Swenson (1991) argues, the expansion of the welfare state has facilitated the expansion of large public sector unions whose interests diverge from private sector blue-collar unions in the export sector (also see Schwartz 1994b). Notable expansion of wages in the public sector often leads to higher inflation and taxes for private sector unions and, in turn, threats to jobs and employment in the price sensitive export-oriented industries. As a result, fissures developed in the 1980s and private export-sector unions aligned with more neoliberal elements in the Finance Ministry and employers in efforts to implement cost controls, efficiency measures, and related public sector reforms.

Against this backdrop of welfare state cost concerns, economic policy change, and some fragmentation of corporatist actors and institutions, the Social Democrats undertook a number of modest initiatives in social welfare policy reform. First, commissions were convened to study ways to curb the growth of several benefit programs, including increasingly expensive sick pay benefits and the demographically driven earnings-related pension (ATP). Moreover, the 1982–91 SAP governments enacted several policy changes that in effect led to cuts in the extensive public health care system. The 1983 Health Care Act decentralized most authority for health care to the county level with subsequent cuts in national subsidies for health care and nationally mandated freezes on the local income tax, effectively constraining health care spending growth. Moreover, the Social Democrats oversaw the initial implementation of market mechanisms for pricing health care services and internal competition within the health care sector (ultimately culminating in the creation of new modes of organization – Diagnosis Related Groups – and new modes of reimbursement that reduced health care spending).[11]

On the other hand, the Social Democrats initiated some moderate extensions of social benefits and rights. SAP increased the child allowance, social services for family and children (and thus public-sector employment), and extended unemployment benefits during the 1982–9 period. As Table 4.1 illustrates, the social wage in Sweden (as estimated by the OECD) increased from 76 to 84 percent of the average unemployed production worker's income between 1980–4 and 1985–9. Most notably, SAP proposed several further expansions of social benefits in its 1988 manifesto. These proposals included, among others, guarantees of child care to all children over 18 months and an extension of parental leave benefits by several weeks. In fact, the 1988 manifesto devoted roughly 25 percent of its policy statements to proposals for defending or bolstering social protection and rights; there were no explicit discussions of retrenchment.[12]

Economic conditions deteriorated in the 1989–91 period, however: growth slowed to .5 percent in 1990 and fell to −1.7 percent in 1991; inflation was 6.4 percent in 1989 and 10.5 percent in 1990. In the wake of declining economic fortunes, the SAP government continued implementation of public sector and health care efficiency reforms and policy

---

[11] During the 1989–91 period, the public health care system experienced some unit closures and layoffs; in addition, new user charges for doctors, hospital services, and prescription drugs were implemented. As Table 4.1 revealed, health care spending in Sweden actually declined from an average of close to 9 percent of GDP in the early 1980s to approximately 7 percent in the 1990s. It is important to note, however, that approximately half of this decrease (1 percent of GDP) was due mainly to accounting changes, primarily as a result of transfer of nursing services to community social service budgets (Diderichsen, 1995).

[12] As I illustrate in Figure 4.3 below, Social Democratic parties throughout the Nordic countries actually increased their ideological support for maintenance and limited expansions of social benefits and rights during the 1980s and early 1990s, and only rarely advocated welfare retrenchment. The gap between Social Democratic and Right parties on the question of the welfare state actually widened in the 1980s.

planning for cost-control measures in social insurance; SAP also initiated a 3 percent reduction in the "base amount" used to calculate social benefits, small cost-saving adjustments to sick pay, and tightened eligibility for early retirement pensions. As Stephens (1996) and others have noted, however, most changes in the Swedish welfare state were relatively minor to this point. Indeed, it is arguably the case that popular approval of the universalist welfare state, SAP electoral strength, the political power of the trade union movement, and – despite the decentralization of collective bargaining – the continuation of social corporatist concertation in social policy making combined to create a bulwark against significant neoliberal restructuring (e.g., Hoefer [1996]; Rothstein [1998]; Svallfors [1995]).

However, with a dramatic fall in the economic growth rate (–2.1 percent in 1992) and commensurate rises in unemployment and deficits, the 1991–4 bourgeois government enacted two main "crisis packages" (largely with the consent of SAP). In fact, a confluence of conditions existed in the early 1990s to pressure nontrivial social policy change: nominal unemployment rates rose to 5.3 percent in 1992, and 8.2 percent in 1993, and the public sector deficit increased to –7.8 percent of GDP in 1992, and to –13.4 percent in 1993. In the context of high international capital mobility and commitments to fixed exchange rates, the Central Bank raised interest rates to as high as 500 percent before eventually allowing the kroner to float in November of 1992. Under this set of pressures, the bourgeois government – in collaboration with SAP – initiated the following changes: the base amount of social benefits was trimmed 3 percent (beyond the change initiated by SAP); sickness benefits were reduced to 65 percent for the second and third days, 80 percent for the remainder of the first year of sickness, and 70 percent of pay after that. One waiting day for sickness benefits was imposed and, to encourage better policing of the system, employers became responsible for the first two weeks of benefits. In addition, the system of work-injury benefits was brought in line with sick pay, and unemployment and social assistance benefits were reduced; a waiting period of five days (and new limits on duration) was introduced for unemployment benefits and new employee contributions for unemployment insurance were initiated. In addition, perhaps the most important change was the initiation of major alterations in the earnings-related pension: in the future, the ATP would be based on lifetime contributions, and not 30 years of contributions for full pension with the "best 15 years" determining pension amounts; new social insurance contributions were planned where the employee would ultimately contribute 9.25 percent of pay to fund ATP. (A new 40-year residence rule, rather than citizenship, was enacted to determine eligibility for the basic, flat-rate pension.)[13] Finally, many new initiatives were taken in 1992 and 1993 to encourage the implementation of market mechanisms in social service delivery and to foster the establishment of private providers (e.g., doctors, child care businesses); additional user fees for a variety of social services were also implemented.

However, despite the conducive context to substantial neoliberal restructuring of the welfare state, several forces combined to offset more significant change. With respect to the bourgeois government, both the centrist Liberal and Centre Parties balked at more substantial neoliberal restructuring of the public sector and social programs; the budgetary policy declarations of the government actually affirmed the fundamental principles of the universal welfare state (e.g., Gynnerstedt [1997]). In addition, as Rothstein (1996) points out, one of the most visible and effective weapons of the Center-Right government in the wake of the economic crisis proved to be Active Labor Market Policy (ALMP), a central component of the social democratic welfare state. In fact, the government substantially increased expenditures for ALMP programs during its tenure. Moreover, the Social Democrats were reelected in 1994. While they preserved many of the social insurance reforms, some neoliberal initiatives encouraging private providers were eliminated; social rights to services for the handicapped, elderly, and children were extended; and the 1994 budget, shaped largely by a deficit in excess of 10 percent of GDP, emphasized modest tax increases over further (major) spending cuts. Together, these changes, along with those of the late 1970s to mid-1990s discussed above, constitute the principal reforms of the Swedish welfare state. Can one conclude that the economic and political forces attendant on internationalization are significant forces in neoliberal reforms? Has the Swedish welfare state substantially moved toward the residual welfare state model?

With respect to the first query, one can frame the question so as to focus on (relatively direct) linkages between international capital mobility and welfare state restructuring. (In Chapter 7, I consider the arguments that the welfare state impacts of internationalization primarily work indirectly through the effects of global capital on macroeconomic policy autonomy and social corporatism.) First, were there relatively direct and immediate

---

[13] In addition to these changes in welfare programs, 1990 marked "the tax reform of the century," in which marginal rates on individuals and capital were reduced substantially (along with the removal of a variety of exemptions, allowances, and deductions in the tax code). See Chapter 7 for an analysis of these changes.

welfare state effects of rises in international capital mobility suggesting competition for investment? Based on the analysis provided above, the answer to this question is generally "no". While there were social policy reforms from the late 1970s to early (pre-crisis) 1990s as international capital mobility accelerated, most policy changes were minor and can be directly linked to domestic socioeconomic or political factors. As in the case of the quantitative analysis, one is hard pressed to find direct, temporally ordered linkages between rises in capital mobility and welfare state retrenchments designed to retain or attract mobile capital. In fact, focusing on the pre-crisis period, when domestic economic and political conditions and the international context were ripe for neoliberal reform (i.e., during the early 1980s), Swedish political institutions and political forces arguably made such reform largely impossible.

Second, is there a linkage between the ascent of domestic and international neoliberal orthodoxy and significant neoliberal welfare state restructuring (the political logic of globalization)? Here again the answer is generally "no". In the context of the partial ascent of neoliberal orthodoxy in Sweden from the late 1970s, it is clearly the case that arguments about the imperatives of international competitiveness and business location – reinforcing the overarching neoliberal program of efficiency-oriented reform – were relevant to the politics of welfare state reform in Sweden. They did not, however, dominate welfare reform debate and policies. Bolstered by relatively strong economic performance, SAP's program (e.g., 1988 party manifesto) continued to emphasize maintenance and refinements to the universal welfare state; even 1980s cost controls were largely oriented to preserving and enhancing the effectiveness of programs as opposed to significant neoliberal retrenchment. Second, even the 1991–4 bourgeois government that presided over the "crisis packages" of welfare reforms generally affirmed the basic principles of the universal welfare state and supported specific components, such as ALMP, over a more dramatic neoliberal program. In sum, the political logic of globalization has arguably had limited impact on the Swedish welfare state (also see the summary comparative analysis below and the analysis of Chapter 7).

Third, are the dynamics of Swedish social policy change consistent with the general finding from the quantitative analysis that international capital mobility exerts general downward pressure on the welfare state primarily under conditions of significant fiscal crisis? Indeed, it is this confluence of conditions in the early 1990s – high international capital mobility and fiscal deficit approaching, and even exceeding, 10 percent of GDP – that produced sufficient pressures for moderate policy reforms in the Swedish system (and these factors explain to an extent the difference between policy changes in the early 1980s and early 1990s). As the theory and research above has suggested, international capital markets charge a premium in the form of higher interest rates on governments who run budget deficits (and threaten price stability and growth prospects with fiscal imbalance). While some have suggested the threshold for budget deficits under high capital mobility is in the range of 3 percent of GDP (Mosley, 1998), my estimates from the quantitative analysis of social welfare provision indicate that the threshold has been probably higher: roughly 10 percent of GDP, on average, across the developed democracies. Indeed, these general estimates fit the Swedish experience well. Together, the quantitative and case evidence combines to highlight this particular conduit of influence of capital mobility on the welfare state.

With respect to the other general question posed above – whether or not the sum of mid-1970s to mid-1990s reforms of the Swedish welfare state constitute a clear and substantial move to a more residual welfare state – again the answer is "no". As the substantive material presented above and similar surveys suggest (e.g., Clasen and Gould [1995]; Gould [1996]; Ståhlberg [1997]; Sainsbury [1996]; Stephens [1996]), the Nordic model of comprehensive, universal, and generous social provision has generally been maintained. Indeed, there are now less generous benefits in some areas, a modest increase in income-testing, tighter eligibility requirements, and, to an extent, some movement toward larger roles for internal markets, as well social insurance-based modes of funding. Despite these changes, however, the Swedish welfare state retains the basic elements of the social democratic model.

In fact, a recent survey by Lindbom (1999) highlights in fine detail the continuity of the universal welfare state in the context of moderate social policy reforms. Specifically, Lindbom clearly documents the moderate cuts, neoliberal reforms, and market-oriented initiatives noted throughout the analysis presented above. His analysis also affirms that the aforementioned 1990s shifts to tighter restrictions on eligibility for certain benefits (primarily for unemployment, sickness, and social assistance) have made it more difficult for some not in the system to gain coverage (also see Palme and Wennemo [1997] on pensions). The author's analysis, however, clearly points to substantial continuity in basic features of the welfare state. Overall replacement rates for major social insurance programs have not declined significantly between 1980 and 1998, and remain high by OECD standards. For instance, Lindbom estimates (with preliminary data) that the average replacement rate for core income maintenance programs was 79 percent of net income in 1980 and 74 percent in 1998.[14] In assessing the reforms of Swedish social and health care services, Lindbom argues that a substantial portion of the impact of reforms fell on secondary personnel. For instance, between 1990 and 1996 (using index numbers), personnel with primary elder care responsibility declined from 100 to 85, yet in-patient operations increased from 100 to 107. Overall, while there has been some increase in liberal program characteristics in the Swedish welfare state, Lindbom's work reveals that Sweden's score on the index of universalism (Esping-Andersen, 1990) has actually risen between 1980 and the mid-1990s.

In addition, recent analysis of trends in means-tested social assistance by Gough et al. (1997) indicates that 7.1 percent of the Swedish population received some form of social assistance in 1992. This is an increase of 2.7 (percentage points of population) from 1980. In relation to total social security expenditure, means-tested social spending amounted to 6.7 percent of total social outlays in 1992. However, in the Anglo-liberal welfare states in 1992, 16.4 percent of the population received means-tested social assistance and these outlays accounted for 45.5 percent of total social security expenditure; these nations also experienced an average increase of recipients of means-tested benefits of 4.0 (percentage points of population) between 1980 and 1992. Overall, the analyses of changes in program attributes by Lindbom and Gough et al. reinforces the impressions that globalization (and other forces) have not produced much if any convergence of the Swedish welfare state with its neoliberal counterparts. I now turn to a general analysis of internationalization and social policy change in the Danish, Finnish, and Norwegian welfare states.

Globalization and the Danish Welfare State

By the early 1980s, Denmark was second only to Sweden in terms of the development of social provision as measured by total social spending and outlays for social services (as percentages of GDP), the social wage, and related measures (see Table 4.1). However, Denmark experienced rising

---

[14] These aggregate income replacement rates are based on averages of pension, unemployment, and sickness net income replacement rates. These were estimated at 72, 75, and 90 percent, respectively, in 1980, and as 72, 71, and 80 percent, respectively, in 1998.

unemployment levels (and associated public sector deficits) in the wake of the two OPEC oil shocks of 1973–4 and 1979–80. In fact, unemployment in Denmark far outpaced Nordic averages in the 1970s and 1980s: between 1980 and 1989 for instance, unemployment rates in Denmark averaged 8 percent of the civilian work force. Comparable rates for Finland, Norway, and Sweden were 4.9, 2.8, and 2.5 percent, respectively. Moreover, inflation accelerated, rising on average 10.8 percent annually between 1973 and 1979. Most observers attribute the relatively early and steep rises in unemployment to a number of factors, including dependence on the agricultural sector and imported energy, greater integration with the EU, relatively weaker Left and trade union actors, relatively stronger Center and Right political parties, and other forces. Most observers also note that, at least in part because of higher 1970s and 1980s unemployment, fiscal stress, and generally weaker economic performance, Denmark embarked on non-incremental social welfare retrenchment earlier than other Nordic countries.

Most important in this respect is the ascent of a series of Center-Right coalition governments (three) that held power between 1982 and 1993. Against the backdrop of 1970s and early 1980s economic problems, the Center-Right government initiated a shift in economic policy similar to that of the mid-1980s Swedish Social Democrats. Emphasis was placed on exchange rate and price stability, restrictive fiscal and monetary policy, private savings and investment (enhanced, for instance, by corporate and marginal personal income tax rate cuts), and efficiency-oriented reforms in the public sector. While these policies contributed to a noticeable improvement in the external balance, inflation, and public sector deficit, high unemployment persisted well into the mid-1980s: unemployment eventually fell to 5.5 percent in 1986 and 5.4 percent in 1987. In this context, moderate reforms to the Danish welfare state have been enacted.

During the 1980s and 1990s, the Danish Center-Right coalition (and the subsequent mid-1990s Social Democratic–led government) initiated a number of moderate rollbacks in social welfare provision. There have been periods of modifications and suspensions of benefit indexation (where benefits were indexed to price levels before 1991; to wages after). There have been new restrictions on eligibility and reductions in benefits in several areas. Much of the focus has been in the area of unemployment compensation. The government froze benefit levels in the early 1980s, initiated more restrictive eligibility criteria, and cut some forms of assistance to the unemployed; the income replacement rate for unemployment assistance has fallen from roughly 70 percent in the early 1980s to 60 percent in the mid-1990s (OECD estimates). As Kvist (1997) makes clear, however, the Danish unemployment compensation system is still very generous to average- and low-income workers: in 1996, workers at one-half the income of the average production worker received replacement of 98.5 percent of income; workers at the average production worker's income received replacement income equivalent to 65 percent.

In addition, there were new restrictions and more means-testing of benefits in a variety of areas including old age and invalidity pensions. In fact, in 1984 an income test was initiated for those 67 to 70 years of age (i.e., for those who had notable private income); this income testing was extended to all elderly in 1991. In 1994, a similar income test was initiated for the ATP (supplemental pension). While this change in pension policy certainly marks a shift to selectivity in a general sense (and one supported by both bourgeois and Social Democratic governments), Kvist (1997) and others have noted that this greater use of income tests does not undercut universalism (i.e., all retirees maintain the claim to basic security and income replacement), but rather introduces need into the calculation of pension benefit. In addition, the basic state pension was made taxable in the mid-1990s (although this effective cut in retirement income has been more than offset by benefit increases). In the area of sickness benefits, the Center-Right government enacted an extension of the "employer period" of benefit responsibility and one waiting day for benefits between 1983 and 1987; however, these measures were rescinded in 1988. Moreover, the bourgeois government initiated a campaign to control the growth of social service spending at the local level.[15] The government imposed fixed budgets, reduced national subsidies, froze local tax rates, and encouraged market mechanisms and privatization in social service delivery. As Table 4.1 suggests, these efforts were somewhat successful with stability and, in some periods, decline in resources devoted to social services between the early 1980s and 1990s.

Despite these rollbacks, the Danish welfare state expanded in some areas from the 1970s to mid-1990s. There has been moderate growth in pension benefits, early retirement provisions, housing allowances, social

[15] Denmark (like Sweden a decade earlier) had decentralized authority for most social services – for families, the elderly, disabled, the sick – to local communes at the beginning of the 1970s. Expenditure on social services at the local level had grown fairly rapidly through the early 1980s (see Villadsen [1996]).

assistance, and maternity leave. For instance, maternity leave was extended from 14 to 24 weeks in 1984; pension benefits were increased by 5 percent for individuals and 7 percent for couples in 1989. Perhaps most significantly, there has been a new emphasis on an "active line" in employment services. There have been increased resources for active labor market policies, employment subsidies, eased conditions for early retirement, and more generous benefits for leave. In fact, members of the unemployment funds can obtain up to 52 weeks of leave for education, family and sabbatical purposes. These policies have been consciously linked to new initiatives in education and public infrastructure. Together with the aforementioned social policy reforms, these extensions and recent reforms constitute the core of social policy change in Denmark from the 1970s to mid-1990s.

Can the cuts and restructuring in the Danish welfare state be linked in a direct sense to international capital mobility? Has the Danish welfare state, under pressures of globalization, begun to converge with its neoliberal counterparts in Anglo political economies? With respect to the first question, forces emanating from the world economy certainly played a role in creating pressure on the Danish welfare state: internationally transmitted energy shocks and their domestic consequences, and problems with productivity in the (consumer goods–oriented) export sector, contributed to weaknesses in 1970s and 1980s economic performance. It is difficult, however, to find direct linkages between economic pressures attendant on rises in international capital mobility on the one hand, and welfare state reform on the other. Increases in international capital mobility in the form of aggregate flows of finance capital, FDI, and liberalization of capital markets do not accelerate to any substantial degree until the mid-1980s; many of the most significant rollbacks in the welfare state were initiated before the weight of the economic logic of international capital mobility could exert strong influences.[16]

Moreover, in the context of improving economic performance and fiscal balance, several of the early and mid-1980s restrictive reforms were rescinded in the 1987 to 1989 era (e.g., in the area of sickness benefits) and several modest new initiatives were taken in the wake of a notable increase in international financial integration. Generally, as Mjøset (1996)

---

[16] Liberalization of Danish capital markets occurred after 1987; the growth in flows of finance and FDI accelerated in 1984, 1985, and 1986 and remained high thereafter.

points out, the principal conduit of influence of international financial integration on Danish national policies was the ascendance of neoliberal orthodoxy. That is, in the most general sense, the political logic of globalization has played a role in general public sector and welfare state reforms: domestic neoliberalism, especially during the bourgeois coalition, provided a conducive context for arguments about business location and global competitiveness, and arguments about the reforms necessitated by international openness reinforced neoliberalism and Center-Right electoral appeals.

However, with respect to actual substantive effects of this political logic of globalization and the extent to which welfare reforms have actually produced substantial retrenchment and convergence, the weight of the evidence clearly indicates the Danish welfare state has not, under pressures of internationalization, lost its basic character as a universalistic welfare state. Indeed, most (although not all) observers have highlighted the absence of significant neoliberal retrenchment in the context of sustained high unemployment, fiscal stress, and a dozen years of Center-Right governance. For instance, J. G. Andersen (1997) has observed that, despite over two decades of very severe welfare state pressures, the Danish welfare state is still a Nordic welfare state; while retrenchments have occurred, basic principles are still in place with new emphases on work (i.e., new emphases on obligations, as well as social rights) and a surprisingly successful avoidance of the social marginalization of workers, particularly young workers. Analyses of the substance of reforms through the mid- to late 1990s by Kvist (1997), Ploug (1998), Christoffersen (1997), and others (c.f., Cox [1997]) all underscore the same general conclusion: while successive governments have engineered moderate neoliberal reforms, the Danish welfare state is still substantially comprehensive, universal, and generous.

K. V. Andersen, Greve, and Torfing (1995) underscore four central reasons for the absence of major neoliberal restructuring. First, given the character of the electoral and party systems, the Right depended on one to three centrist party allies in the 1982–93 coalition governments and there were frequent policy disagreements among the Right and Center on neoliberal restructuring. Similarly, given the parliamentary weakness of the Center-Right, the government had to bargain with the opposition Social Democrats; most observers note that late-1980s rollbacks of neoliberal reforms and modest extensions were the result of this Social Democratic pressure. Third, unions and welfare state interests (what I have called "welfare state programmatic coalitions") resisted neoliberal reforms at each juncture. Finally, Andersen, Greve, and Torfing note (as do most observers of welfare reform in this period) that the universal character of social policy generates and sustains substantial cross-class popular support for social policy in Denmark. Overall, internationalization (even when combined with supportive domestic economic and political conditions) has not led to significant neoliberal retrenchment and convergence of the Danish welfare state.

Internationalization and Finnish Social Policy

As late as the early 1980s, Finland appeared to be a welfare state laggard among the Nordic countries. As data in Table 4.1 suggest, Finnish social welfare policies were "underdeveloped" by social democratic standards. Income replacement rates, social services, and public health spending were lower than in other Nordic nations. Marginal and average tax rates also fell below Nordic averages (see Chapter 7). However, Finland's position had been rapidly changing since the 1960s. Economic development, a reconciliation within the Left and within the trade union movement, and cooperation between the Center and Left political parties had provided opportunities for substantial expansion of the Finnish welfare state. During the 1960s, earnings-related pensions, sickness benefits, and active labor market policies were established. In the 1970s, benefits in these and other areas (e.g., parental leave and child allowances) were extended. Moreover, public health spending and social service provision increased during the 1970s. In the 1980s, additional benefit and coverage increases occurred in social insurance (e.g., the establishment of compulsory unemployment insurance) and more resources were devoted to active labor market policies; some of these extensions of social protection continued up until the advent of severe economic crisis in 1991. As most observers point out, the late but notable expansion of the Finnish welfare state was buoyed by strong economic performance in the 1980s. Export-fueled growth, enhanced by selective currency devaluations, growth in trade with the Soviet Union, and a robust world economy led to 1980s growth rates in Finland second only to Japan among the rich democracies. Indeed, by the late 1980s, the Finnish welfare state had effectively become a Nordic welfare state (Andersson, Kosonen, and Vartiainen, 1993).

It is important to note, however, that, as in other rich democracies, the post-1973 period in Finland was characterized by increasing fiscal pressures for expenditure restraint, and the late but notable expansion of the Finnish welfare state was punctuated with periodic efforts to control social spending. For instance, in 1979, 1982, 1983, and 1985 indexation of pensions was reduced or frozen; as early as 1975 eligibility requirements for some forms of social protection were tightened (e.g., invalidity benefits). Moreover, replacement rates and compensation levels for some benefits were occasionally reduced (e.g., health insurance benefits in the late 1970s). As most observers note, however, Finland did not experience significant rollbacks and restructuring of social provision until the early 1990s.

In the early 1990s, the Finnish economy suffered several dramatic setbacks that had significant repercussions for the welfare state. First, with the collapse of the Soviet Union in 1991, the Finnish economy suffered the immediate loss of 15% of its exports; this external shock coincided with the downturn in the world economy in the early 1990s. As some observers have argued (e.g., Mjøset [1996]; Stephens [1996]; Huber and Stephens [1998]), these exogenous economic shocks interacted with, and were made worse by, a series of domestic policy mistakes and domestic market developments (e.g., the banking crisis following 1980s deregulation and the boom in asset prices). Generally, after the dramatic economic growth performance of the 1980s, the Finnish economy deteriorated rapidly from the latter days of 1991 onward. The growth rate of real GDP per capita in 1991 alone was −7.8 percent and the public sector budget deficit had reached 8 percent of GDP by 1993. Unemployment rates increased rapidly, moving from 3.4 percent of the labor force in both 1989 and 1990 to 13 percent in 1992 and 17.7 percent in 1993.

In the wake of this dramatic crisis, a series of reductions in social welfare effort were made in 1991 and subsequent years. Unemployment compensation replacement rates were cut 3 percent and tighter qualifying conditions for unemployment assistance were enacted. Sickness benefits were reduced: the replacement rate was cut from 80 to 67 percent between 1991 and 1993, employee contributions increased, and the waiting period extended from 7 to 9 days. In addition, the parental benefit was cut from 275 to 263 days, subsidies for prescription drugs were reduced, and many new user fees were enacted for social services. The replacement rate for the earnings-related tier of the pension system was cut from 66 to 60 percent and employee contributions of 6 percent of income were introduced. From 1991 on, indexation of many cash benefits were frozen. In addition, between 1994 and 1997, further reductions in sickness and unemployment benefits were made. Most notable was the creation of a program of active labor support and related changes that resulted in new labor market entrants (and students) being initially excluded from eligibility for sickness and pension coverage. Finally, new pension legislation was enacted in 1996 that modestly reduced the generosity of pension benefits and introduced an income test (for earned income) for pension beneficiaries.

Can these changes in the Finnish welfare state be linked to international capital mobility? Has the Finnish welfare state converged toward the neoliberal model of social protection? With regard to the influence of international financial integration, Finland shares some of the same characteristics as Sweden. That is, few or only minor rollbacks in social protection occurred during several years of substantial increases in international capital mobility.[17] Only after a severe economic crisis hit in the early 1990s were there nontrivial efforts to cut benefits, restrict eligibility, and otherwise introduce reforms to control welfare state costs. In addition, a fixed exchange rate, high capital mobility, and a rapidly accelerating public sector deficit led to a dramatic increase in interest rates until the currency was allowed to float. Thus, as in the case of Sweden, the principal impetus to policy reform was the interaction of economic and fiscal crises on the one hand, and high levels of international financial integration on the other.

Has the Finnish welfare state converged to any substantial degree toward the neoliberal model? Here, as in the case of Sweden and Denmark, the answer is, speaking generally, "no". While most observers cite the moderate reductions in benefits and tighter eligibility standards in unemployment-related programs, the advent of income testing in pensions, and new exclusions connected to the labor support program, the Finnish welfare state has largely retained its character as a relatively comprehensive, universal, and generous system of social protection. Indeed, as recent analyses of Finnish public opinion and welfare state support make clear, there are continuing high levels of support, especially for the universal component of the Finnish welfare state (Kangas, 1995); while this

---

[17] In the Finnish case, inward and outward FDI and financial capital flows accelerated in the mid-1980s although formal capital controls remained the most extensive of the Nordic countries through the late 1980s. Significant deregulation of capital controls, which corresponded with the moderate neoliberal shift in Finnish economic policy, occurred in 1988, 1989, and 1990.

level of support has waned during economic crisis, it has returned to its post-crisis levels in the mid-1990s (Sihvo and Uusitalo, 1995).

Global Capital and Policy Change in the Norwegian Welfare State

Like Finland, Norway enjoyed relatively good economic performance in the 1970s and 1980s; unlike Finland and Sweden, Norway has escaped a dramatic early 1990s economic crisis. Despite a downturn in the Norwegian economy in the late 1980s and the early 1990s world recession, real per capita GDP growth rates have been reasonably strong: 1.6 percent in 1991, 3.4 in 1992, and 3.3 in 1993. By most accounts, Norwegian economic performance is linked to oil reserves, which have provided contemporary governments with an abundant source of revenue since the late 1970s. Indeed, some observers have suggested that Norway has avoided a pronounced welfare state crisis precisely because of oil resources (e.g., Stephens [1996]). In this context, social welfare provision in Norway expanded in the 1970s and 1980s in some areas. Housing allowances were upgraded in the late 1970s and provisions for maternity leave were liberalized in the 1980s; unemployment compensation was expanded and basic pension benefits were increased during this period. In addition, the social assistance benefit level was doubled between 1981 and 1986, maternity leave was further liberalized, and sick leave benefits improved. In addition, as noted above, there have been no major periods of dramatic cuts in income replacement rates, eligibility, or coverage.

However, Norway has experienced economic and political conditions that are conducive to some welfare state retrenchment. In fact, early 1980s nonsocialist governments (and to an extent the subsequent Labor government) pursued neoliberal policies of deregulation and expenditure control. From mid-1986 onward, the new Labor government pursued a hard currency policy and relatively tight monetary and fiscal policy. As Mjøset's (1996) synoptic survey of 1980s and 1990s Nordic economic policies suggests, Norway – like Denmark and Sweden – experienced a shift to a "norms-based" economic policy, where price stability was prioritized and where flexible monetary and exchange rate policies were sacrificed for a fixed exchange rate. With respect to economic performance, the 1986–7 collapse of dollar-denominated oil prices and the late 1980s banking crisis, coupled with the early 1990s world economic downturn, placed substantial pressure on unemployment. Unemployment rates increased from a 1986 low of 2 percent of the labor force to 4.9 percent in 1989, 5.2 percent in 1990, and a peak of 6.0 by 1993.[18] After an annual average budgetary surplus of 5.0 percent of GDP between 1980 and 1989, a small public sector deficit of −.3 percent emerged in 1991.

In this context, most analysts emphasize that there have been a series of incremental rollbacks of social welfare provision since the 1970s. In fact, Marklund (1988) compares Norway to Denmark in discussing a series of cuts and reforms during this period. Specifically, Marklund and other observes have emphasized two major policy thrusts in the 1970s and 1980s. First, there has been a strong emphasis on controlling costs and gaining efficiencies in the health care sector; numerous user fees for health services have been introduced and a number of tighter eligibility standards for health benefits have been introduced. More significantly, there has been a systematic effort to "deindex" many forms of social assistance. In fact, some forms of benefits (for instance, invalidity) have been removed from the "basic amount" that qualifies forms of income maintenance for indexation.

In the late 1980s and early 1990s, despite the absence of a dramatic "economic crisis," a number of additional changes were made. There were stronger work requirements and stricter qualifying conditions for unemployment, as well as imposition of "strictly medical criteria" for disability and sickness benefits. In addition – and unlike Sweden, but like Denmark and Finland – there was increased use of income-testing in pensions and other programs. For instance, there are now income tests for dependent benefits and retirement benefits for those 67 to 70 years of age. In addition, the replacement rate for the supplementary pension has been reduced 3 percent.

Can one reasonably link these moderate cuts and reforms of social welfare provision to rises in international capital mobility? In the case of Norway, one could argue that weak, indirect linkages exist in the form of "the political logic of globalization" and the policy consequences that flow from hard currency policy and high capital mobility. That is, as Mjøset (1996) has pointed out, internationalization has primarily influenced Norwegian national policies through the ways in which internationalization reinforces (and is reinforced by) the ascent of neoliberal policy orientations. Second, the prioritization of price stability and the commitment to

---

[18] Some observers have pointed out that, if one counts individuals on the burgeoning disability rolls (another source of concern over the costs of the welfare state), actual unemployment exceeded 10 percent in Norway in the early 1990s (e.g., Stephens [1996]).

fixed exchange rates in the context of high capital mobility reduces, if not eliminates, traditional monetary (e.g., interest rate) and exchange rate policy flexibility in response to economic downturn (see Chapter 7 for systematic analysis). There was, however, no large surge of unemployment and attendant fiscal problems in Norway, nor was there an interaction between large fiscal deficit and high capital mobility whereby interest rate pressures forced domestic budgetary austerity. In sum, while internationalization is relevant, it has not been a large force in determining social policy reforms.

Has the Norwegian welfare state moved toward convergence with the neoliberal model of social protection? As is the case for the other Nordic political economies, the answer is "no". Most observers agree that from the perspective of the mid-1990s, the Norwegian welfare state has enjoyed the most continuity of the Nordic cases; it retains its social democratic character with relatively comprehensive, universal, and generous programs and services (e.g., Ploug [1998]; Huber and Stephens [1998]; Stephens [1996]). However, one can recognize several trends in Norwegian welfare policy that, while not abandoning basic principles, suggest some small modifications of those principles. First, there is greater emphasis of work, or *arbeidslinje* (work orientation), where benefits are more closely linked with a recipient's self-sufficiency and eventual employment. Second, there is stronger emphasis on family assistance, particularly for families with younger children. Third, there is greater targeting, with increased use of income testing. In addition, there is a greater use of private providers for social and health services and in education; this has taken place with state sanction and subsidy (van Wormer, 1994). Finally, there are some early signs of segmentation of beneficiaries, with upscale employees taking greater advantage of tax preferences and access to private service and benefit providers. Overall, similar to all Nordic welfare states, Norwegian social policy has exhibited both basic continuity and moderate reform.

Globalization, Political Institutions, and Welfare State Reform in the Nordic Countries

Some observers have highlighted the direct roles that international capital mobility (and trade competitiveness) have played in pressuring Nordic governments to retrench the welfare state. For instance, Gould (1993, 1996) has invoked this explanation in his analyses of Nordic policy change and van Wormer (1994) has linked privatization and efforts to control health care costs to globalization pressures. Kosonen (1993) has made the point, reflecting a common version of globalization theory, that the Scandinavian welfare states are particularly susceptible to retrenchment in the contemporary period insofar as they combine a very high level of social protection with high capital mobility. In addition, several observers have offered nuanced accounts of how internationalization interacts with specific domestic and political conditions to pressure moderate welfare state retrenchment and reform. Specifically, Mjøset (1996) has argued that globalization has strengthened the weight of neoliberal economic ideas in countries such as Denmark and Norway and that this neoliberalism leads to efforts to cut spending and implement market-oriented reforms. Finally, as Garrett (1998b) and Moses (2000) have noted, large fiscal imbalances result in high interest rate premiums under conditions of high international capital mobility and governments succumb to interest rate–generated pressures in initiating welfare retrenchments. I will address these points in turn and then return to focal arguments about the roles of national political institutions in shaping the politics of welfare state restructuring.[19]

First, when examining evidence from the four Nordic cases, one can find few temporally ordered and direct linkages between rises in capital mobility and welfare reforms. The case studies simply offer little evidence of such linkages. It is certainly true that there has been a long-term shift toward expenditure restraints, cost control, and efficiency in all four Nordic political economies; linkages of work and benefits have been (re)emphasized in one form or another in all nations. In some Nordic welfare states, privatization and benefit targeting have increased (although this is less true of Sweden), and social insurance modes of finance have made inroads.[20] Additionally, these changes have occurred during the

---

[19] As noted, Huber and Stephens (1998) as well as others (see Martin 1996; Moses, 2000) have argued that a principal impact of international financial integration in the Social Democratic political economies has been to undercut the effectiveness or the availability of traditional economic policy instruments, particulary monetary and exchange rate tools. As a result, unemployment and fiscal crises are exacerbated and universal and generous welfare states purportedly come under irresistible pressures for retrenchment. I will systematically address these arguments in Chapter 7.

[20] With respect to targeting, it is important to note that while all Nordic welfare states experienced a moderate rise in the use of means-tested social assistance (as measured by recipients as a percentage of the population or as shares of the total social security budget), these increases were smaller in absolute terms (and only modestly larger in percentage terms) to those experienced in Anglo-liberal welfare states (Gough et al., 1997). Most important, there remains a large gap between the Nordic and liberal welfare states in relative reliance

period of steady globalization from the mid-1970s to the present; however, the timing of reforms does not correspond, for the most part, to the patterns of internationalization. As Stephens (1996) and others have observed and the case studies make clear, the most substantial cuts in the Nordic welfare states occurred in Finland and Sweden only after severe economic crisis – dramatic rises in unemployment and burgeoning deficits – threatened governments with financial collapse (also see Huber and Stephens [1998]); Finnish and Swedish welfare state rollbacks before that point, during 10 years or so of notable internationalization of markets, had been relatively modest. In addition, many of the most significant cuts in the welfare state in Denmark occurred with the 1970s and early 1980s rise in unemployment and with the early 1980s advent of a Center-Right coalition; that is, many of the most important shifts in Danish social policy occurred before international financial integration proceeded very far. Moreover, 1970s and 1980s rollbacks and modifications of Danish social welfare policy were accompanied by benefit and entitlement expansions in some areas. In Norway, modest 1980s and 1990s welfare state retrenchment and restructuring occurred against a backdrop of nonsocialist government, the ascendance of neoliberal ideas, and moderate economic difficulties; they were also coupled with modest extensions of some social welfare protections. While internationalization may have reinforced or otherwise interacted with domestic and economic pressures on the welfare state, it is very difficult to identify significant neoliberal reforms in the Norwegian case and, in turn, link them directly to capital mobility.

What of the argument that rises in internationalization and the ascent of neoliberalism interact in mutually reinforcing ways to generate greater pressures for welfare state austerity? Certainly, all four Nordic cases offer some evidence for the view; as Mjøset (1996) has pointed out, the effects of internationalization on national policies may come primarily through this conduit. Under Center-Right governments, the neoliberal shift in economic policy orientation was often pronounced; even under Social Democratic governments there was a moderate neoliberal turn. Indeed, Social Democratic parties in all four cases shifted to (or affirmed) priorities and policies of price and currency stability and fiscal austerity, as well as facilitated (through liberalization and deregulation), or presided over, years of

on targeted benefits. As the analysis by Gough et al. (1997) reveals, 1992 means-tested social assistance accounted on average for 6.4 percent of all social spending in the Nordic cases and 45.5 percent in the liberal welfare states.

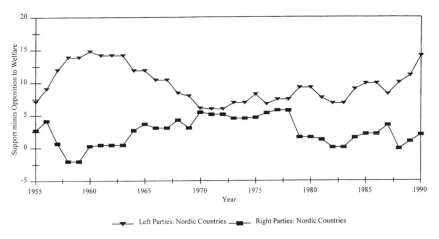

Figure 4.3   Partisan Support for the Welfare State in the Nordic Nations

substantial growth in capital mobility and financial integration. Has this reorientation resulted in a "programmatic neoliberal convergence" between parties of the Right and Left on the questions of welfare state retrenchment and restructuring?

The case studies offer evidence that this may not have occurred: Social Democratic governments have generally attempted to limit neoliberal retrenchment, offer modest extensions of social rights, and reform and improve the effectiveness of the Nordic model of social protection under frequently severe conditions of economic and fiscal stress. In Figure 4.3, I provide systematic evidence on the degree of support for the Nordic welfare state among parties of the Left and Right between the mid-1950s and early 1990s. The data represent the percentage of party manifesto statements in support of the welfare state minus the percent of policy pronouncements that advocate retrenchments in one form or another.[21] If the moderate shift to neoliberal economic policy by Social Democratic parties (and the changing economic fortunes of the 1970s, 1980s, and 1990s) has resulted in a transformation of Left party support for the welfare state, we should observe some "neoliberal convergence" among the parties. Indeed,

---

[21] The data are from the Party Manifesto Project (see Appendix A) and are based on content analysis of party electoral manifestos. See Klingemann, Hofferbert, and Budge (1994) for an extensive discussion of the data and the strong relationships between manifesto programmatic positions of parties and other measures of party policy preferences and actual policies pursued when in government.

155

much of the literature on the comparative politics of advanced industrial societies suggests that one should observe some evidence of party ideological convergence on the need to control or roll back welfare program costs from the 1970s onward. As the figure makes clear, however, there is no evidence that this has occurred in the Nordic polities. In fact, after a decade of significant convergence on social policy (Nordic parties of the Left and Right actually differed little in overall welfare state support between roughly 1968 and 1978), there has been *a notable divergence* in programmatic positions between the late 1970s and early 1990s. Systematic reviews of partisan positions on major issues of social welfare policy in the Nordic countries reveal that this divergence persists through the mid-1990s (Ploug and Kvist, 1994; 1996).

However, in one area, both the quantitative and case-study evidence has underscored the role of international capital mobility in welfare state reform. Specifically, the case analyses support the general finding from the quantitative work of Chapter 3 that capital mobility exerts general downward pressure on the welfare state primarily under conditions of significant fiscal crisis. In fact, there appears to be a confluence of conditions in the early 1990s (in Sweden and Finland most notably) where high international capital mobility and fiscal deficits approaching and even exceeding 10 percent of GDP contributed to moderate retrenchment of the Nordic welfare state. As previous discussions have suggested, international capital markets charge a premium in the form of higher interest rates on governments who run budget deficits (and threaten price stability and growth prospects with fiscal imbalance). As noted above, while some have suggested that the threshold for budget deficits under high capital mobility is in the range of 3 percent of GDP (Mosley, 1998), my estimates from the quantitative analysis of empirical models of social welfare provision indicate that the threshold has been probably higher: roughly 10 percent of GDP on average across the developed democracies. Indeed, these statistical estimates and the Swedish and Finnish experiences lead to the same conclusion: capital mobility matters for the large social democratic welfare states when budget imbalances are excessive.

Internationalization, Political Institutions, and the Nordic Welfare States

The case analysis indicates that internationalization has had limited, indirect, and episodic impacts on Nordic social policy reform. Overall, these welfare states have not moved appreciably toward the neoliberal model under pressures from internationalization. In addition, the conclusions from the case-study analysis also underscore the central finding of the quantitative analysis that national political institutions shape the social policy impacts of internationalization. First, as I have argued above, inclusive electoral institutions buffer systems of social protection from retrenchment pressures in a variety of ways. Some of these mechanisms are clearly evident in the politics of social policy reform in the Nordic polities over the last 20 years. Generally, net of structural features that shape the party system, relatively inclusive systems of electoral representation in all Nordic countries guarantee consequential numbers of votes and seats to parties of the Left; parties of the Center, whose middle-class constituencies have an interest in the preservation of the universal welfare state, also have representation. One immediate consequence of this inclusiveness is to require parties of the Right (historically weak and fragmented) to enlist centrist allies to form governments. The consequences for the enactment and implementation of strong neoliberal reforms are important. For instance, in both Sweden and Denmark, Right and Center party coalition partners often disagreed over the depth or character of neoliberal reforms and more radical neoliberal restructuring was abandoned.

Generally, parties of the Right in the Nordic cases have never enjoyed the status of Thatcher's Conservatives, Reagan's Republicans, or Canadian Progressive Conservatives as single-party majority governments: in the Anglo polities, where institutions of electoral exclusiveness are strong, majority governments of one Right party may well be more responsive to (and conduits of) the economic and political logics of globalization (see Chapter 6). Second, when parties of the Center-Right are in government (often as minority governments), they usually face substantial Social Democratic party oppositions. As the case studies illustrate, this often necessitates the negotiation of policy change – such as particularly extraordinary policy reforms of the early 1990s crisis packages in Sweden – with Social Democrats. In fact, in Denmark, the 1982–93 bourgeois governments were occasionally forced to negotiate with the Social Democratic opposition and, in turn, compelled to drop certain neoliberal reforms or adopt Social Democratic demands for protections of social provision.

Second, as discussed above, analysts have commonly noted that social corporatist systems of interest representation in the Nordic nations – in their general roles as supporters of Social Democratic electoral strength, conduits of union interest representation, or forums for negotiation, compromise, and consensual decision making – have been instrumental in welfare state development and have provided a bulwark against welfare state retrenchment. Indeed, as several observers have noted, extensively organized and centralized unions incorporated in corporatist institutions of national policy making have systematically resisted the more dramatic neoliberal reforms of Nordic Center-Right coalitions during the 1980s and 1990s (e.g., Ryner [1997]; K. V. Andersen, Greve, and Torfing [1995]). As Andersen, Greve, and Torfing's analysis of the Danish case illustrates, in the context of continued corporatist patterns of negotiation over national policy between employers, unions, and the government, unions were able to blunt the more dramatic neoliberal reform efforts of successive Center-Right coalitions. According to the analysts, with a few "minor exceptions," the bourgeois coalition simply avoided direct confrontations with unions over many neoliberal initiatives.

However, as discussed above, the role of social corporatism has been diminished in some cases.[22] This is particular true in Sweden. With the post-1982 decentralization of central bargaining and rising conflicts between private and public sector unions, one can argue that social corporatist underpinnings of the welfare state are being weakened. While I address this issue and the impact of internationalization on social corporatism in Chapter 7, a few points should be made in the present context. First, the weakening of social corporatist institutions in the area of wage setting has been primarily limited to Sweden; relatively centralized bargaining arrangements in Denmark and Finland have not changed that much in the last 15 years and, arguably, have been strengthened in Norway (Wallerstein and Golden, 1997). Moreover, as a recent study of corporatism in Sweden suggests, social corporatist arrangements that deal specifically with social welfare issues – consensus orientations among peak associations in government-mediated bargaining over social welfare policies – have not changed significantly through the mid-1990s (Hoefer, 1996).

With respect to the structure of policy-making authority within the polity, theory as well as systematic evidence from the quantitative analyses has established the case that centralized polities are less likely to engage in internationalization-induced neoliberal restructuring than polities char-

---

[22] In addition, Stephens (1996) points out that in the mid-1980s the LO issued a series of reports that acknowledged the Swedish welfare state had reached its limits. In effect, the LO's position has become that further expansion of the welfare state was not necessary; only reforms of existing programs to improve their effectiveness are called for.

158

acterized by dispersed policy-making authority. Fragmented and decentralized polities, while offering opponents of welfare state retrenchment "institutional veto points," undercut the political capacities of pro–welfare state interests through a variety of mechanisms and tend to foster antistatist values and norms. While the Nordic case studies have not spoken directly to these issues – the structure of policy-making authority in the polity is in large part a long-term structural influence, the characteristics of the Nordic politics and the politics and outcomes of welfare state reform from the 1970s to 1990s are completely consistent with the theory and quantitative evidence. While Finland is characterized by moderate presidentialism and while there is substantial devolution of social service policy making and delivery to counties and municipalities, general and national social insurance policy making authority is relatively concentrated in the Nordic polities. This absence of fragmentation arguably enhances the relative political capacities of welfare state interests in the Nordic case; that is, it contributes (along with other structural properties of the Nordic cases) to the coherence and electoral strength of pro–welfare state parties and the size and coherence of the trade union movements. Concentration also minimizes the conflict and competitiveness-oriented norms and routines of fragmented polities, as well as antistatist orientations often attendant decentralization. Moreover, as discussed above, relatively centralized polities – in that centralization promotes the development of a large welfare state and contributes to the coherence of national-based welfare interests – should have large, coherent, and efficacious welfare programmatic alliances. This is arguably the case for the Nordic nations, and the Danish case is exemplary in this regard. In their comprehensive survey of the welfare retrenchment efforts of the three successive Center-Right governments, K. V. Andersen, Greve, and Torfing (1995) argue that a central political institutional impediment to more notable neoliberal reforms was the size, coherence, and general political strength of national coalitions of welfare state bureaucrats and professionals that systematically pressured the bourgeois governments to moderate neoliberal initiatives.

Finally, analysts of welfare reform in the Nordic cases have highlighted the role of universalism in welfare program structure in blunting neoliberal retrenchment. For instance, Rothstein (1998) offers substantial evidence on the role of universalism in the maintenance of the Swedish welfare state; J. G. Andersen (1997), K. V. Andersen, Greve, and Torfing (1995), and Torfing (1999) have emphasized the role of the universal character of the Danish welfare state as an impediment to significant neoliberal reform initiatives in the 1980s and 1990s. As argued above, the political logic of the universal welfare state weds the self-interests of the poor, working class, and middle class through universal social insurance and services. The electorally crucial middle class receives substantial benefits and insurance against risks in return for significant tax payments (Moene and Wallerstein, 1996; Rothstein, 1998). Moreover, Rothstein (1998) argues that a moral basis of equal respect and concern embodied in program structure, broadly targeted universal benefits, carefully adapted delivery organizations, and participatory administrative processes achieve relatively high levels of contingent consent from the citizenry. Solidarity, trust, and confidence in state intervention are promoted.

In addition, many observers have also emphasized that despite increasing tensions among cross-class coalitions (e.g., between private and public sector unions, upscale and downscale constituencies) and rising criticisms of the universal welfare state as over-bureaucratized and a threat to individual autonomy and self-sufficiency, the high level of mass approval of the universal welfare state and general solidarity among its constituencies persist. For instance, Svalifors (1995) documents sustained high levels of public support for the Swedish welfare state through the mid-1990s, with the exception of declining support for selective programs (e.g., social assistance); Kangas (1995) provides comparable evidence for the Finnish case. Specifically addressing the question of declining cross-class support and solidarity, J. G. Andersen (1997) reports trends in Danish mass opinion through the mid-1990s that underscore the point: while there is declining support for broad goals such as "total equality" and other concerns about welfare policy (e.g., bureaucratization), there is no evidence of declining solidarity among the broad coalition of universal welfare state constituencies. And, as noted above in the Finnish case study, Sihvo and Uusitalo (1995) find sustained high levels of support for the Finnish welfare state that only temporally erode during the early 1990s economic crisis. Overall, the political and normative features of universalistic program structure combined with inclusive electoral institutions, social corporatism, and centralization of the polity have done much to bolster the Nordic welfare states against serious retrenchment pressures over the last two decades.

5

Globalization and Policy Change in Corporatist Conservative Welfare States

In this chapter, I explore the welfare state impacts of international capital mobility in the corporatist conservative welfare states of continental Europe. First, I consider Austria, Belgium, France, Germany, and Italy as a group and then provide analyses of internationalization and social policy change in Germany, France, and Italy. Germany is often regarded as an exemplar of the "corporatist conservative," or Christian Democratic, welfare state and I supplement the analysis of secondary material with interview and other primary data. Given the relatively large size of the French and Italian welfare states and the centrality of the French and Italian economies, I also provide individual case studies of these countries.

I proceed with analysis of the conservative welfare states in the same fashion as I did for the Nordic cases. After an overview of basic features of welfare states, I examine, in turn, trends in international capital mobility and the politics of social welfare reform within individual countries. I conclude with a comparative analysis of the roles of internationalization in influencing social welfare policy change and an assessment of the ways in which national institutions shape the social policy impacts of globalization. As to key hypotheses, globalization theory predicts that we should observe clear evidence of retrenchment subsequent to rises in international capital mobility in the relatively generous and expensive corporatist conservative systems of social protection.[1] On the other hand, my alternative

---

[1] As discussed below, some observers suggest that the conservative welfare states are market-conforming because they leave occupational- and class-status differentials and prerogatives of capital intact. Thus, one might expect that internationalization has less impact on them. In the contemporary globalization literature, however, the generosity of benefits and magnitude of tax burdens of these systems are commonly viewed as threats to profits, competitiveness, and general economic efficiency.

theory argues that we should see differential effects of internationalization across varieties of national political and welfare state institutions. Corporatist conservative welfare states tend to have average levels of social corporatism, moderately high electoral inclusiveness (although France is slightly below average), and (with exceptions) below average dispersion of policy-making authority. As discussed above, the occupationally stratified social insurance system may on balance enhance the representation and capacities of welfare state interests, as well as promote values, norms, and behaviors that mitigate welfare retrenchment. Overall, my argument predicts that we should find muted responsiveness to globalization in these systems.

The Corporatist Conservative Welfare States

Unlike the universalism of social democratic welfare states, rights to social protection in the corporatist conservative welfare states are tied to employment.[2] Rooted in conservative *etatist* traditions and communal corporatism (e.g., skilled craft guilds, mutual societies), public social insurance is designed to both protect workers from market risks and preserve class and occupational status differentials. Generally, these welfare states provide a mix of nationally unified, employment-based social insurance programs that covers the bulk of the workforce and an array of separate insurance programs for workers in specific industries; public sector workers have been traditionally privileged. Social insurance coverage and amelioration of needs is extensive but social aggregates who have not established employment records (e.g., some widows, single female parents) typically receive a "social minimum" or fall through the safety net.

Aside from these groups, the corporatist conservative welfare state provides relatively generous benefits. Influenced by social Catholicism, conservative welfare states (with the exception of Italy) have developed on the basis of the "family wage," or a level of income from employment and social insurance that allows the worker to materially support the family unit. Relatively high benefit ceilings (and the common linkage of benefits to work-life standard of living) also facilitate income security for middle- and high-income workers (and obviate the demand for private insurance). Replacement rates range from roughly 40 to 85 percent of net income and

---

[2] For further discussions of the Christian Democratic model, see Esping-Andersen (1990, 1996c, 1997), Huber and Stephens (1996, 2000), and van Kersbergen (1994, 1995).

are often more generous for married workers with dependents. Reflecting corporatist traditions and the occupational basis of the welfare state, social program administration combines national administrative guidance with decentralized administrative structures that incorporate business and labor as well as professional, constituency, and nonprofit groups.

The corporatist conservative welfare state is also distinguished by its disproportionate use of cash income transfers and low levels of publically funded and provided social services; health care is predominately publically funded, but unlike the Nordic model, administered and delivered by quasi-public and private actors. With the partial exception of France, day-care facilities and other social services that facilitate female employment outside the household are limited. Generally, the influence of social Catholicism as transmitted through Catholic party government, social reformers, and value systems has played a large role in limiting the development of a large public social service sector. Two principles of Catholic social thought are important. First, the principal of subsidiarity stresses the priority of private social provision through the family, church, and voluntary charitable organizations. Second, the Catholic stress on familialism provides a barrier to the development of programs that draw women into the workforce in large numbers.

Recognizing substantial cross-national variations, conservative welfare states have developed in the context of coordinated market structures.[3] These economies are coordinated in two senses. First, they exhibit at least moderate levels of centralization of their labor and industrial relations systems. Second, the economy is structured by high levels of enterprise coordination of essential activities within industrial sectors. Supported by state legal and regulatory frameworks, business trade associations, industry-financial corporate networks, and other cooperative groups typically coordinate research and development activities, export marketing strategy, vocational training, production standards, and some facets of competition and pricing.

As Manow (1998), Huber and Stephens (2001), and Kitschelt, Lange, Marks, and Stephens (1999) have suggested, conservative welfare states

---

[3] For an overview of the institutions and practices of coordinated versus liberal market economies, see Soskice (1999) and Kitschelt, Lange, Marks, and Stephens (1999). For an analysis of the relationships between welfare state models and production regimes, see Kitschelt et al. (1999) and especially Huber and Stephens (2001) and Manow (1998). Austria, Belgium, Germany, and Italy each conform in part to the model of sector-coordinated capitalism, although Germany is closest to a prototype (Hicks and Kenworthy, 1998); France's system of indicative planning and associated policies and structures are distinct.

support essential aspects of the coordinated market economy. These welfare states provide generous social security for workers, social stability for capital, and generally facilitate the cooperative relations necessary for long-term economic development strategies that are impossible in uncoordinated market economies dominated by "spot market" exchanges (Manow 1998). Politically, the integrative functions of the welfare state have been part and parcel of the Christian Democratic party electoral strategy of building cross-class coalitions (van Kersbergen, 1994; 1995).

Table 5.1 brings into concrete relief major elements of the corporatist conservative welfare state. Focusing on the nonrecessionary 1985–9 era, total social expenditure rivaled that of the social democratic welfare states (on average 24.5 and 26.1 percent of GDP, respectively); the conservative welfare state's social wage (43 percent of gross earnings) significantly exceeded the social wage of the Anglo welfare states (30 percent of gross income).[4] Net income replacement rates for pensioners, the disabled, and the sick, while variable, typically average (in the 1990s) in the range of 75 to 85 percent and are often comparable to income replacement in the Nordic welfare states (e.g., Esping-Andersen [1996b]; Ploug and Kvist [1994, 1996]. In addition, conservative welfare states led the advanced democracies in income transfers in the late 1980s (on average 17.5 percent of GDP). However, while expanding in some nations (e.g., France), public social service provision in corporatist conservative systems is roughly comparable to social service benefits in liberal welfare states (.6 and .4 percent of GDP, respectively) and far below the average for the Nordic welfare states (3.6 percent of GDP). Public health care systems, although commonly comprised of quasi-public and private administrative and delivery entities, spent amounts roughly comparable to the Nordic nations in the late 1980s (6.2 and 6.4 percent of GDP, respectively) and higher amounts than the typical liberal welfare state (5.4 percent of GDP). In addition, the public share of total health care expenditure was larger than the Anglo-liberal systems (78.0 to 67.2 percent), although less than the Nordic welfare states (87.4 percent). Finally, moderately funded ALMP benefits have developed in several conservative welfare states as these nations have expanded training, job placement, and employment subsidies in recent years.

---

[4] This average excludes the Italian welfare state, which (by OECD definitions) provides very low statutory direct unemployment benefits. However, the Italian welfare state in practice offers a variety of benefits to unemployed workers including the generous *Cassa Integrazione Guadagni* (Earnings Integration Fund; see below).

Table 5.1. *The Corporatist Conservative Welfare State in Comparative Perspective, 1980–1995*

Part A

	Total Social Protection[a]			Social Wage[b]			Cash Benefits[c]		
	1980–4	1985–9	1990–3	1980–4	1985–9	1990–5	1980–4	1985–9	1990–3
Corp Conservative									
Austria	22.3	23.9	24.4	.32	.35	.32	16.6	18.2	18.3
Belgium	27.5	26.4	25.8	.45	.44	.41	21.2	19.7	18.0
France	25.1	25.7	26.2	.56	.58	.56	17.2	17.5	17.4
Germany[d]	25.5	25.3	26.3	.38	.36	.36	17.8	16.8	17.6
Italy	20.0	21.3	23.2	.01	.05	.11	14.3	15.3	16.5
Average[e]	24.1	24.5	25.2	.42	.43	.41	17.4	17.5	17.6
Nordic-Social Dem	24.4	26.1	30.4	.54	.65	.65	14.2	15.4	18.7
Anglo-Liberal	16.3	15.8	17.8	.30	.30	.30	9.8	9.6	11.7
Average-All Nations	21.8	22.8	24.5	.40	.44	.44	14.1	14.4	16.1

Part B

	Social Services[f]			Public Health[g]			Labor Market Policies[h]		
	1980–4	1985–9	1990–3	1980–4	1985–9	1990–5	1980–4	1985–9	1990–3
Corp Conservative									
Austria	.3	.3	.2	5.5	5.6	5.8	—	.3	.3
Belgium	.3	.3	.2	6.0	6.4	7.0	—	1.4	1.2
France	1.0	1.0	1.0	6.3	6.5	6.9	—	.8	1.0
Germany	.8	.8	.7	7.1	7.1	7.4	—	1.0	1.1
Italy	.3	.3	.3	5.4	5.6	6.4	—	.7	.8
Average	.6	.6	.6	6.1	6.2	6.7	—	1.0	1.0
Nordic-Social Dem	3.2	3.6	4.4	6.6	6.4	6.7	—	1.2	1.7
Anglo-Liberal	.4	.4	.6	5.2	5.4	6.1	—	.5	.5
Average-All Nations	1.3	1.4	1.6	6.0	6.0	6.5	—	.8	1.0

[a] Total social welfare expenditures (OECD definition) as a percentage of gross domestic product (See Appendix A).

[b] "Social Wage:" proportion of gross income for the unemployed average production worker replaced by unemployment insurance and compensation, social assistance, and various entitled welfare schemes.

[c] Cash Benefits: total cash transfers for the elderly, disabled, survivors, families, the unemployed, and poor as a percentage of gross domestic product.

[d] West Germany prior to 1991; Unified Germany for 1991 and after.

[e] Italy not included for average social wage.

[f] Social Services: expenditure for government social services for the elderly, disabled, children, and families as a percentage of gross domestic product.

[g] Government health care expenditures as a percentage of gross domestic product.

[h] Active labor market program (e.g., training, placement) expenditures as a percentage of gross domestic product.

(*continued*)

Table 5.1 (continued)

Part C	Public Health Share[i]			Total Taxation[j]			Social Insurance Share[k]		
	1980–4	1985–9	1990–3	1980–4	1985–9	1990–5	1980–4	1985–9	1990–3
Corp Conservative									
Austria	74.4	75.5	73.5	42.1	42.2	42.6	31.4	32.4	33.5
Belgium	83.2	84.5	88.7	45.9	46.6	45.5	30.9	31.8	34.6
France	78.5	75.9	74.6	42.7	44.1	43.9	43.8	43.2	44.1
Germany	78.1	77.2	77.6	37.7	38.0	41.6	35.6	36.7	38.5
Italy	79.2	77.0	76.5	32.9	36.2	41.2	35.4	34.0	32.0
Average	78.2	78.0	78.1	40.3	41.4	42.9	35.4	36.1	36.5
Nordic-Social Dem	88.5	87.4	85.8	45.3	48.6	48.6	17.7	18.0	20.4
Anglo-Liberal	67.3	67.2	66.7	32.3	33.0	32.6	13.9	15.2	16.1
Average-All Nations	78.2	77.6	77.0	39.1	40.6	41.0	25.1	25.7	26.0

Part D	Poverty Reduction[l]			Inequality-Income/Gender[m]			
	Pre-TR	Post-TR	% Ch	Pre-TR	Post-TR	% Ch	Gender
Corp Conservative							
Austria	—	—	—	—	—	—	.414
Belgium	—	—	—	—	—	—	.366
France	36.4	7.9	78	.385	.285	26	.426
Germany	31.0	6.8	78	.417	.241	42	.396
Italy	—	—	—	—	—	—	.391
Average	33.7	7.4	78	.439	.297	29	.391
Nordic-Social Dem	33.6	5.4	84	.401	.263	34	.624
Anglo-Liberal	27.5	12.0	56	.405	.331	18	.554
Average-All Nations	30.6	9.2	68	.412	.300	25	.513

[i] Government health outlays as a percentage of total public and private health outlays.
[j] Total taxation as a percentage of gross domestic product.
[k] Social insurance contributions as a percentage of total taxation.
[l] Percentage of families below the poverty line (defined as 50 percent of adjusted median income) before and after the effects of income transfers.
[m] GINI index of pre- and post-transfer income inequality for the early 1980s; gender inequality is an index of (1) ratio of female to male labor force participation; (2) ratio of male to female unemployment rates; (3) ratio of female to male industrial wages; and (4) female percentage of political economic elites.

Corporatist Conservative Welfare States

As noted above, a distinctive feature of the corporatist conservative welfare state is the relatively heavy reliance on employer and employee social insurance contributions to fund social welfare provision. As Part C of Table 5.1 illustrates, these welfare states have large general tax burdens (on average 41.4 percent of GDP) and raise revenues disproportionately through social insurance contributions: 36.1 percent of all government revenue is raised through social security levies; comparable tax shares are 18.0 and 15.2 percent in the Nordic and Anglo-liberal welfare states, respectively.[5]

As to the impact of the corporatist conservative welfare state on poverty, as well as income and gender inequality, Part D of Table 5.1 illustrates that the average reduction in pretransfer poverty rates through income maintenance is 78 percent. Comparable figures for the social democratic and liberal welfare states are 84 and 56 percent, respectively. A similar outcome is observed for reductions in income inequality: the reduction of the GINI index of income inequality is on average 29 percent in the corporatist conservative cases, and 34 and 18 percent in the Nordic and Anglo welfare states, respectively. Finally, the table illustrates gender equality on average is low in the conservative welfare states. Indeed, this is not surprising given that these welfare states generally organize benefits according to the "breadwinner model" of social protection (c.f., Bussemaker and van Kersbergen [1996]); women's social benefits are largely derived from their status in the family and conservative welfare states offer relatively low levels of social service and related supports for women's labor force participation and earnings (although see case studies).

A Synopsis of Trends in Social Welfare Protection

Examining changes in social protection in the conservative welfare states between the early 1980s and 1990s, one can not avoid being struck by the high levels of stability in most dimensions of welfare provision. Recognizing small rises in social welfare effort in some areas in Austria and Italy, as well as modest reductions in most areas in Belgium, the general pattern is one of surprising continuity. Average shares of GDP for total social

---

[5] Social security contributions by employers have accounted for the majority of social insurance funds although the share is falling: in 1970, employer social security contributions on average amounted to 64 percent of all contributions in the 5 conservative welfare states; in 1994, the share had fallen to 57 percent.

spending, income transfers, social services, and active labor market policies change little. Income replacement rates, public health shares of total health, and social insurance contributions relative to total taxation change only marginally. The most notable shift occurs in government health care, where spending shares of GDP rise in all countries.

However, a variety of programmatic changes have occurred in the context of substantial pressures on the welfare state. Modest reductions in benefits, tighter eligibility, and increased means-testing have been instituted at various junctures in several countries. In addition, increased tax and social security charges, as well as efficiency-oriented reforms, spending caps, and related policy change in health and social service provision have been relatively common. On the other hand, policy makers in conservative welfare states have also enacted new programs (albeit modest in scope and resources) in income maintenance, social services, and labor market policy to address emergent needs (e.g., the growing population of frail elderly) and the social exclusion of marginalized groups. In addition, in 1990s France and 1980s Italy, there is a shift toward more universal benefits financed by general taxation in health care. Country-specific events (e.g., German reunification) have occasionally played substantial roles in the extension of social welfare. What impact has internationalization had on these policy changes in corporatist conservative welfare states?

Internationalization and Policy Change in the Corporatist Conservative Welfare States

The absolute and relative levels and trends in various dimensions of international capital mobility in corporatist conservative nations are displayed in Figures 5.1 and 5.2. As Figure 5.1 illustrates, the presence of state regulations on international capital movements, as indexed by Quinn's index of liberalization of capital controls, has been generally lower (that is, higher liberalization) in the corporatist conservative economies than in the typical developed democracy. A similar picture emerges for covered interest rate differentials. In the case of both formal-legal controls and interest rates, the data displayed in Figure 5.1, especially that for liberalization, suggest a notable increase in international financial integration in the late 1980s and 1990s. These levels and trends in liberalization and interest rate differentials are the same even if the highly open Belgian economy is excluded.

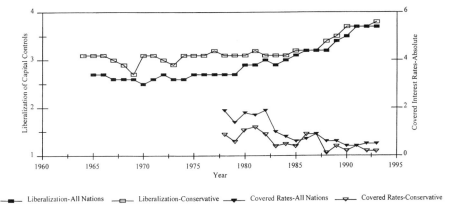

Figure 5.1 Financial Market Integration and Liberalization: All versus Conservative

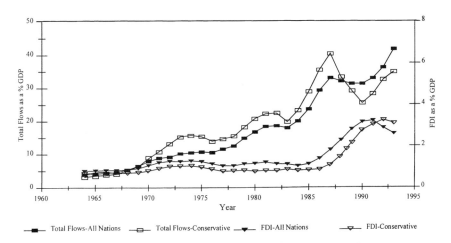

Figure 5.2 Total Flows and FDI: All Nations and Conservative Systems

Figure 5.2 displays levels and trends in two central indicators of the actual magnitude of international capital mobility: total inward and outward movements of capital (i.e., FDI, portfolio investment and bank lending) and the total inflows and outflows of FDI (both as percentages of GDP). As the figure suggests, the magnitude of capital movements in the average corporatist conservative system is modestly higher than the average developed democracy; total capital flows relative to national economic product accelerate in the 1970s and grow even more dramatically in the mid-1980s. The reverse is true for flows of FDI; until the mid-1990s, FDI is modestly lower in the conservative cases and grows notably in magnitude only from the late 1980s.[6] The lower level of FDI is explained by the fact that the Austrian, French, and Italian economies have large public enterprise sectors and attendant constraints on inflows of FDI; Austria has a largely nationally oriented manufacturing sector. Moreover, aspects of the sector-coordinated production regime in some nations (e.g., domestic manufacturing–financial corporate linkages) may also retard international capital flows. Generally, trends in capital flows (and in liberalization and interest rate differentials) tell a similar story in the case of each corporatist conservative nation: capital mobility accelerates most notably from the mid- and late 1980s and continues at high levels in the 1990s.

Globalization and the German Welfare State

The shift in German social policy from expansion to cost containment occurred in the mid-1970s. As Alber (1988) has noted, 81 percent of the 78 major laws governing social protection enacted during the post–World War Two era to 1974 entailed extensions of the welfare state; only 27 percent of the 52 laws enacted between 1975 and 1983 involved welfare expansions, while 56 percent signaled cutbacks (with the remainder devoted to administration).[7] Although the most pronounced efforts to limit welfare expenditure occurred during the 1982–98 Christian Democratic (CDU/CSU)–led governments, initial policies were enacted in the late 1970s and early 1980s under the Social Democrat (SPD)–Free Democrat (FPD) coalition. As such, the shift from notable welfare state expansion in Germany probably began earlier than comparable social policy change in other major European democracies (e.g., Lawson [1996]).

---

[6] Excluding Belgium from the data displayed in Figure 5.2 results in very similar trends but at one-quarter to one-third the levels of FDI and financial capital flows.

[7] German social protection is provided through occupationally based social insurance, which is divided into five "pillars": pensions, health and sickness, injury, unemployment, and (as of 1994) long-term care. Publicly funded and provided social services are relatively modest, as are active labor market programs. Social assistance (*Sozialhilfe*); family and housing allowances, and social housing round out the *Sozialstaat*.

Table 5.2. *Domestic Economic Performance and External Balance in Germany, 1960–1995*

Year	Growth Rate	Unemployment	Inflation	Trade Surplus	Budget Deficit
1960–73	3.7	.8	3.3	1.9	.5
1974–9	2.5	3.4	4.6	2.3	−3.0
1980	.8	3.2	5.4	−.5	−2.9
1981	−.1	4.5	6.3	.8	−3.7
1982	−.5	6.4	4.2	2.4	−3.3
1983	2.3	7.9	3.3	2.0	−2.6
1984	3.4	7.9	2.4	2.5	−1.9
1985	2.6	8.0	2.1	3.1	−1.2
1986	2.5	7.7	−.1	4.5	−1.3
1987	1.6	7.6	.2	4.3	−1.9
1988	3.1	7.6	1.3	4.4	−2.2
1989	2.7	6.9	2.8	4.6	.1
1990	2.3	6.2	2.7	3.3	−2.1
1991	2.0	6.7	3.6	−.1	−3.3
1992	1.4	7.7	5.1	.0	−2.6
1993	−1.8	8.8	4.5	.5	−3.2
1994	2.6	9.6	2.7	.7	−2.4
1995	1.6	9.4	1.8	.8	−3.3

Note: All economic performance indicators apply to West Germany to 1990; from 1991, they apply to the united Germany.

Definition of Variables:

Growth Rate: Annual percentage change in real per capita GDP.

Unemployment: Percentage of civilian labor force unemployed (standard OECD definitions).

Inflation Rate: Annual percentage change in consumer price index.

Trade Surplus: Difference in exports and imports of goods and services as a percentage of GDP.

Budget Deficit: Difference in outlays and receipts for the general government sector as a percentage of GDP.

Source of data: See Appendix A.

Social Policy Change in the 1970s and 1980s. As Table 5.2 illustrates, German growth, unemployment, and inflation rates, as well as fiscal balance, deteriorated after the first OPEC oil shock of 1973–4. The economic environment was further conditioned by the adoption of monetarism and restrictive economic policies by the Bundesbank.[8] After some improvements in economic performance in the late 1970s, inflation accelerated again in the wake of the 1978–9 OPEC oil shock, fiscal deficits remained high, the trade balance deteriorated, and high interest rates in the United States led to capital export (to dollar-denominated instruments) and a declining DM. In the context of these pressures, monetary policy turned decidedly restrictive in 1979.[9] The confluence of these macro-economic conditions placed substantial pressure on fiscal policy in the early 1980s. Economic growth rates turned negative in 1981 and 1982, unemployment soared to over 6 percent, and the nominal deficit for general government rose to nearly 4 percent of GDP in 1981. Overall, these macroeconomic and fiscal pressures provided the immediate impetus for the social policy reforms of the late 1970s and early 1980s.

Beginning with the Budget Structure Act of 1975, and for most years through 1983, German governments pursued moderate cost containment and efficiencies in social welfare provision.[10] In 1975, the budget mandated tighter qualifying conditions for unemployment compensation (*Arbeit-slosengeld*) and new restrictions on unemployment assistance (*Arbeitslosen-hilfe*). In 1977, controls over the duration of unemployment assistance were strengthened and new initiatives were enacted to control both pension and health care costs (e.g., temporary postponement of the index-ation of pension benefits and "concerted action" for efficiencies in health care). In each year from 1978 through 1981, increases for social assistance were held below the inflation rate; in 1981, family allowances were

---

[8] For material on German economic structure, performance, and policy, I rely on Betz (1996); Carlin (1996); Giersch, Paqué, and Schmieding (1992); Hall (1997); Kloten, Ketterer, and Vollmer (1985); Manow and Seils (1999); OECD (various years), *Economic Survey: Germany*; Scharpf (1991); M. Schmidt (1994); and Streeck (1997), as well as numer-ous reports and analyses by Federal Ministries and German interest associations and parties.

[9] As Scharpf (1991) points out, the Bundesbank did not necessarily have to pursue a pro-nounced restrictive policy in order to promote strong and balanced economic perfor-mance. The alternative would have been to allow the DM to fall, thereby generating export growth and resulting positive domestic economic impacts (e.g., on growth, employment, and fiscal imbalance).

[10] In this and subsequent sections, I rely heavily on: Alber (1988, 1996); Clasen (1997); con-tributions to Clasen and Freeman (1994); Clasen and Gould (1995); Döring (1997); Hauser (1995); Hinrichs (1995); Lawson (1996); Manow and Seils (1999); Meyer (1998); Mushaben (1997); OECD (selected years, b), *Economic Surveys: Germany*; Schmähl (1993); Toft (1997); and Wilson (1993), as well as reports and analyses by the Federal Ministries, interest associations, and political parties.

reduced, co-payments for several health care services were increased, cuts in unemployment benefits were made, and contribution rates for unemployment insurance were increased.

In a program of fiscal consolidation for the 1982 budget, family allowances, housing benefits, and social assistance payments were restricted.[11] In addition, co-payments for medical services and unemployment contribution rates were further increased and a number of job creation programs were scaled back or eliminated. The SPD-FPD government initiated (in 1982) an additional program for 1983 fiscal consolidation that included substantial cost containment measures; many of these measures, adopted and strengthened by the CDU/CSU–FPD government that took office in September 1982, formed the basis of the 1983 austerity program. Small adjustments to pension benefits and tighter qualifying conditions for invalidity pensions were enacted. Family allowance, social assistance, and unemployment benefits were limited. Finally, cash sickness benefits became subject to contributions to the pension and unemployment funds and, in turn, were effectively lowered.

Overall, mid-1970s to early 1980s social policy reforms in Germany resulted in no structural changes in the corporatist conservative model of welfare provision. Pension benefits were lower than they would otherwise have been, although they kept pace with wage growth (Alber, 1988). New emphases on efficiency and increased co-payments were implemented in health care, and sickness benefits were indirectly reduced; however, the health "pillar" was not structurally altered and retained a redistributive character (Hinrichs, 1995).The most notable rollbacks of social provision occurred in the areas of unemployment benefits and social assistance; yet many of these retrenchments were moderate in character and effectively reversed during the mid- and late 1980s (see below).

The German economy performed well on most indicators of economic performance in the years from 1984 to 1989. As Table 5.2 illustrates, economic growth, inflation, and, most notably, the trade surplus improved between 1984 and 1990. As Betz (1996), Streeck (1997), and others have argued, Germany engaged in significant export-oriented economic modernization during the 1980s, reinforcing its commitment to "diversified quality production" of upscale manufacturing goods. As most observers note, however, the one blemish on Germany's economic

---

[11] Within the SPD-FPD government, the Free Democrats pressed for a shift to supply-side policies to enhance business investment and work effort; FPD proposals included significant spending cuts.

performance during this period is the persistence of relatively high unemployment rates. Although unemployment subsequently declined from its high of 8 percent of the workforce in 1985, it remained above 6 percent until accelerating with the structural shocks attendant on unification (e.g., the privatization of enterprises in the former East Germany).[12]

German social policy change during the remainder of the 1980s was marked by both a continuation of cost-oriented restructuring and a series of extensions of social protection that addressed new needs and the burdens of structural adjustment. Despite neoliberal commitments to end overreliance on entitlements, restore individual responsibility and initiative, and promote market efficiency (embodied in the *Wende*, or "turnaround"), the 1980s Center-Right governments led by Chancellor Helmut Kohl pursued a social welfare policy of moderate cost containment and partial restructuring. In health care, 1985 and 1989 Health Reform Acts instituted moderate cost control measures (e.g., reforms limited insurance coverage to predetermined costs in some areas), increased patient co-payments for certain services, and encouraged preventive care. In the area of social housing, the 1980s Center-Right governments followed a well established OECD-wide trend of shifting from the subsidization of the production of social housing to reliance on means-tested housing allowances.

However, the most significant reform of the Sozialstaat during this period occurred with the 1989 pension reform (to be implemented as the Pension Reform Law of 1992). Explicitly motivated by adverse demographic predictions and the desire to hold pension contribution rates down (e.g., Schmähl [1993]), the 1992 Act tightened eligibility for pensions under special circumstances (e.g., unemployment among older workers) and adopted the net-wage (as apposed to gross wage) adjustment principle for determining benefits. It also increased the retirement age to a unified 65 years for men and women (as of 2001); the effective retirement age had been 60 and 65 years of age for women and men, respectively (with flexible retirement for men at 63). On the revenue side, the reform limited federal supplements to the pension fund and mandated pension contribu-

---

[12] See Giersch, Paqué, and Schmieding (1992) for a critical assessment of the capacity of the German model to cope with unemployment and other economic problems. These authors present the largely neoliberal indictment of the impacts of structural rigidities (e.g., labor market regulation), welfare state costs, and flaws in the industrial relations system. For more positive yet cautious assessments (emphasizing, among other factors, the comparative advantage of Germany's coordinated market economy), see Carlin (1996), Hall (1997), Manow and Seils (1999), and Streeck (1997).

tions for the unemployed. These reforms in health, housing, and pensions, along with modest or unsuccessful efforts to tighten program eligibility (e.g., for disability pensions) constitute the major cost containment and market-oriented reforms of the 1984–9 period.

Concomitant with these measures, a number of extensions of social protection occurred. In 1984, the Pre-Retirement Act liberalized early retirement provisions and the duration of unemployment benefits were extended from 12 to 32 months for older workers. Moreover, between 1985 and 1988, spending for active labor market programs and social assistance was increased. As the result of a ruling by the Constitutional Court declaring an investment-oriented tax on high income earners unconstitutional, the Kohl government was pressured to increase support for the lower-income strata; benefits for social assistance, which had recently been held below inflation, were increased from 1985 (through 1992) to 1970s real levels (Alber, 1996). In addition, new education allowances were established, parental leave rights were legislated, and child-rearing benefits initiated; in the 1992 pension law, pension credits for time spent in child rearing were expanded and pension benefits for low-income workers improved. Overall, one might argue that German social policy change during the mid- to late 1980s involved as many modest extensions as it did limited retrenchments. However, with formal reunification of a divided Germany in 1990, the German Sozialstaat entered of period of dramatic new challenges.

Social Policy Change in the Post-Unification Era. Generally, German unification created significant new pressures on the German Sozialstaat.[13] With the privatization of state-owned enterprises, roughly 40 percent of employment was lost in the former East Germany (e.g., OECD [selected years, b]). The financial burdens of this unemployment, as well as direct privatization costs, infrastructure modernization, and the transfer of the social insurance pillars to the East were substantial: the annual costs of German unification have consistently been estimated in the range of 4–6 percent of the former West German Gross Domestic Product (e.g., BMF [1996]; IMF [1995]; OECD [selected years, b]; M. Schmidt [1994]). Public

---

[13] Unless otherwise noted, figures for economic performance in this section are taken from the International Monetary Fund's (1995) synoptic analysis of the "economics of unification." Additional characterizations and interpretations are taken from those sources referenced in earlier notes and cited material.

sector borrowing increased substantially, as did new taxes: the VAT was increased (from 14 to 15 percent), a 7.5 percent surcharge on income tax liabilities was intermittently levied, and social insurance contributions were raised (see below). In addition, annual price rises began to accelerate in the post-1989 period, reaching 5.1 percent annually in 1992.[14] In response to accelerating inflation, generally, and labor's strong wage demands and rising government spending and deficits specifically, the Bundesbank shifted monetary policy in a decidedly restrictive direction. While growth was still positive in the East, the overall economy was thrown into a recession in 1993: real GDP declined 1.8 percent and unemployment rose to 8.8 percent.

In the context of these macroeconomic pressures, burdens of unification, and other domestic and international forces, several initiatives were taken in the 1990s to roll back the costs of the German welfare state.[15] The first major effort took the form of the 1993 "Solidarity Pact," or the 1993 Federal Consolidation Program. While much of this program focused on general government finance, the Solidarity Pact was accompanied by the 1993 Federal Assistance Act and the "second stage" of health care reform in 1993 (following the 1989 reform). After growth in the real value of Sozialhilfe from the mid-1980s to early 1990s, the 1993 social assistance law fixed the rate of growth in benefit levels in advance (irrespective of real wage growth and inflation). It also mandated that, from 1996 on, the amount of the basic benefit and housing allowance provided by social assistance could not exceed the average earnings of a low-income worker. The 1993 health reform increased co-payments for drugs and dentures, fixed health fund reimbursements for some drugs and various

---

[14] Fueled by high wage demands in 1991 and 1992, the rise in the price level in the Eastern *Länder* (as measured by the GDP deflator) was 16.6 percent in 1991 and 18.2 percent in 1992. As many observers have noted (e.g., M. Schmidt 1994), while the transfer of the German model of high-wage and high-quality production to the East was fraught with problems (also see Streeck [1997]), labor in the East – supported by national trade union leaders – pursued a dramatic increase in wage levels in the early 1990s. From the perspective of Western unions, such a strategy also worked to stem labor migration from East to West.

[15] Particularly important were the pressures to maintain or lessen social insurance contribution rates in order to alleviate "tax wedge" effects on employment growth and to lower nonwage costs of employers. As I discuss below, concerns about international competitiveness and the (dis)advantages Germany offers as a location for business investment (the Standort problem) became factors in the formation of social policy in the 1990s.

treatments, and effectively capped budgets (by limiting spending to fund revenues through 1995).[16]

One of the most significant reforms of the German Sozialstaat of the early to mid-1990s was the 1994 Saving, Consolidation, and Growth Act. This legislation included direct and indirect reductions in child benefits, housing allowances, and student grants (and other domestic programs). At the center of the act's social welfare cuts was a reduction in unemployment benefits and new restrictions on duration of benefits. Specifically, the act reduced the income replacement rate for the unemployment insurance benefit from 63 and 68 percent of earnings (for those without and with children, respectively) to 60 and 67 percent of earnings; comparable changes in unemployment assistance benefits moved replacement rates to 53 and 57 percent. In addition, a series of measures were enacted in the mid-1990s that either raised contributions or further reduced benefit levels or eligibility in some areas. For instance, the 1996 budget raised pension contributions from 18.6 to 19.2 percent of earnings; in 1995, the maximum duration for unemployment benefits to older workers was cut from 32 to 24 months.

However, a number of initiatives of Kohl's Center-Right government to legislate even more significant rollbacks of social welfare spending were withdrawn or defeated. In 1995, a measure that would have extended and strengthened the 1993 reductions in Sozialhilfe was rejected by the (SPD-controlled) Bundesrat. In 1996, the Program for Growth and Employment proposed a reduction in the (employer-paid) first six weeks of sick pay from 100 to 80 percent of current earnings. This proposed measure drew withering criticism from the unions and Left parties; it also led to an anti-plan protest by 350,000 citizens in Bonn. After extensive negotiations, the measure was passed so as to allow for sick pay income replacement of 80 percent, if agreed to in private employee-employer bargaining. However, in practice most workers have continued to receive 100 percent sick pay (e.g., Clasen [1997]; Manow and Seils [1999]).

---

[16] The act also initiated the practice of cross-subsidization of health funds where transfers from funds with low risk beneficiaries to funds with high-risk members would be allowed. More controversial provisions, such as those for setting individual health care contributions by health risks of citizens and full scale choice and competition between the 1,100 health funds, were not legislated in the new act and were intensely debated through the mid-1990s. Hinrichs (1995) argues that these measures, if fully adopted, along with cross-fund subsidization, risk undercutting the egalitarian character of German health insurance.

Despite political opposition, other aspects of the 1996 Program and related legislation were enacted (with the ultimate consent of the unions and SPD). In 1996, the government and social partners agreed on a plan for restricting the flow of older workers into early retirement pensions. Social assistance work requirements were further tightened (i.e., a 25-percent benefit reduction when suitable employment was refused). In addition, as part of the general initiatives to improve work incentives, recipients of social assistance were allowed to combine six months of wages with receipt of benefits. Unemployment assistance benefits were also (further) reduced by a change in the method of calculating benefits. Finally, the Pension Reform Act of 1999, one of the most significant and contested reforms of the contemporary period, was passed in 1997 and contained significant reductions in benefits and eligibility; however, after the 1998 Bundestag elections and the formation of the SPD-Green government, the 1997 law was rescinded.[17]

Welfare Expansions. Despite the significance of some of the aforementioned reforms, the German welfare state was also expanded during the 1990s. First, the Sozialstaat was transferred virtually in toto to the East (e.g., Hauser [1995]; Mangen [1994]; and M. Schmidt [1994]). Indeed, one might argue that much of the subsidization of mass unemployment in the East was provided by the social welfare system. As Manow and Seils (1999) point out, the West German unemployment compensation system was transplanted to the East and the unemployment system funds of East and West were merged. An unemployment fund surplus in the West (DM 117 billion) and an increase in unemployment contribution rates from 4.3 to 6.8 percent of wages in 1991 financed unemployment benefits; generous provisions for part-time work (for roughly two million workers), extensions of early retirement benefits (for 400,000), and active labor market programs further cushioned the blow of significant rises in joblessness.[18]

---

[17] The major provisions of the act include reform and tightening of the provisions for qualification for disability pensions and tightening eligibility for early retirement for older unemployed and part-time workers; in 2012 these early retirement options would have been abolished. In addition, and most significant, the 1999 Pension Reform Act incorporated life expectancy into the calculation of benefits. As a result, average retirement benefits would have been reduced as life expectancy increases (e.g., from 70 to 64 percent of net wages for those with 45 years of contributions; see Schiltz [1998]).

[18] The pension system was also transferred on relatively generous terms with the effect of raising the pension level of employees and dependents in the Eastern Länder (compared

In addition, the German social welfare state has also been expanded in limited ways to address new needs and economic stress in the West. Pension reform acts actually strengthened guarantees and generosity of child-rearing credits. As a result of rulings in 1990 and 1992 by the Constitutional Court, tax credits and family allowances were improved to insure that the post-tax income of poorer families reached the subsistence level. In 1992, the right to a nursery school was made universal (to be implemented in 1996). In addition, there were modest extensions of active labor market policy to buffer workers in the West from recession and the costs of unification.[19] Finally, a fifth "pillar" was added to the German system of social insurance. Directly motivated by rising needs and the fiscal strain on Sozialhilfe of long-term care costs, and emerging in the context of relatively intense conflict over program structure, the Long-Term Care Insurance Act of 1994 created a new social insurance program for the costs of caring for citizens requiring long-term residential or institutional medical care.[20]

In sum, the post-Unification period is characterized by both cost containing and efficiency-oriented reforms and extensions of social welfare protection. What role has globalization played in post-1970 German social policy change? As a result of the accumulation of policy reforms, has the welfare state moved toward a market-conforming model of social protection under international pressure, as predicted by globalization theory? I now turn to these questions.

to the former East German system). As Manow and Seils (1999) note, the pension funds for West and East were merged two years earlier than planned (1992) when the deficit in the Eastern Länder was DM 75 billion and the surplus in the fund for the West was DM 71 billion (and pension contribution rates were increased from 18.7 to 20.3 percent of earnings between 1990 and 1997).

[19] As a result of the confluence of economic conditions and the restrictive policies of the Bundesbank, the DM had appreciated in the early 1990s and enterprises engaged in significant labor shedding; this, in combination with the 1993 recession and general upward pressures on unemployment, created substantial pressure to devote more resources to combat general and long-term unemployment in the West.

[20] The program provides financial support (formally as direct cash transfers to the citizen) for in-home medical care (implemented in 1995) and institutional care (implemented in 1996). It is financed by employee and employer social insurance contributions of 1.7 percent of earnings (1.0 in 1995, and 1.7 in 1996 and thereafter). However, reflecting the contemporary political economic pressures on the Sozialstaat, expenditures are directly limited to the growth of contributions and employers are compensated for their contribution. In the final compromise before passage of the law, workers gave up one paid holiday to offset new employer costs.

The Impact of International Capital on German Social Policy Change.
As observers have noted (e.g., V. Schmidt [1999]), the German economy
for decades has had a high level of exposure to international markets.
Reflecting the strong export orientation of manufacturing, Germany has
consistently registered a relatively high level of trade openness (exports
and imports as shares of GDP averaged 47.7 percent in the years from
1990 to 1995). Second, the international orientation of the German
economy is also reflected in the relatively high level of liberalization of
capital controls. As illustrated in Table 5.3, restrictions on financial flows
were completely liberalized in the post-1980 era. However, with respect
to actual international movements of capital, Germany has long experienced relatively low levels of FDI and financial capital flows; actual capital
movements have generally remained at 50–60 percent of the average for
the developed democracies. As Table 5.3 suggests, after modest growth in
the early 1980s, all forms of financial flows increased appreciably after
1985. As in the case of many European countries, the expansion of German
capital flows from 1985 onward commonly reflects (the post–Single
Europe Act) efforts of German manufacturing and financial enterprises to
position themselves for the advent of the integrated European market at
the end of 1991.[21] In the 1990s, there was some contraction in outward
FDI, modest growth in international bank activity, and significant expansion of borrowing on international capital markets (all influenced by the
financial requirements of unification).

Can this pattern of expansion of capital mobility be directly and systematically linked to neoliberal reforms of the German welfare state?
To simplify analysis of this question, it is useful to consider the impact of
international capital mobility across the three stages in economic performance and policy change I have discussed above: the mid-1970s–early
1980s period of post-OPEC economic performance problems; the 1984–9
period of improving economic performance and modernization, and the
post-Unification era of the 1990s. With regard to the first phase of welfare
state cost containment, it is hard to make the case that rises in international capital mobility directly contributed to the initial wave of social
policy reforms. While the final liberalization of capital controls occurred
in 1981, most forms of capital flows did not increase appreciably in the

---

[21] For instance, the lion's share of German outward foreign direct investment bound for
Europe (or the United States) is oriented to marketing, service, and other supports for
German exports in new or expanding markets (OECD selected years, b).

Table 5.3. *International Capital Mobility for Germany, 1960–1995*

Year	Absence of Capital Controls[a]	Borrowing on Capital Markets[b]	FDI Inflows[c]	FDI Outflows	International Banking[d]	Corporate Capitalization[e]
1960–73	3.9	.05	.5	.3	10.6	2.2
1974–9	3.8	.06	.3	.5	11.1	3.2
1980	3.5	.02	.1	.5	13.5	2.3
1981	4.0	.05	.1	.6	—	—
1982	4.0	.20	.1	.4	—	—
1983	4.0	.42	.3	.5	—	—
1984	4.0	.31	.1	.7	—	—
1985	4.0	.51	.1	.8	14.5	2.5
1986	4.0	1.32	.1	1.1	—	—
1987	4.0	.88	.2	.8	—	—
1988	4.0	.98	.1	1.0	—	—
1989	4.0	.98	.6	1.2	—	—
1990	4.0	.64	.2	1.5	18.3	4.8
1991	4.0	1.01	.2	1.4	—	—
1992	4.0	1.09	.1	1.0	18.2	2.2
1993	4.0	2.45	.1	.8	20.3	2.4
1994	4.0	2.29	.1	.8	19.9	4.2
1995	4.0	3.63	.4	1.4	20.8	5.6

[a] Absence of Capital Controls: 1–4 Scale (see Chapter 2) where 4 indicates a complete absence of capital controls.

[b] Borrowing on Capital Markets: Total borrowing through international and foreign bonds, international bank and bank consortiums, issuance of equities, and miscellaneous financial securities as a percentage of GDP (OECD [1996] definition of international capital markets.)

[c] FDI Inflows/Outflows: Foreign direct investment inward flows and outward flows as a percentage of GDP.

[d] International Banking: International liabilities (e.g., borrowing) and lending (e.g., assets) of the banking sector as a percentage of total bank assets and liabilities; values for 1960–73 and 1974–9 are for 1970 and 1975, respectively.

[e] Corporate Capitalization: Share of nonfinancial corporate sector finance accounted for by equities; values for 1960–73 and 1974–9 are for 1970 and 1975, respectively.

Source for data: See Appendix A, except for international banking and corporate capitalization data, which are from Deutche Bundesbank and are given in Table 0 of OECD, *OECD Economic Surveys, 1995–1996: Germany.*

late 1970s and early 1980s. It is the case, however, that international financial flows did contribute indirectly to the initial round of social policy reforms. Specifically, in the wake of the collapse of the Breton Woods system, flows of short-term capital among currencies tended to exacerbate domestic economic problems and fiscal stress. In the case of Germany, this development began in 1979 when the U.S. Federal Reserve shifted to restrictive monetary policy. This policy shift, coupled with the effects of expanding U.S. deficits, resulted in high U.S. interest rates and a concomitant depreciation of the DM (e.g., Scharpf [1991]). As discussed above, the depreciation of the DM reinforced the shift of the Bundesbank to especially restrictive monetary policies in the early 1980s. This, in turn, intensified the budget imbalances that stand as the proximate cause of early-1980s fiscal consolidation programs.

In the mid- and late 1980s, flows of international capital mobility increased noticeably (see Table 5.3). Moreover, during this period the export-oriented modernization of the German economy, combined with accelerating European Community trade integration, increased the already high trade openness of Germany. However, while the economic logic of globalization suggests we should see some acceleration of neoliberal reforms (e.g., formal neoliberal restructuring to maintain and attract capital), there was actually a rough balance of moderate cost containment measures on the one hand, and extensions of the welfare state on the other. As discussed above, many of the retrenchments of the mid- and late 1980s were oriented to controlling health care costs and adverse impacts of demographics on the pension system. In addition, most observers agree that these reforms were also directed at holding down contribution rates in order to alleviate tax wedge effects on employment and the political problems associated with projected future tax increases (e.g., Clasen [1997]). Moreover, many of the extensions of social protection (e.g., early retirement and unemployment coverage for older workers) appear to be direct compensations for the dislocations of export-oriented modernization (and inability of the German economic model to create new jobs).

Generally, as noted above, much of the additional capital mobility can be linked (in terms of timing and substance) to the expansion of European integration and exports, generally. While concerns over the economic impacts of insurance contribution rates and overall welfare state costs on domestic investment, profitability, and employment played a large role in social policy reform, the *Standortdebatte* had not begun in earnest. That is, debates over the need to improve Germany as a location of investment and to promote international competitiveness – prominent in the 1990s – are not central to welfare state conflicts during the earlier period.[22]

In the early and mid-1990s, liberalization of capital mobility and financial integration remained high, as it had for much of the last 25 years. International bank activity increased moderately and borrowing on international capital markets accelerated on pace with the financial costs associated with unification. After peaking in 1990, FDI outflows remained relatively constant – around 1 percent of GDP through the mid-1990s (and inflows of FDI remained relatively marginal, as they had for much of the last 25 years). During the early and mid-1990s, however, there is some evidence that FDI outflows increasingly involved the international movement of production facilities in search of lower labor costs (and other advantages): German producers of textiles, clothing, leather goods, and chemicals all moved some production outside Germany (e.g., OECD [selected years, b]; Manow and Seils [1999]). Yet, examined alone, this relatively moderate increase in international capital mobility over 1980s levels can not explain the vigorous renewal of efforts at cost containment and welfare state retrenchment that occurred in the 1990s.

On the other hand, it is arguably the case that the interaction of globalization with fiscal stress provided the real impetus for the efforts at retrenchment of the German Sozialstaat in the 1990s (e.g., Borchert [1996]; Clasen [1997]; Hauser [1995]). The palpable rise in the long-term level of unemployment in Germany, coupled with demands generated by rises in health care costs and adverse demographic forces (rising life expectancy and declining fertility), had placed substantial cost pressures on the German welfare state before unification. With unification, these cost pressures were multiplied significantly. In addition, not only did these developments contribute to fiscal imbalance, they also fueled a rise in social insurance contribution rates: the combined employer and employee rate rose from 32 percent in 1980 to 41 percent in 1996. In this context,

---

[22] Analyses of the German economy and welfare state in the 1980s by the OECD as well as the Ministries of Finance and Economics and Bundesbank commonly highlighted the impacts of health care costs, demographics, and higher general and long-term unemployment rates on welfare state costs and the impact of these expenses on general profit and investment levels and, in turn, employment. Concerns over nonwage labor costs and trade competitiveness were occasionally stressed, although it is not until the early 1990s that arguments about Germany's international competitiveness and suitability as a location for business investment come to the forefront of debates in the economic and social policy communities. See annual surveys of Germany by the OECD (selected years, b) and the academic and government analyses cited therein.

the Standortdebatte takes on much greater salience and arguments emphasizing the deterioration in the environment for (internationally mobile) business investment take on more plausibility among political actors and the mass electorate.

At the same time, the character as well as relatively modest levels and growth rates of international capital flows in Germany in the 1990s suggest that the political logic of globalization (and not the weight of economic imperatives) is the most important aspect of the linkages between globalization and welfare state reform. As Hinrichs (1995) points out, globalization has undergirded the political mobilization of employers for more extensive welfare state reforms, and this mobilization is particularly pronounced after the Center-Right victory in the 1994 Bundestag election and the accumulation of the costs of unification. Related, Manow and Seils (1999) point out that the employment impacts of international capital mobility are moderate, at best, and that the real impact of globalization has probably been to enhance the credibility of the exit option of capital. These points are underscored by the social policy positions and actions of the employers. For instance, in a major analysis of the problems of German social welfare policy in 1994 (Confederation of German Employers' Associations [BDA], 1994), German employers called for a series of reforms of the German Sozialstaat, including a number of neoliberal policies, such as increased emphases on targeting, some privatization and market competition in service provision, possible benefit reductions, and limits to income redistribution, urging legislators "to act in good time." In the document, the BDA emphasized the important consequences of the interaction of demographic trends and global economic change and, in turn, the adverse effects of the current and future costs of the Sozialstaat on investment and work effort, international competitiveness, and business location.[23]

In addition, some observers have stressed the additional weight accorded general neoliberal arguments for welfare state retrenchment in Germany generated by internationalization of capital (e.g., Clasen and

---

[23] While only 10 percent of German FDI outflows went to the formerly Communist economies in Eastern Europe in the 1990s and much of this is related to facilitating new markets for German exports (OECD selected years, b), the BDA has also emphasized that Eastern Europe not only offers the opportunity for low-wage production, but that the infrastructure and human capital of Eastern Europe can support German high-quality manufacturing (Interview, BDA, Cologne, December 1996). Here and in subsequent pages I cite observations made in a series of interviews I conducted in December 1996 in Bonn, Cologne, and Düsseldorf with all major political parties, key Federal Ministries (Finance, Economics, and Labor and Social Affairs), and the social partners (BDA and DGB).

Gould [1995]; Hinrichs [1995]). Examining the Center-Right government's policy analyses and statements advocating or concretely proposing economic and social policy reforms in the 1990s, it is clear that the CDU/CSU government increasingly justified general neoliberal economic and welfare state reforms on the basis of the need to improve the investment environment and international competitiveness of Germany.[24] For instance, in a major policy analysis released in 1996, the Ministry of Finance emphasized the large impact of the costs of unification on the expansion of the public economy and welfare state, yet went on to argue:

On the other hand, the negative economic and social consequences of an overextended public sector are independent of the causes of such development. . . . For companies engaged in tough competition it is immaterial whether taxes and contributions rise because of misdirected policy decisions or because of welcome national events. They will respond in either case by reducing investments, laying off workers or relocating production. This trend is aggravated by the increasing globalization of markets and the emergence of large, regional economic areas (such as EU, NAFTA, and ASEAN). For this reason, too, the state must cut back, no matter how urgently the funds are needed by the public sector (BMF, 1996: 29).

The importance of the political logic of globalization is also illustrated by the degree to which international capital mobility (and trade competitiveness) is emphasized by the major social policy actors that contested the larger reforms of the German Sozialstaat. As discussed above, the employers have emphasized the imperatives created by globalization, and its interaction with forces such as demographic trends, in calling for a series of neoliberal reforms. Aside from the Social Christian wing, the governing Center-Right parties have consistently highlighted the need to pursue significant neoliberal restructuring in order to maintain and attract investment and to promote the competitiveness of German exports. On the other hand, the SPD and the unions, while acknowledging the challenges of globalization, have largely rejected the position that international capital mobility and general trade openness require substantial neoliberal

---

[24] It is important to note that the commonly understood heterogeneity of the CDU/CSU is also manifest during this period. The "Social Christian" wing of the party, most directly represented by the Catholic workers faction in the Bundestag (CDA) and by pro-worker Ministers, such as Nobert Blum at Labor and Social Affairs, has generally adopted a more modest position on the depth and extent of neoliberal reforms than the rest of the party. For instance, while acknowledging the importance of globalization pressures and the necessity of examining all areas of the Sozialstaat for potential savings, the CDA has not supported real benefit reductions for core pillars of social insurance (Interview, CDA Faction, Bonn, December 1996).

reforms.[25] For instance, in its 1994 and 1998 election manifestoes, the SPD advocated a multifaceted approach to globalization that emphasizes the strengths and opportunities of the German economy with regard to the growing internationalization of markets. The party has also stressed that international policy coordination (e.g., through the EU, WTO, G-7) is needed to promote currency stability and low interest rates, as well as retard tax competition and social dumping. In fact, the SPD and the unions have explicitly rejected the need or feasibility of competing with economies with low labor costs through cuts in wages or through significant reductions in nonwage costs (Interviews, SPD, Bonn; DGB, Düsseldorf, both December 1996).[26]

Overall, this survey of the ways in which globalization has affected the reforms of the German Sozialstaat over the last two decades leads to a small, but relatively clear, set of conclusions. First, there is little evidence that rises in international capital mobility have directly and systematically caused cost containment and efficiency-oriented reforms of the German Sozialstaat. There is support, however, for the view that internationalization of capital matters in that it interacts with episodes of fiscal stress to reinforce domestic pressures for cost containment and retrenchments and that the political logic of globalization has grown more important in 1990s welfare politics. From the perspective of the mid- to late 1990s, have the cumulative policy changes initiated a dismantling (*Abbau*) of the German welfare state, where one can perceive movement to a market-conforming system of social protection? Or, is it more accurate to

---

[25] So, too, have the Greens, who have emphasized a series of environmental-oriented energy taxes and other environmental protections, as well as maintenance of generous levels of social benefits and a variety of policies to combat social exclusion and improve the position of women in the labor market and in the welfare state (see the 1994 and 1998 Green Party Election Manifestoes).

[26] Instead, the SPD, largely with union support has called for a series of supply- and demand-side policies consisting primarily of significant resource commitments to education, training, and public infrastructure, as well as policies to encourage investment and employment in high-technology industries (e.g., research and development supports, reductions in company taxes). They have also stressed the need to reduce tax burdens on workers. At the same time, the SPD (with strong support from the Greens) has also advocated improvements in family benefits, as well as reforms of labor market regulations and social policy provisions that enhance female labor force participation and gender rights. Finally, the SPD and Greens have advocated the development of a universal means-tested social minimum benefit within the social insurance system that would obviate the need of low-income pensioners and other social aggregates to rely on stigmatized social assistance. Again, globalization has not been viewed as a systematic restraint on maintenance or limited expansion of the welfare state.

Table 5.4. *Change and Continuity in the German Welfare State in Comparative Perspective*

	Germany	Sweden	Britain
Unemployment Gross Earnings Replacement Rate for Production Worker at:			
100 Percent Average: 1981	38.0	71.5	27.8
1995	35.0	74.5	17.4
66 Percent Average: 1981	40.7	90.2	38.3
1995	37.0	90.0	26.1
Net Replacement Rate (married couple, one earner, two children):			
Unemployment: 1994	71.0	83.0	58.0
Social Assistance: 1994	71.0	107.0	58.0
Social Insurance Contributions (% of Total Taxes Collected)			
1980: Total	34.3	28.8	16.6
Employees	15.8	.1	6.4
Employers	18.4	27.6	10.1
1996: Total	40.6	29.8	17.3
Employees	17.6	4.5	7.2
Employers	20.5	24.9	9.6
Private Social Welfare (as percentage of total):			
1995	8.4	6.9	16.8

Source of data: Gross Unemployment Earnings Replacement Rates are from OECD *Unemployment Replacement Rate Data Base* (Paris: OECD, 1996); Net Unemployment and Social Assistance Replacement Rates are from Hansen (1998); Social Insurance Contributions are from OECD, *Revenue Statistics 1960–1996* (Paris: OECD, 1997); and Private Social Welfare Share (Voluntary and mandatory private risk insurance and services) is from Adema (1999).

characterize German social policy change as restructuring (*Umbau*), where reforms address pressures, but preserve basic principles and levels of social protection?

Abbau versus Umbau? At first glance, it might be tempting to argue that the German welfare state has been on the slippery slope of dismantlement by degrees; however, the evidence does not seem to support that conclusion. A relatively comprehensive (and comparative) perspective on German social policy change can be obtained by examining the patterns in measures of social protection and welfare state structure in Table 5.4. The first panel of the table displays changes between 1981 and 1995 in the gross income replacement from unemployment benefits for single workers at 100 and 66 percent of the average production worker's earnings. As the table indicates, while there has been a modest reduction in German replacement rates, those cuts do not approach the degree of retrenchment in the British case, and the overall position of Germany is roughly unchanged (compared to a typical Social Democratic and largely liberal welfare state). The second panel draws on 1994 data on net income replacement rates for unemployment and social assistance benefits (including family and housing allowances) from Hansen (1998); the table displays the replacement rates for married couples with two children (one earner). Germany's relatively generous benefits place it moderately behind Social Democratic Sweden and appreciably ahead of the United Kingdom.

The bottom panels of the table display trends and levels in financial structure of the welfare state and the role of private benefits in total social protection. While both Social Democratic Sweden and largely liberal Britain register moderate levels of reliance on social insurance contributions with small increases of insurance contributions as shares of total taxes, Germany clearly continues to rely on the social insurance mode of financing. In fact, this reliance on social insurance contributions (as shares of total taxation) increases over time. In Germany as well as in Sweden and the United Kingdom, employee contributions have risen in importance between 1980 and 1996, but in Germany so have employers' social insurance contributions (relative to total taxes). In addition, the reliance on private social welfare schemes (e.g., employer-provided health and retirement benefits) is relatively low: private insurance and other benefits constitute less than 10 percent of all German (and Swedish) social spending in the mid-1990s, while private benefits constitute 16.8 percent of social outlays in Britain (with much higher percentages in the other Anglo-liberal welfare states).

Generally, these patterns suggest little structural change in the German welfare state and only modest declines in generosity through the mid-1990s. In fact, one might conclude that the reform of the German welfare state, shaped by the variety of political economic dynamics discussed above (including indirect and episodic globalization pressures), can be characterized as moderate restructuring with maintenance of basic principles and relatively generous levels of social protection (also see Clasen and Gould [1995]; Lawson [1996]; Toft [1997]). While the continuing costs of unification, the pressures of sustained high unemployment, and needs and demands of a variety of groups continue to place substantial pressure on the German Sozialstaat, there is still little evidence of Abbau (dismantling) or the emergence of a German neoliberal welfare state.[27]

[27] See Manow and Seils (1999) for a detailed discussion of late 1990s prospects for the German economy and welfare state.

Global Markets and the French Welfare State

The contemporary era of welfare state reform in France begins in the late 1970s.[28] As post-1973 French economic performance deteriorated, macro-economic policy under the 1974–6 Chirac government was reflationary; as a consequence of this policy stance and increased demands, social expenditure accelerated in the mid-1970s. However, macroeconomic policy became progressively more restrictive and the control of social costs became much more prominent in the Barre Center-Right government of 1976–81. Although no major welfare state retrenchments occurred during these years, a variety of modest expenditure controls and revenue enhancements were initiated. For instance, various efficiency measures were introduced in the health care sector (e.g., experimental efforts at "global budgeting" for hospitals).[29]

After the Socialist ascendance to power in 1981, the French welfare state experienced a brief yet dramatic period of expansion as the goal of greater social protection was linked to growth and employment-oriented economic policy ("Keynesianism in one country"). The early 1980s expansion of the French welfare state was substantial. The minimum wage (SMIC) was increased by 55 percent (with repercussions for subsequent welfare reform), a fifth week of paid vacation was added, and the work week was reduced to 39 hours. The minimum income support for elderly without sufficient pensionable contributions (*minimum vieillesse*) was increased substantially: support for the lone aged increased 65 percent and assistance to a married couple was expanded by 51 percent. The Socialists also lowered the retirement age to 60 from 65 years of age, establishing full pension rights for those with 37.5 years of employment.[30] In addition,

---

[28] For material in this section, I rely on contributions to Ambler (1991), Bonoli and Palier (1998), Bouget (1998), Hantrais (1996), OECD (selected years, a), Palier (1997), and miscellaneous government reports and analyses. I cite further works below.

[29] During the years of the Barre government, economic performance improved as growth rebounded and the general government deficit moved toward balance. However, unemployment continued to inch upwards, inflation increased, and the social security budget balance deteriorated. As a result of these conditions and the ascendance of neoliberal orthodoxy, control of social costs was emphasized. At the same time, one can identify some extensions of social protection during this period, such as expansion of family and early retirement benefits.

[30] This policy was implemented in 1983 and in effect contained provisions that slowly reduced pensionable amounts for early retirees from 1983 onward. In essence, the new retirement plan replaced the *garantie de ressources*, a de facto early retirement program that had guaranteed 70 percent of salary to unemployed workers between 60 and 65 years of age.

resources for housing and ALMP programs were expanded. In the area of family policy, basic allowances were increased by 25 percent and supplements for lone parents, housing, and other special benefits were enhanced; in 1985, paid leave for the birth and care of a third child was introduced. However, the Socialists shifted family policy away from support of larger (often affluent) families: supports for the second child were increased while those to the third reduced, a ceiling was placed on child tax deductions, and some benefits became means-tested.[31]

In one of the most widely analyzed policy changes of the contemporary era, the Socialists reversed the course of economic and social policy in 1982.[32] By the summer of that year, macroeconomic conditions and the general government and social security budget balances had deteriorated noticeably. Generally, the French economy weakened in several major respects after 1980: the unemployment rate rose from 7.4 to 8.1 percent of the labor force between 1981 and 1982, and inflation hovered in the range of 12–14 percent in the early 1980s. Reflecting what is widely regarded as a policy-related fall in business confidence, private nonresidential capital investment declined moderately, falling 4.6 percent in 1982 and 3.0 percent in 1983. On the international side, the current account balance worsened in 1982 and the extent mix of economic conditions and policies placed substantial pressure on the French franc.[33]

---

[31] The programmatic structure of the French welfare state is highly complex, with roughly 500 funds (*caisses*). The principal plan, the *régime général*, covers most workers in general industry and trade; it is divided into three major components for health and sickness insurance, pensions, and family programs. Unemployment compensation is organized into a separate régime. The régime général is complemented by roughly 120 plans for public sector workers (*régimes spéciaux* and *régimes particuliers*) and a variety of additional schemes for agricultural workers, the self-employed, and other groups. Social housing and cash allowances, a variety of social services, and social assistance programs round out the welfare state.

[32] Among others, see Christofferson (1991), Hall (1986, 1987), Loriaux (1991), and contributions to Ross, Hoffman, and Malzacher (1987) for analyses of French Socialist economic policy during this period.

[33] As Loriaux (1991) and others have noted, the franc had sustained a relatively high value through the 1970s (in part because of the issuance of foreign bonds that supported demand for francs). However, in the context of expansionary policies and high inflation in France, widespread deflationary policy in other countries, and the general international economic downturn, the franc was subjected to speculative trading. Moreover, the economic downturn in Germany and a rise in French relative labor costs significantly constrained French reflationary policy; so did high real U.S. interest rates, which increased the value of the dollar and hence the costs of increasingly large shares of dollar-denominated imports (e.g., Christofferson [1991]; Hall [1986, 1987]). However, it is important to note that while

In response to these conditions, the government sharply reversed economic policy in 1982. Expenditure controls and tax increases were announced by mid-1982, a June–October 1982 freeze on wage and price rises was enacted, additional capital controls were temporarily imposed, and three successive devaluations of the franc were made through March 1983. Furthermore, plans to pursue major domestic and international liberalization of financial markets, industrial restructuring, anti-inflationary policies, and a stable franc (*franc fort*) were announced and tax reductions and investment incentives for business were enacted. The *plan de rigeur* that unfolded in 1982 and 1983 effectively moved France closer to the deflationary policies, austerity, and liberalization characteristic of Center-Right governments in other Western democracies.

In this context, the Socialists initiated a second wave of social welfare policies designed to reduce the growth of social expenditure, as well as significantly increase revenues to fund an increasingly generous and encompassing welfare state.[34] On the benefit side, the Socialists tightened eligibility for unemployment benefits in 1982 and 1983 and shortened the maximum duration of standard unemployment compensation in 1984. In 1982, housing allowances were decoupled from the cost-of-living adjustment index (and began falling in real terms). As noted above, the complex set of changes surrounding early retirement introduced in 1983 effectively reduced guarantees to full pensions for early retirees. In addition, the government began reforms of the health care system. Doctors' fees, prices for pharmaceutical goods, and, for the short-term, sickness benefits were effectively frozen. Daily charges for hospital beds were introduced, medical procedure guidelines streamlined, and a variety of medical reimbursements were reduced. Most significantly, global budgets for hospitals were introduced in January of 1983, ushering in the use of annual hospital budget caps. In 1984, a variety of reforms designed to achieve efficiency in the health care system were introduced and several pharmaceutical companies were nationalized (partially as a strategy to stabilize prices).

international competitiveness and exchange rate pressures played a role in the reversal of welfare expansion, capital movements – outward flows of financial capital and inward and outward flows of FDI – did not exhibit dramatic year-to-year movements or step-level increases during this time.

[34] This new era in social welfare policy was marked by the June 1982 appointment of Pierre Bérégovoy as Minister of National Solidarity and Social Affairs (and the dismissal of previous Social Affairs Minister Nicole Questiaux). Between mid-1982 and 1985, Bérégovoy and allies within the government made a number of social policy changes that actually brought the social security budget into line relatively quickly.

On the revenue side, social insurance contributions for pensions and unemployment compensation were increased and the income ceiling on social insurance contributions was raised. Social security contributions were applied to unemployment and early retirement benefits. Higher taxes earmarked for social insurance purposes were imposed on pharmaceuticals, car insurance, alcohol, and tobacco. Perhaps most significant, a 1 percent tax on most forms of income (*contribution sociale généralisée*, or CSG) was legislated to bolster social security fund balances; it was later lifted in 1985. Together with benefit cost controls and reductions, these revenue increases substantially improved the fiscal health of the social insurance system and, to a degree, shifted funding away from social contributions and toward general taxation. In the end, however, the combined effect of these changes did not actually involve significant retrenchment or neoliberal restructuring: many of the pre-1983 increases in social protection remained in place, although with higher tax burdens and more restricted benefits in some areas.[35]

The loss of the Socialists and their allies in the 1986 National Assembly elections resulted in the formation of the Center-Right coalition of the Union for French Democracy (UDF) and Gaullists headed by former Premier Jacques Chirac. However, despite the ostensible ideological commitment by Chirac to *liberalisme*, actual reforms in the area of social welfare policy reflected a substantial continuity with the post-1982 Socialist policy initiatives. Initially, the Chirac government had announced the consideration of a major overhaul of the entire social security system, including partial privatization. After a substantial wave of criticism, however, lobbying, and protests by the Left, unions, and a broad array of interest groups (culminating in a 200,000-person demonstration in March of 1987), restructuring and privatization plans were shelved.

In practice, successful 1986–8 reforms focused on selective tax increases, limited spending controls, and new anti-unemployment measures. On the revenue side, the government increased pension contributions, levied new taxes on tobacco, and enacted a new special .4 percent social security tax on general income. In the area of spending controls, the government

---

[35] In comparison to the late 1970s, social provision appears more generous in the mid-1980s. For instance, even with significant efforts to curb the growth of unemployment benefits, the social wage actually increased from roughly 37 percent during the Barre government to 55 percent by 1985 (and this figure factors in post-1982 reforms). Other indicators suggest, at minimum, an absence of substantial retrenchment or similar increases.

changed the indexing system for housing benefits that, in turn, reduced the real value of benefits for many recipients. In the area of health care, the government continued to tighten medical procedure guidelines, reduce reimbursements for some items, and encourage "contracting out" of certain health care functions to the private sector. A campaign against medical care cost increases was launched that attempted to bring together health care providers, administrators, and other actors to cooperate on new cost control initiatives. In response to both youth and long-term unemployment, the Chirac government initiated a new series of training and employment subsidy programs. Together, these policies constitute the major reforms of the Chirac government.

After victory in the 1988 National Assembly elections, the 1988–93 Socialist governments pursued reforms that entailed a continuation of spending controls, selective benefit reductions, tax increases, and a handful of major new extensions of social protection. The environment of these policy changes, although distinct from the early-1980s conditions, was characterized by continuing demographic, economic, and budgetary pressures on the social welfare system. In this context, the Socialists undertook a number of major studies of the social welfare system in the late 1980s and early 1990s. As the OECD (selected years, a) pointed out in its 1980s and 1990s annual reviews of the French economy, these government reports (as well as independent studies and the OECD's own analysis) pinpointed key pressures, discounted the importance of other forces, offered possible solutions and, in turn, shaped the government's social policy orientation in the late 1980s and 1990s. First, despite the emphasis by employers' associations and neoliberal politicians on the role of social costs in dampening international competitiveness and business location, most analyses downplayed this factor as an element of the social insurance crisis: French unit labor costs were roughly comparable to the average among its principal trading partners (e.g., OECD [selected years, a] and the studies cited therein; Hantrais [1996]). Second, most analyses documented the cause-and-effect dynamics involving strong demographic and health cost pressures on social security and, in turn, the substantial employment "tax wedge" created by rising social security contributions to cover these costs. In other words, in the eyes of many policy makers and analysts these pressures had created a situation where the net wage employers could offer (especially at lower ends of the labor market) was often too low relative to the net wage potential employees would accept (and to the high minimum wage itself) to generate requisite employment.

In sum, the principal challenges to the 1988–93 Socialist governments, the 1993–7 Center-Right governments of Balladur and Juppé, and even the 1997 Socialist government of Lionel Jospin, were to fashion social welfare reforms that would adequately address the spending pressures of aging, health care cost rises, and unemployment, as well as mitigate welfare state cost effects on the persistently high unemployment rates. After 1992, the increasing pressure for policy reform from the interaction of rising deficits and the Maastricht convergence criteria (i.e., annual deficit at 3 percent and public sector debt at 60 percent of GDP or below) added an additional and significant immediate pressure to welfare state reform (e.g., Bonoli and Palier [1998]). The principal difference between the Socialists on the one hand, and the Balladur and (especially) Juppé Center-Right governments on the other, is the depth and scope of proposed benefit reductions and structural reforms.

In the late 1980s, the Socialists enacted a number of spending and tax policies that continued the post-1981 emphasis on cost control and revenue increases. On the social benefits side, the government continued initiatives to reduce the rising costs of ambulatory care and drugs; a number of measures were taken to restrain doctors' fees, pharmaceutical costs, and achieve general efficiencies in the health care system (e.g., better health care planning). In 1991 and 1992, a reduction in unemployment benefits was enacted. After negotiations between the unions and employers, the government enacted changes in the unemployment system where a two-day waiting period would be required and benefits would be reduced by 15–25 percent every four months to stimulate greater work effort. On the revenue side, several major policies were enacted. In 1989, employee health contributions were increased 1 percentage point and the .4 percent special income tax was renewed. In 1990 and 1991, however, the .4 percent income tax was eliminated and employee pension and employer family policy contributions were reduced. In their place, the government reinstated the CSG (the *contribution sociale généralisée*, which had been in effect between 1983 and 1985) at a rate of 1.1 percent on most forms of income. In addition, a solidarity fund of new taxes on spirits and soft drinks and a small share of social security contributions was initiated to pay for nonfunded components of the pension system.

At the same time, the Socialists undertook some extensions of social protection. Continuing an emphasis of the 1981–6 governments, additional day-care facilities and related services for families and working mothers were created. In 1990 and 1991, ALMP was again bolstered with increased placement services for the unemployed and new tax subsidies for employers hiring youth and the long-term unemployed. In 1990, initiatives were taken to bolster basic housing allowances, which had been eroding in real value since 1982, and to improve social housing for low income groups (Besson Law). However, two additional initiatives overshadowed these policies. First, the government enacted a new program establishing a minimum insertion income (*revenu minimum d'insertion*, or RMI) for individuals that had exhausted other social protection and failed to reap benefits of ALMP. Designed to combat growing social exclusion, the RMI was means-tested social assistance targeted at the long-term unemployed and other disadvantaged groups.[36] Second, the Socialists commissioned major studies and began planning for a major reform of the pension system. In fact, a 1991 White Paper on social security reform and the 1992 Cottave Report outlined the major parameters of the pension reforms that were actually undertaken by the 1993 Center-Right government of Edouard Balladur.

After the defeat of the Socialists in the 1993 National Assembly elections, the Center-Right government of Balladur initiated significant social policy reforms. After extensive negotiations among the government, the Socialists, and the social partners (Bonoli, 2001), and building on the base laid out in previous studies, the Balladur government enacted in 1993 a significant change in the pension component of the *régime général* (covering the bulk of private sector workers). The Balladur reforms made three basic changes: calculation of benefits would be made on the basis of the 25, not 10, best years of income, the contribution period for full pension would be extended to 40 from 37.5 years, and pension benefits would be indexed to prices, not net wages. The estimated effect of these changes was that the average income replacement rate to pensioners covered by the pension reform (previously in the range of 80 percent of gross income for typical production workers) would be reduced by roughly 2–4 percent by 2020; pension spending growth would continue, but would be 1.75 percent of GDP less than under the current system by 2010 (OECD

---

[36] The notion of social exclusion had originated in France in the 1970s and was a broad concept used to refer not only to economic exclusion of the unemployed, but also to social exclusion of minorities, those with AIDS, and other disadvantaged groups (e.g., Spicker [1997]). RMI not only addressed the needs of excluded groups but in effect significantly extended the fragmented and decentralized system of social assistance that had served to provide a minimum safety net to those who "fell through the cracks" of the extensive and generous social insurance system.

selected years, a [1994 edition] and studies cited therein). Beyond the pension reforms, the Balladur government also legislated a variety of moderate social policy changes: additional resources were given to jobs and housing programs, additional efficiencies were sought in health care, and paid leave for the second child was enacted.

In the aftermath of the 1995 Presidential election victory of Jacques Chirac and the replacement of Balladur with Alain Juppé, a second round of policy changes was initiated. As the government assumed office, demographic, economic, and fiscal pressures on social security continued (e.g., the general government budget deficit had reached 6.0 percent of GDP in 1994). As noted above, the Maastricht convergence criteria for fiscal balances (3 percent of GDP) created yet another impetus for reform. In response to these pressures, the Juppé government proposed several significant changes in the pension system and structure of the health care system. In addition, it proposed changes in the policy-making, administrative, and funding structure of social security, as well as a variety of miscellaneous new social policy reforms. First, the plan called for an extension of the Balladur pension reforms to the supplementary pension schemes for public sector workers. Second, the plan proposed, in effect, gradually moving the health care system from a pay-as-you-go social insurance plan to a universal social program that would be funded from income tax (rather than contributions); a variety of initiatives were taken to increase public control of the health care system, as well as to strengthen health care planning and cost control. To finance the reformed health care system, the CSG was increased from 1.1 to 3.4 percent on most forms of general income in 1996. Additional funding measures were taken to reduce the fiscal stress on the social security system; most importantly, a new social debt refunding tax at .5 percent of income was enacted. In addition, policy-making and administrative reforms were undertaken. From 1996 (by constitutional amendment), parliament would set annual social security spending and revenue levels and determine trends in social spending; the presence of government personnel on social insurance fund boards would be increased. Finally, the Juppé plan proposed a system of supplementary private pensions and means-tested basic family allowances.

In the aftermath of the initial announcement of the Juppé plan in November of 1995, major strikes and demonstrations spread throughout France in late November and December in protest over its major elements. Among the three main unions, only the moderate Catholic CDFT voiced support for components of the plan; the communist CGT and the public

196

sector-based FO, as well as the parties of the Left and a broad array of national interest groups, vehemently denounced major provisions of the plan. As Bonoli (2001) points out, unlike the 1993 Balladur reforms, the Juppé plan had not been based on extensive negotiations among the parties and social partners and, as such, had a distinctly confrontational character. In the wake of this political resistance, the pension components of reforms (as well as planned educational reforms) were withdrawn; however, other elements of the plan described above survived. The most notable exceptions are the initiatives to encourage private pensions and to means test family allowances, which the 1997 Socialist government canceled. The new government approved most other elements of the plan and even accelerated some (CSG funding of health care).

Internationalization and Reform of the French Welfare State. To what extent can actual reforms of the French welfare state be clearly linked to internationalization? While the late 1970s–mid-1990s has been marked by one period of major expansion and several episodes of moderate extensions of social protection, the last 20 years of social policy reform have been dominated by continuing efforts to contain the growth of social welfare spending, to increase revenues, and, most recently, restructure core features of the system of social protection. As the preceding analysis has illustrated, however, it is very difficult to systematically and directly link reforms of the French welfare state – their timing and depth – to rises in international capital mobility. In the mid- to late 1980s and 1990s, as capital mobility and financial integration were accelerating, concerns over trade competitiveness and business location – while highlighted to a degree by business and neoliberal partisans – seemingly played a secondary role in welfare state restructuring. On the other hand, pressures from continued fiscal stress and sustained high unemployment, as well as concerns about the direct policy impacts of aging and the budgetary consequences of health care cost rises, can be systematically implicated in moderate retrenchment efforts and restructuring throughout the last two decades. Indeed, the dynamic linkages between demographic trends and health care costs on the one hand, and higher social contributions and the attendant employment "tax wedges" on the other, have played major roles in shaping social policy reform efforts.[37]

---

[37] As Gary Freeman (1994) has argued, the principal forces driving social policy makers in governments of both the Left and Center-Right have been fiscal constraints (largely

Has the ascent of domestic and international neoliberalism systematically influenced French social welfare reforms? At first glance, the casual
observer might respond, "yes", based on the ostensibly neoliberal policy
pronouncements of the Center-Right Barre, Chirac, Balladur, and, especially, Juppé governments (as well as the u-turn of early 1980s Socialists).
However, upon closer inspection, the answer is not so clear: the rise in
neoliberal economic orthodoxy – reinforced by the rhetoric of internationalization – appears to be a relatively weak influence on actual policy
change. As Spicker (1997) points out, despite statements of neoliberal
ideology, the actual social policy initiatives of the 1980s and early 1990s
Center-Right governments were weak reflections of Reagan-Thatcher
policy programs. In fact, the concrete policies of these governments consisted of policy initiatives to control spending growth, raise revenues, and
selectively and modestly reduce benefits; each government also initiated
or expanded social policies in several areas (e.g., to address long-term
unemployment). As noted above, there is little in the way of evidence that
a belief in the "imperatives" of international competitiveness and business
location systematically drove social policy change during the tenure of
Center-Right or post-1982 Socialist governments.

Instead of relatively direct and systematic linkages between the economic and political pressures attendant internationalization and neoliberal
welfare state reforms, the real impacts of internationalization of markets
in the French case appear to be indirect, conjunctural, and limited in effect.
That is, similar to the effects of international financial integration in the
case of Germany and the Nordic political economies, international market
forces become important at specific historical junctures and in the presence of additional adverse conditions. With regard to the watershed era
of the early 1980s, the 1970s transition to flexible exchange rates and the
associated financial flows played a significant role in the early 1980s reversal of Keynesian reflationary policy and, in turn, the end of extensions of
social protection. As Loriaux's (1991) analysis makes clear, the transition
to flexible exchange rates created a volatile climate for French economic
policy strategy. The French model had largely hinged on extensive control
of credit to French industry, generously distributed in what Loriaux calls
the "overdraft economy," and selective devaluations of the franc to offset
the adverse effects of domestic inflationary pressures. However, while the

shaped by demographic and economic needs) on the one hand, and a continuing desire to
promote social justice and accommodate claimant groups on the other.

franc had remained strong in the 1970s, the confluence of pressures in the early 1980s resulted in significant downward pressure on the franc, as well as pressures to reform the French model. In the short term, these changes entailed the reversal of Keynesian reflationary policy and the halt of welfare state expansions, as well as devaluation; in the long term, policy change entailed a fundamental reform of the "overdraft economy" with financial liberalization, price and exchange rate stability, and industrial restructuring.

Second, in the early 1980s downturn, concerns over the trade competitiveness of French industry emerged as policy makers focused on recent declines of world market shares, foreign penetration of domestic markets, and rising relative labor costs (e.g., Christofferson [1991]). In addition, as Hall (1986, 1987) has noted, the international integration of the French economy had risen by the early 1980s: the above concerns, as well as the adverse effects of increasingly expensive dollar-denominated imports and the economic downturn in Germany (and other trading partners), contributed to economic policy reversal and the shift from welfare expansion to cost control and revenue raising. Yet, together, these international forces constituted one of several sets of pressures that ultimately reversed the extension of social welfare.

Has French social policy reform during the 1970s–90s era produced an appreciable shift toward the residual model of welfare provision? Some observers such as Bruno Palier (1997) have argued that there is a discernable "liberal dynamic" in the reforms of the French welfare state. In Palier's analysis, tax reforms that shift the burden from employers to employees and flat-rate income taxes, reductions in benefits, and the increased use of means-tested benefits may well entail a "recommodification" of labor and a turn toward the residual model. Other scholars disagree, however. Bouget's (1998) analysis of the Juppé plan and the future course of the French welfare state suggests three concomitant trajectories: a continuity in core Bismarckian features of French social policy; a move toward universalism in the area of health care; and the development of a neoliberal component, especially in the area of targeted benefits. In addition to these insights, several points might be added. First, despite intense fiscal and demographic pressures, the French welfare state in the mid- to late 1990s is hardly significantly less generous and encompassing than it was in the mid- to late 1970s; many of the early 1980s extensions of social protection have not been rolled back, a number of new social benefits have been added, and the actual reductions in benefits have been moderate. Second, the change in relative share of social security contributions provided by employees has been modest and employers still contribute the majority of contributions at amounts (as shares of GDP) that have been relatively stable in the 1990s.[38]

As to means testing, the advent and rising importance of RMI and the increase in means-tested family benefits (from 38 to 45 percent of total family benefits between 1981 and 1995) could be interpreted as an indication of (partial) neoliberal restructuring of the French welfare state. However, as late as 1992, only 6.4 percent of total social security benefits were comprised of mean-tested social assistance in France; the percentage for the liberal welfare states in 1992 was 45.5 percent (Gough et al., 1997). In addition, the advent of the RMI is not as clear an example of residualism as might appear. As Spicker (1997) argues, the RMI was motivated by the absence of a nationally unified social safety net for the rising numbers of socially excluded citizens; it is based on the foundational principle of solidarity and the need to reintegrate marginalized citizens into French society and economy. In other words, RMI is qualitatively different than typical residual social assistance in liberal welfare states.[39]

In sum, while there is ample evidence to conclude that notable reforms and partial restructuring of the French welfare state have occurred, the French welfare state has not significantly converged toward the neoliberal model. A more apt description would emphasize two basic thrusts of social policy since the 1970s. First, there has been significant policy continuity: the Bismarckian structure and the general level of social provision have been preserved. Second, there have been policy changes within the context of this overarching continuity: a pluralism of structural reforms (including neoliberal ones), expansions of social protection to meet new needs,

---

[38] Using 1970 and 1996 as the base years, the employer share of social security contributions has fallen from 73 to 62 percent of total contributions. In terms of shares of GDP for the comparable period, the employers' contribution has risen from the equivalent of 9.3 to 12.2 percent of GDP (where the peak is 12.5 percent of GDP in 1985).

[39] As Spicker (1997) points out, a central underlying principal of French welfare state development is solidarity. Essentially Catholic in origin, the concept refers to the network of relationships and obligations that promote social cohesion. Together with the principle of subsidiarity (see above), social policy development has been motivated by considerations of fostering solidarity or redressing problems that threaten solidarity. The Catholic variant is supported by secular traditions, such as the Rousseauian concept of *solidarite*, or the view that the state has the responsibility of promoting diverse interests through social inclusion. Programs that redress the problem of social exclusion, either through means-tested benefits or other devices, have been heavily influenced by these principles.

strong constraints on spending growth, and revenue reforms. Finally, it is also the case that these reforms of the French welfare state have not occurred under direct and systematic pressures of globalization; the role of internationalization in shaping French social policy reforms has certainly been more complex (i.e., conjunctural and limited) than conventional globalization theories suggest.

Internationalization and the Italian Welfare State

Compared to other corporatist conservative welfare states, the Italian welfare state (*stato sociale*) developed late.[40] While social protection was extended during the 1950s and early 1960s, many of the programs and policies that structure the contemporary system of social provision were not enacted until the late 1960s and 1970s. In 1969, the pension system was substantially reformed. Workers with 35 years of contribution could retire at 70 percent of past earnings (with no age criteria), while men with requisite contributions could retire at the full pension rate of 80 percent of earnings at age 60 (women at 55); legislation bolstered generous pensions for civil servants available after short contribution periods. Beginning in 1975, pensions were indexed by wages (themselves subject to the automatic inflation adjustment of the scala mobile). Also in 1975, the ordinary and special earnings integration funds (*cassa integrazionne ordinario* and *cassa integrazionne straordinario*) were reformed and uprated: unemployed workers displaced by economic restructuring could receive temporary unemployment benefits at 80 percent of previous earnings for up to 2 years (with the possibility of extensions). In 1978, the National Health Service (*Servizio Sanitorio Nazionali*, or SSN) was created to provide free and universal health care to all Italians and make health care subject to public control. Under the original plan, revenue collection (a combination of social insurance and general tax revenues) and aggregate

[40] I rely heavily on the following sources for material: Ferrera (1995, 1997); Ferrera and Gualmini (1998); Niero (1996); OECD (selected years, c); Pitruzzello (1997); contributions to Rhodes (1997); Saraceno and Negri (1994); and Trifiletti (1999). Generally, the Italian welfare state conforms to the corporatist conservative model. Pensions are structured by four major funds for employees and categories of the self-employed (managed by the National Institute of Social Insurance, INPS), a separate fund for civil servants (managed by the Treasury), and 40 minor funds. Contributory unemployment benefits and invalidity pensions exist and social insurance is supplemented by a variety of non-contributory social assistance programs provided at both the national and local levels. See the text in this section on health care and other welfare state areas.

budget making are performed at the national level; revenues are disbursed to regional governments who in turn distribute funds to Local Health Units (*Unità Sanitorie Locali*, or USL) and perform regulatory functions. USLs, themselves subject to partisan control through local councils, oversee the delivery of health care.[41]

Italian economic performance in the 1970s and 1980s was affected by a series of events in the late 1960s to mid-1970s; economic dynamics, in turn, significantly shaped 1980s welfare state development.[42] As Locke (1995) and others have noted, the strikes and labor militancy of the "hot autumn" of 1969 produced a series of reforms of the labor and industrial relations system that led to rigidity in the wage system, the tight regulation of hiring and (especially) firing, the elimination of overtime, and a slowdown in the pace of work. The 1970s Workers Charter strengthened union organization and restricted antiunion practices. In addition, the oil shock of 1973–4 significantly boosted inflation and, in interaction with the scala mobile (which required automatic indexation of wages to inflation), facilitated the development of a wage-price spiral and strong inflationary expectations. The breakdown of the Bretton Woods system of fixed exchange rates in the 1971–3 period led to the devaluation of the lira and placed additional upward pressures on the price level. Restrictive measures to remedy the declining external balance in the early 1970s were followed by expansionary measures; a stop-go economic policy cycle began to develop. Finally, the combination of generous increases in social protection, benefit indexing under conditions of high inflation, and slower growth contributed to substantial fiscal stress: the general government budget deficit increased sharply to an annual average of 9.2 percent of GDP in the years from 1974–9.

---

[41] As observers have noted (e.g., Rhodes [1997]; Trifiletti [1999]), the Italian welfare state is also somewhat distinct from other conservative welfare states in that it has been shaped by notable features of the broader political system. The imprints of relatively high levels of clientelism, partisan fragmentation, ideological polarization, and administrative inefficiency are evident. In addition, social protection is even more significantly skewed toward covered employees in the core sectors of the economy (than in the typical occupationally based system). The absence of supplements for families, no universal minimum benefits, and low means-tested benefits and services leave workers in informal labor markets and those outside of the labor market with low and uncertain support.

[42] I rely on a number of analyses of Italian economic performance in this and subsequent sections. Especially helpful are: Ferrera and Gualmini (1998); Lange and Regini (1989); Locke (1995); OECD, *Economic Surveys: Italy* (various years); Regini and Regalia (1997); Rossi and Toniolo (1996); and Treu (1994).

In reaction to this decline in economic performance, employers, unions, and the state pursued a variety of strategies, individually and in cooperation with one another, that sought to improve economic efficiency and ease inflation. As I discuss below, these developments had substantial consequences for the development of the Italian welfare state. In bilateral negotiations and pacts (employers and unions, or unions and the state) or in tripartite concertation (*concertazione*) between the mid-1970s and mid-1980s, government and the social partners attempted to negotiate improvements in labor market flexibility and dampen inflation.[43] For instance, unions agreed in a 1978 bargain with government to pursue wage restraint. In 1983, a modification of the *scala mobile* was negotiated between the social partners and, in 1984, unions and employers agreed to create more labor market flexibility with the introduction of part-time and fixed-term contracts, work sharing, and related measures. Negotiated anti-inflation measures, such as the reform of the scala mobile, were reinforced by actions of the state; in 1979, the lira joined the European Monetary System. In addition, the institutional independence of the Bank of Italy was partially established by early-1980s reforms (the "divorce" of the Bank from the Treasury); from 1981 the Bank pursued a more restrictive, high-interest monetary policy. Finally, both small- and medium-sized enterprises and large employers increasingly pursued efficiency-oriented restructuring and modernization as the 1980s progressed. As in Germany, economic restructuring often involved substantial labor shedding.

The 1970s and early 1980s economic performance shocks and the subsequent adaptive responses of unions, employers, and the state had significant repercussions on social welfare policy. Even more clearly than in the French and German cases, Italian expansions of extant programs and new social welfare initiatives provided compensation for displaced workers, supplemented incomes, and often provided the cement that held together fragile pacts between employers and unions for labor market reform. For

---

[43] Although the trade union movement enjoys moderately high union density rates (e.g., 40 percent of wage and salary earners in 1990), it has traditionally been fragmented among three central confederations (affiliated with Communist, Catholic, and Socialist Parties): CGIL (*Confederazione Generale Italiana del Lavoro*), CISL (*Confederazione Italiana Sindicati Lavoratori*), and the UIL (*Unime Italiana del Lavoro*). Although coordination among these confederations has increased in the contemporary period, efforts at unification have failed. On the employer side, the principal peak association is *Confindustria*, although other associations exist (e.g., public sector employers). In recent years, Confindustria has become more encompassing, absorbing the smaller peak federations. For overviews, see among others Treu (1994) and Regini and Regalia (1997).

instance, the (ultimately unsuccessful) 1978 union commitment to wage restraint was exchanged for increased programs to combat youth unemployment and additional funds for active labor market programs. The 1983 negotiations between unions and employers over reform of the scala mobile were facilitated by government commitments to bolster family allowances for workers and to subsidize the social security contributions of employers. The *Cassa Integrazionne Guadagni* (earning integration funds) and general active labor market policies (e.g., the Wages Guarantee Fund) played a significant role in supporting displaced workers.[44]

However, while 1970s welfare state expansion continued into the 1980s, some limited efforts at cost containment were in fact initiated. In 1983, the government increased targeting of welfare benefits by establishing income ceilings for recipients of minimum pensions and multiple program benefits. In 1984, invalidity pension rules were tightened. In the mid-1980s, social insurance contributions were raised (especially on the self-employed) and, in 1986, quarterly indexation of pensions was shifted to twice-yearly adjustments. Various proposals were made to initiate more significant reforms (especially in the area of pensions), but political resistance or government instability commonly led to the defeat or withdrawal of the plans. Generally, the most substantial cost control reforms were made in the area of health care: in 1983, a 15 percent co-payment for prescription drugs was created; this was expanded to 25 percent in 1986, and to 30 percent in 1989. New expenditure limits on health service units at the regional government–level were imposed in 1983 and reduced reimbursements for some forms of health services were initiated in 1986. Overall, these policy changes notwithstanding, most observers point out that a major "reform of the reform" in health policy did not occur until the 1990s.

The adaptive responses of unions, employers, and the state (as facilitated by social welfare policy) arguably led to some notable improvements in economic performance in the 1980s. Inflation fell to single digits in 1985 and continued a downward trend throughout the 1980s and 1990s. Both general economic growth rates and external balances improved notably after 1982: real per capita GDP growth exceeded 2 percent each

---

[44] For instance, as Ferrera and Gualmini (1998) point out, the *Cassa Integrazionne Straordinario* absorbed 20,000 workers in 1980 in the wake of the crisis at Fiat. In 1981, the "pre-retirement" pension (*prepensionamento*) for unemployed workers within three years of normal retirement was significantly expanded.

year between 1984 and 1990, and a consistent string of trade surpluses was registered after 1985. However, unemployment did not fall below 10 percent after 1982 (with notably higher unemployment rates in the South), and the general government budget balance between 1981 and 1991 exceeded 10 percent of GDP every year but one (1989). In fact, it is the extraordinarily large and sustained budget deficit and concomitant build-up in public sector debt (for instance, 104 percent of GDP by 1990), in interaction with early 1990s developments, that finally precipitated a series of significant reforms of the stato sociale.

As observers have suggested, the confluence of severe domestic fiscal crisis, the ratification of the Maastricht Treaty, and the crisis and reform of the political system during the *Tangentopoli* ("Bribe City") investigations created a unique opportunity for nonincremental social policy change (e.g., Ferrera [1997]; Ferrera and Gualmini [1998]; Pitruzzello [1997]). With respect to fiscal crisis, relatively generous and late expansion of the Italian welfare state, sustained high unemployment, and social compensation of workers placed substantial upward pressures on social spending throughout the 1980s. Sociodemographic changes (e.g., exceptionally low fertility rates) had increased the population share of the elderly to 14.4 percent by 1990 (and potentially to 22.8 percent by 2020 [George, 1996]) and, in turn, fueled fiscal stress as well as intensified pressures for pension and health care reform. The ratification of the Maastricht Treaty in 1992 and impending European Monetary Union created an imperative for dramatic fiscal consolidation; the concomitant speculative attacks on the lira and its withdrawal from the Exchange Rate Mechanism in 1992 reinforced the "European imperative." In the context of the corruption scandals, the shift in electoral behavior in the 1992 elections and subsequent electoral reforms resulted in the substantial restructuring of the Italian party system: the collapse of the long-lived *pentapartito* governments of the Christian Democrats, Socialists, Social Democrats, Liberals, and Republicans, the advent of a series of reform-minded technocratic governments (i.e., the Amato, Ciampi, and Dini governments), and the 1994 election of the right-wing Berlusconi government (comprised of the new *Forza Italia*, ascendent *Lega Nord*, and *Alleanza Nazionale*) changed the political context of social welfare reform notably.

With these developments, three major social welfare reform packages – two of the pension system and a "reform of the reform" in health care – as well as a series of smaller policy changes were proposed, negotiated, and enacted between 1992 and 1995; a major reform package proposed by the Berlusconi government in 1994 was defeated in the wake of widespread and intense political opposition. In 1992, the Amato government enacted a relatively significant reform of the pension system. Under the new legislation, the retirement age would be increased from 55 years of age for women and 60 for men to 60 and 65 years of age, respectively, by 2008. There would also be a gradual increase in minimum years of contribution from 10 to 20 years and the last 10 years, as opposed to 5, of earnings would be used as the basis for calculating benefits. Seniority pensions would be awarded after 36 years of contributions for both public sector and private employees, instead of the present 35 years for private employees (and the much shorter period of 20 years for civil servants). Contribution rates were also increased. The Amato government pension reform of 1992 was followed by additional initiatives by the Ciampi technocratic government in 1993. Most important, tighter restrictions were imposed on disability pensions and a temporary freeze on new seniority pensions was initiated.

In addition to pension policy change, the "reform of the reform" in health policy was enacted in 1992. Structurally, the new plan severed the ties between the USLs and local councils, converting the Local Health Units into public enterprises to be run by a professional manager; larger hospitals themselves were also reorganized as independent agencies within the USLs, with efficiency-oriented management and strict budgetary requirements. The national government would continue to formulate general health care policy and would allocate funds to regions based on strict reimbursement guidelines within annual budgets; regions that exceeded spending limits would have to cover excess health expenditures from their own sources. In addition, the reform encouraged contracting out with private providers for health services, allocation of space for physicians' private patients, and the development of alternative (i.e., private) health plans beginning in 1995. Finally, with the 1992 reform and subsequent initiatives in 1993 and 1994, the patient co-payment system was extended to require higher user fees.[45]

After the 1994 elections, the right-wing Berlusconi government proposed additional measures to retrench the welfare state. Unlike other

---

[45] It is important to note that while the user fees have increased during the 1980s and 1990s, there are significant exemptions from payment. For instance, children under 10 and those over 60 years of age, those subject to chronic illness, and pregnant women are typically exempt.

governments in the 1990s, Berlusconi's Forza Italia explicitly advocated movement to a neoliberal model of publicly provided basic benefits and a large second tier of private insurance (Niero, 1996); Berlusconi's government also proposed the major reforms without negotiating and building consensus with the unions (Pitruzzello, 1997). In September of 1994, the government announced legislation that would have substantially reduced pension benefits, lengthened contribution periods, fully harmonized private and public sector pensions, and indexed pensions with the targeted inflation rate. A variety of additional measures were proposed, such as further cuts in health services (e.g., closing smaller hospitals). The response from the unions, Center-Left parties and organizations, and the electorate was highly negative. A series of strikes and massive protest marches, including a November 1994 demonstration of 1.5 million people in Rome, as well as intense conflict within the governing coalition led to defeat of the proposals and eventual resignation of the government in December 1994.

In the wake of the collapse of the Berlusconi government, the Dini technocratic government was invested on January 17, 1995. With the support of the broad range of Left-Center parties, the Dini government initiated a series of reforms to address the deficit-debt crisis, including a major pension reform. Unlike the Berlusconi government, the Dini government negotiated the content of the pension reform with the unions (with intermittent involvement of *Confindustria*); on May 8 a consensus between the government and unions (with partial support of Confindustria) was reached, and, on August 4, the Parliament approved the new pension plan. The 1995 reform went beyond the 1992 pension legislation in several ways. First, although the "pay-as-you-go" structure was kept, a major element of the reform was a shift from an earnings-related to contributions-based method of calculating benefits; by 2013 pension benefits would be calculated on the basis of life-time contributions to the system. In addition, benefits would be calculated to account for life expectancy at pensionable age; under the new system, retirement could occur between 57 and 65 years of age. Next, stricter requirements were imposed on "seniority pensions" and a minimum age of 57 for seniority pension eligibility was established. The plan also called for a gradual yet full harmonization of public sector and private employee pension plans and stricter rules for disability pensions. In addition, income limits on the accumulation of pensions benefits and means tests for survivor benefits were established. Finally, guidelines were created to usher in a second tier of supplementary (private) occupational pension plans. To what degree has internationalization systematically shaped these social policy reforms from the late 1970s to the mid-1990s?

The Impact of Globalization on the Italian Welfare State. Similar to Germany, the export orientation of the Italian economy is more pronounced than the typical larger economy. For instance, in the contemporary era (1991–5), the average export-to-GDP share for the G-7 economies was 15.5 percent, while for Italy it was 22.3 percent. On the other hand, international capital mobility has not been great. Full liberalization of restrictions on financial flows did not occur until 1988 in the wake of Single Europe Act. Moreover, actual flows of financial capital and FDI have been relatively small: total inflows and outflows of FDI rarely exceeded 1 percent of GDP through the mid-1990s; borrowing on international capital markets has rarely surpassed 2.5 percent of GDP in the 1980s and 1990s.[46] With respect to change, international capital mobility does increase appreciably after the 1970s. With the general acceleration of international market integration in the late 1970s and early 1980s, Italy's membership in the EMS in 1979, and the higher interest rate policy of the Bank of Italy after its "divorce" from the Treasury, Italy became more open to international capital markets. Covered interest rate differentials fell after 1982 and financial inflows from international capital markets increased from a 1974–9 average of .6 percent of GDP to 1.8 percent in the 1981–90 period. Along with the aforementioned forces and economic restructuring of the Italian economy, FDI increased notably, as well. This is particularly true for FDI outflows, which rose from .1 percent of GDP in the 1974–9 period to .4 percent of GDP in the years 1981–90.

The trend toward internationalization continues in the late 1980s and 1990s. In the wake of the Single Europe Act, Italian capital controls were liberalized in 1988. Covered interest rate differentials fell further in the late 1980s and 1990s and FDI outflows continued to increase (from .4 percent of GDP in the 1980s to .6 percent of GDP in the 1991–5 period). Borrowing on international capital markets remained relatively high in the 1990s at just under 2 percent of GDP. Is it possible to systematically link

---

[46] Generally, most forms of international capital flows in Italy are two-thirds to three-quarters the average for the developed democracies. For instance, in the 1991–3 period, total inflows and outflows of FDI, portfolio capital, and bank lending average roughly 32 percent of GDP in Italy and 42 percent for the typical developed democracy.

this pattern of rises in international capital mobility with retrenchment of the Italian welfare state?

In direct contradiction of the conventional globalization thesis, it is arguably the case that the relationship between rises in international capital mobility (and trade openness) and the development of the Italian welfare state to about 1990 fits the "compensation" thesis well. That is, if one examines only the 1970s and 1980s, internationalization of the Italian economy proceeds apace with the later stages of the expansion of the Italian welfare state in the 1970s and with 1980s extensions of early retirement, the Cassa Integrazionne Guadagni, active labor market spending, and other programs. In fact, as the above analysis has suggested, many of the late-1970s and 1980s program expansions were in effect designed to buffer Italian workers from the costs of economic change and to seal bipartite and tripartite bargains to cope with inflation and promote efficiency of labor markets. The modest cuts that did occur were often targeted at specific problems of particular programs (e.g., the cost controls in the health care system) and were not systematically and significantly influenced by considerations of investment environment and international competitiveness.

On the other hand, the 1990s welfare state impact of internationalization – broadly defined to encompass Europeanization, as well as the pressures attendant on general rises in trade openness and financial integration – is arguably negative. As discussed above, the ratification of the Maastricht Treaty placed significant and direct pressures on Italy to initiate substantial reductions in expenditure. As observers have noted (e.g., Ferrera and Gualmini [1998]; Pitruzzello [1997]), the treaty not only imposed specific budget deficit and public debt criteria on Italy, as well as the ultimate threat of nonmembership in the European Monetary Union, but it signaled new levels of exposure to European markets (and implicitly exposure to the pressures of global markets). However, it is also fair to suggest that the Maastricht Treaty, itself, as well as the more general concerns over international competitiveness and the moderate 1990s increase in international financial integration and flows (over 1980s levels) would not by themselves have precipitated the reforms in the stato sociale that actually occurred in the 1992–5 period.

As noted above, and consistent with the pattern of evidence adduced from the quantitative and previous case-study analyses, the ratification of the Maastricht Treaty (and attendant international pressures) occurs concurrently with, and reinforces the reform pressures of, domestic political economic crises and change. Specifically, it is the interaction of a step-level increase in European economic integration (and broader internationalization) with the severe domestic fiscal crisis and the crisis and reform of the political system during the Tangentopoli investigations, that created the economic and political conditions for nonincremental social policy change in the 1990s. As such, both the general internationalization of markets as well as the specific features of international capital mobility matter for Italian social policy change; however, they matter in complex ways that are hardly consistent with the economic and political logics of globalization as commonly understood.

Have the cumulative reforms of the stato sociale moved Italy appreciably closer to the neoliberal welfare state model? In comparative perspective, the Italian welfare state still possesses the broad features of a corporatist conservative system of social protection. The relative magnitude of means-tested benefits in 1992 (9.1 percent of total benefits) is only slightly above the average for continental European welfare states (6.7 percent) and far from the degree of reliance on these benefits by liberal welfare states (45.5 percent). A similar position for Italy is achieved for use of mandatory or voluntary social welfare provision: private benefits in 1995 account for 6.7 percent of total social welfare provision in Italy, 5.7 percent in the typical corporatist conservative welfare state, and 21.5 percent on average in the liberal welfare states. Finally, an examination of the 1995 social insurance contribution share of total revenues indicates that Italy still conforms well to the funding structures of the corporatist conservative model: social insurance levies account for 34.2 percent of total revenues in Italy, 37.0 percent in the average corporatist conservative system, and 14.6 percent in the typical liberal welfare state.

Beyond these broad structural indicators, one might argue that the 1992–5 reforms of pensions and health care (the dominant components of the system as noted above) will in the future significantly move the stato sociale toward the liberal model. However, it is important to note that while the pension reforms will reduce average income replacement of retirees significantly, the reforms have a number of protections for current workers and future retirees.[47] As Pitruzzello (1997) argues, both younger

---

[47] Pitruzzello (1997) estimates that the reforms, when implemented, will reduce income replacement from the 70–80 percent–range for a typical pension beneficiary to 55–60 percent.

and older workers are protected through the transition mechanisms built into the reforms (e.g., those with 18 years or more of contributions can opt out of the new system); moreover, significant state supports for new supplemental pensions (tax incentives, earnings supplements) have been built into to the reforms. In a similar fashion, the 1992 "reform of the reform" of the health care system represents both significant change and limited retrenchment. As Ferrera (1997) points out, while the 1990s health reforms are certainly a shift away from "democratic universalism," the movement toward managerial efficiency and cost control, with greater reliance on private service provision and insurance, is also notable for its lack of significant use of internal markets and competition (as has been the case in reforms of the National Health Service in Britain). Overall, while the recent reforms of the Italian welfare state have been significant, they have not produced a new residual system of social protection in Italy. It is also the case that the recent and substantial changes that have occurred in the stato sociale have not been systematically and directly driven by internationalization; the impacts of globalization, generally, and capital mobility, specifically, have been contingent on a confluence of domestic fiscal stress, political crises, and structural changes.

Globalization, Political Institutions, and Corporatist Conservative Welfare States

In the preceding pages, case studies and quantitative analysis (from Chapter 3) have suggested that there is no systematic and direct relationship between the notable post-1960s internationalization of markets and retrenchment of the corporatist conservative welfare state. Instead, analysis has pointed to the conclusion that, as in the case of the Social Democratic welfare states, the impacts of capital mobility (and trade openness) are largely episodic and contingent: internationalization interacts in often complex ways with domestic fiscal stress, itself produced by complex domestic structural changes and system "shocks" (e.g., German Unification), to produce pressure for welfare state retrenchment. In addition, theory as well as quantitative and case-study evidence suggests that, at least in some periods, significant internationalization has occurred concomitantly with (if not as a cause of) modest expansions of social protection. Increased "compensation" of workers in the wake of economic modernization and attendant labor shedding and limited expansions of social protection to address new needs (e.g., social exclusion, the growth of the frail elderly) is present in all of the corporatist conservative countries. Ultimately, the evidence indicates that while there have been moderate and occasionally substantial changes in social welfare protection, the corporatist conservative welfare model is still largely intact.

In addition, country studies and quantitative work demonstrate that democratic political institutions and welfare state structures have played substantial roles in mediating the welfare state impact of internationalization. Most notably, the institutional structure of the corporatist conservative model, social corporatist interest representation, and relatively inclusive electoral institutions have all facilitated the ability of pro–welfare state interests to act to maintain present program benefits or otherwise resist and shape proposed neoliberal reforms. While the welfare state impacts of the organization of decision-making authority in the polity are less direct and variable in these cases, some impacts do stand out. With respect to welfare state structure, theory and evidence from the focal cases suggest that direct interest representation of the social partners in administration of social insurance funds often provides constituency groups and the trade unions leverage in routine, if not major, episodes of social policy making. For instance, Ebbinghaus and Hassel (2000) point out that in the case of France, the social partners have full management responsibility for unemployment and early retirement pension funds, and thus welfare restructuring in these programs has involved bipartite negotiations between the social partners. In Germany, extensive social partner administration of social insurance funds has often created the necessity of more general engagement of unions and employers in contemporary national social policy reform (Schmähl, 1993).

As prefigured in theory, the nature of the corporatist conservative model also cultivates broad political coalitions of working- and middle-class beneficiaries, as well as public sector employees. Major neoliberal plans for welfare state restructuring and retrenchment were commonly met with high levels of cross-class political resistence in all of the focal countries; reforms that had not been subject to extensive negotiations and consensus building across parties and the social partners (e.g., Berlusconi's 1994 reform proposals in Italy; features of the 1995 Juppé plan in France; Kohl's 1996–7 pension and austerity package) were defeated legislatively or withdrawn in the face of overwhelming political resistance. Indeed, taking Germany as paradigmatic, the basic structure of the social insurance model offers relatively comprehensive social insurance to a wide range of employees encompassing the working and middle classes (Wilson, 1993).

212

Upgrades (e.g., imputed earnings) for lower-income wage earners, the equivalence principle linking high contributions and generous benefits for middle-class beneficiaries, and generous provisions for public sector employees create a broad cross-class coalition that supports the welfare state (e.g., Toft [1997]). Thus, in the case of Germany (Alber, 1988; Lawson, 1996; Clasen, 1997) as well as France (Hantrais, 1996) and Italy (Niero, 1996; Ferrera and Gaulmini, 1998), significant neoliberal retrenchment of the welfare state has been typically blunted by the mobilization of working- and middle-class constituencies, civil servants, and specific constituency groups, such as pensioners.

Moreover, the structure of the conservative model tends to promote high levels of legitimacy and the values of "cross-class solidarity," trust, and confidence in the system of social insurance; such widespread orientations reinforce the economic interests of broad coalitions of beneficiaries.[48] Constitutional guarantees to the right of subsistence (e.g., Italy and Germany) and legal determinations that claims to social insurance benefits are in effect property rights (e.g., Germany) create a high degree of legitimacy for the prevailing system. As Clasen (1997), Clasen and Gould (1995), Hinrichs (1995) and others have noted for Germany (and as Niero [1996] and Spicker [1997], among others, have argued for Italy and France, respectively), the structure of the conservative welfare state model has linked working- and middle-class interests, facilitated the integration of labor and capital, offered a formula for sharing the proceeds of national economic growth, and promoted a "culture of solidarity" and trust in the welfare state.

With regard to social corporatist institutions, social welfare reform in both Germany and Italy has been systematically conditioned by either

---

[48] Reinforcing the arguments that the conservative model leads to broad cross-class support based on economic interests and on the generation and maintenance of legitimacy and the values of solidarity and trust, data generated by the International Social Survey on the Role of Government demonstrates that corporatist conservative welfare states have enjoyed comparatively high levels of mass support and this has been sustained through at least the early 1990s (e.g., Döring [1997]; Pettersen [1995]). Country-specific public opinion polls have shown consistently high support for most features of the social insurance systems as well (on France, see Hantrais [1996]; on Germany, Clasen [1997] and Lawson [1996]; on Italy, see Niero [1996]). However, one should note that issues surrounding the ability of the model to address problems of social exclusion – of immigrants, the long-term unemployed, single female-headed households, and those in irregular labor markets – have created fissures in broad supportive political coalitions. Perhaps the most notable example of decline in support for a major element of the social insurance model is the mid-1990s decrease in positive attitudes to the Italian health system (Ferrera, 1997).

formal or informal concertation between the social partners and the government. Even in France, where union density and centralization are low, informal incorporation of the social partners has played a role in shaping contemporary social policy change. In the case of Germany, Ebbinghaus and Hassel (2000) make clear that the German system of wage bargaining has operated without either formal government involvement or income policies; recent efforts to formally negotiate tripartite social pacts have also largely failed. However, most analysts of social policy reform also make clear that trade unions (and employers) have been integral partners, either through direct participation in negotiations or through explicit representation by the political parties, in major social welfare reforms. As Alber (1996), Clasen and Gould (1995), Lawson (1996), and others have argued, unions have been consistently incorporated in consensus-oriented social policy making throughout the last two decades. For instance, in the 1989 pension – and other large-scale – reforms, specific elements of the policy were adjusted to incorporate demands of the trade unions (and employers), and the ultimate reform reflected the typical concertation among the social partners and the governing and opposition political parties (Schmähl, 1993).

In Italy, regularized corporatist concertation has been a more recent development. As discussed in the case-study analysis, regular social pacts in the late 1970s and 1980s facilitated bargains on wage restraint and economic restructuring. As Treu (1994) and others have pointed out, corporatist social pacts played a large role in the latter stages of development of the Italian welfare state and 1980s extensions of social protection. In addition, most observers have suggested that corporatist concertation and systematic integration of the social partners in national policy making have become more institutionalized in the 1990s (Ferrera and Gualmini, 1998; Regini and Regalia, 1997; Treu, 1994). In fact, analysts of the reforms of the 1990s have highlighted not only the greater institutionalization of concertation, but also the increasing necessity for governments (e.g., the Amato and Dini technocratic governments) to negotiate major reforms and restructuring with the social partners (Ebbinghaus and Hassel, 2000; Ferrera and Gualmini, 1998; Regini and Regalia, 1997). As a result, the interests of welfare state constituencies and the unions have been at least in part protected (Pitruzzello, 1997).[49]

---

[49] Even in the case of France, where union density and centralization are low and where tripartite concertation has generally failed (Ebbinghaus and Hassel, 2000), negotiations

The presence of relatively inclusive electoral institutions has also facilitated the development and defense of the welfare state. As noted in Chapters 2 and 3, the corporatist conservative welfare states (with the exception of France) possess relatively high levels of electoral inclusiveness: proportional representation and multiparty parliamentary chambers and cabinets are typical of these systems. In fact, in the 1980–95 era of substantial welfare state retrenchment efforts, electoral representation and government participation across the Social Democratic, Christian Democratic, and the secular Center-Right parties was highly balanced. For instance, average votes for Left, Christian Democratic, and Center-Right parties in parliamentary elections for lower chambers were 43, 29, and 28 percent, respectively. Cabinet participation among the party groups was even more equally distributed: the percentage of cabinet portfolios held by Social Democratic, Christian Democratic, and secular Center-Right parties in the average year between 1980 and 1995 in the corporatist conservative welfare states was 36, 38, and 26 percent, respectively.

The welfare state consequences of the presence of relatively inclusive electoral institutions may be illustrated by the case of Italy. As Ferrera (1995), Ferrera and Gualmini (1998), Niero (1996), and others have pointed out, the Center-Left governments of the late 1970s–early 1990s played a large role in shaping the latter stages of development of the Italian welfare state and responsiveness of social policy to domestic and international economic change. For instance, the pentapartito governments of the 1980s (Christian Democrats, Socialists, Social Democrats, Liberals, and Republicans) represented the welfare state interests of the Center and Left, enhanced the role of unions in concertation, and generally served as "veto players" over welfare state change (Ferrera and Gaulmini, 1998). Even with the shift to more majoritarian electoral institutions and reconstitution of the Italian party system in the mid-1990s, the technocratic governments of Amato, Ciampi, and Dini relied on, and incorporated the interests of, the Center-Left parties in major mid-1990s social welfare reforms (Pitruzzello, 1997). For the most part, Italy and the remainder of the conservative welfare states have experienced multipartism and the

between unions and governments have often occurred and proven crucial to the success of social policy reforms. For instance, the Balladur government's 1993 reforms were based on consensus building among the unions, parties, and government, and were successfully proposed and enacted with little political resistance; Juppé's 1995 reforms were consciously introduced without concertation and were significantly modified in the wake of mass political opposition.

attendant dynamics of consensus building among a relatively broad spectrum of interests; representation and consensus building inclusive of pro–welfare state interests has been typically absent with respect to the significant social policy reforms of the single-party majority governments of the Anglo-liberal welfare states.

Finally, with respect to the structure of decision-making authority within the polity, evidence about institutional effects on welfare state restructuring is less clear. Generally, the polities of the corporatist conservative welfare states span a range from relatively high formal concentration of policy-making power (e.g., France), to relatively decentralized and dispersed decision-making authority (e.g., Germany). It is important to point out, however, that, in most cases, the core programs of the social insurance model have been developed and institutionalized at the national level of government during periods of political centralization. In fact, despite historical traditions of fragmentation and decentralization, Germany has a strong legacy of centralized welfare state institutions (e.g., M. Schmidt [1989]). As Alber (1996) points out in his comparative analysis of means-tested social assistance in Germany and the United States during the era of retrenchment, Germany's welfare state is built on the basis of national program structures supported by federal-level constitutional guarantees; this concentration focuses political attention and facilitates the construction of strong supportive national coalitions. This centralization stands in direct contrast to the more fragmented structure of the U.S. welfare model, in which national coalitions have been undercut by notable institutional fragmentation of both the welfare state itself and the polity; such dispersion of authority has reflected and reinforced antistatist values and norms.

Overall, Germany is the case that most notably stands apart from the theory's predictions about welfare state retrenchment in systems of dispersed authority. That is, in all or most of the polities of high dispersion of authority – Australia, Canada, Switzerland, and the United States – country-specific evidence, as well as theory and quantitative analysis, suggests that dispersion of authority has retarded welfare state development (and hence contemporary welfare programmatic coalitions), strategically and organizationally fragmented pro–welfare state actors and national coalitions, and reinforced biases against central state intervention. As such, pro–welfare state interests and coalitions are weak and policy-making orientations tend to favor welfare state retrenchment (despite the presence of institutional veto points). In Germany, however the relatively recent post–World War Two construction of the institutions of the Federal Republic has had few of the anti–welfare state effects of the long-standing institutional fragmentation of other polities of dispersed decision-making authority. Instead, the German case analysis of welfare state retrenchment has to a degree highlighted the role of institutional veto points, especially the role of the SPD-controlled Bundesrat during the 1990s Center-Right government's tenure: as discussed above, the Bundesrat effectively blocked (or contributed to the reformulation of) a number of welfare state reform measures during the era of post-Unification welfare state restructuring.

In sum, configurations of national political and welfare state institutions have played large roles in shaping the welfare state impacts of the economic and political pressures generated by internationalization. Welfare state structures of the social insurance model, social corporatist interest representation, and inclusive electoral institutions have all been systematically important for social welfare policy reform: each of these institutional dimensions have promoted representation, political capacities, and supportive norms and values for pro–welfare state interests, and, in turn, blunted neoliberal reform. The structure of decision-making authority has also mattered, but in complex ways that reflect the multiple linkages between institutional structures, political power, and policy change.

6

Internationalization and Liberal Welfare States: A Synopsis

The predominately liberal welfare states of Britain, North America, and Australasia are characterized by a mixture of moderate to low flat-rate, social insurance, and extensively means-tested benefits, as well as significant private social insurance and relatively small public commitments to government-provided social services. Comparative data presented in preceding chapters have highlighted these features of liberal welfare states, as well as their relatively modest impacts in ameliorating poverty and income inequalities. As I have also illustrated, programmatic features of some of these welfare states create significant departures from the liberal prototype. Most notably, Britain (especially prior to 1980) exhibits significant elements of universalism in program structure (especially through the National Health Service and flat-rate benefits based on citizenship). In addition, the Australian (and New Zealand) welfare state represents an interesting variation of the liberal model. Prior to the 1980s, low and heavily means-tested social benefits have been embedded in a state regulated system of relatively high minimum wages, protectionism for domestic industry, and progressive taxation (e.g., Castles [1996]; Castles and Mitchell [1993]). Although public social protection is modest, (pre-1980s) wage compression and full employment have combined with social welfare programs to create a "wage earners welfare state" (Castles, 1985).

In this chapter, I provide succinct case studies of contemporary social welfare policy change and the sources of that change in two liberal systems, the United States and Britain, and brief analyses of globalization, political institutions, and social welfare state reforms in Australia, Canada, and New Zealand. For Britain and the United States, I first provide chronologies of what are, in effect, relatively extensive neoliberal reforms of social welfare provision. I then assess the ways in which the economic and political logics

218

of globalization have influenced these reforms and how institutional features of the polity and welfare state have shaped social policy change. Emphasis is placed on the United States and Britain given their weight in the world economy, their roles in neoliberal policy innovations, and widespread debates over the sources and impacts of U.S. and British social policy change.

Social Welfare Policy Change in the United States

As Benjamin Page (1997) has noted, the expansion of redistributive social (and tax) policy in the United States was arguably reversed during last two Democratic (Carter, Clinton) and Republican (Reagan, Bush) presidential administrations. In fact, nearly all of the increase in U.S. social spending since 1975 (in real dollar or GDP share terms) can be directly traced to socioeconomic and demographic pressures on social programs enacted in the 1930s (i.e., the New Deal legislation of the Roosevelt Administration) and the 1960s (i.e., Kennedy-Johnson Great Society Initiatves).[1] During the last 25 years, new U.S. social policy legislation has in nearly all cases promoted cost containment, market-oriented restructuring, or reductions in social welfare provision.

The social policy initiatives during the 1977–80 presidency of Jimmy Carter form the groundwork for subsequent (and more significant) market-oriented reforms and welfare retrenchment of the Reagan-Bush and Clinton eras. Within the context of a broader shift to deregulation and restrictive macroeconomic policies, the Carter administration proposed (unsuccessfully) modest reductions in old-age and survivors pensions benefits, as well as (successfully) initiated social security tax increases and tighter eligibility rules for disability insurance. In addition, labeling extant means-tested social assistance antiwork and antifamily, the Carter administration proposed the Program for Better Jobs and Income (PBJI), which mandated work for recipients of means-tested assistance (principally Aid to Families with Dependent Children; hereafter AFDC). Although the PBJI was not enacted into law, it foreshadowed significant reforms of

---

[1] For analysis of the origins and singular importance of these two periods of policy innovation, see Hicks (1999, 2000). For my synopsis of the development of U.S. social policy, I rely heavily on: Brady and Volden (1998), Champagne and Harpham (1984), Estes (1991), Gottschalk (1988), Howard (1997), Noble (1997), Pierson (1994, 1998), Quadagno (1991), Skocpol (1995), Stoesz (1996), Stoesz and Karger (1992), Waddam (1997), and Weaver (1998).

means-tested social supports that emphasized work, self-sufficiency, and flexibility at the low end of the labor market. In fact, perhaps the most notable social welfare reform of this period was the 1978 extension of the work-oriented 1975 Earned Income Tax Credit (hereafter EITC) that offered tax reductions and (within limits) cash rebates to low-income employees.

The 1980 election of Ronald Reagan to the presidency and presence of a Republican party majority in the Senate marked the beginning of moderate to significant retrenchment of the American welfare state (c.f., Pierson [1994]). With the support of conservative (principally southern and border-state) Democrats in the House of Representatives, the Reagan administration initiated a series of significant retrenchments in means-tested cash and in-kind social programs (primarily in the 1981 Omnibus Budget and Reconciliation Act), reductions in health programs, moderate cuts in social insurance programs for workers (e.g., unemployment and disability insurance), and long-term reductions in old-age pensions. In fact, excluding Medicare and Medicaid spending, which, despite cost containment and efficiency-oriented reforms, accelerated under the pressure of significant health care cost inflation (Graig, 1999), nonhealth social welfare spending as a share of GDP declined during the Reagan-Bush era from an 1975–9 annual average of 10.5 percent to 9.2 percent in 1991–5. This decline occurred in the face of significant upward demographic and economic pressures on social expenditure, including significant increases in unemployment, poverty, and declining incomes at the low end of the income distribution.[2]

Income maintenance and social service programs for the poor, as well as social insurance for those in the labor force, were significantly reduced during the first years of the Reagan-Bush presidential administrations. Primarily through restrictive changes in eligibility rules, 1982 and 1983 fiscal year expenditure for AFDC was trimmed by roughly 14 percent, while Food Stamp outlays were cut by approximately 17 percent; roughly 400,000 families lost AFDC benefits and 300,000 had benefits reduced

---

[2] Total U.S. social spending (as a percentage of GDP and using OECD definitions) increased from 14.1 to 15.5 between the 1975–9 to 1991–5 periods. On the increases in unemployment, poverty, and inequality and their interaction with the welfare state in the United States, see, among others, Levy (1998); for a comparative perspective on the relatively large increases in U.S. poverty and income inequality, see OECD (1995b) and contributions to McFate, Lawson, and Wilson (1995).

during the Reagan administration (see contributions to Bawden, 1984; Stoesz and Karger, 1992). Combined with significant post-1973 reductions in the real value of AFDC benefits through the absence of cost-of-living adjustments (e.g., Alber [1996]), low-income support through AFDC was significantly retrenched during the 1980s. In addition, the Family Support Act was passed in 1988. While the program provided increased funds for child care and authorized training funds through the Job Opportunities and Basic Skills (JOBS) program, the act established the principle that the receipt of benefits required work: states were mandated to enroll stipulated percentages of their AFDC populations in work or training programs and work requirements for two-parent AFDC families were initiated.

Means-tested social services, housing assistance, and labor market programs were consolidated into block grants to the states and significantly reduced. Real outlays for social services for the poor, housing assistance programs, and training and education programs declined by 30 percent between 1978 and 1994 (Mollenkopf, 1998). Stricter eligibility rules for disability insurance enacted during the Carter presidency were further tightened in the first years of the Reagan administration and unemployment insurance benefits were cut. For instance, the administration raised the unemployment level required to "trigger" extended unemployment benefits. In fact, the long-term trend for the social wage provided by the U.S. welfare state fell from an early-1980s level of 28 percent to 24 percent of gross wages for the average production worker by the 1991–5 period.

In the area of health care, expenditures under existing budgetary projections for Medicare and Medicaid were reduced by $20 and $15 billion, respectively, between 1981 and 1987 (Estes, 1991). Generally, the Reagan administration promoted reductions in health outlays through tighter federal and state eligibility rules (e.g., for home health care), incentives to the states to reduce utilization, direct cost containment (e.g., the shift to prospective reimbursement systems), increases in co-payments and deductibles, and privatization. With respect to the latter, direct and indirect policy changes (e.g., cuts in supports of public day care) encouraged increased use of private service providers. Although there were small extensions of health care coverage during the Bush administration (principally the extension of Medicaid to children in families at or below 133 percent of the poverty line), trends toward program cuts, cost containment, and efficiency-oriented reforms continued during the 1989–92 period (e.g., increased deductibles and tightened health care provider reimbursements for Medicare). An expansion of the public role in health care, the Medicare Catastrophic Insurance Act, was initially enacted in 1988 and then rescinded in 1989.[3]

The U.S. system of old-age pensions, created by the 1935 Social Security Act and expanded through the early 1970s, was also the target of retrenchment during the Reagan administration. Although tax increases were enacted during the Carter presidency, adverse demographic trends and the early 1980s recession of the U.S. economy engendered severe fiscal pressure on the system by the time the new Republican president and senatorial majority took office. Initial administration proposals to trim $45 billion (primarily in an effort to effect large and immediate general budget cuts) generated withering political resistance by Democrats, unions, the interest associations of the elderly, and a large majority of the public; these proposals were summarily rejected by Congress (e.g., Light [1985]; Pierson [1994]). However, continued fiscal stress and efforts to seek substantial public expenditure cuts resulted in 1983 legislation that moderately reduced old-age pension benefits and increased social security taxes. On the benefit side, early retirement benefits were reduced, the retirement age was scheduled for future increases, and the benefits of high-income workers were taxed; modest reductions through changes in the benefit formula were made and the COLA adjustment was frozen for six months. Revenues were enhanced by increasing social security contribution rates, bringing new federal government workers into the system, and increasing taxes on the self-employed. In addition to the increased costs of taxation, the 1983 legislation reduced income replacement rates during the 1985 to 2030 period from roughly 64 to 51 percent for low-income workers and from 41 to 36 percent for average earners (e.g., Pierson [1994]).

The 1992 election of Democrat Bill Clinton to the White House did not significantly alter the general trajectory of U.S. social policy. Although Clinton succeeded in passing the 1993 Family and Medical Leave Act in 1993 (after failures of this legislation in 1985, 1988, and 1991), this legis-

---

[3] During the Bush administration, the most notable programmatic expansion was the 1990 extension of the EITC. This program provides income support to low-income workers and, hence, hinges on nontrivial earnings. As such, it is consistent with market-conforming social policy reform (see Myles and Pierson [1997]). As Howard (1997) has noted, the program has quickly rivaled AFDC as the main form of cash income support for the poor. In addition, the 1990 Budget Enforcement Act contained modest increases for some social service programs (replacing some expenditures eliminated during the Reagan years); however, roughly one-half of the additional revenues for social programs consisted of increases for the EITC (Stoesz and Karger, 1992).

lation provided no income supports for medical or maternity leaves and exempted roughly 40 percent of employers from the act's provisions. In addition, a modest 1993 economic stimulus package, which provided some expansion of social service, training, and health programs for the poor, largely failed in Congress (in part due to a filibuster in the Senate). In even more dramatic fashion, the 1993 Health Security Act, which offered virtually universal health coverage through a national system of managed care and federal guidelines, failed to win legislative approval. Although the Clinton administration won some small increases in budgetary support for antipoverty programs and presided over the 1993 increase in the EITC, the 1994 congressional elections returned a Republican majority to the House. House Republican proposals in 1995 and 1996 included significant cuts in planned Medicare outlays (e.g., a $270 billion multiyear cut that was vetoed by Clinton) and a major restructuring of means-tested programs.

After Clinton assumed office in 1993, major proposals were developed to honor the pledge "to end welfare as we know it." The administration generally supported AFDC reforms that would mandate work and training (with additional child and health care supports during transition to employment), improved child support payment enforcement, and time limits on receipt of AFDC. The House Republican initiatives went significantly beyond the administration's policies in most areas, effectively proposing the abrogation of the federal role in most forms of means-tested social welfare. The compromise legislation, the 1996 Personal Responsibility and Work Opportunities Act, transferred AFDC, JOBS funds, and administrative responsibilities to the states. The act also approved five-year time limits on receipt of AFDC, stringent work requirements, and provisions for state discretion to impose family caps (i.e., limits on assistance irrespective of additional children) and other restrictions on benefits. In effect, while the federal role in Food Stamps and Medicaid was maintained, the 1996 Act ended national entitlement to income support for the poor.

Internationalization and U.S. Social Welfare Reform

At first glance, domestic social policy in the United States may seem somewhat insulated from the immediate economic and political pressures associated with globalization. Other than indirect policy effects that derived from America's hegemonic position in the international political economy, and from the routine politics of international economic policy, relatively low levels of trade and capital flows for much of the postwar era palpably resulted in a relatively weak linkage between internationalization and American social policy development. However, further liberalization of already low capital and financial controls in the 1970s and 1980s, and a significant expansion of trade flows from roughly 10 percent to 20 percent of GDP between the 1960s and late 1980s, have arguably increased substantially the potential for international pressures on social welfare (and other domestic) policies. So, too, have the acceleration of capital flows in the wake of the collapse of the Bretton Woods system, subsequent developments of international markets, and reductions in transaction costs for FDI. Generally, the impact of post-1973 internationalization on the reform and retrenchment of the American welfare state comes through two interrelated channels.[4]

First, as King and Wood (1999) suggest, retrenchment of the American welfare state has been part of an overall neoliberal response to the inability of 1970s policies (e.g., cyclical macroeconomic management) in liberal market economies (LME hereafter) to address stagflation and problems attendant on globalization. Complementary analyses by Krieger (1986), and Borchert (1995, 1996) have also stressed that the post-1970s shift to a broad program of neoliberal reform by U.S. policy makers (and those in Britain) was in part driven by a "politics of relative economic decline," where perceptions of a secular fall in trade competitiveness and increases in outward flows of foreign investment – and the resulting job and income losses – was a factor in liberalization and fiscal retrenchment. Building on the work of Soskice (1999), King and Wood (1999) argue that, within the context of the LME, American (and British) policy makers did not have recourse to, for instance, corporatist management of wage costs or the advantages associated with high levels of state-regulated business cooperation characteristic of nationally or sectorally coordinated market

---

[4] As I have noted above, beyond the causal mechanisms highlighted in this section, the systematic relationship between globalization and social welfare retrenchment in the liberal cases uncovered in quantitative analysis may also be a function of the relationship between a broad neoliberal program of domestic and international liberalization of markets and concomitant or subsequent rollbacks of social welfare protections. As I demonstrate here, however, a source of the overarching neoliberal reform program is internationalization itself. Furthermore, exogenous economic change and political action, as I also demonstrate, clearly link internationalization and welfare state retrenchment, as well. In all cases, democratic institutions condition the linkages between internationalization, liberalization, and social policy change.

economies. In the absence or infeasibility of these and related institutions and state-guided responses, American (and British) policy makers pursued substantial fiscal retrenchment, deregulation, and labor market reforms in order to enhance overall market flexibility and to reduce the social wage that undermines the low-cost production strategy of LMEs. In fact, observers of the character of American (and other liberal system) social policy reform have consistently noted that, by reducing the social wage and reinforcing work incentives, reductions in cash income transfers, "work-fare," increases in programs such as the EITC, and related policy changes are a coherent approach to enhancing flexibility at the low end of the labor market (e.g., Banting [1997]; Myles [1996]; Myles and Pierson [1997]).[5]

Second, exemplifying the political logic of globalization, the social policy impacts of internationalization have been shaped by the political mobilization of American business. Rises in the U.S. trade deficit and concerns over international competitiveness initially contributed to 1970s business mobilization (e.g., Ferguson and Rogers [1986]; Page [1997]; Quadagno [1991]). This well documented era of new levels and forms of collective action consisted of the post-1972 refurbishing of extant business organizations (e.g., Business Council, Chamber of Commerce, Council of Economic Development, National Association of Manufacturers) as well as the establishment of new organizations such as the Business Roundtable (Edsall [1984]; McQuaid [1994]). Political action from the mid-1970s consisted of substantial increases in funds for Political Action Committees, lobbying, and conservative think-tanks, as well as a wave of advertising and publication activity that linked the problems of the U.S. economy, including the perceived loss of competitiveness, outflows of FDI, and related international economic problems, to the Keynesian welfare state (e.g., Edsall [1984]; Page [1997]; Piven and Cloward [1982]). As Edsall and Edsall (1991) and most of the aforementioned scholars note, the systematic claims that social welfare spending and the taxes that support it undercut competitiveness and contribute generally to international economic difficulties strongly reinforce the appeal of general neoliberal economic

---

[5] It is also important to point out that King and Wood (1999) argue that not only is the neoliberal response to post-1970 economic performance problems and the challenges of internationalization functional in LME, but that Reagan's and Thatcher's policies were strategic political constructions, as well. In the case of both the Republican and Conservative parties, such policies were designed to weaken core constituencies of their oppositions and otherwise promote their electoral success under extant late-1970s political conditions.

orthodoxy (i.e., that the welfare state contributes to the diminution of work incentives, saving, and investment). Together with ascendent neoconservative social theories that link the welfare state to a wide set of social pathologies, widely publicized arguments about the deleterious domestic and internationalization economic performance impacts of the welfare state have contributed to the neoliberal policy reforms of the last 25 years.[6]

A series of popular magazine articles and books in the 1980s and 1990s by business executive Peter G. Peterson, founding member of Concord Coalition for U.S. entitlement reform, is illustrative of the popularization of these arguments by business economists and executives.[7] For instance, in the October 1987 *Atlantic Monthly* article, "The Morning After," Peterson argues that curbing U.S. entitlement spending, especially social security pensions and Medicare, is essential to restoring U.S. competitiveness and the relative performance of the U.S. economy. Specifically, Peterson argued that notable growth in entitlement spending is at the heart of the rise of federal government deficits; post-1980 deficits are singled out as the key factor in declining U.S. saving and investment rates and, in turn, sagging productivity and competitiveness. In addition, Peterson highlights the argument that post-1980 rises in deficits and debt have led to a dramatic growth in foreign borrowing and, in turn, increasing exposure of the U.S. economy to the volatility of international capital markets and preferences of foreign investors.[8] This and related arguments (e.g., the rise in

---

[6] On the social and economic theory of "the new Right" in America and Britain, see King (1987) and King and Wood (1999) and the large literature on the topic they survey. For an insightful analysis of the rise of monetarism in Britain, see Hall (1993). With respect to business policy preferences, C. J. Martin (2000) has pointed out that while elements of American business have tentatively supported social spending for human resources (including modest levels of large business support for Clinton's Health Security Act), neoliberal arguments concerning threats to profits and other business interests – including threats to international competitiveness – have typically dominated debates within American business and subsequent social policy positions. For a theoretical and empirical analysis of conditions under which business has supported social interventions, see Swank and C. J. Martin (forthcoming).

[7] Observers (e.g., Myles [1996]) note that Peterson's Concord Coalition has been influential in 1990s policy debates and government reports on long-term social insurance reform. For instance, the 1994 Entitlement Commission chaired by Democratic Senator John Kerry and Republican Senator John Danforth recommended significant increases in means-testing of social insurance, a position championed by Peterson.

[8] It is also important to note that as U.S. budget deficits rose in the 1980s and early 1990s, anticipations of the reaction of international bond markets by U.S. fiscal policy makers may well have added pressures for early-1990s balanced budget legislation and further fiscal restraints (e.g., Noble [1997]).

foreign debt entails the transfer of U.S. assets to nonresidents), were increasingly common in the 1980s and early 1990s (e.g., see Phillips [1990, Ch. 5] for a review of the popular and academic literature). Overall, while the specifics of Peterson's critique of American social policy is somewhat distinct (with its criticism of Reagan administration policies and its emphasis on the mediating role of the deficit and a mean-tested solution for U.S. entitlement spending reform), the general logic of linking U.S. social spending to domestic and international performance problems of the American economy is typical of much post-1972 business and neoliberal partisan attack on the welfare state.

Political Institutions and Policy Change in the American Welfare State

The moderate to substantial retrenchment of the American welfare state from the mid-1970s to mid-1990s, and the role of globalization in that policy change, was arguably facilitated by the structural features of the American polity and welfare state. In sharp contrast to the Social Democratic and corporatist conservative systems, the absence of inclusive electoral institutions and social corporatist institutions in the United States has certainly reduced the veto and leverage points through which pro–welfare state interests can defend their material and ideological interests; weakened (in the long-term) pro–welfare state parties, unions, and other pro–welfare state collective actors; and contributed to the absence of prevailing norms of compromise and consensus in which all interests are accounted in the formulation of social policy reform. The liberal structure of the welfare state has also contributed to the development of political conditions conducive to retrenchment. As analysts have noted, the absence of universal social citizen rights and the means-tested character of substantial components of the American welfare state has fragmented lower- and middle-class support; the association of 1960s Great Society antipoverty programs with inner-city African Americans has further fragmented collective actors (e.g., the Democratic party) and national redistributive coalitions across racial lines (e.g., Noble [1997]; Quadagno [1994]; Skocpol [1995]).

The one arguable exception to these generalizations occurs with respect to Social Security (i.e., old-age pensions), and the important 1983 reform of this major element of the American welfare state. Light (1985), Pierson (1994), and others have pointed out that the 1983 reform was negotiated in the context of significant working- and middle-class support for the program and among representatives of labor, the aged, the Democratic party on the one hand, and spokespersons for the Reagan administration, congressional Republicans, and business on the other. However, in comparison to both the Social Democratic and conservative welfare states, the ability of pro–welfare state interests to defend old-age income maintenance seems limited. In the context of economic recession and long-term structural problems of the U.S. economy, benefit cuts and disincentives to early retirement were enacted relatively early in the 1980s (and under less onerous demographic shifts than faced by European policy reformers in the 1990s). In addition, while tax increases were shared by employers and the affluent elderly, lower- and middle-income employees (and not higher-income earners, given the program's cap on wages and salaries subject to taxation) bear a substantial portion of increased social security costs. In cross-national comparison to old-age pension reform in the European welfare states, one might argue that stronger representative institutions would have resulted in reforms somewhat more favorable for pro–welfare state interests.

Finally, the structure of decision-making authority in the American polity has certainly played a role in shaping the course of welfare state reform. In previous chapters, I have argued that the dispersion of policy-making authority in the polity should, on balance, foster welfare state retrenchment under economic and political pressures attendant on globalization; I argued this should be true despite the veto points accorded pro–welfare state interests in fragmented polities. While institutional fragmentation certainly offers opportunities to block retrenchment in the short term, the long-term impacts of fragmentation on the political capacities of pro–welfare state interests and the prevailing character of the policy process suggest that fragmented polities will be particularly conducive to welfare retrenchment over the course of time. Theoretically, the case seems strongest for decentralization of decision-making authority. Subsequent analysis has indeed demonstrated that decentralization (and not separation of powers) has the strongest (negative) direct effects on the welfare state and plays the pivotal role in enhancing pressures generated by globalization.

The role of decentralization seems particularly important to understanding American social policy reform in the contemporary period. As discussed, decentralization (especially federalism itself) has fragmented pro–welfare state actors and coalitions and promoted antistatist orientations, conflict, and competition within the American political system.

Federalism has played a general role in promoting regional, ethnic, and racial divisions within the national Democratic party, fissures that seem increasingly problematic for the ability of the Democratic party to defend social welfare programs over the last 25 years. Moreover, while federal and state authority and responsibility are inextricably linked in the formation and implementation of substantial components of American social policy, program structure allows substantial latitude for autonomous federal policy change (and hence few formal veto points for the states). Instead, federalism offers numerous opportunities for retrenchment-minded national administrations to devolve increasing responsibility for social policy to the states. With limited fiscal capacities, exacerbated by post-1973 economic problems, and the tendency to engage in interstate competition for economic resources, 1980s and 1990s decentralization of means-tested policy-making and financial responsibilities to the states, as well as federal retrenchment in programs such as unemployment insurance, in which the states play significant roles, may well be a successful example of what Paul Pierson (1994) has labeled systemic retrenchment. While strong U.S. bicameralism, which creates an additional national veto point, is closely tied to the federal structure of the American polity through the territorially based Senate, the overall impact of decentralization of the political system in the United States has been to facilitate retrenchment.[9]

Internationalization and Retrenchment of the British Welfare State

As in the United States, the era of retrenchment and restructuring of the British welfare state begins in the mid- to late 1970s under Left party government.[10] In 1976, the balance-of-payments crisis necessitated emergency International Monetary Fund loans to Britain. Under significant IMF pressure for public expenditure controls, pressures that reinforced the Labour government's shift to expenditure containment in the wake of the

---

[9] While this argument may be at odds with those of some who have contended that the fragmented structure of the U.S. polity versus the British political system can explain generally less severe U.S. welfare retrenchment (e.g., King and Wood [1999]; Borchert [1995, 1996]), my argument and subsequent analysis is consistent with the view that the separation of powers establishes more significant institutional impediments to retrenchment in the United States than in parliamentary Britain.

[10] For material on the British welfare state, I rely on Graig (1999, Ch. 7), Erskine (1997), King (1987), King and Wood (1999), Perry (1988), Pierson (1994, 1996), Rhodes (2000b), Taylor-Gooby (1996), and Williamson (2000), as well as sources cited in the text.

1975 "sterling crisis," Labour Prime Minister James Callaghan initiated a series of budgetary reductions, reversing earlier expansions of social welfare legislated in 1974 and 1975 by the Labour government (e.g., Hall [1986, Ch. 4]; Holmes [1985]; King [1987]; Krieger [1986]; Wickham-Jones [1996]). Significant initiatives to retrench the British welfare state, however, do not begin until the 1979 parliamentary election victory of the Conservative party and the government of Prime Minister Margaret Thatcher.

Market-oriented restructuring of the British welfare state during the Thatcher government and that of her successor, John Major, has arguably been extensive (c.f., Pierson [1994, 1996]; Castles and Pierson [1996]). Significant retrenchment and efficiency-oriented reforms have occurred in old-age pensions, income supports for the working-age population, and health care and social services. With respect to public pension provision, the Thatcher-Major governments legislated a series of significant changes in British pension policy. First, the universal flat-rate "basic pension," created as a means-tested pension in 1908 and made universal in 1925, has been scaled back. In effect, 1980 welfare reform legislation reduced the value of the basic pension by shifting the indexing method from wage increases to changes in price levels. As Pierson (1994) and others have noted, this reform in effect allows economic growth to erode the importance of the basic pension over time: the value of the basic pension declined (relative to pre-1980 policies) by roughly 20 percent during the 1980s.

While the Thatcher government's 1985 proposals for major and rapid restructuring of the State Earnings Related Pension System (SERPS) met with substantial political resistance, the 1986 Social Security Act significantly reformed the earnings-related tier of public pensions. The benefit formula was altered to reduce general income replacement rates from 25 to 20 percent of earnings; provisions to base benefits on the "best 20 years" of earnings were changed so that benefit calculations would be made on lifetime earnings. In addition, significant tax incentives were created to encourage workers to opt out of SERPS and establish personal pensions (or take advantage of private occupational pensions). The 1986 pension legislation was extended by 1995 pension reforms during the Conservative government of John Major: the retirement age for women was increased from 60 to 65 years of age (by 2010), benefit formula modifications made public pensions even less generous, and the costs of indexing occupational pensions were shifted from the government to employers. As Williamson (2000) has illustrated, the long-term effects of these reforms are, in comparative perspective, rather dramatic. While virtually all other nations experience (sometimes huge) rises in shares of GDP committed to public pensions from 1990 through 2050 (often despite benefit cuts and other cost controls), the pension outlay share of GDP in Britain is projected to decline from 4.2 to 3.4 percent during this period (Williamson, 2000, Table 1). Furthermore, as Helen Fawcett (1995) has pointed out, while Thatcher-Major era reforms might be interpreted as consistent with path dependency in pension policy, the cumulative effect of 1980s and 1990s Conservative Party policy change has been to residualize public pensions, significantly weaken political support for public old-age provision, and, in turn, lay the groundwork for future retrenchment of the system.

Significant rollbacks in benefits have also occurred in the area of income supports for the working-age population. Unemployment and disability insurance as well as sick pay have been cut significantly. As Pierson (1994, 1996) and others have documented, replacement rates for British unemployment benefits have been incrementally reduced through a series of piecemeal reforms. For instance, 1980 social welfare legislation (implemented in 1982) ended supplemental unemployment benefits and began taxation of benefits. The real value of basic unemployment benefits was allowed to fall in the 1980s and tougher eligibility standards were enacted in 1989. In 1996, income supports and insurance for the unemployed were largely consolidated into Jobs Seekers Allowances. Duration of benefits was restricted to six months (from one year) and strict work and training requirements were mandated. In the area of sick pay, early-1980s legislation transferred costs to employers for the first six weeks of sickness and phased out employer subsidies of these costs. Indexation was shifted from wages to price levels and the real value of benefits was reduced roughly 15 percent by 1988.

In the wake of the early-1980s recession and concomitant unemployment benefit cuts, means-tested programs and other income supports became increasingly important to the expanding numbers of unemployed. The recipients of the Supplemental Benefit and Family Income Support (FIS) programs grew substantially (and eligibility for the FIS was expanded). Although these programs experienced only modest benefit cuts and restructuring as the 1980s progressed (e.g., modest late-1980s budget cuts in the consolidated Income Supplement and Family Income Support program), eligibility and the real value of benefits were reduced for other important income maintenance programs such as housing assistance and the Family Credit. Using OECD data, the social wage, defined as the percentage of gross income replaced by unemployment insurance and income supports for the average unemployed production worker, declined from a 1975–9 annual average of 28 percent to 18 percent by the 1991–5 era.[11]

Market-oriented restructuring and retrenchment has also occurred in the areas of health care, social housing, and social services. Efficiency-oriented reforms in public service provision have been widespread and include the contracting out of services, implementation of private sector management methods, and internal markets. The two most notable reforms (aside from extensive market-oriented education reforms) have occurred in the areas of housing policy and health care. In the area of housing policy, the Housing Act of 1980 established the "right to buy" entitlement for residents of council housing; roughly one-fifth of council housing was sold under provisions favorable to purchasers by the early 1990s. Early 1980s- and subsequent policy reforms also dramatically reduced new construction of social housing, significantly cut subsidies to local housing authorities, and increased rents. While the emphasis in housing policy was the nurturing of the private housing market and a shift to cash allowances (to replace social housing construction and support), cash housing assistance was restricted, especially for those over the poverty line.

In the area of health care, policy proposals of the early 1980s to radically restructure the National Health Service (including significant privatization) were met by strong political resistance and withdrawn. However, the market-oriented proposals of the 1989 Government White Paper, "Working for Patients," were enacted by the Conservative Party's parliamentary majority the following year. While the 1990 National Health Service and Community Care Act preserved the basic NHS principles of publicly financed, universal, and comprehensive care that was free at the point of delivery, it entailed substantial reform of the highly centralized

[11] Others such as Stephens, Huber, and Ray (1999) and Ploug and Kvist (1994, 1996) have reported similar or even larger estimates for reductions in income replacement rates for British unemployment, sick pay, and other programs. However, as virtually all analysts of the Thatcher era recognize, demographic shifts and new needs (e.g., the rise in single-parent families), as well as significant post-1979 increases in poverty and unemployment, placed substantial pressures on social welfare budgets: total social spending shares of GDP rose from 21 to 24 percent across the years of the Thatcher budgets (1980–91).

British health care system (Graig, 1999). The central innovation in the NHS was the creation of internal markets (i.e., competition) within the system. Under strict budgetary controls, purchasers (primarily District Health Authorities) would contract for services with NHS hospitals, newly autonomous self-governing trust hospitals, and private and public general practitioners, clinics, and other health care providers. A variety of additional provisions encouraged efficiency in management and service delivery (including contracting out some NHS functions) and provided incentives for the growth (and integration with NHS) of private sector health care providers. In the context of general public spending constraints and the 1990s reforms, and in spite of the dramatic acceleration of health care costs, the public health spending share of GDP expanded moderately from an annual average of 5.2 to 5.7 percent between the 1980–4 and 1991–5 periods; the public share of total health care outlays declined from 88 to 84 percent during the same years (OECD Health Data 98, as described in Appendix A).

Internationalization, Political Institutions, and the British Welfare State

Unlike the United States, Britain was relatively open to external economic pressures prior to the post-1970 acceleration of international market integration. Although significant financial controls were in place until full liberalization of capital movements and international payments in 1979, the de facto integration of British and international financial markets and relatively high financial and trade flows resulted in notable exposure of British domestic economic and budgetary policy to international influences. For instance, while annual capital flows (inward and outward movements of FDI, portfolio investment, and direct bank loans) averaged 6 percent of GDP in the typical Anglo-liberal democracy in the 1960s, the annual GDP share of these financial flows in Britain exceeded 10 percent. Annual average trade openness in the 1960–73 era (i.e., exports and imports of goods and services as shares GDP) was 41 percent, while trade flows in the United States averaged roughly 10 percent of GDP during the same period. In the wake of the breakdown of the Bretton Woods system, technological and institutional changes, and liberalization of barriers to financial and trade movements, integration of British and international markets increased significantly: both total flows of FDI, portfolio investment, and direct bank lending, as well as trade flows, averaged 60 percent of GDP in the 1990–5 period; the monetary value of annual cross-border trade in bonds and equities exceeded 1000 percent of GDP by the early 1990s.[12]

As discussed above, the 1975 "sterling crisis," the 1976 extension of IMF credits to Britain, and concomitant pressures for budgetary retrenchments are exemplary of the impact of internationalization on the British welfare state. In fact, some scholars have argued that postwar Labour governments have been systematically constrained by real and anticipated reactions of international financial markets to Social Democratic expansions of welfare provision and related interventionist policies. Glyn (1986) notes that not only was the 1974–9 Wilson-Callaghan Labour government ultimately forced to roll back Keynesian welfare state policies by international financial markets, but also that the 1960s Labour government of Harold Wilson was similarly constrained upon taking office in 1964. Wickham-Jones (1995) argues that the 1987–92 Labour Party policy review and moderation of traditional manifesto positions, and the accompanying Labour Party initiatives to win approval of its more centrist policy orientations from British and foreign capital, was a conscious strategy to preempt the collapse of confidence and investment that would result from business anticipation of a Labour Party electoral victory. Similarly, Hay (1999), Kreiger (1999), and others argue that subsequent reforms of Labour party policy positions under the leadership of Tony Blair are a function of the Party's acceptance of the "logic of no alternative." That is, in their view, the "modernization" of the Labour Party's ideological orientations and programmatic positions – or the general acceptance of major features of the preceding Conservative governments' neoliberal economic policies and market-oriented reforms and retrenchments of the welfare state – is a function of the belief that alternative, interventionist policy strategies are untenable in the contemporary era of significant globalization.

Beyond the (real and perceived) constraints on interventionism by the Labour Party, the post-1970 acceleration of internationalization, the domestic and international economic performance problems in the 1970s,

---

[12] Measures of capital mobility and trade openness cited in this section are identical to those defined in Chapter 2 and utilized throughout this volume (see Appendix A for all data sources). Cross-border trade in financial instruments is based on Bureau of International Settlements data, as reported in the Economist (1995). See, among others, Kreiger (1999) for a relatively detailed analysis of the relationship of the British economy to international markets and how globalization has affected domestic economic structure.

and the failure of Keynesian welfare state policies during the 1974–9 Wilson-Callaghan governments combined to enhance the appeal of neoliberal economic and social policies (e.g., Borchert [1995, 1996]; King and Wood [1999]; Krieger [1986]). In terms of the political logic of globalization, rising and adverse international financial flows in the 1970s and general international integration of capital and goods markets both contributed to the political acceptance of monetarism and the sound money and price stability it promised (e.g., Gamble [1994a]). Extensive commentary in the business and popular press as well as widely read academic analysis of the scope and consequences of globalization (e.g., Ohmae [1991, 1996]; Reich [1992]) underscored the decline of national autonomy in an era of globalization and, in turn, reinforced the appeal of Conservative party neoliberal economic and social policies and the transformation of the Labour Party in the 1980s and 1990s (Hay and Watson, 1998; Hay and Marsh, 2000).

From a structural perspective on the British political economy, King and Wood (1999) argue that the Thatcher governments' economic and social policies constitute a neoliberal response to the inability of Keynesian welfare state policies to address stagflation and problems attendant on globalization (also see, among others, Krieger [1986]; Borchert [1995, 1996]; Gamble [1994b]).[13] As in their complementary analysis of the American political economy, King and Wood suggest that within the context of a liberal market economy (LME), British policy makers could not successfully pursue social corporatist management of wage costs or industrial policy strategies that depended on high levels of state-regulated business cooperation characteristic of coordinated market economies. As in the case of the United States, British policy makers alternatively pursued substantial domestic and international liberalization, as well as retrenchment and neoliberal restructuring of the welfare state, in order to enhance overall market flexibility and to reduce the social wage that undermines the low-cost production strategy of LMEs. International liberalization itself, and subsequent rises in external flows (e.g., FDI), was

---

[13] As many scholars have noted, the Thatcher government was also motivated by ideological goals that, while related to the contemporary domestic and international economic challenges facing Britain, extended to restoring individual responsibility and entrepreneurial spirit, as well as destroying the legacy or future prospect of socialism in Britain (e.g., Gamble [1994a, 1994b]; King [1987]; King and Wood [1999]). In addition, Thatcher's program was not only functional economically, but was successful in terms of undercutting political opposition and bolstering Conservative party electoral fortunes, as well (e.g., Boix [1998, Ch. 7]; King and Wood [1999]).

designed to further promote industrial consolidation and efficiency-oriented restructuring of the British economy (e.g., Gamble [1994a]; Krieger [1999]; V. Schmidt [1999]); domestic and international liberalization and the subsequent rises in international exposure of the British economy (e.g., substantial inward flows of FDI in the wake of market-oriented reform) created additional constraints on 1990s British social policy makers (Rhodes, 2000b).

Political Institutions and Reform of the British Welfare State. As in the case of the United States, the retrenchment and neoliberal restructuring of the British welfare state, and the impact of internationalization on those policy changes, has been fundamentally conditioned by institutional characteristics of the British polity and welfare state. With regard to the polity, perhaps most important is the character of systems of electoral and collective interest representation. Indeed, the absence of inclusive electoral institutions and associated features of consensus policy making, or the strong majoritarian character of British electoral-party systems, is central to understanding the success of neoliberal reforms. Specifically, Thatcher Conservative government majorities in the House of Commons after the 1979, 1983, and 1987 parliamentary elections were 53.4, 61.1. and 57.8 percent of total seats, respectively. These seat shares were based on 43.9, 42.4, and 42.3 percentage points of the popular vote, respectively. Institutional mechanisms for the direct incorporation of interests materially harmed by, or ideologically opposed to, neoliberal reforms, as well as structural-normative features of the policy process that result in formal or informal negotiations of policy change among all affected interests, do not exist.

The absence of routine, long-lived formal or informal social corporatist interest representation in Britain is also important. During the Thatcher-Major governments, regularized incorporation of labor in tripartite economic bargaining or formal policy-making forums, or a pattern of informal consultations among the social partners, or between the social partners and government, was virtually nonexistent. As is commonly understood, the Labour Party initiated a strategy for corporatist bargaining and wage restraint when in opposition during the early 1970s. When in government after 1974, policies of full employment–oriented demand management, industrial restructuring, and welfare state expansion (e.g., the 1975 creation of SERPS) were combined with negotiated wage restraint to form a new "social contract" (e.g., Holmes [1985]; Krieger [1986]; Wickham-

Jones [1996]). However, structural problems of the British economy, the macroeconomic consequences of the 1973 OPEC oil shock, the organizational character and ideology of functional economic interest associations (e.g., the decentralization of authority in the trade union movement), and other forces contributed to the effective collapse of the social contract (e.g., Hall [1986, Ch. 4]; Scharpf [1991, Ch. 5]). The 1978–9 "winter of discontent" among (especially public sector) trade unions and the post-1979 Thatcher government's reforms of labor and industrial relations law (significantly reducing the organizing and collective action capacities of trade unions) spelled the end to any prospects of developing social corporatist institutions in Britain during the contemporary era.[14]

Finally, the character of British welfare state institutions themselves is important. While universal elements of the 1970s British welfare state suggest the cultivation of strong political and normative bulwarks against neoliberal retrenchments (and high levels of cross-class political support for the NHS is an exemplar of this), a closer examination of programmatic structure reveals that the liberal characteristics of some major programs facilitated rollbacks of public social protection. Perhaps most important is the structure and reform of British pension policy from 1980 through the 1990s. As illustrated above, the consequence of 1980, 1986, and 1995 reforms has been to actually reduce significantly GDP shares committed to public pension spending into the first half of the 21st century; in comparison, virtually the whole of developed democratic capitalist Europe will experience significant, if not dramatic, increases in pension claims on national resources during this period.

The institutional structure of the system of British pensions in late 1970s arguably facilitates these notable policy changes. First, as Pierson (1994) has pointed out, the relatively late addition of a significant earnings-related public pension in 1975 (SERPS), overlaid on the basic (universal flat-rate) pension, creates a fragmented constituency for defense of extant pension policy; the late development of SERPS also decreases the relative size and intensity of vested interests in the program. Moreover, the late-1970s British pension system was also characterized by a significant liberal component: the existence of nontrivial private occupational

---

[14] As I have discussed above, some scholars have also emphasized that the parliamentary character of the British polity, or the absence of veto points associated with the separation of powers, was a contributor to the success of the Thatcher government's neoliberal reform effort relative to that of the United States (e.g., Borchert [1995, 1996]; King and Wood [1999]; Stephens, Huber, and Ray [1999]).

pensions. In fact, as Williamson (2000) notes, a modest second-tier earnings-related pension (the graduated pension) was introduced in 1959. At that time, employees were allowed to opt out of the public graduated pension and elect a private occupational pension. While private occupational pensions were typically modest in income replacement, OECD (1992) data suggest that in the 1978–80 period, private pensions supplied 15 percent of the gross income of citizens 65 to 74 years of age in Britain; comparable figures in the universal Norwegian and Swedish welfare states were 1 percent or less. As a result, not only was the system of public pensions politically vulnerable to retrenchment, but private pension alternatives and provisions for opting out were clearly established. These institutional features of the British pension system have facilitated retrenchment and trends toward privatization during the contemporary era (Williamson, 2000).

An Overview: Australia, Canada, and New Zealand

Social welfare policy change in both Britain and the United States has been characterized by relatively early and continuing retrenchment and neoliberal restructuring over the past 25 years. The political and economic pressures generated by globalization, along with domestic political economic forces, have played significant roles in fostering these reforms. The institutional character of the polity and the welfare state in these systems has facilitated rollbacks of public social protection and market-oriented restructuring of the welfare state. Generally, similar linkages between internationalization, political institutions, and neoliberal reform can be identified in other liberal systems. In addition, variations among political and welfare state structures within the Anglo-liberal systems are also important.

In the case of Canada, the economic and political pressures attendant on globalization, in conjunction with demographic and domestic socioeconomic and political factors, have been central forces in promoting neoliberal policy reforms of the welfare state (Banting 1997, 1998). Canadian social protection has been the subject of benefit reductions, increased means-testing (e.g., in old-age pensions), significant cost controls in health care and social services, and work-oriented reforms in unemployment and social assistance; with the exception of health care, citizenship entitlements to social protection have been effectively abolished (Banting 1997, 1998; Myles 1996). Furthermore, neoliberal reforms, most of which follow the

1984 ascendance of the Progressive Conservative government of Prime Minister Brian Mulroney, have accelerated in the wake of the early-1990s recession (e.g., Graig [1999, Ch. 6]) and with the ratification of the North American Free Trade Act (e.g., Borchert [1995]).

However, at the same time, comparatively high levels of Canadian social protection (e.g., a generous social wage; universal health care) have not converged with those of the United States as of the mid-1990s and the relatively moderate character of neoliberal reforms in some areas has cushioned citizens from increases in poverty and income inequality of the magnitude seen in the American case (e.g., Banting [1997]; Myles [1996]). Observers (e.g., Graig [1999, Ch. 6]; Myles [1996]) point out that the comprehensiveness and generosity of the Canadian welfare state relative to the United States, exemplified by universal health care, creates substantial cross-class support for the welfare state, as well as reflects and reinforces higher levels of collectivism in the Canadian polity. Generally, Canadian pro–welfare state interests share many of the same institutional disadvantages as do those in the United States, including the direct representational and long-term structural disadvantages of exclusive electoral institutions, pluralist interest representation, and decentralization (e.g., the fragmentation of coherent national redistributional coalitions and the prospect of subnational fiscal stress and competition with devolution of social welfare responsibilities by the federal government).[15] However, the political consequences of programmatic features of the Canadian welfare state, in contrast with those of the United States, have slowed retrenchment.

In the antipodes, the Australian and New Zealand welfare states have followed neoliberal reform trajectories generally similar to those of other liberal welfare states. In the late 1970s, the Liberal-led government of Malcolm Fraser initiated neoliberal reforms of the Australian welfare state; the Hawke-Keating Labor governments of the 1980s and 1990s accelerated these reforms. As many observers have noted, pressures associated with globalization – a collapse in the 1970s "resources boom," growing dependence on international capital markets, and a concern for declining international competitiveness – in conjunction with domestic

---

[15] As Banting (1986), Myles (1996), and other scholars of the Canadian welfare state commonly note, policy development in the decentralized Canadian polity, while sharing some anti—welfare state biases with the United States, has at times been favorable to welfare state development (e.g., by promoting national integration at important historical junctures).

socioeconomic and political forces have shaped Australian economic and social policies since the late 1970s (e.g., Bell and Head [1994]; Castles [1988, 1996]; Jennett and Stewart [1990]). Similar pressures stemming from internationalization have contributed to neoliberal reforms of the New Zealand welfare state (e.g., contributions to Castles, Gerritsen, Vowles [1996]; Castles and Pierson [1996]).

In the context of domestic and international liberalization, decentralization of the wage arbitration system, and other efficiency-oriented reforms associated with the new "economic rationalism" (see contributions to Castles, Gerritsen, and Vowles [1996]; Jennett and Stewart [1990]), the Australian welfare state was subject to significant budgetary restrictions on public expenditure and market-oriented reforms of public services during the 1980s and 1990s (Castles and Pierson, 1996). Specifically, new restrictions on conditions of entitlement and eligibility, including more stringent means and assets tests, were enacted in old-age pensions (asset tests), unemployment, and social assistance; the universal child benefit became means-tested (Castles, 1996). In addition, 1990s social policy change has been characterized by new emphases on work and training and a relative diminution of cash assistance, as typified by policies initiated after the 1994 government report, "Working Nation" (Wiseman, 1998). At the same time, however, increases in the social wage, including new programmatic initiatives, were used to cushion the burdens (e.g., declines in real wages) created by significant neoliberal restructuring of the economy (e.g., Castles [1996]; Schwartz [2000]). For instance, modest benefit increases were enacted for single-age pensions, rent assistance, and working family supports. In the mid-1980s, the Labor government reinstated Medicare (the National Health Care System) – a program enacted by the early-1970s Labor government and abrogated by the Liberal-led Fraser government in the late 1970s. In 1989, the Government formalized a mandatory private pension scheme (superannuation) to be financed by employers (contributions equal to 3 percent of base wages); the program was further upgraded in 1992.

In the case of the New Zealand welfare state, the 1984–90 "Fourth Labour government" combined modest increases in income maintenance and social services, policies that were designed to compensate workers for neoliberal restructuring (Schwartz, 2000), with increasing cost controls and efficiency-oriented reforms of social programs. Modest benefit reductions and stricter eligibility, primarily through more stringent means tests, affected most program areas; the real value of some benefits was allowed to drop, early retirement provisions were phased out, user charges were increased, and a surcharge was placed on the relatively generous benefits of the national superannuation system (e.g., Castles and Pierson [1996]; Schwartz [2000]). In the late 1980s, with the ascent of the neoliberal wing of the Labour party, the government proposed relatively more widespread and severe reductions in benefits and restrictions on eligibility. The 1990 election of a right-wing National party government resulted in notably more extensive neoliberal restructuring of the New Zealand welfare state than legislated or planned by the Labour Party in the late 1980s: benefits were cut significantly in many areas of social protection (especially social assistance), the effective tax rate was increased on old-age pensions, and indexation of pensions was abandoned for two years. In addition, the child benefit was abolished; programmatic means-testing, user charges, and work incentives were significantly increased; privatization of social insurance and social services was fostered; and internal markets and private sector managerial principles were initiated in health and social services (e.g., Castles [1996]; Castles and Shirley [1996]; Schwartz [2000]).

Overall, as the cumulative analysis of the scholars cited above underscores, the direct effect of institutional characteristics of the polity and welfare state on the opportunity structure of representation (e.g., the adverse impacts on welfare state interests of exclusive electoral institutions and liberal program structure) significantly contributed to the scope and depth of neoliberal social policy reform in both cases. So, too, do the long-term structural impacts of institutional structures on the political capacities of pro–welfare state actors and coalitions and the character of the policy process. In fact, variations in institutional structures across these Anglo-liberal welfare states help explain some significant differences in policy reform, especially with regard to the divergence between Australian and New Zealand welfare state restructuring after the mid-1980s.

The course of social policy change in Australia may be characterized as limited retrenchment and neoliberal restructuring of social welfare, in combination with social compensation for economic restructuring; in New Zealand, from 1987, and especially from 1990, the retrenchment of the welfare state has been significant. A significant part of these divergent trajectories can be explained by the development of social corporatist bargaining (the Accords) between the Australian Labor Party government and the Australian Council of Trade Unions (ACTU) during the 1983–95 period.[16] During this time, wage restraint and other concessions to enhance competitiveness-oriented restructuring of the economy (e.g., the acquiescence to partial enterprise bargaining) was exchanged in centralized bargaining between the Labor government and ACTU for increases in the social wage and the new pension and health care programs discussed above (Castles and Pierson, 1996; Schwartz, 2000). In New Zealand, fragmentation of the trade unions, conflicts between the Labour party and trade unions, and the absence of a commitment to economic modernization by the unions contributed to the abandonment of the early Labour party commitment to develop corporatist institutions (Easton and Gerritsen, 1996). As Castles and Pierson (1996) observe – and a point consistent with a central argument of this volume – the absence of social corporatist representation in New Zealand deprived welfare state interests of a major institutional mechanism through which to resist significant retrenchment of the welfare state.

[16] The fragmentation of national business interest associations, and failures to develop a cohesive national peak association of employers in the 1980s, have minimized business participation in post-1983 Australian corporatism, or what some have suggested may be "corporatism without business" (e.g., Matthews [1991]).

7

Assessing Long-Term Impacts: The Effect of Globalization on Taxation, Institutions, and Control of the Macroeconomy

Despite the evidence against conventional globalization theory generated in the preceding chapters, it may still be the case that increases in international capital mobility and financial integration contribute indirectly to rollbacks in social protection and otherwise constrain democratically elected governments from pursuing their social policy goals. Specifically, international capital mobility may contribute to the retrenchment of the welfare state through its impacts on the funding basis of the welfare state, the strength of political institutions that support the welfare state – most notably social corporatism – and the efficacy of macroeconomic policy to control unemployment and promote economic growth (and hence prevent fiscal stress that can lead to retrenchment). In the pages that follow, I go beyond my treatment of these issues in early sections of the volume and provide more detailed assessments of each argument. In the case of taxation, I provide a relatively developed analysis of the widely debated relationship between globalization and revenue raising by extending arguments I have offered elsewhere about internationalization and tax policy (Swank 1998) and by providing new evidence on international capital mobility's effects on tax burdens on capital, labor, and consumption, as well as on the tax share of GDP. In the case of the linkage between internationalization and social corporatism, I review the arguments, weigh the best recent evidence, and provide some new analysis. Finally, I provide a succinct assessment – relying on the best recent treatments of the topic, as well as analytic summaries of my case-study evidence – of the view that the decline in the efficacy of monetary, exchange rate, and related policies associated with rises in capital mobility forces governments, through a deterioration in economic performance (most notably, escalating

243

unemployment rates), to rollback social protection to restrain rising welfare state costs.

International Capital Mobility and Taxation

Much of the writing on internationalization and domestic politics and policy has highlighted the impact of international capital mobility on taxation. This is a particularly important relationship because, of course, the ability of the governments in advanced democratic polities to pursue social protection and other democratically determined goals inevitably hinges on (often) substantial taxation on a variety of economic activities and resource bases. It is also important because, if conventional propositions about capital mobility-induced tax competition and reduction in redistributive taxes are correct, not only will the revenue base of the welfare state be reduced as capital mobility increases, but egalitarian effects of the welfare state will be diminished by the movement toward less progressive tax structures.

In the preceding analyses, the causal chain from capital mobility to taxation and, in turn, to social welfare policies has been assessed indirectly. Rises in transnational capital mobility may produce downward pressures on taxation and these in turn may be translated relatively quickly into reductions in social protection. The evidence offered in the preceding chapters suggests that this has not occurred systematically to any significant extent through the early 1990s, or, if it has, tax-mediated pressures on the welfare state have been offset by other forces. However, globalization may result in reductions in tax burdens (or constraints on their expansion) that are not immediately translated into social policy change; as the preceding discussion has suggested, both social and tax policy reform can be "sticky" even in those political institutional contexts most conducive to neoliberal policy reforms. In other words, it is possible that internationalization produces cuts or restraints in taxation that accumulate over time, incrementally contribute to fiscal stress or crisis, and ultimately lead to welfare state retrenchment. Indeed, the findings in preceding chapters on the welfare impact of fiscal stress underscore the potential importance of this linkage.

Thus, in light of these considerations, I assess below the direct impacts of international capital mobility on taxation. I briefly present the theoretical argument, prefigured in preceding discussions, about how international capital mobility affects the revenue-raising capacity of the state, and

I further provide an overview of the relevant empirical research. I then offer an alternative argument: rises in capital mobility have occurred simultaneously with reductions in nominal tax rates on corporate and personal income across the developed democracies. Concomitant with these tax policy changes, however, the income tax base has been broadened through the elimination of a variety of exemptions, allowances, and deduction. Given that the net revenue effects of these "market-conforming" reforms is modest and that a variety of socioeconomic and political forces place upward pressures on taxes (e.g., needs of an expanding aged population), we might expect to find little relationship between internationalization and effective tax rates and overall tax burdens. To assess these arguments, I present new systematic evidence about the direct impact of international capital mobility on effective tax rates on capital, labor, and consumption, as well as the tax share of GDP.

An Overview of Theory and Evidence

Scholars have long argued that capital mobility constrains the fiscal capacities of the state to tax mobile assets. The basic notion dates at least to Adam Smith who states the argument succinctly (1976 [1776]: 848–9):

> The . . . proprietor of stock is properly a citizen of the world, and is not necessarily attached to any particular country. He would be apt to abandon the country in which he is exposed to a vexatious inquisition, in order to be assessed a burdensome tax, and would remove his stock to some country where he could, either carry on his business, or enjoy his fortune at his ease. A tax that tended to drive away stock from a particular country, would so far tend to dry up every source of revenue, both to the sovereign and to the society. Not only the profits of stock, but the rent of land and the wages of labour, would necessarily be more or less diminished by its removal.

Many contemporary economists concur with the implicit policy recommendations of Smith. That is, in theoretical models of taxation in small economies with fully mobile capital, the optimal rate of tax on income from capital is thought to be zero; shortfalls of revenue are offset by shifting the tax burden to relatively less mobile factors, such as labor and land (e.g., Gordon [1986]; Razin and Sadka [1991]; Gordon and Mackie-Mason [1995]).

Several contemporary scholars have made the direct linkage between capital mobility and actual tax policy change more explicit, arguing that internationalization is empirically associated with specific tax policies and reforms that shift revenue from capital to less mobile factors and otherwise undercut the revenue base of governments. Taking a historical perspective, Bates and Lien (1985) suggest that revenue-dependent governments have generally imposed lower rates on mobile assets and incorporated the preferences of these asset holders into policies and even institutions. Steinmo (1993, 1994) and McKenzie and Lee (1991), among other contemporary observers, have argued that capital mobility has effectively led governments to reduce tax burdens on corporate profits and high income–earners, substantially reducing tax-based income redistribution and the revenue-raising capacities of the state. Vito Tanzi (1995) has argued that transfer pricing and other mobility-related tax avoidance strategies have led to tax policy change: the risk of capital flight and the absence of new foreign investment, as well as new difficulties in tax collection associated with capital mobility, lead to tax competition among national governments; this, in turn, reduces taxes on mobile assets, generates reforms not dictated by efficiency or democracy (e.g., creation of tax havens), and generally threatens the revenue base of national governments.

However, there are several reasons to believe that rises in international capital movements may not necessarily result in significant reductions in the tax burdens on capital or in overall government revenues. First, most research on foreign direct and portfolio capital investment has shown that, while important in determining the rate of return on capital investment and ultimately the decisions of international enterprises, tax policy constitutes only one of several important factors shaping investment decisions (e.g., Giovannini, Hubbard, and Slemrod [1993]; IMF [1991]; OECD [1990, 1991]).[1] Second, some formal analysis in political economy questions the globalization-taxation linkage. Importantly, Wallerstein and Przeworski (1995) extend their well-known work on "structural dependence" to the case of internationally mobile capital. They find that as long as the cost of investment is fully deductible (i.e., through depreciation), governments can collect substantial revenues from a stable tax on uninvested profits even when capital is fully mobile. In their analysis, Wallerstein and Przeworski find that capital investment by business will only

---

[1] The actual relationship between taxation and international investment is complex. Jun (1990) has argued that tax-related aspects of investment decisions depend on (1) the tax treatment of foreign income; (2) the tax treatment of profits generated from domestic investment (i.e., the relative return between domestic and foreign investment); and (3) the tax treatment of external funds across different countries (also see Slemrod [1990]).

decline during the period between the announcement and implementation of new taxes on profits. Third, international investors may value certain public goods such as political stability, human capital, and modern infrastructure (Garrett [1998b]). In the presence of fiscal stability (i.e., the absence of large budget deficits, low inflation), the benefits of these public goods may well offset the costs of the taxes required to finance them.

A number of new studies have addressed the question of the actual impacts of capital mobility on tax policy.[2] Specifically, Geoffrey Garrett (1996, 1998a, 1998b) has reported evidence that the liberalization of capital controls is largely unrelated to total revenues, general categories of taxation (as shares of GDP), or the effective tax rate on capital in the developed democracies. Similar findings are reported by Dennis Quinn (1997): in samples of developed and developing nations, Quinn finds substantively small and positive relationships between liberalization of capital flows and corporate taxes (as percentage shares of GDP and of total taxation) at both levels of economic development. Hallerberg and Basinger (1998) study 1986–90 changes in corporate and personal income tax rates in a sample of advanced democracies and find that changes in tax rates are, at best, only indirectly related to the liberalization of capital markets. Generally, the number of veto players who may slow tax policy reform is an important determinant of the pace of 1986–90 changes in tax rates. In my own study of business taxation (Swank 1998), I show that corporate income taxes and employer social security and payroll taxes (both standardized by aggregate operating income) are positively associated with rises in actual capital flows and liberalization; however, the increases in business taxes associated with rises in capital mobility are small. On the other hand, Dani Rodrik (1997) reports results that support conventional theory: he finds that trade openness and, at high levels of trade openness, capital control liberalization are negatively associated with effective tax rates on capital; increasing trade openness is also associated with increases in taxes on labor. While Rodrik's findings represent an important exception to the pattern, the weight of the evidence leads to the unanticipated impression that international capital mobility may be unrelated (or even positively related) to capital taxation.

---

[2] I do not explicitly analyze the tax policy impacts of European economic integration in the present work. For an overview of theory and research and an interesting analysis of tax competition and efforts at coordination of corporate tax policy within the EU, see Radaelli (1997).

In previous work (Swank 1998), I drew on theory, the policy record of individual nations, and the secondary literature to offer an interpretation for the absence of systematic, downward pressure on overall tax burdens on business from internationalization. I argued that one should focus on the policy "rules" governing business taxation, how these have changed in the contemporary era, and the general political and economic context of tax policy reform. That is, one should focus on the set of assumptions, beliefs, and prescriptions about relationships between taxes, investment, and economic performance that cohere and persist among partisan policy makers and specialists across time and countries. Ample evidence exists to suggest that there was a shift in tax policy orientations during the period of expansion of capital mobility in the developed democracies. However, the empirical record indicates that, while heavily influenced by the ascendance of neoliberal economic orthodoxy – a change that complements and is reinforced by rises in internationalization – the shift in tax policies did not produce the outcomes predicted by the structural dependence–diminished democracy theory.[3]

As to tax policy change in the 1980s and 1990s, comparative case studies of national experiences (e.g., Boskin and McClure [1990]; Pechman [1988]) and detailed surveys of national and aggregate directions of reform (e.g., OECD [1989, 1991, 1993b]) paint a clear picture of policy change that involved a shift from market-regulating to marketing-conforming policy "rules." Specifically, beginning most notably with the tax reform of 1984 in Britain, and closely followed by the tax legislation of 1986 in the United States, national policy makers have cut tax rates on corporate profits in a majority of advanced democracies: the maximum marginal tax rate on corporate profits fell on average from 49 to 37 percent between 1981 and 1992, and a large majority of nations experienced appreciable declines in corporate income tax rates. However, policy makers have simultaneously emphasized base-broadening. This has primarily involved, in a majority of nations, elimination of investment reliefs that had theretofore effectively lowered taxes paid by capital substantially. Some nations

---

[3] The sources of this shift in tax policy rules (in the context of the broader liberalization of domestic and international markets) is largely beyond the scope of the present inquiry. I might note, however, that it in all likelihood stems from the interaction between ideas, ideology, and interests – societal and state-centered – in the context of 1970s and 1980s economic performance problems and structural change. (See C. J. Martin [1991] for a particularly interesting and insightful analysis of U.S. tax policy changes of the sort discussed here.)

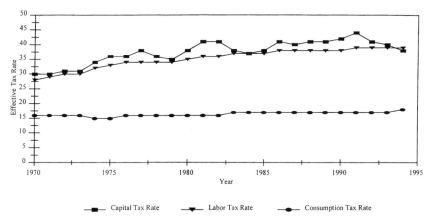

Figure 7.1   Trends in Effective Tax Rates Averages – 13 Developed Democracies

(e.g., Australia, and the pioneers of the policy reform, the United Kingdom and the United States) have done away with investment allowances, credits, and grants entirely, while others (e.g., Austria and Finland) have lowered them substantially.[4]

As previously cited studies and publications of the Fiscal Affairs Secretariat of the OECD make clear (see particularly OECD [1987, 1993b]), tax policy makers in Ministries of Finance and throughout OECD governments have been influenced by two principles in the adoption of these reforms. First, while business income tax rate cuts were viewed as economically advantageous, policy makers emphasized the need to make overall changes in revenue neutral, or otherwise protect the revenue needs of the state (OECD, 1987: 25). Thus, rate cuts should be offset, in particular, by the elimination of allowances, credits, exemptions, and other special business tax provisions for regional or sectoral development. In fact, as Figure 7.1 makes clear, the effective tax burden on capital has not fallen notably between the early 1970s and 1990s.[5] Second, tax-based

---

[4] I should note that standard depreciation for most capital investment has been maintained in all of the advanced democracies. See OECD (1991, 1993b) for a detailed, comparative review of depreciation methods and remaining investment reliefs.

[5] For instance, between 1980 and 1993, the effective tax rate on capital has hovered within a percentage point or two of 40 percent. The effective tax rate on capital income equals taxes on property income and immovable property plus taxes on unincorporated and corporate enterprise profits plus taxes on capital and financial transactions, all as a percentage of operating surplus, as suggested by Mendoza, Razin, and Tesar (1994). See the Appendix for sources of all data on items used in calculating tax rates.

investment incentives, once believed to be essential for encouraging investment, were now viewed as inefficient. As an OECD (1993b: 56–7) report indicates, investment reliefs have become associated with inefficient allocation of investment, tax avoidance, lost tax revenue and, interestingly, ineffective outcomes in that they do not apparently produce the investment they were designed to promote. Thus, the emphasis in business income tax policy has become the creation of a level playing field where the market will presumably allocate investment in the most efficient manner.

The upshot of the trends in the taxation of business income is that both the conscious redistributive and economic management roles of corporate taxation are being reduced. That is, while increases in the taxation of capital to fund new social policy initiatives are unlikely, so too is the systematic use of investment reliefs in corporate taxes to target and spur domestic investment and to engineer favorable climates for international investors. Indeed, there appears to have been a rejection of this policy strategy in most market-oriented democracies. As Slemrod (1990) has pointed out, a strategy of mixing a low tax rate with few investment reliefs makes sense for many nations in an internationally interdependent economy. This is so because low rates retain taxable income that would otherwise be shifted through transfer-pricing to low-tax nations. That is, low rates "defend the treasury" in an international economy. Moreover, increasing the tax burden on investment (that is, on profits that are invested) also "defends the treasury" in the sense that more revenues from foreign investment are collected if that investment comes from countries with tax credits for foreign taxes paid and with ample rates of investment taxes themselves. Slemrod believes that the "low tax rate/no investment break" strategy certainly makes sense for countries like the United States and probably many more advanced market-oriented democracies in a world with globally integrated markets.

Moreover, similar trends toward lower nominal rates, a broader tax base, and little change in overall revenue collection can be seen in changes in the taxation of personal income. In fact, between the mid-1980s and mid-1990s, the highest (central government) marginal rate on personal income has fallen on average from 56 to 43 percent in the advanced democracies. However, as in the case of corporate income taxes, governments have eliminated a variety of deductions, exemptions, and allowances; in addition, citizens in the typical advanced democratic nation have experienced some increase in social security contributions.[6] Figure 7.1 high-lights the fact that, after increasing from the early 1970s to mid-1980s, the overall effective tax rate on labor income has actually remained relatively stable. In addition, despite some notable exceptions, near universal reductions in marginal personal income tax rates (with fewer tax brackets) have not produced a trend toward substantially lower effective tax rates for higher income–earners.[7]

The effective tax rate on consumption and the tax share of domestic product are also relatively stable. As Figure 7.1 illustrates, the effective tax rate on consumption has held steady at about 17 percent.[8] If anything, total tax burdens have inched up slightly between the early 1980s and mid-1990s as capital mobility and financial integration increased rapidly: the OECD average for total tax shares of GDP was 38 percent in 1980 and 41 percent in 1994. Overall, while the shift in tax policy toward market-conforming orientations is clear (i.e., lower rates with fewer exemptions, allowances, and deductions), there does not appear to be a notable redistribution of tax burdens from capital to labor and consumption (within relatively constant levels of total taxation).

Certainly, part of the explanation of this relative stability in taxation, in the context of the shift to more market-conforming orientations in tax policy, is related to public expenditure pressures. Concomitant with

---

[6] While many countries have added new tax reliefs, the majority of developed democracies have broadened the tax base by eliminating allowances, exemptions, and credits (e.g., OECD [1993b]). Employee social security taxes have increased steadily in the majority of nations over the last 25 years. For instance, between 1970 and 1994, employee social security collections in the average OECD country rose from 1.8 to 3.2 percent of GDP (OECD, 1995a). Averages for the OECD or developed democracies pertain to the 15 focal nations of this study.

[7] Effective taxes on higher income–earners refer to the percentage of income paid in taxes by workers at 200 and 400 percentage of the gross earnings of the average production worker. Effective taxes on labor income is computed as: taxes paid on wages and salaries plus total social security contributions and payroll taxes as a percentage of total wages and salaries plus employers' social security taxes, as suggested by Mendoza, Razin, and Tesar (1994). As the OECD (1997) illustrates, only in the United States, the United Kingdom, and in Sweden were average taxes significantly lowered in the middle and high ends of the income distribution; small declines in effective tax rates at the high end of the income distribution were recorded for Australia and Germany, as well.

[8] The effective consumption tax rate is computed as: general goods and services taxes plus excise taxes as a percentage of private and government consumption spending minus consumption by producers of government services, goods and services taxes, and excise tax payments, as suggested by Mendoza, Razin, and Tesar (1994).

downward pressures on taxes associated with neoliberal macroeconomic orthodoxy and internationalization, governments have simultaneously faced significant political pressures to maintain extant programmatic commitments, as well as meet rises in needs and demands for additional social spending (e.g., such as those that come from the "crisis of aging"). Given that upper limits on debt and deficits had in all likelihood been reached in the 1980s and early 1990s in most nations, spending pressures have probably made it much more difficult for many governments to substantially reduce the aggregate volume of tax collections from levies on capital or other relatively mobile factors, such as skilled labor. Given the difficulty in retrenching the welfare state and public sector as a whole, these pressures contribute to policy maker emphases on revenue neutrality of tax reforms.

However, it is quite difficult to draw any firm conclusions about the myriad forces shaping tax policy from a perusal of descriptive data. The extant studies reviewed above, including my own, provide evidence about the tax effects of only one or two dimensions of capital mobility (primarily liberalization of capital controls) and, with a few exceptions, use relatively imprecise measures of tax burdens. Thus, I empirically assess the relationships between the five dimensions of capital mobility utilized in previous chapters and the effective tax rates on capital, labor, and consumption, as well as the total tax share of GDP.

Assessing the Tax Impacts of International Capital Mobility

To examine the actual consequences of capital mobility for the levels and distribution of tax burdens, I utilize the measures of effective tax rates on capital, labor, and consumption developed by Mendoza, Razin, and Tesar (1994) and defined above. I also extend the models of taxation that I developed in my earlier research on tax policy (Swank 1992, 1998). In that work, I hypothesized that business (and other) tax burdens are functions of past levels of taxation, the funding requirements of programmatic outlays, macroeconomic factors (inflation, economic growth), and partisan politics: Left and Christian Democratic parties will generally favor higher levels of taxes. Tax burdens on capital may be also be influenced by specific domestic business conditions, such as recent investment and profit rates. Following Cameron's (1978) seminal study (and contra the globalization thesis), I also hypothesized that tax burdens would be higher in economies more open to international trade. Personal income and social security levies on labor, as well as general taxation, should also be influenced by the unemployment rate. I directly extend these hypotheses to the present case.[9]

I utilize econometric procedures similar to those discussed above in relation to social welfare models to test for direct effects of the five dimensions of international capital mobility on taxation during the period from the mid-1960s to mid-1990s: models are estimated with Ordinary Least Squares regression; panel correct standard errors are used for computation of t-tests; and potentially significant unit (nation) effects are incorporated in models by the inclusion of dichotomous variables (if t-statistics >1.00). Data limitations constrain the analysis of tax rates on capital, labor, and consumption to the period between 1970 and 1993 for 13 nations; the empirical models for the total tax share of GDP cover 1965–93 data for 15 nations.[10]

I present tests for the direct linear effects of the different dimensions of international capital mobility on taxation in Table 7.1. Tax policy effects of each of the five international capital mobility variables are estimated in separate equations. To highlight the tests of the central hypotheses about internationalization and taxation, as well as to minimize the volume of reported findings, I present the full results for each tax dimension for only the equation that includes total capital flows. The tax effects of other causal variables are virtually the same across the five individual equations for each tax variable.

---

[9] I discuss rationales for the inclusion and specific operationalization of political and economic variables in my earlier papers on tax policy (Swank 1992; 1998). There, as well as in the present analysis, I use the following control variables in a general model of taxation: the lagged tax rate; present levels of government outlays (as a percentage of GDP); lagged levels of trade openness; the proportion of cabinet portfolios held by parties of a particular ideological type (here, Left and Christian Democratic parties); lagged levels of inflation, unemployment, and economic growth; and lagged percentage changes in real investment in machinery and equipment and in total real business profits. All lags are one year. Further information and data sources are given in Appendix A.

[10] As noted above, one might explicitly model the autoregressive process by inclusion of the lagged dependent variable (see Beck and Katz [1996]). Tests of the residuals for remaining autocorrelation in the models of Table 7.1 suggest that this procedure is appropriate here (e.g., rhos, the coefficients of first-order autocorrelation are virtually 0.00). I also test the robustness of findings by using two alternative estimators of tax models: full fixed effects (i.e., controlling for all time and nation effects) with the lagged endogenous variable and generalized error correction, where changes in tax variables are regressed on lagged levels and changes of taxes and levels and changes in capital mobility variables. The 13 nations consist of the 15 focal nations of this study, minus Austria and Denmark. For these two countries, some of the requisite data for computation of effective tax rates are unavailable.

Table 7.1. *Global Capital and Taxation, 1966/71–1993*

	Tax Rate on Capital	Tax Rate on Labor	Tax Rate on Consumption	Total Taxes (% of GDP)
Global Capital				
Total Capital Flows	−.0121	−.0069	−.0021	−.0054
	(.0135)	(.0046)	(.0024)	(.0034)
Direct Investment	.0833	−.0696	−.0345	−.1084*
	(.2259)	(.0859)	(.0534)	(.0536)
Capital Markets	.0315	−.0084	−.0054	−.0071
	(.1974)	(.0573)	(.0442)	(.0418)
Capital Liberalization	.8301*	−.1192	.0459	.0281
	(.4892)	(.1465)	(.1361)	(.1285)
Interest Rate Differentials	−.4666	−.0381	.0405	−.0413
	(.3511)	(.1007)	(.0795)	(.0679)
General Model				
Tax Rate$_{t-1}$	.7924*	.8464*	.8416*	.8610*
	(.0498)	(.0370)	(.0362)	(.0270)
Government Outlays$_t$	.2448*	.1124*	−.0117	.0957*
	(.0788)	(.0345)	(.0221)	(.0211)
Trade Openness$_{t-1}$	.0032	.0138	.0149*	.0088*
	(.0312)	(.0087)	(.0050)	(.0036)
Left Government	.0239*	.0028	−.0035	.0056*
	(.0136)	(.0045)	(.0031)	(.0030)
Christian Democrat	−.0038	.0127*	.0073	.0027
Government	(.0180)	(.0076)	(.0063)	(.0048)
Inflation$_{t-1}$	.0878	.0210	−.0181	.0077
	(.0650)	(.0216)	(.0154)	(.0172)
Growth$_{t-1}$	.6935*	.0541	−.0221	.1384*
	(.1539)	(.0391)	(.0288)	(.0279)
Investment$_{t-1}$	.0363	—	—	—
	(.0372)			
Profits$_{t-1}$	−.0787*	—	—	—
	(.0389)			
Unemployment$_{t-1}$	—	−.0498	.0184	−.0656*
		(.0320)	(.0271)	(.0258)
intercept	−2.2207	.2406	1.0546	.6613
standard error of the estimate	3.4854	1.2345	.9371	1.1511
mean of the dependent variable	37.8070	35.5300	16.5270	37.2710
Buse R^2	.9157	.9857	.9881	.9789

Note: The effects of each of the five international capital mobility variables on a specific type of tax are estimated in five separate equations. As indicated, the table reports for each tax variable the tax policy effects of general model variables in the equation that includes Total Capital Flows. The significance and general magnitude of effects for various political and economic factors do not vary appreciably across the five separate equations and thus I only report one set of findings. Each model is estimated with 1971–93 data (or 1966–93 data for the total tax share equation) by Ordinary Least Squares; models for interest rate differentials are estimated with 1979–93 data. The table reports OLS unstandardized regression coefficients and panel correct standard errors. For discussion of this econometric technique, see Beck and Katz (1995, 1996). All models include nation-specific dichotomous variables (if $t > 1.00$) to account for unmodeled country effects.

As Table 7.1 illustrates, the conventional academic wisdom about internationalization and taxation does not seem to be accurate. Focusing on the first column of the table, it is clear that rises in international capital mobility are not generally related to the effective tax rate on capital. The coefficients for each dimension of actual cross-border capital flows and convergence in covered interest differentials are substantively tiny and statistically insignificant. Moreover, and contrary to conventional theory, the relationship between the liberalization of capital controls and the effective tax rate on capital is positive and statistically significant. This result suggests that as capital controls were lifted, concomitant changes in tax policy (e.g., cuts in rates, base broadening, and related tax policy reforms) produced moderate increases in tax revenues from capital; there is no evidence that rises in international capital mobility produce significantly lower profits (i.e., a lower denominator) and in turn a higher effective average tax rate.[11]

Turning to the effects of capital mobility on labor, consumption, and overall taxation, the table reveals that there is little evidence that tax burdens have shifted away from capital or that internationalization has produced a general reduction in taxation. In nearly all cases, the relationship between international capital mobility and labor and consumption taxes is not statistically different from 0.00; most coefficients are trivial in magnitude. The one exception to the overall pattern of findings occurs in the case of the relationship between direct foreign investment and total taxation (as a percentage of GDP). Here, analysis indicates that, net of other forces, increases in direct foreign investment are associated with small declines in the overall tax share of GDP. However, this finding is not reproduced in the alternative econometric analyses: when controlling for all country and time points, or when examining the impact of changes in direct investment on changes in total tax burdens (in the context of general error correction models), this relationship disappears.

One might also highlight other results that bear on the focal questions of this study. First, trade openness is not generally related to taxes on capital or labor; it is positively associated with consumption taxes and total taxation.[12] Cameron's (1978) original finding of a positive and significant

---

[11] In complementary work (Swank and Steinmo, 2000), I find in systematic empirical analysis that, if anything, rises in capital mobility (and trade openness) are associated with higher profits.

[12] Flat-rate general consumption taxes (value added and sales taxes) are often touted as efficient alternatives to graduated income and capital taxes in that they are the least intrusive

effect of trade openness on various measures of public sector size has also been confirmed for the contemporary period in other studies: trade openness and associated measures such as volatility in terms of trade are positively related to various measures of public sector intervention in markets (e.g., Garrett [1998a]; Rodrik [1997]; c.f. Iversen [2001]). Second, the table indicates that partisan governments have clear effects on taxation. Left governments levy higher tax burdens on capital and produce higher overall tax burdens, while Christian Democratic governments prefer higher taxes on labor (income and social security taxes relative to wages and salaries). Finally, it is important to note that these partisan effects on taxation are not generally diminished as capital mobility increases. That is, on balance, the effects of Left governments on capital and total taxation and of Christian Democratic governments on labor tax rates hold at low and high levels of international financial intergration.[13]

Generally, it seems clear that the dramatic rises in international capital mobility have not produced significant changes in the distribution of tax burdens across capital, labor, and consumption or in the overall level of taxation. That is, there is no evidence for the period from the 1960s through the mid-1990s that the economic and political pressures associated with international capital mobility have dramatically shifted tax burdens from capital to other factors of production or substantially undercut the general fiscal capacity of governments to raise revenues. Democratically elected governments can still maintain relatively extensive networks of social protections and services if they so choose. In other words, there appears to be no overriding internationally generated structural imperatives for tax reduction that force all welfare states to "run to the bottom."[14]

in the efficient operation of markets. As such, they may be the preferred alternative in an economy relatively open to competitive international markets. I also tested for the prospect that, following Rodrik's (1997) finding, increases in international capital mobility would produce downward pressure on the tax burdens on capital at high levels of trade openness. Examining the capital tax effects of individual measures of flows, liberalization, and interest rate convergence across levels of trade openness, I found no support for this hypothesis.

[13] Examining the interaction of parties and international capital mobility in Table 7.1 models (results not shown), only 3 of the 15 possible interactions – party variables in the capital, labor, and total tax equations with the 5 measures of capital markets – are significant. That is, partisan effects are not generally contingent on the level of capital mobility.

[14] Two points are in order. First, the shift toward market-conforming policies in the areas of business and personal income taxation eliminates some tools governments have used to

Internationalization and Political Institutions: The Case of Social Corporatism

International capital mobility may shape welfare state restructuring through its effects on political institutions that support the welfare state. The impact of globalization on social corporatist interest representation is particularly salient and important. As noted in Chapter 2, a number of scholars have suggested that large welfare states may be weakened by the internationalization-induced decline of social corporatist institutions and practices (e.g., Huber and Stephens [1998]; Kurzer [1993]; Mishra [1993]; Moses [2000]). This proposition is especially important because, as demonstrated in the preceding analysis, social corporatism is positively related to an array of features of social welfare protection and a principal institutional mechanism that blunts the potentially negative welfare state impacts of internationalization.

Rises in capital mobility are commonly thought to engender a shift of power resources away from labor and government to capital (e.g., Huber and Stephens [1998]; Kurzer [1993]; Moses [2000]). In turn, this shift of power to capital may well contribute to the weakening of core features of social corporatism, such as centralized wage bargaining and union density.[15] A number of mechanisms linking capital mobility to the decline of social corporatism have been highlighted in the literature. The relative gains from bargaining for wage restraint (and engagement in tripartite social pacts) to increasingly mobile enterprises may be diminished because capital mobility may present relatively more advantageous options for employers (e.g., Kurzer [1993]); even if centralized collective bargains are struck, mobile enterprises may choose subsequently to invest internationally, thereby weakening the prospects of future corporatist exchange

achieve social and economic policy objectives (Steinmo, 1998). Second, many nations have begun to rely more heavily on taxes of a regressive nature; the 1990s reforms initiating new employee social security taxes in Sweden and higher employee social security taxes in post-1990 Germany are just two examples of this trend. While these reforms do not suggest that redistributive taxes are a thing of the past, they do point to the prospect that a cumulative process of tax reform may produce less egalitarian tax structures in a large majority of developed nations in the not-so-distant future. As such, the redistributive impacts of the contemporary welfare state will be reduced.

[15] As commonly understood, social corporatism is construed as a system of densely and well-organized trade unions, well-organized employers' associations, centralized collective bargaining, and associated incorporation of unions (and employers) in bipartite and tripartite concertation over major economic and social policies.

(Moses, 2000). Internationally mobile employers may seek more flexibility in work organization and this, in turn, may diminish the attractiveness of unions (e.g., Scruggs and Lange [1999]; Western [1997]). From the perspective of Hecksher-Ohlin-Samuelson trade theory (see Chapter 2), globalization creates declining incomes and employment prospects among often unionized semi- and unskilled workers (while increasing the income of skilled workers); potential increases in wage inequality fragment trade union movements, and declining jobs and income among lower skilled workers may diminish the attractiveness of unions (see Golden and Londregan [1998], for theorizing along these lines).

In sum, scholars have emphasized that international capital mobility may simultaneously weaken unions and strengthen employers. Moreover, according to some observers, domestic political economic changes are pushing the actual preferences of increasingly mobile capital in the direction of decentralization and deregulation of labor and industrial relations systems. Huber and Stephens (1998), building on the work of Iversen (1996), Pontusson and Swenson (1996), and others, have suggested that in moderate to very strong social corporatist systems (most notably Sweden), post-Fordist flexible, specialized production of high quality goods and the compression of wage differentials (an outcome of past corporatist exchange) have created strong incentives for employers to press for decentralization of collective bargaining; the exit option enhances the power of employers to press for such change. Is there evidence to support these views?

Globalization and Social Corporatism: Empirical Evidence

An examination of trends in major elements of social corporatism over the last three decades might initially appear to support the globalization thesis. Figure 7.2 displays annual 15-nation averages for two major features of social corporatism highlighted in the literature (and two elements that anchor the index of social corporatism developed in Chapter 2): union density and the level of wage bargaining.[16] As the figure suggests, both

---

[16] The 15 nations are the same countries utilized in analyses throughout this study. Union density is computed as the percentage of employed wage and salary workers belonging to unions and the level of bargaining is a 0.0–3.0 scale ranging from enterprise-level bargaining (0.0) to economy-wide bargaining with sanctions (3.0).

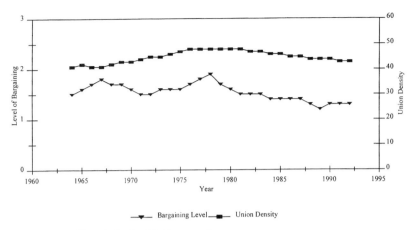

Figure 7.2 Trends in Social Corporatism

union density and the level of collective wage bargaining have declined from the late 1970s or early 1980s; the timing of these decreases generally corresponds with the acceleration of international financial integration.

With respect to union density, the figure highlights the fact that after peaking at 48 percent in the late 1970s and early 1980s, average union density drops after 1982 and reaches a low of 43 percent in 1992. However, the cross-national average masks considerable variability in post-1970s national trends in union density rates. As Western (1997) has demonstrated, high–union density countries (Belgium, Denmark, Finland, and Sweden) have actually experienced rises in unionization rates in the 1980s. In addition, Western's analysis of the determinants of union growth indicates that institutions – most notably the Ghent system of union-administered unemployment insurance, centralized bargaining itself, and strong Social Democratic parties – foster unionization and may well buffer unions from adverse political economic forces. With respect to other sets of countries, nations with moderate levels of unionization rates (e.g., Canada, Germany, Italy, and the United Kingdom) have experienced both stability and decline in the share of union workers in recent years. Low–union density countries (e.g., France, the United States) have commonly witnessed further decreases in union density rates in the 1980s. Generalizing from Western's argument, one might argue that these declines in part reflect the weakness or absence of institutions (e.g., the

259

Ghent system) that could buffer unions from the adverse domestic and international changes of the 1980s and 1990s.

With regard to the centralization of bargaining, similar national diversity (in the context of a general trend of moderate decentralization) exists. As discussed in Chapter 4, the early-1980s decentralization of the highly corporatist Swedish system is a prototype of corporatist decline. In 1983, centralized economy-wide bargaining between the Swedish Employers' Association (SAF) and the Swedish Confederation of Trade Unions (LO) was abandoned. Motivated by the desire for more flexibility in wage negotiations and influenced by a variety of forces, the Engineering Employers' Association (VF) persuaded the Metalworkers Union (Metall) to engage in independent bargaining; this development effectively decentralized wage setting. In subsequent years, unions and employers periodically returned to economy-wide negotiations (with supplemental industry-wide bargaining), although the dominant trend has been decentralization. Symbolizing this change, SAF disbanded its central bargaining unit in 1990 and withdrew representatives from some corporatist boards of state agencies in 1991. On the other hand, the Swedish trend is not representative of the Nordic cases. As Wallerstein and Golden (1997) point out, wage bargaining in Finland and Norway has remained relatively centralized and decentralization in other social corporatist cases (Denmark) has been less dramatic than in Sweden.

In addition, a number of recent studies suggest that concomitant with globalization (and perhaps as a consequence of it), some nations have experienced a reconstitution or new development of relatively centralized wage setting, supplemented with formal and informal social pacts. For instance, Visser and Hemerijck (1997) argue that, in the wake of the 1982 Wasenaar Accord, Dutch corporatism was revitalized with concertation between unions and employers over wage restraint, labor market flexibility, and employment. Perez (1998) has pointed out that in Southern Europe, the social partners and the state in Italy and Spain have increasingly engaged in concertation to achieve national framework agreements over wages; sectoral and enterprise bargaining takes place within the context of these frameworks. Other scholars (e.g., Ebbinghaus and Hassel [2000]; Rhodes [2001]) have also documented the development of "competitive corporatism" in the Netherlands, Italy, and other countries (e.g., Ireland). In this contemporary form of corporatism, bargaining over wage restraint and employment is commonly supplemented with social pacts over labor market, economic, and social policies. Certainly, these examples of reconstituted or newly developed corporatism involve more decentralization than traditional corporatist concertation. However, they also involve more coordination and representation of union interests than do the deregulated labor markets and decentralized enterprise-based bargaining common in liberal political economies.

Is globalization systematically associated with a decline in corporatism, as theory and some country-specific evidence suggest? Or, alternatively, have countries followed divergent paths during the era of increasing internationalization of markets?[17] Two recent studies shed light on this question. First, Golden and Londregan (1998) examine the effects of the liberalization of financial flows, as well as trade openness and trade volatility, on a battery of dimensions of the labor and industrial relations system: union density, the share of union members in confederations, the intra-confederal concentration of members, and confederal and government involvement in wage setting. Employing pooled–time series analysis of 1950–92 data for 16 nations (the 15 focal nations of the present study plus Switzerland), they find no evidence of any relationship between liberalization of international finance (or trade openness) and variations in labor and industrial relations systems. The only statistically significant relationships occur between trade volatility and union density (a negative relationship) and trade volatility and the share of union members in confederations (a positive relationship). In sum, the authors produce little evidence to support the conventional globalization thesis.

The second study adopts similar methodology and explores the impact of financial liberalization, flows of foreign direct investment (FDI), and trade openness on union density in the same 16 nations between 1960 and 1995 (Scruggs and Lange, 1999). In pooled–time series models of union density rates, the authors find no direct and systematic relationships between liberalization of capital controls, FDI, and trade openness on the one hand, and variations in union density on the other. This set of findings lends weight to the conclusions generated by Golden and Londregan.

---

[17] Of course a number of rival hypotheses on the origins of corporatist decline exist. For instance, the direct effects of technological change and the shift to post-Fordist flexible manufacturing of diversified high-quality products (Pontusson and Swenson 1996); employers' desire to reduce wage compression in some social corporatist systems (Huber and Stephens, 1998; Wallerstein, Golden, and Lange, 1997); the deregulatory impetus of neoliberal orthodoxy and governments (e.g., Streeck [1993]); and the rise in white-collar or public-sector unions within trade union movements (e.g., Garrett and Way [1999]) may all play roles in corporatist decline.

However, the authors also examine the effects of international capital mobility across different institutional contexts. They find that where labor market institutions are strong (e.g., the presence of the Ghent unemployment system), liberalization of capital markets is not related to variations in union density; where such institutions are weak, liberalization is negatively associated with density.[18] As such, these findings converge with predictions from Western's (1997) theory and suggest that the impact of capital mobility on unions might be contingent on broader institutions in much the same way as globalization's impacts on the welfare state are determined by national political institutions.

To further assess the possibility that capital mobility may negatively affect social corporatism, I estimated the impacts of the liberalization of capital controls, total capital flows, and flows of FDI on the strength of social corporatism using the focal measure of corporatism employed in the present study (a factor score index of density, confederal power, and the level of bargaining).[19] Tests for the effects of FDI are especially important, as much of the theorizing and debate over globalization's impacts on unions and corporatist institutions directly or indirectly stresses the importance of the ability of enterprises to move production or create jobs internationally through direct investment.

The effect of each of these three dimensions of capital mobility was estimated with 1965–92 data for the 15 focal nations of this study. To explore the possibility that the impact of international capital mobility on social corporatism varies depending upon the type of political economic institution, I also estimated the models for subsets of nations where countries were grouped as social democratic, corporatist conservative, and liberal political economies.[20] All else being equal, one might expect that

[18] With somewhat contradictory implications, Scruggs and Lange also report that under strong labor market institutions – especially central bargaining and corporatist interest intermediation – FDI actually has a larger negative effect on density than under weak labor market institutions.

[19] All variables are operationalized as above. I also estimated the effects of the broader 0–14–point scale of financial liberalization developed by Quinn, borrowing on international capital markets, and covered interest rate divergence. However, the effects of these dimensions of capital mobility on social corporatism are insignificant (or in one case significant and positive).

[20] See the discussions of previous chapters on the general pattern of institutional attributes of each type. For instance, social democracies possess universalistic welfare states, high levels of social corporatism (and typically other labor market institutions favorable to unions, such as the Ghent system), inclusive electoral institutions, centralized polities, and other attributes of coordinated market economies.

unions and their allies will be better able to resist decentralization and deregulation of labor and industrial relations systems where political institutions promote representational opportunities and political capacities of downscale interests (e.g., moderate-to-strong social corporatism itself and inclusive electoral institutions) and where economic models (i.e., coordinated versus uncoordinated capitalism) systematically incorporate labor. Thus, consistent with arguments discussed in this section as well as my theoretical argument throughout this volume, capital mobility might be expected to have little relationship to social corporatism in social democratic and conservative cases, but have negative effects in liberal political economies.

Empirical models control for trade openness and a full set of dichotomous country and year variables to account for country-specific and general temporal effects. A variety of additional factors (e.g., business cycle variables) were added to the empirical models; none of these additional controls altered the reported estimates of effects of capital mobility. Similar to previous pooled–time series analysis in this study, models were estimated as first-order autoregressive processes with OLS; panel correct standard errors were computed using procedures suggested by Beck and Katz (1995, 1996).

The results of these simple tests are presented in Table 7.2. As indicated in the table, none of the dimensions of capital mobility are significantly related to corporatism across the full sample of developed democracies. Reinforcing conventional theory (Cameron [1978]; Stephens [1979]; and see Chapter 2), trade openness is positively associated with social corporatism across the full set nations. An identical pattern of results for capital mobility obtains for the social democratic and conservative political economies: liberalization of capital controls, total cross-border flows of capital, and FDI are unrelated to social corporatism. However, FDI is negatively related to social corporatism in liberal systems (although the coefficients for liberalization and total flows, while possessing the correct negative signs, only have t-statistics of roughly 1.0). This negative effect of the level of FDI on social corporatism is highly robust to the addition of a variety of controls for business cycle dynamics.

Overall, while far from conclusive, these preliminary tests tend to confirm findings and reinforce conclusions from recent empirical assessments of the impacts of globalization on unions and social corporatist institutions. First, there is no evidence of systematic and direct effects of rises in international capital mobility on core features of social corporatism.

263

Table 7.2. *The Impact of Internationalization on Social Corporatism, 1965–1992*

	All Nations	Social Democratic	Corporatist Conservative	Liberal
Global Capital				
Capital Liberalization	−.0377	.0173	.0054	−.0642
	(.0239)	(.0618)	(.0239)	(.0550)
Total Capital Flows	−.0000	.0055	−.0002	−.0014
	(.0009)	(.0055)	(.0013)	(.0015)
Foreign Direct	−.0087	.0231	−.0067	−.0604*
Investment Flows	(.0198)	(.0410)	(.0287)	(.0350)
Trade	.0068*	−.0019	.0014	.0057
	(.0021)	(.0048)	(.0018)	(.0063)

Note: The effects of each of the three international capital mobility variables on social corporatism for each set of countries are estimated in three separate equations. The table reports the trade effects on social corporatism from the equation that includes Capital Liberalization. Each model for the full set of countries is estimated with 1965–92 data for 15 countries by Ordinary Least Squares (df = 377). Each model for the subsets of countries defined by welfare state type is estimated with 1965–92 data for five nations (df = 107). All equations include $N - 2$ and $t - 2$ dummy variables to control for unit and annual effects, respectively. The table reports OLS unstandardized regression coefficients and panel correct standard errors. For discussion of this econometric technique, see Beck and Katz (1995, 1996).
* Significant at the .05 level or below.

Second, international financial integration may be associated with decreases in union density, (further) decentralization of wage bargaining, and weakening in other features of social corporatism in more liberal political economies. This proposition, however tentative, is certainly consistent with the results reported here, the implications of Western's (1997) theory, and findings reported by Scruggs and Lange (1999). At the same time, these two preliminary conclusions do not rule out the possibility that international capital mobility may have enhanced the ability of employers to pursue decentralization in a small number of cases (e.g., Sweden), while in other cases social corporatist institutions might have been maintained (e.g., Norway), reconstituted (e.g., the Netherlands), or developed (e.g., Italy). With regard to the central focus of this inquiry, it appears to be the case that international capital mobility has not shaped welfare state restructuring indirectly through systematic downward pressures on social corporatism. While some features of social corporatism have certainly weakened in the 1980s and 1990s, there is no evidence for the common claim that globalization is substantially responsible for the decline.

Globalization and Control of the Macroeconomy

While a thorough examination of the impact of globalization on macro-economic policy is beyond the parameters of this study, it may be useful to consider the argument that capital mobility creates pressure for welfare state retrenchment primarily through its impact on macroeconomic policy autonomy and, in turn, economic performance pressures on the welfare state. Specifically, according to some analysts, rises in international capital mobility result in the loss of crucial economic instruments for maintaining low unemployment in larger welfare states; rises in unemployment create substantial fiscal stress or even crisis and, in turn, force rollbacks in the welfare state. While variations of this argument appear regularly in debates about the domestic impacts of globalization, I will focus on two important studies of globalization and economic policy and performance in large welfare states to explicate the proposition.[21]

In a recent analysis of crisis and change in social democratic political economies, Huber and Stephens (1998) argue that retrenchment of the generous welfare states of these systems only occurred after steep rises in unemployment rates. Indeed, these authors and others (e.g., Martin [1996]; Visser and Hemerijck [1997]) assert that the relatively large universalistic and corporatist conservative welfare states of Western Europe are generally dependent on relatively low unemployment rates; rapid rises in unemployment and long-lived joblessness at substantial levels create unsustainable fiscal burdens on unemployment compensation, social assistance, early retirement (and often disability) pensions, and active labor market policies. In the view of Huber and Stephens (1998), the late 1980s and early 1990s expansion of unemployment rates – more gradual and modest in Norway and Austria, while relatively rapid and dramatic in Finland and Sweden – is primarily a function of the loss of crucial supply-side policies of the social democratic model that had been instrumental in promoting growth and jobs.

---

[21] At a general level, the specific argument considered here is based on the common Mundell-Flemming model of monetary policy in open economies. At its most elemental level, the model asserts that national policy makers can only achieve two of three goals among the set of fixed exchange rates, capital mobility, and monetary policy autonomy. For a nontechnical overview, see Cohen (1996); for an accessible yet rigorous presentation of a variety of models in this theoretical perspective, see Shepherd (1994). A related argument that I do not consider here is that globalization – both international financial integration and trade openness – directly increases unemployment in the developed capitalist democracies, and hence precipitates welfare state fiscal stress. For a review of the literature on globalization effects on unemployment, see Martin (1996).

Specifically, according to Huber and Stephens (and see Chapter 4 above), social democratic political economies have relied heavily on a battery of supply-side economic policies (and only modestly on counter-cyclical demand management) to promote growth and low unemployment in the contemporary era. In addition to tax-based investment incentives (e.g., investment credits, allowances, tax-free investment reserve funds), these supply-side policies consist primarily of general and selective credit allocation through the control of interest rates and the operation of various industrial policies that channel domestic credit; direct state intervention (e.g., bank or enterprise ownership) has been higher in Finland, Norway, and Austria than in Sweden. The post-1960s increase in international capital mobility, both in the form of multinationalization of production and increasing international financial flows, directly weakens the capacity of governments to control interest rates and channel domestic credit. For instance, the advent of high–interest rate policies in the United States in the late 1970s and early 1980s, coupled with further liberalization in leading economies and the development of international capital markets, significantly undercuts the efficacy of domestic interest rate control in the social democratic systems (Huber and Stephens, 1998: 374–5).[22]

Moses (2000) emphasizes related but distinct elements of the economic policy mix of the Nordic social democracies. According to Moses, the pre-1990s employment success of the Norwegian and Swedish political economies hinged on the combination of selective exchange rate depreciations in the late 1970s and 1980s, which notably expanded Nordic exports, and economy-wide bargains for domestic wage restraint; the latter blunted domestic inflationary pressures attendant on currency depreciation and allowed export gains to be translated into employment gains. In fact, Moses documents selective currency devaluations, supportive policies, and subsequent employment gains from the mid-1970s to early 1980s in Norway and Sweden. However, in Moses' view, by the early to mid-1980s, capital mobility and the inability of governments and the social partners to control the inflationary aspects of successive devaluations

---

[22] As discussed in the previous section of this chapter, Huber and Stephens (1998), like Moses (2000) and others, also argue that international capital mobility weakens social corporatist mechanisms for wage restraint. In addition, Huber and Stephens argue that unemployment expansions and crises were in part created by a series of 1980s policy mistakes in the majority of social democratic cases.

undercut the model.[23] With notable rises in international capital mobility, Moses argues that Nordic central banks found it increasingly difficult to counter speculative attacks on currencies. In addition, with the shift of power from labor and government to capital that accompanied capital mobility, Moses suggests that globalization contributed to the collapse of centralized bargaining in Sweden (and general decentralization elsewhere). In the end, both Sweden and Norway shifted to a fixed currency position (1982 and 1986, respectively) and eventually a European Currency Unit peg.

Together, the analyses of Huber and Stephen and Moses suggest that the exogenous pressures of internationalization of production and financial markets stripped policy makers of key supply-side and monetary policy instruments that had been crucial in sustaining full or near-full employment in the 1970s and 1980s. In turn, the absence of these instruments in the late 1980s and especially 1990s left social democratic political economies vulnerable to the unemployment consequences of external shocks (e.g., the collapse of Soviet markets for Finland's exports) and business cycles (e.g., the early-1990s economic downturn across the developed democracies). The resultant "unemployment crises" engendered "welfare state crises" and social welfare protection was retrenched. Does this argument identify a key (albeit indirect) linkage between globalization and welfare state reform?

First, while the argument is plausible for the Nordic cases (although see below), there are clear limits on its generalizability as a systematic explanation of how capital mobility shapes welfare state retrenchment. To take the three main corporatist conservative welfare states analyzed in Chapter 5, the argument is at least partly applicable to France, but much less so for Germany or Italy. In the case of France, increased international competitiveness and short-term currency market pressures on the franc interacted with inflationary pressures, expanding fiscal deficits, and declining investment in the early 1980s to produce a shift in national economic policy from "Keynesianism in one country" to restrictive fiscal and monetary policies, a stable currency position, and subsequent financial liberalization. As a result, key French economic policy instruments, especially the state

---

[23] Of course, wage drift (wage increases beyond the parameters of central bargains), strong wage rises in the sheltered sector of the economy (e.g., those initiated by public sector unions), and related forces had much to do with the build-up of inflationary pressure.

credit control in what Loriaux (1991) calls the "overdraft economy" and the flexibility for supportive exchange rate devaluations, were lost. Arguably, the abandonment of these economic policy instruments can be cited as one cause of the inability of French policy makers to abate rises in unemployment rates in the 1980s and 1990s. As the analysis of Chapter 5 illustrated, concerns over tax wedge effects of welfare state costs on unemployment have been a significant impetus to French welfare reform since the late 1980s.

On the other hand, in the cases of Germany and Italy, one finds it difficult to link rises in international capital mobility to notable reforms in economic policy strategy and, subsequently, sharp upturns in unemployment and welfare state retrenchment. As discussed in Chapter 5, the German political economy has long been oriented to production for export markets and has long maintained high levels of formal liberalization of capital controls. German adaptation to post-1960s economic performance problems and rises in internationalization has played on the strengths of the German model. From the late 1970s to early 1990s, economic modernization to bolster exports of diversified, high-quality manufactured goods has been facilitated by the educational and vocational training system, consensual industrial relations system, industry-finance linkages, and a framework of supportive state policies. Macroeconomic policy has been characterized by the late adoption of the principles of Keynesian countercyclical demand management and the early-1970s embrace of monetarist orthodoxy by the Bundesbank. Although the expansion of international capital markets and movements has reinforced the restrictive monetary policies of the Bundesbank at times (e.g., in the late 1970s and early 1980s), increases in capital mobility did not result in significant losses of economic policy instruments or institutional reforms during the era from the late 1970s to early 1990s.

In the case of Italy, one can argue that there is a similar absence of linkages between international capital mobility, significant loss of key economic policy instruments, and unemployment and welfare state crises. While domestic economic performance problems (including unemployment) contributed to the fiscal crisis of the early 1990s and the initiation of significant welfare state restructuring, adaptation to economic performance problems and higher levels of international economic integration from the late 1970s to the early 1990s involved reforms in the Italian economic model that actually contributed to welfare state expansion (e.g., compensation for structural adjustment) and, on some dimensions, better economic policy performance (see Chapter 5). The early-1990s crisis involved the interaction of excessive general government deficit and debt, dramatic political system change, and the impetus of Maastricht Treaty convergence criteria and, as such, extended far beyond the unemployment crises emphasized by the theory discussed here.

A second problem with the macroeconomic autonomy argument is that losses in key policy instruments may well be due to other forces (especially where governments consciously abandon instruments for the neoliberal policies of financial deregulation, hard currency, and so forth). In fact, although Huber and Stephens (1998), Moses (2000), and others generally assume that loss of key instruments is in large part the result of internationalization, other scholars have offered alternative interpretations of the causes of the shift to the neoliberal economic policies described above. They have also explicitly questioned any overriding, independent effect of international financial integration. Two recent, complementary sets of work are representative of a broader literature on the origins of 1980s shifts toward neoliberal policy orientations. First, Notermans (1993) and Forsyth and Notermans (1997) have argued that the early to mid-1980s shift to more restrictive monetary and fiscal policies, a formally or informally fixed currency, and associated neoliberal reforms (e.g., central bank independence, deregulation of international and domestic financial controls) was a conscious response of national policy makers to the inability of extant Keynesian policy prescriptions and instruments and domestic political economic institutions (e.g., corporatist wage setting) to adequately control post-1960s inflationary pressures. Thus, the desire to establish the credibility for commitments to price stability (and not ineluctable pressures from capital mobility) was the principal impetus behind the initiation of reforms that eliminated or weakened the use of a variety of monetary and supply-side instruments.[24]

In addition, McNamara's (1998) analysis of the causes of the development of the European Monetary Union sheds additional light on the origins of the shift to restrictive policies, fixed exchange rates, and related reforms. For McNamara, these policy changes represent an emergent neoliberal consensus among national policy makers in Europe around the desirability to control inflation generally, and to pursue hard currency

---

[24] In addition, as discussed at various junctures in preceding chapters, much of the expansion in most areas of capital mobility and financial integration often occurred after the shift to more neoliberal policy orientations.

policies specifically. In fact, McNamara explicitly rejects the argument that the neoliberal consensus was directly driven by the imperatives of international capital mobility and financial integration. Instead, she argues that the development of the neoliberal consensus across the larger welfare states of Europe – a system of shared beliefs and redefined common interests among national policy makers – was caused by three sets of additional forces. First, in McNamara's view, the emergence of neoliberal consensus was assisted by the common experiences of the weakness of Keynesian prescriptions and policies in the face of post-1960s economic performance problems. Second, the monetarist macroeconomic paradigm offered explanations and policy prescriptions for 1970s and early-1980s performance problems and policy failures and, in turn, was diffused through the economic and national policy communities of the developed democracies. Finally, the German experience of inflation control through restrictive monetary policy by an independent central bank and hard currency policies created an example for emulation across Europe. Overall, McNamara's and Notermans's arguments highlight the roles of long-term patterns in economic performance, macroeconomic ideas, political interests, and their interaction in shaping the conscious choices of governments to change economic policy regimes; the imperatives of international financial integration, alone, play a small role in the views of these authors.

In addition, a number of scholars have suggested that alternative economic policies and institutions have been developed by governments of large welfare states that, in the intermediate- to long-run, mitigate unemployment and general economic performance problems (and hence weaken pressures to retrench the welfare state). Other scholars have emphasized the continuity of (relatively successful) features of interventionist economic policies in large welfare states and the limited effects on national policy autonomy of globalization. While the relevant literature is large, I will focus on two important sets of studies that bear on the question of whether governments – despite the ostensible loss of some monetary and supply-side instruments – can weather high unemployment, maintain generous welfare states, and promote employment growth.

First, Visser and Hemerijck (1997) offer the Dutch case as an example of how large welfare states might cope with sustained unemployment crises. Specifically, these authors argue that in the wake of the early-1970s collapse of corporatist institutions and the notable rise of unemployment rates to roughly 10 percent by the early 1980s, it was in fact possible to "regain" the advantages of corporatist concertation and associated policies.

270

That is, in the Dutch case, governments and the social partners have reconstituted institutions for wage restraint and the negotiation of labor market flexibility and job creation while maintaining many features of the relatively generous Dutch welfare state. While a variety of economic performance problems remain (and some of the gains of the Dutch "miracle" are questionable), post-1982 bipartite concertation among the social partners contributed to substantial wage restraint (and hence modest growth in labor costs) and labor market flexibility (e.g., part-time contracts, deregulation of shop hours and business licenses). These reforms, in turn, have contributed to relatively good employment performance. For instance, job creation has been strong and formal unemployment rates have declined significantly (by EU standards). In addition, while a number of welfare state reforms have reduced benefits and eligibility (especially in the disability assistance that had supported large numbers of the unemployed), created new openings for private insurance and market competition, and reasserted government control over the administration of social insurance, the employment "miracle" has been created without significantly dismantling the Dutch welfare state. As Visser and Hemerijck point out, economic reforms and performance gains have been made while maintaining social insurance for workers (including extensions to part-time workers) and avoiding increases in income inequality typical of neoliberal welfare states.[25]

Second, recent work by Geoffrey Garrett (1998a, 1998b) and Carles Boix (1998) directly confronts the argument that internationalization has significantly eliminated the ability of governments to actively pursue economic growth and employment while maintaining redistributive public policies (also see Garrett and Lange [1991]). For Garrett, redistributive governments, strong unions and social corporatist institutions, and "vibrant capitalism" form a "virtuous circle" of complementary elements. Generous and comprehensive social protection and additional government interventions cushion workers against adverse economic impacts and new risks associated with trade and capital openness; material well-being,

---

[25] As Visser and Hemerijck (1997, esp. Ch. 6) document, reforms along the lines indicated have been significant (also see Cox [1993]; Stephens, Huber, and Ray [1999]). Examining the broad features of the Dutch welfare state, however, one can detect surprising continuity in generosity and aggregate state welfare effort. For instance, the social wage (as defined in the present study) actually increased from 65 percent of gross wages in 1980 to 70 percent in 1995. Total welfare expenditure remained stable across the 1980s and 1990s, at roughly 28 percent of GDP.

271

equality, and social stability in the presence of potential income and employment volatility is maintained. Strong trade union movements and social corporatist institutions can mitigate many of the deleterious effects of interventionist governments; wage restraint and cooperative adaptation to domestic and international economic changes can promote economic performance. Moreover, increasingly mobile enterprises can be attracted, and overall performance enhanced, by education, active labor market, and infrastructure policies that promote both social stability and economic efficiency.

As Boix (1998) points out, internationalization does not constrain these latter policies, which operate to enhance the productivity of human and physical capital. According to Boix, Left parties in particular have, in the 1980s and 1990s, continued to pursue activist supply-side policies that entail substantial government intervention. In empirical analyses of fiscal policy instruments and the scope of the public economy, Garrett (1998a, 1998b) highlights the finding that the principal costs of significant intervention to governments in a world of international finance involve the high interest premiums that accompany fiscal deficits. Overall, the central implication of Garrett's, Boix's, and related work is straightforward: while some governments have largely lost autonomy in exchange rate and domestic monetary policy – and faced new constraints on other instruments – significant policy options still remain for the active promotion of employment and general economic performance in the presence of global markets.

Summing Up

Does international capital mobility create pressures for significant welfare state retrenchment through its negative impacts on the revenue-raising capacities of the state, social corporatism, and macroeconomic policy autonomy? Generally, the answer is "no". As the preceding analyses have demonstrated, internationalization is not systematically related to reductions of tax burdens on capital, the shift of tax burdens to relatively immobile factors, or cuts in overall tax shares of GDP. Furthermore, there is no clear systematic relationship between international capital mobility and core elements of social corporatist systems of interest representation across the developed capitalist democracies during the last three decades or so. In addition, there is little evidence that globalization, itself, has systematically eliminated all of the economic policy tools necessary to promote low unemployment and, in turn, a sustainable welfare state of generous and comprehensive proportions.

However, while the preceding sections of this chapter have offered ample theory and evidence in support of these conclusions, it is also necessary to point out that internationalization of markets generally, and international capital mobility specifically, may have had limited, adverse effects on the welfare state through these indirect channels of influence. First, the shift to market-conforming tax policy regimes – which itself involves a loss of tax-based policy instruments and potentially less redistribution, if not lower revenues – occurred concomitantly with internationalization. Policy-maker perceptions about the benefits of lower nominal rates and broader tax bases (and the limits on tax increases) were certainly shaped by the economic and political logics of international financial integration. Second, while there is no systematic negative relationship between international capital mobility and elements of social corporatism, case evidence and quantitative analysis suggest that, under some political economic conditions and in some institutional contexts, globalization may have contributed to decentralization and other reforms of social corporatist institutions. Finally, although policy makers have been influenced by a variety of forces in shifting to more neoliberal macroeconomic policy orientations (and although instruments for interventionist economic guidance remain), the promotion of economic growth and employment through targeting of domestic credit (i.e., through tax, interest rate, and industrial policy), efficacious domestic monetary policy, and selective exchange rate policy is highly constrained in smaller, more open economies at 1990s levels of international financial integration. In sum, while the arguments assessed above strongly overstate the indirect consequences of internationalization for the welfare state, globalization has certainly not been irrelevant for taxation, trends in social corporatism, and macroeconomic control.

8

Conclusions: National Welfare States in
a Global Economy

In the preceding chapters, I have assessed the argument that internationalization, especially the dramatic increases in international capital
mobility over the past 25 years or so, has contributed significantly to the
retrenchment of the welfare state in the developed capitalist democracies.
As I have discussed, the heart of the globalization thesis is an argument
about "diminished democracy," or the general diminution of the ability
of democratically elected governments to pursue social policy goals that
depart from market-oriented principles. I have also offered and assessed
an alternative theory about the relationship between internationalization
of markets and contemporary social welfare policy change. In this alternative view, the domestic policy impacts of internationalization vary
notably across political contexts. The institutional structures of the polity
and welfare state shape the structure of opportunities for representation
of pro–welfare state interests (i.e., programmatic coalitions, collective
actors, and national alliances). Institutions also have long-term structural
effects on the relative political capacities of pro–welfare state interests and
on the prevailing norms and values embedded in the policy process.
Hence, configurations of national institutions play a large role in determining the ways in which national policy makers respond to the economic
and political pressures associated with globalization.[1] Overall, the evidence
has been disproportionately in favor of this latter view.

In the subsequent pages, I state my principal conclusions about the
relationships between international capital mobility and policy change in

---

[1] As I have also argued, some national political institutional contexts are particularly conducive to the economic and political logics of internationalization, generally, and to the
actions of neoliberal collective actors, specifically.

274

developed welfare states and about how national political institutions shape the social welfare impacts of globalization. I also offer a summary of the supporting empirical evidence for each conclusion and discuss any qualifications that are merited on the basis of the empirical record. In addition, I discuss the general contributions of the present volume for theories about contemporary welfare states and about the consequences of globalization for the domestic political economy and autonomy of the nation-state in advanced capitalist democracies. Finally, I highlight the implications of my conclusions and findings for future trajectories of social welfare states themselves.

Principal Conclusions and Summary of Findings

International capital mobility is not systematically and directly related to social welfare policy change in the contemporary era. In the preceding chapters, I have documented a number of rollbacks in benefit levels and restrictions in eligibility, cost controls and privatizations of social services, and related neoliberal policies across the developed capitalist democracies. There is no evidence, however, that these policy changes have been driven directly and systematically by globalization in the developed democracies as a whole, or in the largest welfare states. A quite different picture has emerged. In Chapter 3, quantitative analyses of direct impacts of multiple dimensions of international capital mobility on aggregate social welfare effort and several specific aspects of social welfare protection – cash transfers for income maintenance, the social wage, and government health effort (and the public share of total health spending) – offered no evidence in support of the conventional globalization thesis. If anything, findings of no relationships and small positive associations between capital mobility and welfare effort lend modest support to the "compensation thesis," or the argument that social programs have expanded to protect populations whose incomes and employment have been adversely affected by globalization.

In addition, in a set of supplementary tests for welfare state convergence toward a neoliberal model of social protection, results suggested that international capital mobility does not place systematic pressure on larger welfare states to "run to the bottom" or "run to a middle ground" of more market-conforming social policy. Contra this common proposition, the quantitative analysis generated modest evidence that large welfare states may diverge more from residual, market-oriented welfare states at higher levels of capital mobility. Finally, the quantitative analysis produced little support for the proposition that trade openness exerts systematic, downward pressure on social welfare protection in the contemporary era. General aspects of trade openness (aggregate trade flows as shares of GDP or flows between developed and "low-wage" economies) and the interaction of trade openness with international capital mobility are unrelated to the dimensions of the welfare state analyzed here.[2]

Case-study analysis of the social democratic and corporatist conservative welfare states strongly support the results of the quantitative analysis. (I defer summary of the evidence from the Anglo-liberal welfare states until the section on political institutions below.) With regard to the Nordic social democratic cases, there has been a moderate long-term shift toward expenditure restraints, cost control, and limited neoliberal reforms (e.g., new work orientations, increased targeting, inroads for private social insurance and services) to varying degrees in all of the focal countries. And, these changes have occurred during the period of steady globalization from the mid-1970s to the mid-1990s. However, the timing of reforms does not correspond closely to the internationalization of capital markets, and the immediate political economic impetus behind reforms is often inconsistent with forces highlighted in conventional globalization theory. As discussed in Chapter 4, the most substantial cuts in the Nordic welfare states occurred in Finland and Sweden only after severe economic crisis threatened governments with financial collapse (also see Huber and Stephens [1998]); Finnish and Swedish welfare state rollbacks before that point, during 10 years or so of notable internationalization of markets, had been relatively modest. Many of the cuts in the welfare state in Denmark occurred with the 1970s and early-1980s rise in unemployment and with the early-1980s advent of a Center-Right coalition, and thus before international financial integration proceeded very far. Furthermore, moderate rollbacks and restructuring of Danish social welfare policy were accompanied by benefit and entitlement expansions in some areas, as was the case in Norway. In addition, the neoliberal shift in economic policy orientation, present to a degree among even Nordic social democratic

---

[2] Again, while I have assessed the welfare state impacts of general attributes of trade openness in the quantitative analyses and influences of concerns over trade competitiveness in the case studies, this overview is far from thorough and comprehensive (e.g., in terms of empirical indicators of relevant dimensions of trade openness and competitiveness). As such, my conclusions regarding trade and the welfare state must be regarded as preliminary.

governments and arguably a conduit for globalization pressures (Mjøset, 1996), has not produced any notable convergence of social democratic and bourgeois parties on matters pertaining to social welfare protection.

With respect to the corporatist conservative welfare states of continental Europe, case studies of social welfare policy reforms in the French, German, and Italian welfare states also suggested that there is no systematic and direct relationship between the notable post-1960s internationalization of markets and retrenchment of the welfare state. As in the social democratic systems, it is very difficult to find any systematic linkage over time between capital mobility and consistent retrenchment and neoliberal restructuring of social policy. As discussed extensively in Chapter 5, adverse demographic trends, rises in health care costs, the growth in general and long-term unemployment (and the consequent fiscal imbalances) have been far more consistent motivations for welfare state retrenchments. For instance, in the case of Germany, late-1970s and early-1980s fiscal consolidation, which was largely shaped by fiscal stress and inflationary pressures, was followed by nearly a decade of limited cost-control efforts in pensions and health care, as well as some extensions in social protection (e.g., expansions of early retirement and unemployment benefits for older workers, active labor market policies). During this time frame, Germany experienced substantial increases in capital mobility (as well as an export-oriented modernization). In fact, in all of the corporatist conservative cases, globalization has been accompanied by moderate retrenchments, increased "compensation" of workers in the wake of economic modernization, and limited expansions of social protection to address new needs (e.g., social exclusion, the growth of the frail elderly).

International capital mobility is negatively related to social welfare effort at high levels of domestic fiscal stress. The empirical analysis in preceding chapters did indicate that internationalization may have episodic and conjunctural effects on social welfare effort. In the quantitative analysis, tests of the interaction between international capital mobility and fiscal stress indicted that where general government fiscal stress is high (e.g., budget deficits approaching or exceeding 10 percent of GDP), increases in international capital mobility are associated with reductions in social welfare effort; at average levels of budget imbalance for the contemporary era (i.e., 1960s–90s average budget deficits approaching 5 percent of GDP), capital mobility is largely unrelated to social welfare effort. When budgets are in balance, capital mobility is associated with small positive increments to social welfare spending. Consistent with arguments made by Garrett

(1998b), my analysis suggests that when budget deficits become high, international capital markets and mobile asset holders may well expect higher inflation, higher taxes, and other adverse outcomes in the wake of severe fiscal imbalance and, in turn, bid down the value of currency; currency depreciation itself will create a substantial interest rate premium for the focal nation. In such a political economic environment, policy makers may well turn to retrenchment of social welfare spending.[3]

The case-study evidence offered in Chapters 4 and 5 strongly underscores the general conclusion that international capital mobility and budget deficits interact to create significant pressures for social expenditure controls in even larger welfare states. The interaction of high capital mobility and significant fiscal stress, often in the context of political or economic "shocks" (e.g., German Unification, Italian political system restructuring), certainly accounts for key episodes in the contemporary reform of welfare states. As discussed in Chapter 4 for the Nordic cases, there appears to be a confluence of conditions in the early 1990s (in Sweden and Finland, most notably) where high international capital mobility and fiscal deficits approaching and even exceeding 10 percent of GDP contributed to moderate retrenchment of the Nordic welfare state. Moreover, in each of the corporatist conservative welfare states, it is arguably the case that the most notable welfare state retrenchments occurred under similar conditions. In early-1980s France, pressure on the franc from expanding international currency markets and concerns over increased international competitiveness interacted with the deterioration of domestic economic performance and rising budget imbalances to reverse welfare expansion and usher in cost control, revenue increases, and efficiency-oriented reforms in social policy. In 1990s Germany, substantial fiscal stress attendant on early-1990s recession and Unification interacted with continuing internationalization of capital and political pressures from the neoliberal wing of the Christian Democrats and the peak

---

[3] As several commentators on my work have pointed out (also see Garrett [1998a]), expansions of international capital markets may facilitate deficit finance (e.g., lessen domestic "crowding out" effects that may occur when governments and private borrowers compete for limited pools of finance). As such, international capital mobility may actually alleviate pressures for social spending cuts by making deficit finance easier. However, given high levels of domestic fiscal stress, international capital mobility may well be negative in its effect, as international capital markets impose higher interest rates on high-deficit countries. Results of both quantitative and case-study analyses certainly indicate that this systematically occurs.

associations of business (who stressed the Standort problem) to produce moderate welfare state retrenchments. Finally, in 1990s Italy, notably high fiscal stress, coupled with political system change, interacted with Maastricht convergence criteria and generally higher levels of internationalization of markets to produce moderate retrenchments and reforms in pensions and health care.

In sum, the case-study evidence, in combination with the results of the quantitative analysis, all point to the conclusion that international capital mobility has had a contingent effect across the developed welfare states: capital mobility interacts with substantial domestic fiscal stress to engender some retrenchment in social protection. At the same time, however, it must be recalled that extensive surveys of the secondary literature and primary data presented in the case studies indicate that the reforms flowing from the confluence of fiscal stress and internationalization have actually been relatively moderate; there is no compelling evidence that the social democratic and corporatist conservative welfare state models have broken down and moved substantially in the direction of the neoliberal model.

The direction and magnitude of social welfare effects of international capital mobility are significantly shaped by domestic political institutions, namely, the structure of systems of collective group and electoral representation, the structure of decision-making authority in the polity, and the structure of welfare state institutions. Standing in contrast to the absence of support for conventional globalization theory, the quantitative findings presented in Chapter 3 strongly point to the conclusion that the social welfare effects of notable post-1960s rises in international capital mobility are largely mediated by domestic political institutions. The economic and political pressures generated by globalization appear to operate as conventional theory would suggest in the context of pluralist systems of interest representation, exclusive electoral institutions, and polities of historically embedded decentralization of policy-making authority. They also appear to operate in accordance with the globalization argument where welfare states are structured according to liberal programmatic principles. It is in these institutionally defined contexts that the globalization thesis of internationally influenced welfare state retrenchment is confirmed. Where universalistic and corporatist conservative welfare state structures are strong and in political institutional contexts of moderate-to-strong social corporatism, inclusive electoral institutions, and centralized policy-making authority, the conventionally hypothesized globalization dynamics are absent. Internationalization has no direct and systematic impact on social welfare policy change, or it is related to small positive increments in social protection in these institutional contexts. This set of findings emerges from the systematic analysis of the ways in which domestic political institutions shape the influence of multiple dimensions of international capital mobility on aggregate social welfare effort. The conclusion is also strongly supported by results of the disaggregated analysis of the determinants of multiple features of social welfare protection within distinct clusters of nations defined by welfare state structure (and indirectly by political institutional context).

The case-study analysis also underscores the basic conclusions about the role of domestic political institutions. As I have argued for the Nordic social democracies, relatively inclusive systems of electoral representation in the Nordic countries guarantee consequential numbers of votes and seats to parties of the Left; parties of the Center, whose middle-class constituencies have some interest in preservation of the universal welfare state, also have representation. Immediate consequences of this inclusiveness are to require parties of the Right (historically weak and fragmented) to enlist centrist allies to form governments and for bourgeois governments (often with slim majorities or minority status) to negotiate reforms with opposition Left parties. Social corporatist systems of interest representation – in their general roles as supporters of Social Democratic electoral strength, conduits of union interest representation, or forums for negotiation, compromise, and consensual decision making – have also provided a bulwark against welfare state retrenchment. Extensively organized and centralized unions incorporated in corporatist institutions of national policy making have systematically resisted the more dramatic neoliberal reforms of Nordic Center-Right coalitions during the 1980s and 1990s. In addition, the relatively centralized polities of the Nordic social democratic cases contribute to the coherence and electoral strength of Nordic pro–welfare state parties and the size and coherence of the trade union movements. Centralization also minimizes the conflict and competitiveness-oriented norms and routines of fragmented polities, as well as antistatist orientations often attendant on historically rooted decentralization of decision-making authority in the polity. The size, coherence, and general political strength of national coalitions of welfare state bureaucrats and professionals, a common feature of centralized political systems, have also played a role in blunting neoliberal initiatives. Finally, as discussed in Chapter 4, research by Rothstein (1998), J. G. Andersen (1997), K. V. Andersen, Greve, and Torfing (1995), Torfing (1999), and many others have highlighted the roles of the political and moral logics of the universal welfare state – manifested in significant and sustained mass-support for the systems of generous and comprehensive programs – as significant buffers against neoliberal retrenchment efforts in the Nordic cases.

With regard to the corporatist conservative welfare states, the structure of generous occupationally based social insurance, moderately strong social corporatist institutions, and inclusive electoral institutions have played especially important roles in blunting neoliberal reform in all or a majority of the cases. With respect to the institutional characteristics of the social insurance model, theory and evidence from all of the corporatist cases suggest that direct interest representation of the social partners in administration of social insurance funds often provided constituency groups and the trade unions leverage in routine, if not major, episodes of social insurance policy making. In addition, the nature of the occupationally based model of social insurance cultivates broad political coalitions of working- and middle-class beneficiaries, as well as public sector employees; it also tends to promote high levels of legitimacy and the values of "cross-class solidarity," trust, and confidence in the system; such widespread orientations reinforce the economic interests of broad coalitions of beneficiaries and contribute to widely diffused welfare state support and active mobilization in defense of the system of social protection. As the case studies of Chapter 5 illustrated, major neoliberal plans for welfare state restructuring and retrenchment were commonly met with high levels of cross-class political resistance in all of the focal countries.

With regard to social corporatist institutions, social welfare restructuring in both Germany and Italy has been systematically conditioned by either formal or informal concertation between the social partners and the government. As the analysis of Chapter 5 makes clear, trade unions (and employers) have been integral partners, either through direct participation in negotiations or through explicit representation by the political parties, in major German social welfare reforms. In Italy, increasingly regularized corporatist concertation in the late 1970s and 1980s facilitated bargains on wage restraint and economic restructuring; social pacts that extended welfare protections were often instrumental in cementing these bargains. In the 1990s, governments have arguably found it increasingly necessary to negotiate major reforms and restructuring with the social partners. With regard to the presence of relatively inclusive electoral institutions (in all conservative welfare states except France), analysis illustrated that the electoral system has generally facilitated the development and defense of the welfare state in the contemporary era. In the 1980s–90s, electoral representation and government participation across Social Democracy, Christian Democracy, and the secular Center-Right was in fact highly balanced in the corporatist conservative welfare states. As illustrated by the majority of cases, multipartism, and the attendant dynamics of consensus building among a relatively broad spectrum of interests, has commonly facilitated the protection of pro–welfare state interests during major reforms of the contemporary period.

The roles of institutional features of the polity and welfare state have also been highlighted in the succinct case studies of social policy change in the Anglo-liberal welfare states. In Australia, Britain, Canada, New Zealand and the United States, internationalization contributed to significant economic and political pressures for rollbacks of social protection and neoliberal restructuring of the welfare state. Analysis suggested that strongly majoritarian electoral institutions, generally pluralist systems of interest representation, and liberal programmatic structures provided a conducive environment for neoliberal reforms of social policy in these systems; in the case study of the United States, analysis illustrated the multifaceted roles of decentralization of the polity in bolstering retrenchment. Moreover, comparative analysis of social policy change within the set of largely liberal welfare states also highlighted the role of political institutions. For instance, divergent trajectories of social policy change in Australia and New Zealand can in part be explained by the relative strength of post-1983 social corporatism in Australia.

Globalization has limited systematic effects on taxation, social corporatist institutions, and macroeconomic policies for full employment. While I ended my analysis and discussion in Chapter 7 by highlighting how internationalization of markets has had limited relevance to all three phenomena of interest – the revenue-raising capacity of the state, trends in social corporatism, and the available macroeconomic tools for promoting low unemployment – it is important to reiterate that the weight of the evidence is clearly against more general assertions that globalization undermines the welfare state indirectly through relatively strong impacts in these three areas. In the case of taxation, relatively extensive quantitative analysis indicated that internationalization is not systematically related to reductions of tax burdens on capital, the shift of tax burdens to labor and consumption, or cuts in overall tax shares of GDP. The shift in the structure of tax policy from high marginal rates and extensive tax allowances to lower rates and a broader base certainly occurred concomitantly with liberalization of capital markets, but the effective tax rates on capital and overall revenue shares of GDP have not systematically declined as internationalization proceeded.

Second, there is little question that key features of social corporatist institutions and practices have on average weakened in the 1980s and 1990s; union density and the level of collective bargaining in the typical developed democracy have declined. However, in recent and extensive analyses by other authors and in the results from quantitative analysis presented here, there is no clear systematic relationship between international capital mobility and core elements of social corporatist systems of interest representation across the developed capitalist democracies. In fact, case evidence indicates that, the Swedish experience notwithstanding, social corporatist institutions (albeit characterized by "competitive corporatism" and attendant social pacts) have been reinstituted or newly developed in some countries and that this trend, itself, is related to globalization. Finally, there is only limited evidence that globalization has systematically eliminated the economic policy tools necessary to promote low unemployment and, in turn, a sustainable welfare state of generous and comprehensive proportions. While high levels of international capital mobility and fixed exchange rates certainly eliminate conventional monetary policy tools as central instruments of full employment (and the broad national strategy of general credit control and selective exchange depreciations), other policy instruments and overarching employment strategies exist.

Contributions to Theories of the Welfare State and Globalization

While my arguments have relied on strong foundations built by other scholars, I wish to briefly highlight several features of the present work that contribute to extant theory on the welfare state, especially theory on welfare state retrenchment, and to debates on how the internationalization of markets shapes the domestic political economy, generally, and the autonomy of national policy makers, specifically. My theoretical argument recognizes, even emphasizes, the importance of class-based actors and the relative distribution of political capacities across them as central features of welfare state politics. As such, my argument draws on, and provides some support for, a "power resources" theory of the welfare state (e.g., Korpi [1983]; Stephens [1980]). However, similar to recent work in the "power resources" tradition (e.g., Esping-Andersen [1990, 1996]; Hicks [1999]; Huber and Stephens [forthcoming]) I also stress the roles played by collectivist Christian Democratic parties and groups, the middle class, and the welfare state programmatic coalitions that have emerged as significant actors in the postwar era. Most importantly, I emphasize the features of democratic political institutions that facilitate the mobilization of class-based actors, cross-class coalitions, and programmatic coalitions in defense of the welfare state. While the distribution of extant political capacities across pro– and anti–welfare state actors is central to understanding trajectories of welfare states, democratic institutions define the opportunities for representation of pro–welfare state actors (and shape interests and strategic interactions in important ways), and, in the long term, fundamentally shape political capacities and cultural contexts that determine the balance of political power, policies and programs of the national state, and economic and social outcomes of state action (e.g., the extent of inequality).

Current theorists of welfare state retrenchment have tended to dispute the ability of traditional power resources theory (as well as theories that emphasize broad features of state structure and capacities) to offer convincing explanations for social welfare policy outcomes in developed capitalist democracies in the post-1970s era. For instance, in an influential theory of welfare state retrenchment, Paul Pierson (1994, 1996) argues that analysts who attempt to explain patterns of welfare state retrenchment as functions of trade union power or state structures do not get very far (Pierson, 1994: 28–39). In Pierson's view, the politics of retrenchment are different from the politics of welfare expansion: governments practice blame-avoidance as the inherent nature of retrenchment involves taking away concentrated benefits from well-defined constituencies in return for promises of diffuse and long-term payoffs. Welfare states are path dependent, and extant program structure, including the character and strength of specific programmatic coalitions, defines the scope and range of retrenchment. Clearly, my own theory has drawn heavily from Pierson's work in some respects. However, my argument has emphasized – and the extensive quantitative and qualitative analysis has supported – an approach to retrenchment politics that also recognizes the importance of the political capacities of traditional class and cross-class coalitions and the direct and structural effects of institutional features of the broader polity on the distribution of political power across traditional actors. For instance, and perhaps most important, the preceding chapters have illustrated that social corporatist interest representation, defined as the incorporation of broadly organized and centralized trade union federations in tripartite bargaining and policy making, has consistent and large effects on contemporary

284

welfare state trajectories and on the degree to which globalization is associated with neoliberal reforms of the developed welfare states. The institutional structures of *both* the welfare state and broader polity, and their immediate and structural impacts on the political power of traditional and contemporary welfare state actors and coalitions, is essential to a theory of welfare state retrenchment.

With respect to globalization theory, first, the present volume adds to recent evidence that the globalization of markets for capital, goods, and labor rarely if ever has uniform effects on national social systems and political economies of developed capitalist democracies. Specifically, recent scholarship (e.g, contributions to Berger and Dore [1996]; Keohane and Milner [1996]; Kitschelt, Lange, Marks, and Stephens [1999]) has consistently found that various dimensions of internationalization of markets have commonly had divergent impacts on domestic economic performance and policies, national production regimes, and other features of the domestic political economy across nations. As Zysman (1996) and others who have contributed to this literature argue, national political economic models of innovation and investment have distinct economic and political logics; these "varieties of capitalism," through distinct political economic institutions, interests, and policies, have a notable capacity to refract pressures from the internationalization of markets, maintaining some continuity while following divergent paths of adaptation to globalization. The present volume has offered an extensive analysis of the impacts of internationalization on social policy, and the political sources of cross-national variations in those impacts, to firmly establish the point for national welfare states.

Second and relatedly, moreso than in previous research, the current work offers systematic theory and an extensive array of supportive evidence on the political mechanisms that link globalization to specific actions of the democratic state and, in turn, to continued divergence in social welfare states. To recapitulate the central argument at the most general level, the economic and political pressures generated by internationalization have fundamentally important impacts on both the material and ideological interests of a broad array of domestic actors. Central features of domestic political institutions shape the representational advantages of "winners" and "losers," directly embody or indirectly influence the relative political capacities of these actors and coalitions among them, and promote (or impede) configurations of norms, values, and behaviors embodied in national policy-making routines that favor (or disfavor) slow adaptation to

285

the pressures of globalization and the inclusion of all interests in that process.

Third, the present work contributes to the debate over the degree to which governments in the developed democracies have responded to globalization with "compensation" and, hence, have maintained the postwar compromise of embedded liberalism, or have begun to abandon the model (of international openness with domestic compensation) for a more encompassing program of domestic and international liberalization. Indeed, much of the theorizing and evidence in the present volume speaks directly to this question. To restate my principal conclusions from this perspective, social democratic welfare states and corporatist conservative systems have not generally dismantled their specific forms of post–World War Two embedded liberalism. Governments in these political economies have restructured social policy to a degree, adapting to crises and long-term pressures with widespread, yet limited, retrenchments of social protection and modest extensions of social welfare provision. However, despite the economic and political forces that have accompanied 1980s and 1990s evolution of international markets (and concomitant domestic structural changes), the political forces and institutions that have long supported an internationally oriented capitalism with significant domestic compensation (through the welfare state and other policies) have blunted the economic and political pressures for encompassing liberalization. On the other hand, however, theory and findings suggest that the compromise of embedded liberalism has begun to unravel in the Anglo democracies. This is not only a function of the political success of neoliberal parties, neoliberal economic orthodoxy, or international enterprises and institutions that championed international financial liberalization in the 1970s or domestic liberalization in the 1980s; it is also a function of the weakness of domestic redistributive coalitions and the character of institutions that condition their ability to defend national systems of social protection.

Implications: Future Trajectories of Developed Welfare States

To conclude, I wish to succinctly outline some of the implications of my theory and empirical analysis for future trajectories of the welfare state, emphasizing how welfare state retrenchment *might* actually go further than I have suggested in previous analysis. First, the theory and findings of this volume on the direct welfare state influence of the decentralization of policy-making power in the polity and on its role in mediating the economic and political pressures attendant on globalization have some notable implications for future welfare state change. The creation of federalism in Belgium, quasi-federal institutions in Britain, and extensive devolution of policy-making power to regions throughout much of the developed democratic world may well fragment and otherwise weaken national welfare state coalitions in the long run. To the extent that decentralization refocuses collective actors on inter- or intraregional distributive conflicts, intensifies social divisions within national pro–welfare organizations, and creates a more tenuous fiscal foundation for systems of social protection, the welfare state will be weakened. From a different perspective, future transfers of social welfare policy-making power to a confederal European Union also suggests a weakening of the social welfare state in Europe (also see Huber and Stephens [1992] for a similar argument). Institutional veto points for opponents of social welfare expansion and nationally fragmented European redistributive coalitions and pro–welfare state constituencies, to name two structural aspects of a federal European welfare state, suggest that the development of a more residual European-level social policy is possible.

Second, the theory and findings of this volume have also highlighted the significant and large direct and mediating effects of social corporatist institutions on the welfare state. Thus, despite the absence of support for the proposition that international capital mobility, itself, directly and systematically weakens social corporatist institutions, the present work clearly indicates that documented (albeit moderate) declines in union density and the decentralization of collective bargaining will, in the immediate future, weaken the ability of national trade unions and associated Social Democratic parties to defend the welfare state. In addition, the economic growth and efficiency orientation of new "competitive corporatist" arrangements suggests that the welfare state has been – and will continue to be – moderately weakened. Indeed, the linkage of labor market reform and other issues of economic restructuring with social welfare issues (Ebbinghaus and Hassel, 2000) and the participation and engagement of both productivity and distributional coalitions in new corporatist arrangements (Rhodes, 2001) suggest not only a continuation of the ability of unions to bargain for maintenance of social protection, but the potential of a long-term shift to more productivist social policies with less generous and costly general income maintenance.

In addition, the success of pro–welfare state interests in largely defending the corporatist conservative welfare state, coupled with the absence of labor market reform and employment-generating economic policies, has potentially adverse effects on the long-term viability of generous social protection in continental Europe.[4] Specifically, limited retrenchments in many areas of welfare policy, the maintenance and even expansion of social protection in other areas in the face of economic restructuring (e.g., early retirement), and the (upward spending) impacts of demographic patterns and new needs (see Chapter 5) have combined with insufficient employment growth and generally high unemployment rates to foster the syndrome of "welfare without work" (e.g., Esping-Andersen [1996c]). In fact, the two processes are now commonly linked, as evinced by the OECD (1995a) "jobs study" and academic analyses by welfare state scholars (e.g., Hemerijck, Manow, and van Kersbergen [2000]; Manow and Seils [2000]; Scharpf [2000]). The principal and interrelated mechanisms commonly cited as sources of the "welfare without work" syndrome are the negative impacts of welfare state generosity on labor market participation and "tax-wedge" effects, as well as a variety of labor market rigidities, such as strong employment protection and restrictions on business creation. Tax-wedge effects on employment occur where the net wage (the wage after income and social security taxes) employers can offer is too low relative to the net wage potential employees will accept to generate appreciable growth in jobs and reductions in unemployment rates. Thus, the corporatist conservative welfare states, given their generous income replacement rates and high social insurance contributions, are thought to be particularly vulnerable to "welfare without work." Consequentially, these welfare states face continuing pressures for retrenchment in the generosity of income replacements, tax reforms favorable to capital, and other policy change (e.g., reductions in strong employment protections) that may weaken social protection in the future.

It is arguably the case, however, that an alternative to dramatic neoliberal social and labor policy reforms exists. National policy makers may be able to increase productivity through policies and innovations that foster rises in human capital investment (e.g., effective active labor market policies) and physical capital investment, as well as initiate moderate reforms in social, labor market, and tax policy that both reinforce supply-side

---

[4] As observers have suggested, the strong functional complementaries between the corporatist conservative welfare state and coordinated market economic model reinforce the political defense of the welfare state (e.g., Hemerijck, Manow, and van Kersbergen [forthcoming]; Manow and Seils [2000]).

policies and maintain (relative to the Anglo-liberal cases) social protection, solidarity, and equality. While such reforms are politically and economically very difficult to achieve, they are not impossible, as the Dutch experience (at least partially) illustrates (Hemerijck, Manow, and van Kersbergen, 2000). As discussed in Chapter 7, in the post-1970s Netherlands, reinvigorated social corporatism (e.g. negotiated wage restraint), labor market reforms (e.g., the use of part-time contracts), and welfare state reforms (e.g., the reduction of costs associated with unemployment-related rises in disability) have been at least partially successful in generating job growth without rises in insecurity, poverty and inequality associated with welfare state reform in the Anglo-liberal cases (e.g., Visser and Hemerijck [1997]).

Finally, to the extent that incremental neoliberal changes in social policy accumulate, the political supports provided by the institutional frameworks (i.e., universalism and comprehensive and generous occupational social insurance) of large social democratic and corporatist conservative welfare states of course weaken. In turn, the diminution in positive political support (i.e., a weakening of the political and moral logics of these welfare states) may well result in a more ready translation of international and domestic pressures into retrenchment (see van Kersbergen [2000] for a similar argument). While I have provided extensive analysis and citations to supportive studies on the resilience of the universal and conservative welfare state models, a continuation of reforms toward increased targeting, private risk insurance, internal markets, and privatization of services would ultimately change the structural character of the welfare state and, in turn, its political viability. However, as I discussed in Chapters 4 and 5 (and as others have noted), neoliberal reforms have often been accompanied by new universalism in conservative welfare states (e.g., in French health care) and contributory social insurance in social democratic welfare states (e.g., in Swedish pensions). The political consequences of this actual shift to greater "welfare pluralism," within the context of the continuation of many basic features of long-lived welfare institutions, are unclear.

Appendix A: Data Sources

Data for Computation of Variables Measuring Internationalization

Total inflows and outflows of direct foreign investment, portfolio investment, and bank lending in millions of current U.S. dollars. *Source*: IMF, *Balance of Payments Statistics*. Washington, DC, selected years; OECD, *Foreign Direct Investment in OECD Countries*. Paris: OECD.

Index of restrictions on capital flows. *Source*: Dennis Quinn, School of Business, Georgetown University. See Dennis Quinn and Carla Inclan, "The Origins of Financial Openness." *American Journal of Political Science* 41 (July 1997): 777–813.

Exports and Imports of goods and services in millions (billions for Italy and Japan) of national currency units. *Source*: OECD, *National Accounts of OECD Member Countries*. Paris: OECD, various years.

Bilateral flows of merchandise exports and imports in millions of U.S. dollars. *Source*: IMF, *Direction of Trade*. Washington, DC: IMF, selected years.

Covered interest rate differentials. Shepherd (1994).

Gross domestic product in millions of current U.S. dollars. *Source*: OECD, *National Accounts of OECD Member Countries*. Paris: OECD, selected years.

Data for Computation of Variables Measuring Aspects of Policy/Government/Politics

See below on socioeconomic data used for some standardizations.

Surplus/deficit and total outlays of general government as a percentage of GDP. *Source*: OECD, *Economic Outlook, National Accounts of OECD Member Countries*. Both Paris: OECD, selected years.

Total social welfare outlays. *Source*: for 1991–3, and for some countries for 1980–93, OECD, *Social Expenditure Statistics of OECD Member Countries*. Labour Market and Social Policy Occasional Papers, No. 17. Paris: OECD, 1996. For 1961–91 for most nations, OECD, *New Directions in Social Policy in OECD Countries*. Paris: OECD, 1994.

General government current revenues and social transfers (social security, social assistance, unfunded employee welfare benefits of general government, transfers to institutions serving households) in millions (billions for Italy and Japan) of national currency units at current prices. *Source*: OECD, *National Accounts of OECD Member Countries*. Paris: OECD, selected years.

Social service and active labor market program spending (millions of national currency units, except for Italy and Japan, where data are in billions). *Source*: OECD, *Social Expenditure Statistics of OECD Member Countries*. Labour Market and Social Policy Occasional Papers, No. 17. Paris: OECD, 1996.

Public health expenditures as a percentage of GDP. *Source*: for 1991–93, and for some countries for 1980–93. *Source*: OECD, *Social Expenditure Statistics of OECD Member Countries*. Labour Market and Social Policy Occasional Papers, No. 17. Paris: OECD, 1996. For 1961–1 for most nations, OECD, *New Directions in Social Policy in OECD Countries*. Paris: OECD, 1994.

Inequality and poverty data: GINI index of income inequality for late 1970s/early 1980s–mid-/late 1980s for most countries. *Source*: OECD, *Income Distribution in OECD Countries*. Social Policy Studies, No 18. Paris: OECD, 1995. Pre- and post-fisc GINIs and poverty rates (Mitchell, 1991). Gender inequality index (Siaroff, 1994).

Total and categorical tax revenues (millions of national currency units, except Italy and Japan, where data are in billions). *Source*: OECD, *Revenue Statistics of Member Countries*. Paris: OECD, various years.

Percentage of Left (Right, Center, Christian Democratic) party manifesto programmatic statements composed of statements advocating expanding or maintaining (cutting or controlling) social security, social services, support for the needy, and so forth. (If more than one Left/Right/Center/CD party, variable value is mean for all parties in group.) For definition of "Left" and other party classifications, see below on measurement of Left party government control). *Source*: for 1955–88 data for all nations, except for Finland and Switzerland,

Economic and Social Research Council Dataset CMPr3, *Comparative Manifestos Project: Programmatic Profiles of Political Parties in Twenty Countries, 1945–1988*. ESRC Data Archive, University of Essex. For 1989–90 manifestoes and for Finland and Switzerland, *Comparative Manifestos Project*, data set update, supplied by Professor Richard Hofferbert, State University of New York, Binghamton.

Average tax rate on a production worker at 66 percent (and 200 percent) of average production worker's income; one-earner couple, two children. Data are complete for 1978, 1981, 1985, 1989, 1992 for all countries except Austria, Ireland, New Zealand, and Switzerland. *Source*: OECD, *The Jobs Study: Taxation, Employment and Unemployment*. Paris: OECD, 1995.

Gross income replacement rate for first year of benefits – unemployment insurance, assistance, guaranteed income, and other entitlement benefits – for a worker (mean of single, married-dependent spouse, married-working spouse) at the average production worker's income. Data are biennial for 1961–95. *Source*: OECD *Database on Unemployment Benefit Entitlements and Replacement Rates*. Paris: OECD, forthcoming.

Left party cabinet portfolios as a percentage of all cabinet portfolios. *Source* (for portfolios): Eric Browne and John Dreijmanis, *Government Coalitions in Western Democracies*, (Longman, 1982); *Keesings Contemporary Archives* (selected years). *Source* (for classification): (1) Francis Castles and Peter Mair, "Left-Right Political Scales: Some 'Expert' Judgments," *European Journal of Political Research* 12 (1984): 73–88. (2) *Political Handbook of the World* (New York: Simon and Schuster, selected years.) (3) Country-specific sources.

Political Institutions: Union membership. *Source*: Jelle Visser, "Trade Union Membership Database," Typescript, Sociology of Organizations Research Unit, Department of Sociology, University of Amsterdam, March, 1992; "Unionization Trends Revisited," Centre for Research of European Societies and Industrial Relations (CESAR), Research Paper 1996/2, February 1996; data on elements of confederal power, level of wage bargaining, and related union measures are from Miriam Golden, Michael Wallerstein, and Peter Lange, "Union Centralization Among Advanced Industrial Societies," typescript, Department of Political Science, UCLA; data on degree of proportional representation, federalism, bicameralism, and use of referendums are from Huber, Ragin, and Stephens (1993) and country-specific sources.

Legislative seats and votes for parties are from Mackie and Rose, *The International Almanac of Electoral History* and annual "political data handbooks" in *European Journal of Political Research.*

Welfare State Institutions: Ranking of nations by univeral, occupational, and residual elements, as defined above, are from Esping-Andersen (1990).

Socioeconomic Data

Consumer price index (1980 = 100). *Source*: IMF, *International Financial Statistics.* Washington, D.C.: IMF, various years.

Percentage of the civilian labor force unemployed, wage and salary employees, civilian labor force, female labor force participation, population, population 65 and older. *Source*: OECD, *Labor Force Statistics.* Paris: OECD, various years.

Gross fixed capital formation, investment deflator, GDP deflator, Gross Domestic Product, net operating surplus of domestic producers, national income, machinery and equipment expenditures (including transport equipment), compensation of employees by resident producers, private consumption expenditure, compensation of producers of government services, operating surplus of unincorporated enterprises, household property and entrepreneurial income, wages and salaries paid, and operating surplus for nonfinancial and financial corporate and quasi-corporate enterprises, where national account aggregates other than deflators are in millions of national currency units (billions for Italy and Japan). *Source*: OECD, *National Accounts.* Paris: OECD, various years.

Real Per Capital GDP in constant (1985) international prices. *Source*: *The Penn World Table* (Mark 5.6). National Bureau of Economic Research (http://www.nber.org).

Appendix B: Alternative Estimators

As a final step in this analysis, I present in Table B.1 the results from alternative estimations of the "baseline" model of preceding sections. To minimize the proliferation of results (and because results are very similar for any dimension of capital mobility), I focus on the liberalization of capital markets. The liberalization of capital markets is significantly related to other dimensions of capital mobility (e.g., 1960–92 correlations of lagged liberalization with total flows, direct investment, and capital market borrowing are statistically significant and substantively moderate or large). Also, in the case of every direct effect and interaction effect from Tables 3.2 to 3.5, two of the three alternative estimators confirm the findings; in the large majority of cases, all three alternative estimators produce the same result.

As discussed in the section on methodology in Chapter 3, I present (along with my "baseline" model) a "full" fixed effects model with a lagged endogenous variable and a generalized error correction model. To make the table manageable, I report complete model results (institutions and general controls) for the equations that estimate the linear effects of capital liberalization on social welfare effort. I present results for the individual interactions that are obtained from individual estimations of the complete model with the focal interaction and display significance levels, but not standard errors for the interactions.

As Table B.1 reveals, the primary findings about the welfare state effects of international capital mobility and its mediation by national political institutions are systematically confirmed. There is no evidence of direct negative effects of capital mobility on the welfare state. There is, however, pervasive evidence that the welfare state effects of capital mobility vary across institutions of interest representation, the organization of decision-making authority in the polity, and welfare state structures. In terms of the nature of the institutionally mediated effects, the error correction model of column 4 displays some useful information. Lagged year-to-year changes in capital mobility are not related to contemporary year-to-year policy changes. However, variations in lagged levels of capital mobility are, net of the panoply of other forces affecting welfare effort in these models, related to current movements in social welfare protection over time. Specifically, this pattern of findings suggests that subsequent social policy change proceeded in lock-step with past variations in capital mobility over the long term, the direction of that relationship determined fundamentally by the extant configuration of domestic political institutions. Taken together, these findings support the view that short-term policy responses to the immediate pressures attendant on globalization do not systematically occur; long-term, institutionally mediated responses to the economic pressures and political logic of globalization do indeed occur and characterize the relationship between international financial integration and the evolution of social policy in the contemporary era.

Table B.1. *Global Capital, National Institutions, and Social Welfare Effort, 1965–1993: Alternative Estimators*

	Baseline	Fixed Effects	Fixed Effect/LEV	Error Correction
Global Capital				
Capital Liberalization	.5790*	.4676*	.3755*	.4783*
Change Capital Liberation	—	—	—	-.1282
Global Capital by Institutions				
Level Cap Lib*Social Corporatim	.8112*	1.0562*	.4384*	.2926*
Change Cap Lib*Social Corporatism	—	—	—	-.0188
Level Cap Lib*Electoral Inclusiveness	.3645*	.4465*	.2004*	.2084*
Change Cap Lib*Electoral Inclusiveness	—	—	—	-.2068
Level Cap Lib*Decentralization	-1.8834*	-.7976*	-.5611	-.4702*
Change Cap Lib*Decentralization	—	—	—	.6447
Level Cap Lib*Universalism	.2188*	.2860*	.1164*	.0385*
Change Cap Lib*Universalism	—	—	—	-.0874
Level Cap Lib*Conservatism	-.0178	.0040	.0529*	.0159
Change Cap Lib*Conservatism	—	—	—	-.0042
Level Cap Lib*Liberalism	-.1376*	-.1805*	-.0723*	-.0356*
Change Cap Lib*Liberalism	—	—	—	.0370
National Political Institutions				
Social Corporatism	.8820*	.5517*	.1191	.0490
	(.3614)	(.3904)	(.2427)	(.1756)
Inclusive Electoral	1.3011*	.8677*	.4575*	.4522*
Institutions	(.3251)	(.3647)	(.2306)	(.1425)
Dispersion of Authority	-4.8053*	-2.7003*	-1.7399*	-1.0648*
	(.7393)	(1.5602)	(.8985)	(.2482)

296

General Model				
Social Welfare$_{t-1}$	—	—	.8599* (.0331)	-.1572* (.0293)
Old$_{t-1}$	.8075* (.1143)	.2374 (.2080)	-.1784 (.0946)	.0146 (.0398)
Unemployment$_{t-1}$	.3794* (.0585)	.2127* (.0655)	-.0036 (.0353)	-.0472 (.0279)
Inflate$_{t-1}$	.0404* (.0212)	-.0132 (.0222)	.0299* (.0177)	.0404* (.0144)
Growth$_{t-1}$	-.1284* (.0219)	-.0692* (.0218)	-.0723* (.0229)	-.1088* (.0234)
Affluence$_{t-1}$	.8060* (.0969)	.1050 (.1978)	.2604* (.1108)	.1715* (.0381)
Left Government	-.0038 (.0078)	-.0139 (.0076)	.0028 (.0029)	.0030 (.0028)
Christian Democratic Government	.0066 (.0132)	-.0013 (.0118)	.0038 (.0044)	.0094* (.0046)
Trade$_{t-1}$	.0253* (.0130)	-.0502* (.0182)	-.0311* (.0107)	.0083 (.0062)
intercept	-6.4900	4.7810	1.3040	.5700
standard error of the estimate	.9120	.8380	.8090	.8510
mean of the dependent variable	19.6570	19.6570	19.6570	.4770
Buse R²	.8160	.8620	.9880	.2700

Note: Each model is estimated with 1965–93 data by Ordinary Least Squares; equations are first-order autoregressive unless a lagged dependent variable is included. The table reports OLS unstandardized regression coefficients and panel correct standard errors. For discussion of this econometric technique, see Beck and Katz (1995). The baseline models include nation-specific dichotomous variables (if $t > 1.00$) to account for unmodeled country effects and dichotomous variables to control for series breaks in the dependent variable. Fixed effects contains $N-2$ and $t-2$ dummies to control for all unit and time effects; Fixed-LEV contains full unit and time dummies and a lagged endogenous variable; Error Correction consists of models that regress the change in social welfare effort on lagged levels of social welfare, the variables of the control model – institutions and general model factors (and nontrivial unit effects), and levels and changes of the capital mobility variable. The interaction models include both the interaction between an institutional factor and the level and the institutional factor and the change in the capital mobility factor.

* Significant at the .05 level.

^{a} Significant at the .10 level.

297

References

Adema, Willem. 1999. "Net Social Expenditure." Labour Market and Social Policy Occasional Paper No. 39. Paris: Organization for Economic Cooperation and Development.

Alber, Jens. 1988. "Germany." In *Growth to Limits: The Western European Welfare Sates Since World War II*. Volume 2. Peter Flora, ed., 1–154. New York: Walter de Gruyter.

1996. "Selectivity, Universalism, and the Politics of Welfare Retrenchment in Germany and the United States." Presented at the Annual Meeting of the American Political Science Association, August 29–September 1, San Francisco, CA.

Alesina, Alberto and Nouriel Roubini with Gerald Cohen. 1997. *Political Cycles and the Macroeconomy*. Cambridge, MA: MIT Press.

Ambler, John. 1991. *The French Welfare State: Surviving Social and Ideological Change*. New York: New York University Press.

Amenta, Edwin. 1998. *Bold Relief: Institutional Politics and the Origins of Modern American Social Policy*. Princeton, NJ: Princeton University Press.

Andersen, Bent Rold. 1993. "The Nordic Welfare State under Pressure: The Danish Experience." *Policy and Politics* 21 (3): 109–20.

Andersen, Jørgen Goul. 1997. "The Scandinavian Welfare Model in Crisis? Achievements and Problems of the Danish Welfare State in an Age of Unemployment and Slow Growth." *Scandinavian Political Studies* 20 (1): 1–31.

Andersen, Kim Viborg, Carsten Greve, and Jacob Torfing. 1995. "Reorganizing the Danish Welfare State: 1982–93: A Decade of Conservative Rule." *Scandinavian Studies* 68 (2): 161–87.

Andersson, Jan-Otto, Pekka Kosonen, and Juhana Vartiainen. 1993. *The Finnish Model of Economic and Social Policy-From Emulation to Crash*. Åbo: Åbo Akademis tryckeri.

Aspinwall, Mark. 1996. "The Unholy Social Trinity: Modelling Social Dumping under Conditions of Capital Mobility and Free Trade." *West European Politics* 19 (1): 125–50.

299

Banting, Keith. 1986. "The State and Economic Interests: An Introduction." In *The State and Economic Interests*, Keith Banting, ed., 1–33. Toronto: University of Toronto Press.

1997. "The Social Policy Divide: The Welfare State in Canada and the U.S." In *Degrees of Freedom*, Keith Banting et al., eds., 267–309. Toronto: McGill-Queen's University Press.

1998. "The Internationalization of the Social Contract." Typescript, Center of European Studies, Harvard University.

Bates, Robert and Da-Hsiang Donald Lien. 1985. "A Note on Taxation, Development and Representative Government." *Politics and Society* 14 (1): 53–70.

Bawden, D. Lee, ed. 1984. *The Social Contract Revisited: Aims and Outcomes of President Reagan's Social Welfare Policy*. Washington, DC: Urban Institute Press.

Beck, Nathaniel and Jonathan Katz. 1995. "What to Do (and Not To Do) With Time-Series – Cross-Section Data in Comparative Politics." *American Political Science Review* 89 (3): 634–47.

1996. "Nuisance versus Substance: Specifying and Estimating Time-Series – Cross-Section Models." *Political Analysis* 6: 1–36.

Béland, Daniel and Randall Hansen. 2000. "Reforming the French Welfare State: Solidarity, Social Exclusion and the Three Crises of Citizenship." *West European Politics* 23 (1): 47–64.

Bell, Stephen and Brian Head. 1994. *State, Economy, and Public Policy in Australia*. New York: Oxford University Press.

Berger, Suzanne and Ronald Dore. 1996. *National Diversity and Global Capitalism*. Ithaca: Cornell University Press.

Betz, Hans. 1996. "The German Model Reconsidered." *German Studies Review* 19 (2): 303–20.

Birchfield, Vicki and Markus Crepaz. 1998. "The Impact of Constitutional Structures and Competitive and Collective Veto Points on Income Inequality in Industrialized Democracies." *European Journal of Political Research* 34 (2): 175–200.

Block, Fred. 1977. "The Ruling Class Does Not Rule: Notes on the Marxist Theory of the State." *Socialist Revolution* 33: 6–27.

1987. "Social Policy and Accumulation: A Critique of the New Consensus." In *Stagnation and Renewal in Social Policy*, Martin Rein et al., eds., 13–34. Armonk, NY: M. E. Sharpe.

Boix, Carles. 1998. *Political Parties, Growth, and Inequality: Conservative and Social Democratic Party Strategies in the World Economy*. New York: Cambridge University Press.

Bonoli, Giuliano. 2001. "State Structures and the Process of Welfare State Adaptation." In *The New Politics of the Welfare State*, Paul Pierson, ed., 238–64. New York: Oxford University Press.

Bonoli, Giuliano and Bruno Palier. 1998. "Changing the Politics of Social Programmes: Innovative Change in British and French Welfare Reforms." *Journal of European Social Policy* 8 (4): 317–30.

Borchert, Jens. 1995. *Die Konservative Transformation des Wohlfahrtsstaates: Grossbritannien, Kanada, die USA und Deutschland im Vergleich*. Frankfurt: Campus.

References

1996. "Welfare State Retrenchment: Playing the National Card." *Critical Review* 10 (1): 63–94.

Boreham, Paul and Hugh Compston. 1992. "Labour Movement Organization and Political Intervention." *European Journal of Political Research* 22 (2): 143–70.

Boskin, Michael and Charles McClure. 1990. *World Tax Reform*. San Francisco: International Center for Economic Growth.

Bouget, Denis. 1998. "The Juppé Plan and the Future of the French Social Welfare System." *Journal of European Social Policy* 8 (2): 155–72.

Boyer, Robert. 1996. "The Convergence Hypothesis Revisited: Globalization But Still the Century of Nations." In *National Diversity and Global Capitalism*, Suzanne Berger and Ronald Dore, eds., 29–50. Ithaca: Cornell University Press.

Boyer, Robert and Daniel Drache, eds. 1996. *States Against Markets: The Limits of Globalization*. New York: Routledge.

Bradford, Neil and Jane Jenson. 1992. "Facing Economic Restructuring and Constitutional Renewal: Social Democracy Adrift in Canada." In *Labor Parties in Postindustrial Societies*, Frances Fox Piven, ed., 190–211. New York: Oxford University Press.

Brady, David and Craig Volden. 1998. *Revolving Gridlock: Politics and Policy from Carter to Clinton*. Boulder, CO: Westview.

Bruno, Michael and Jeffrey D. Sachs. 1985. *Economics of Worldwide Stagflation*. Cambridge, MA: Harvard University Press.

Bundesministerium der Finanzan (Federal Ministry of Finance [BMF]). 1996. *Finanzpolitik 2000 (Fiscal Policy 2000)*. Bonn: Federal Ministry of Finance.

Burrows, Roger and Brian Loader, eds. 1994. *Towards a Post-Fordist Welfare State*. New York: Routledge.

Bussemaker, Jet and Kees van Kersbergen. 1996. "Gender Inequality and the Conservative Welfare State: A Four-Nation Comparison." Presented at the Annual Meeting of the American Political Science Association, August 29–September 1, San Francisco, CA.

Cameron, David. 1978. "The Expansion of the Public Economy: A Comparative Analysis." *American Political Science Review* 72 (4): 1243–61.

Carlin, Wendy. 1996. "West German Growth and Institutions, 1945–1990." In *Economic Growth in Europe Since 1945*, Nicholas Craft and Gianni Toniolo, eds., 455–97. New York: Cambridge University Press.

Carnoy, Martin. 1984. *The State and Political Theory*. Princeton: Princeton University Press.

Carnoy, Martin et al. 1991. *The New Global Economy in the Information Age*. University Park, PA: Pennsylvania State University Press.

Castles, Francis, ed. 1982. *The Impact of Panties*. Beverly Hills, CA: Sage.

1985. *The Working Class and Welfare: Reflections on the Political Development of the Welfare State in Australia and New Zealand, 1890–1980*. Sydney: Allen and Unwin.

1988. *Australian Public Policy and Economic Vulnerability: A Comparative and Historical Perspective*. Sydney: Allen and Unwin.

301

1996. "Needs-Based Strategies of Social Protection in Australia and New Zealand." In *Welfare States in Transition: National Adaptations in Global Economies*, Gøsta Esping-Andersen, ed., 88–115. Thousand Oaks, CA: Sage.

1998. *Comparative Public Policy: Patterns of Post-war Transformation*. Brookfield, VT: Edward Elgar.

Castles, Francis, Rolf Gerritsen, and Jack Vowles, eds. 1996. *The Great Experiment: Labour Parties and Public Policy Transformation in Australia and New Zealand*. Sydney: Allen and Unwin.

Castles, Francis and Robert D. McKinlay. 1979. "Public Welfare Provision, Scandinavia, and the Sheer Futility of the Sociological Approach to Politics." *British Journal of Political Science* 9 (2): 157–72.

Castles, Francis and Deborah Mitchell. 1993. "Worlds of Welfare and Families of Nations." In *Families of Nations: Patterns of Public Policy in Western Democracies*, Francis Castles, ed., 93–128. Brookfield, VT: Dartmouth.

Castles, Francis and Christopher Pierson. 1996. "A New Convergence? Recent Policy Developments on the United Kingdom, Australia, and New Zealand." *Politics and Policy* 24 (3): 233–45.

Castles, Francis and Ian Shirley. 1996. "Labour and Social Policy: Gravediggers or Refurbishers of the Welfare State." In *The Great Experiment: Labour Parties and Public Policy Transformation in Australia and New Zealand*, Francis Castles, Rolf Gerritsen, and Jack Vowles, eds., 88–106. Sydney: Allen and Unwin.

Cerny, Philip. 1996. "International Finance and the Erosion of State Power." In *Globalization and Public Policy*, Philip Gummett, ed., 83–104. Brookfield, VT: Edward Elgar.

Champagne, Anthony and Edward Harpham. 1984. *The Attack on the Welfare State*. Prospect Heights, IL: Waveland Press.

Christoffersen, Henrik. 1997. "Social Policy in Denmark." In *The Politics of Social Policy in Europe*, Maurice Mullard and Simon Lee, eds., 170–87. Lyme, NH: Edward Elgar.

Christofferson, Thomas R. 1991. *The French Socialists in Power, 1981–1986*. Newark: University of Delaware Press.

Clasen, Jochen. 1997. "Social Insurance in Germany – Dismantling or Reconstruction?" In *Social Insurance in Europe*, Jochen Clasen, ed., 60–83. Bristol, UK: The Policy Press.

Clasen, Jochen and Richard Freeman, eds. 1994. *Social Policy in Germany*. New York: Harvester Wheatsheaf.

Clasen, Jochen and Arthur Gould. 1995. "Stability and Change in Welfare States: Germany and Sweden in the 1990s." *Policy and Politics* 23 (3): 189–201.

Clayton, Richard and Jonas Pontusson. 1998. "Welfare State Restructuring Revisited: Entitlement Cuts, Public Sector Restructuring, and Inegalitarian Trends in Advanced Capitalist Democracies." *World Politics* 51 (1): 67–98.

Cohen, Benjamin. 1996. "Phoenix Risen: The Resurrection of Global Finance." *World Politics* 48 (January): 268–90.

Confederation of German Employers' Associations (BDA). 1994. *Social Provision in Germany: The Welfare State at the Crossroads*. Cologne: author.

References

Cox, Robert H. 1993. *The Development of the Dutch Welfare State: From Workers' Insurance to Universal Entitlement.* Pittsburgh: University of Pittsburgh Press. 1997. "The Consequences of Welfare Retrenchment in Denmark." *Politics and Society* 25 (3): 303–26.

Crafts, Nicholas and Gianni Toniolo. 1996. *Economic Growth in Europe Since 1945.* New York: Cambridge University Press.

Crepaz, Markus and Vicki Birchfield. 2000. "Global Economics, Local Politics: Globalization and Lijphart's Theory of Consensus Democracy and the Politics of Inclusion." In *Democracy and Institutions. The Life Work of Arend Lijphart,* Markus Crepaz, Thomas Koelble, and David Wilsford, eds., 197–224. Ann Arbor: University of Michigan Press.

Crouch, Colin and Wolfgang Streeck. 1997. *Political Economy of Modern Capitalism: Mapping Convergence and Diversity.* Thousand Oaks, CA: Sage.

Cummins, Jason G., Kevin A. Hassett, and R. Glenn Hubbard. 1995. "Tax Reforms and Investment: A Cross-Country Comparison." National Bureau of Economic Research Working Paper No. 5232.

Daley, Mary. 1997. "Welfare States under Pressure: Cash Benefits in European Welfare States over the Last Ten Years." *Journal of European Social Policy* 7 (2): 129–46.

De Villiers, Bertus, ed. 1994. *Evaluating Federal Systems.* Boston: Martinus Nijhoff.

Diderichsen, Finn. 1995. "Market Reforms in Health Care and the Sustainability of the Welfare State: Lessons from Sweden." *Health Policy* 32: 141–53.

Doremus, Paul N., William W. Keller, Louis W. Pauly, and Simon Reich. 1998. *The Myth of the Global Corporation.* Princeton: Princeton University Press.

Döring, Deither. 1997. "Is the German Welfare State Sustainable?" In *Restructuring the Welfare State: Theory and Reform of Social Policy,* Peter Koslowski and Andreas Føllesdal, eds., 38–61. Berlin: Springer-Verlag.

Döring, Herbert. 1994. "Public Perceptions of the Proper Role of the State." *West European Politics* 17 (3): 12–31.

Drache, Daniel. 1996. "From Keynes to K-Mart: Competitiveness in a Corporate Age." In *States Against Markets: The Limits of Globalization,* Robert Boyer and Daniel Drache, eds., 31–61. New York: Routledge.

Eastan, Brian and Rolf Gerritsen. 1996. "Economic Reform: Parallels and Divergences." In *The Great Experiment: Labour Parties and Public Policy Transformation in Australia and New Zealand,* Francis Castles, Rolf Gerritsen, and Jack Vowles, eds., 22–47. Sydney-Allen and Unwin.

Ebbinghaus, Bernhard and Anke Hassel. 2000. "Striking Deals: Concertation in the Reform of Continental Conservative Welfare States." *Journal of European Public Policy* 7 (1): 44–62.

Economist. 1995. "Who's in the Driving Seat? A Survey of the World Economy." October 7.

Edsall, Thomas Byrne. 1984. *The New Politics of Inequaliy.* New York: W. W. Norton.

Edsall, Thomas Byrne and Mary D. Edsall. 1991. *Chain Reaction: The Impact of Race, Rights, and Taxes on American Politics.* New York: W. W. Norton.

Eichengreen, Barry. 1996. *Globalizing Capital: A History of the International Monetary System*. Princeton, NJ: Princeton University Press.

Epstein, Gerald and Herbert Gintis. 1992. "International Capital Markets and the Limits of National Economic Policy." In *Financial Openness and National Autonomy: Opportunities and Constraints*, Tariq Banuri and Juliet B. Schor, eds., 167–97. Oxford: Clarendon Press.

Ervik, Rune and Stein Kuhnle. 1996. "The Nordic Welfare Model and the European Union." In *Comparative Welfare Systems: The Scandinavia Model in a Period of Change*, Greve, Brent. ed., 87–107. New York: St. Martin's Press.

Erskine, Angus. 1997. "The Withering of Social Insurance in Britain." *Social Insurance in Europe*, Jochen Clasen, ed. Bristol, UK: The Policy Press.

Esping-Andersen, Gøsta. 1990. *Three Worlds of Welfare Capitalism*. London: Polity Press.

ed. 1996a. *Welfare States in Transition: National Adaptations in Global Economies*. Thousand Oaks, CA: Sage.

1996b. "After the Golden Age: Welfare State Dilemmas in a Global Economy." In *Welfare States in Transition: National Adaptations in Global Economies*, Gøsta Esping-Andersen, ed., 1–31. Thousand Oaks, CA: Sage.

1996c. "Welfare States Without Work: The Impasse of Labour Shedding and Familialism in Continental European Social Policy." In *Welfare States in Transition: National Adaptations in Global Economies*, Gøsta Esping-Andersen, ed., 66–87. Thousand Oaks, CA: Sage.

1997. "Hybrid or Unique? The Japanese Welfare State between Europe and America." *Journal of European Social Policy* 7 (3): 179–90.

Estes, Carroll. 1991. "The Reagan Legacy: Privatization, the Welfare State, and Aging in the 1990s." In *States, Labor Markets, and the Future of Old-Age Policy*, John Myles and Jill Quadagno, eds., 59–83. Philadelphia: Temple University Press.

Evans, Peter. 1997. "The Eclipse of the State? Reflections on Stateness in an Era of Globalization." *World Politics* 50 (1): 62–87.

Fawcett, Helen. 1995. "The Privatisation of Welfare: The Impact of Parties on the Private/Public Mix in Pension Provision. *West Europe Politics* 18 (4): 150–69.

Feldstein, Martin and Charles Horioka. 1980. "Domestic Savings and International Capital Flows." *Economic Journal* 90 (June): 314–29.

Ferguson, Thomas and Joel Rogers. 1986. *Right Turn: The Decline of the Democrats and the Future of American Politics*. New York: Hill and Wang.

Ferrera, Maurizio. 1995. "The Rise and Fall of Democratic Universalism: Health Care Reform in Italy." *Journal of Health Politics, Policy and Law* 20 (2): 275–302.

1996. "The 'Social Model' of Welfare in Southern Europe." *Journal of European Social Policy* 6 (1): 17–37.

1997. "The Uncertain Future of the Italian Welfare State." *West European Politics* 20 (January): 231–49.

Ferrera, Maurizio and Elisabetta Gaulmini. 1998. "The Adjustment of National Employment and Social Policy to Economic Internationalization: The Case of Italy." Typescript. Cologne: Max Planck Institute for the Study of Societies.

References

Flora, Peter, ed. 1988. *Grow to Limits: The Western European Welfare States Since World War II.* New York: Walter de Gruyter.

Forsyth, Douglas and Ton Notermans. 1997. *Regime Changes: Macroeconomic Policy and Financial Regulation from the 1930s to the 1990s.* Providence: Berghahn Books.

Frankel, Jeffrey. 1991. "Quantifying International Capital Mobility in the 1980s." In *National Saving and Economic Performance*, B. Douglas Bernheim and John B. Shoven, eds., 227–60. Chicago: University of Chicago Press.

Frankel, Jeffrey and Andrew Rose. 1996. "Currency Crashes and Emerging Markets: An Empirical Treatment." *Journal of International Economies* 41: 51–66.

Freeman, Gary P. 1994. "Financial Crisis and Policy Continuity in the Welfare State." In *Developments in French Politics* (revised edition), Peter Hall, Jack Hayward, and Howard Machin, eds., 188–200. London: Macmillan.

Freeman, John R. no date. "Globalization, Welfare, and Democracy." Unpublished manuscript. Department of Political Science, University of Minnesota.

French, Kenneth and James Poterba. 1991. "Investor Diversification and International Equity Markets." NBER Working Paper No. 3609.

Frieden, Jeffry. 1991. "Invested Interests: The Politics of National Economic Policies in a World of Global Finance." *International Organization* 45: 425–51.

Frieden, Jeffry and Ronald Rogowski. 1996. "The Impact of the International Economy on National Policies: An Analytical Overview." In *Internationalization and Domestic Politics*, Robert Keohane and Helen Milner, eds., 25–47. New York: Cambridge University Press.

Friedrich, Robert. 1982 "In Defense of Interaction Terms in Multiple Regression Equations." *American Journal of Political Science* 26: 797–833.

Gamble, Andrew. 1994a. *The Free Economy and the Strong State: The Politics of Thatcherism.* London: Macmillan.

1994b. *Britain in Decline: Economic Policy, Political Stategy, and the British State.* New York: St. Martin's Press.

Garrett, Geoffrey. 1996. "Capital Mobility, Trade, and the Domestic Politics of Economic Policy." In *Internationalization and Domestic Politics*, Robert Keohane and Helen Milner, eds., 79–107. New York: Cambridge University Press.

1998a. *Partisan Politics in a Global Economy.* New York: Cambridge University Press.

1998b. "Global Markets and National Policies: Collision Course or Virtuous Circle?" *International Organization* 52 (4): 787–824.

Garrett, Geoffrey and Peter Lange. 1991. "Political Responses to Interdependence: What's 'Left' for the Left?" International Organization 45 (4): 539–64.

1996. "The Impact of International Economy on National Policies: An Analytic Overview." In *Internationalization and Domestic Politics*, Robert Keohane and Helen Milner, eds., 48–75. New York: Cambridge University Press.

Garrett, Geoffrey and Deborah Mitchell. Forthcoming. "Globalization and the Welfare State: Income Transfers in the Advanced Industrialized Democracies, 1965–1990." *European Journal of Political Research.*

Garrett, Geoffrey and Christopher Way. 1999. "Public Sector Unions, Corporatism, and Macroeconomic Performance." *Comparative Political Studies* 32 (4): 411–34.

George, Vic. 1996. "The Future of the Welfare State." In *European Welfare Policy: Squaring the Welfare Circle*, Vic George and Peter Taylor-Gooby, eds., 1–30. New York: St. Martin's Press.

George, Vic and Peter Taylor-Gooby, eds. 1996. *European Welfare Policy: Squaring the Welfare Circle*. New York: St. Martin's Press.

Giersch, Herebert, Karl-Heinz Paqué, and Holger Schmieding. 1992. *The Fading Miracle: Four Decades of Market Economy in Germany*. New York: Cambridge University Press.

Gill, Stephen and David Law. 1988. *The Global Political Economy*. Baltimore: Johns Hopkins University Press.

Giovannini, Alberto, R. Glen Hubbard, and Joel Slemrod, eds. 1993. *Studies in International Taxation*. Chicago: University of Chicago Press.

Glyn, Andrew. 1986. "Capital Flight and Exchange Controls." *New Left Review* 155 (January–February): 37–49.

1995. "Social Democracy and Full Employment." *Nordic Journal of Political Economy* 22: 109–26.

Golden, Miriam and John Londregan. 1998. "Globalization and Industrial Relations." Typescript, Department of Political Science, UCLA.

Goodman, John B. and Louis W. Pauly. 1993. "The Obsolescence of Capital Controls? Economic Management in an Age of Globalization." *World Politics* 46 (1): 50–82.

Gordon, Margaret. 1988. *Social Security Programs in Industrial Countries*. New York: Cambridge University Press.

Gordon, Roger H. 1986. "Taxation of Investment and Savings in a World Economy." *American Economic Review* 76 (5): 1086–102.

Gordon, Roger H. and Jeffrey K. Mackie-Mason. 1995. "Why is There Corporate Taxation in a Small Open Economy?" In *The Effects of Taxation on Multinational Corprations*, Martin Feldstein et al., eds., 67–91. Chicago: University of Chicago Press.

Gottschalk, Peter. 1988. "Retrenchment in Antipoverty Programs in the United States: Lessons for the Future." In *The Reagan Revolution?*, B. B. Kymlicka and Jean Matthews, eds., 131–45. Chicago: Dorsey.

Gough, Ian et al. 1997. "Social Assistance in OECD Countries." *Journal of European Social Policy* 7 (No. 1): 17–43.

Gould, Arthur. 1993. *Capitalist Welfare States*. New York: Longman.

1996. "Sweden: The Last Bastion of Social Democracy." In *European Welfare Policy: Squaring the Welfare Circle*, Vic George and Peter Taylor-Gooby, eds., 72–94. New York: St. Martin's Press.

Graig, Laurene. 1999. *Health of Nations: An International Perspective on U.S. Health Care Reform* (3d ed.). Washington, DC: Congressional Quarterly Press.

Greene, William. 2000. *Econometric Analysis 4ᵗʰ Edition*. Upper Saddle River, NJ: Prentice-Hall.

References

Greve, Brent, ed. 1996. *Comparative Welfare Systems: The Scandinavia Model in a Period of Change*. New York: St. Martin's Press.

Grieder, William. 1997. *One World, Ready or Not*. New York: Simon and Schuster.

Gynnerstedt, Kerstin. 1997. "Social Policy in Sweden: Current Crises and Future Prospects." In *The Politics of Social Policy in Europe*, Maurice Mullard and Simon Lee, eds., 188–206. Lynne, NH: Edward Elgar.

Hagen, Kåre. 1992. "The Interaction of Welfare States and Labor Markets." In *The Study of Welfare State Regimes*, Jon Eivind Kolberg, ed., 124–68. Armonk, NY: M. E. Sharpe.

Hall, Peter. 1986. *Governing the Economy: The Politics of State Intervention in Britain and France*. Cambridge: Polity Press.

   1987. "The Evolution of Economic Policy under Mitterrand." In *The Mitterrand Experiment: Continuity and Change in Modern France*, George Ross, Stanley Hoffman, and Sylvia Malzacher, eds., 54–72. New York: Oxford University Press.

   1993. "Policy Paradigms, Social Learning, and the State: The Case of Economic Policy Making in Britain." *Comparative Politics* 25 (3): 275–96.

   1997. "The Political Economy of Adjustment in Germany." In *Ökonomische Leistungsfähigkeit und institutionelle Innovation: Da deutsche Produktions- ind Politikregime im globalen Wettbewerb*, WZB Jahrbuch 1997, Frieder Naschold et al., eds. Berlin: Wissenschaftszentrum Berlin für Sozialforschung.

Hall, Peter and Rosemary Taylor. 1996. "Political Science and the Three New Institutionalisms." *Political Studies* 44 (5): 936–57.

Hallerberg, Mark and Scott Basinger. 1998. "Internationalization and Changes in Tax Policy in OECD Countries: The Importance of Domestic Veto Players." *Comparative Political Studies* 31 (3): 321–53.

Hansen, Erik Jørgen, et al. 1993. *Welfare Trends in the Scandinavian Countries*. Armonk, NY: M. E. Sharpe.

Hansen, Hans. 1998. "Transition from Unemployment Benefits to Social Assistance in Seven European OECD Countries." *Empirical Economics* 23: 5–30.

Hantrais, Linda. 1996. "France: Squaring the Welfare Circle." In *European Welfare Policy: Squaring the Welfare Circle*, Vic George and Peter Taylor-Gooby, eds., 51–71. New York: St. Martin's Press.

Hauser, Richard. 1995. "Problems of the German Welfare State after Unification." *Oxford Review of Economic Policy* 11 (3): 44–58.

Hay, Colin. 1998. "Globalization, Welfare Retrenchment, and 'the Logic of No Alternative': Why Second-best Won't Do." *Journal of Social Policy* 27 (4): 525–32.

   1999. *The Political Economy of New Labour: Labouring under False Pretences?* Manchester: Manchester University Press.

Hay, Colin and David Marsh, eds. 2000. *Demystifying Globalization*. New York and London: St. Martin's Press, Macmillan.

Hay, Colin and Matthew Watson. 1998. "Rendering the Contingent Necessary: New Labour's Neo-Liberal Conversion and the Discourse of Globalization." Presented at the Annual Meetings of the American Political Science Association, September 3–6, Boston.

Helleiner, Eric. 1994. *States and the Reemergence of Global Finance*. Ithaca: Cornell University Press.

Hemerijck, Anton, Philip Manow, and Kees van Kersbergen. Forthcoming. "Welfare without Work? Divergent Experiences of Reform in Germany and the Netherlands." In *The Survival of European Welfare States*, Stein Kuhnle, ed. London: Routledge.

Herring, Richard J. and Robert E. Litan. 1995. *Financial Regulation in the Global Economy*. Washington, DC: Brookings Institution.

Hibbs, Douglas A., Jr. 1987a. *The American Political Economy: Macroeconomics and Electoral Politics in the United States*. Cambridge, MA: Harvard University Press.

1987b. *The Political Economy of Industrial Democracies*. Cambridge, MA: Harvard University Press.

Hicks, Alex. 1988. "Social Democratic Corporatism and Economic Growth." *Journal of Politics* 50 (3): 677–704.

1994. "Introduction to Pooling." In *The Comparative Political Economy of the Welfare State*, Tomas Janowski and Alexander Hicks, eds., 169–217. New York: Cambridge University Press.

1999. *Social Democracy and Welfare Capitalism*. Ithaca: Cornell University Press.

2000. "Social Democrats in Traditional Shackles: Democrats, Dixiecrats, Republicans, Social Security, and Comparative Politics." Paper presented at the Annual Meeting of the American Political Science Association, Washington, DC.

Hicks, Alex and Lane Kenworthy. (1998). "Cooperation and Political Economic Performance in Affluent Democratic Capitalism," *American Journal of Sociology* 103 (6): 1631–72.

Hicks, Alexander and Duane Swank. 1984. "On the Political Economy of Welfare Expansion: A Comparative Analysis of 18 Advanced Capitalist Democracies, 1960–71." *Comparative Political Studies* 17 (1): 81–120.

1992. "Politics, Institutions, and Social Welfare Spending in the Industrialized Democracies, 1960–1982." *American Political Science Review* 86 (September): 658–74.

Hinrichs, Karl. 1995. "The Impact of German Health Insurance Reforms on Redistributioin and the Culture of Solidarity." *Journal of Health Politics, Policy, and Law* 20 (3): 653–87.

Hirst, Paul and Grahame Thompson. 1996. *Globalization in Question*. Cambridge, MA: Blackwell.

Hoefer, Richard. 1996. "Swedish Corporatism in Social Welfare Policy, 1986–1994: An Empirical Examination." *Scandinavian Political Studies* 19 (1): 67–81.

Holmes, Martin. 1985. *The Labour Government, 1974–79: Political Aims and Economic Reality*. New York: St. Martin's Press.

Howard, Christopher. 1997. *The Hidden Welfare State: Tax Expenditures and Social Policy in the United States* . Princeton, NJ: Princeton University Press.

Huber, Evelyne and John D. Stephens. 1992. "Economic Internationalization, the European Community, and the Social Democratic Welfare State."

References

Paper presented at the Annual Meetings of the American Political Science Association.

1996. "Political Power and the Making of the Social Democratic Service State." Paper presented at the Annual Meeting of the American Political Science Association, August 28–September 1, San Francisco, CA.

1998. "Internationalization and the Social Democratic Welfare Model: Crises and Future Prospects." *Comparative Political Studies* 33 (June): 353–97.

2001. "Welfare State and Production Regimes in an Era of Retrenchment." In *The New Politics of the Welfare State*, Paul Pierson, ed., 107–45. New York: Oxford University Press.

Huber, Evelyne, Charles Ragin, and John Stephens. 1993. "Social Democracy, Christian Democracy, Constitutional Structure and the Welfare State." *American Journal of Sociology* 99 (3): 711–49.

Immergut, Ellen. 1992. *The Political Construction of Interests: National Health Insurance Politics in Switzerland, France and Sweden.* New York: Cambridge University Press.

International Monetary Fund. 1991. *Determinants and Consequences of International Capital Flows.* Washington, DC: International Monetary Fund.

1995. *United Germany: The First Five Years. Performance and Policy Issues.* IMF Occasional Papers 125. Washington, DC: International Monetary Fund.

Iversen, Torben. 1996. "Power, Flexibility, and the Breakdown of Central Wage Bargaining: Denmark and Sweden in Comparative Perspective." *Comparative Politics* 28 (4): 399–436.

2001. "The Dynamics of Welfare State Expansion: Trade Openness, Deindustrialization, and Partisan Politics." In *The New Politics of the Welfare State*, Paul Pierson, ed., 45–79. New York: Oxford University Press.

Jäntti, Markus, Olli Kangas, and Veli-Matti Ritakallio. 1996. "From Marginalism to Institutionalism: Distributional Consequences of the Transformation of the Finnish Pension Regime." *Review of Income and Wealth* 42 (4): 473–91.

Jennett, Christine and Randal G. Stewart. 1990. *Hawke and Australian Public Policy: Consensus and Restructuring.* Melbourne: Macmillan.

Jessop, Bob. 1996. "Post-Fordism and the State." In *Comparative Welfare Systems: The Scandinavia Model in a Period of Change*, Brent Greve, ed., 165–83. New York: St. Martin's Press.

Jones, Catherine, ed. 1993. *New Perspectives on the Welfare State in Europe.* New York: Routledge.

Judge, George et al. 1985. *The Theory and Practice of Econometrics, Second Edition.* New York: John Wiley and Sons.

Jun, Joosung. 1990. "U.S. Tax Policy and Direct Investment Abroad." In *Taxation in the Global Economy*, Assaf Razin and Joel Slemrod, eds., 55–78. Chicago: University of Chicago Press.

Kangas, Olli. 1995. "Attitudes on Means-Tested Social Benefits in Finland." *Acta Sociologica* 38: 299–310.

Kangas, Olli and Joakim Palme. 1993. "Statism Eroded? Labor-Market Benefits and Challenges to the Scandinavian Welfare States." In *Welfare Trends in the*

Scandinavian Countries, Erik Jørgen Hansen et al., eds., Armonk, NY: M. E. Sharpe.

Kant, Chandler. 1996. *Foreign Direct Investment and Capital Flight*. Princeton: International Finance Section, Department of Economics, Princeton University.

Kapstein, Ethan B. 1994. *Governing the Global Economy: International Finance and the State*. Cambridge, MA: Harvard University Press.

Katzenstein, Peter. 1985. *Small States in World Markets*. Ithaca: Cornell University Press.

Keohane, Robert and Helen Milner, eds. 1996. *Internationalization and Domestic Politics*. New York: Cambridge University Press.

King, Desmond. 1987. *The New Right: Politics, Markets, and Citizenship*. Chicago: The Dorsey Press.

King, Desmond and Stewart Wood. 1999. "The Political Economy of Neoliberalism: Britain and the United States in the 1980s." In *Continuity and Change in Contemporary Capitalism*, Herbert Kitschelt, Peter Lange, Gary Marks, and John Stephens, eds., 371–97. New York: Cambridge University Press.

King, Gary, Robert Keohane, and Sidney Verba. 1994. *Designing Social Inquiry: Scientific Inference in Qualitative Research*. Princeton, NJ: Princeton University Press.

Kitschelt, Herbert, Peter Lange, Gary Marks, and John Stephens. 1999. "Conclusion: Convergence and Divergence in Advanced Capitalist Democracies." In *Continuity and Change in Contemporary Capitalism*, Herbert Kitschelt, Peter Lange, Gary Marks, and John Stephens, eds., 427–60. New York: Cambridge University Press.

Kleinman, Mark. 1996. *Housing, Welfare, and the State in Europe: A Comparative Analysis of Britain, France, and Germany*. Brookfield, VT: Edward Elgar.

Klingemann, Hans-Dieter, Richard Hofferbert, and Ian Budge. 1994. *Parties, Policy, and Democracy*. Boulder, CO: Westview.

Kloten, Norbert, Karl-Heinz Ketterer, and Rainer Vollmer. 1985. "West Germany's Stabilization Performance." In *The Politics of Inflation and Economic Stagnation*, Leon Lindberg and Charles S. Maier, eds., 353–402. Washington, DC: Brookings.

Knight, Jack. 1992. *Institutions and Social Conflict*. New York: Cambridge University Press.

Köhler, Peter A. and Hans F. Zacher, eds. 1982. *The Evolution of Social Insurance 1881–1981: Studies of Germany, France, Great Britain, Austria, and Switzerland*. New York: St. Martin's Press.

Korpi, Walter. 1983. *The Democratic Class Struggle*. London: Routedge and Kegan Paul.

Korpi, Walter and Joachim Palme. 1998. "The Paradox of Redistribution and Strategies of Equality: Welfare State Institutions, Inequality, and Poverty in the Western Countries." *American Sociological Review* 63 (5): 661–87.

Kosonen, Pekka. 1993. "Welfare Policy In Sweden." In *Scandinavia in a New Europe*, Thomas P. Boje and Sven E. Olsson Hort, eds., 39–70. Oslo: Scandinavian University Press.

References

Krieger, Joel. 1986. *Reagan, Thatcher, and the Politics of Decline*. New York: Oxford University Press.

1999. *British Politics in the Global Age: Can Social Democracy Survive?* New York: Oxford University Press.

Kurzer, Paulette. 1993. *Business and Banking: Political Change and Economic Integration in Western Europe*. Ithaca: Cornell University Press.

Kvist, Jon. 1997. "Retrenchment or Restructuring? The Emergence of a Multi-tiered Welfare State in Denmark." In *Social Insurance in Europe*, Jochen Clasen, ed., 14–39. Bristol, UK: The Policy Press.

Lange, Peter and Geoffrey Garrett. 1985. "The Politics of Growth: Strategic Interaction and Economic Performance in Advanced Industrial Democracies." *Journal of Politics* 47 (3): 792–827.

Lange, Peter and Marino Regini, eds. 1989. *State, Market, and Social Regulation: New Perspectives on Italy*. New York: Cambridge University Press.

Lawson, Roger. 1996. "Germany: Maintaining the Middle Way." In *European Welfare Policy: Squaring the Welfare Circle*, Vic George and Peter Talyor-Gooby, eds., 31–50. New York: St. Martin's Press.

Leibfried, Stephan and Paul Pierson, eds. 1995. *European Social Policy: Between Fragmentation and Integration*. Washington, DC: Brookings Institution.

Lehmbruch, Gerhard. 1984. "Concertation and the Structure of Corporatist Networks." In *Order and Conflict in Contemporary Capitalism*, John Goldthorpe, ed., 61–80. Oxford: Clarendon Press.

Lessard, Donald R. and John Williamson. 1987. *Capital Flight and Third World Debt*. Washington, DC: Institute for International Economics.

Levy, Frank. 1998. *The New Dollars and Dreams: American Incomes and Economic Change*. New York: Russell Sage Foundation.

Lewis-Beck, Michael. 1988. *Economics and Elections: The Major Western Democracies*. Ann Arbor: The University of Michigan Press.

Light, Paul. 1985. *Artful Work: The Politics of Social Security Reform*. New York: Random House.

Lijphart, Arend. 1984. *Democracies: Patterns of Majoritarian and Consensus Government in Twenty-One Countries*. New Haven: Yale University Press.

1999. *Patterns of Democracy: Government Forms and Performance in Thirty-Six Countries*. New Haven: Yale University Press.

Lijphart, Arend and Markus M. L. Crepaz. 1991. "Corporatism and Consensus Democracy in Eighteen Countries." *British Journal of Political Science* 21 (2): 235–56.

Lindbeck, Assar et al. 1994. *Turning Sweden Around*. Cambridge, MA: MIT Press.

Lindblom, Charles. 1977. *Politics and Markets*. New York: Basic Books.

Lindbom, Anders. 1999. "Dismantling the Social Democratic Model? Has the Swedish Welfare State Lost Its Defining Characteristics?" Paper presented at the Joint Session of Workshops of the Euroepan Consortium for Political Research, Mannheim, Germany, March 26–31.

Locke, Richard. 1995. *Remaking the Italian Economy*. Ithaca: Cornell University Press.

311

Locke, Richard, Thomas Kochen, and Michael Piore, eds. 1995. *Employment Relations in a Changing World Economy*. Cambridge, MA: MIT Press.

Loriaux, Michael. 1991. *France After Hegemony: International Change and Financial Reform*. Ithaca: Cornell University Press.

Mahon, James. 1996. *Mobile Capital and Latin American Development*. University Park, PA: Pennsylvania State University Press.

Mangen, Steen. 1994. "The Impact of Unification." In *Social Policy in Germany*, Jochen Clasen and Richard Freeman, eds., 42–57. New York: Harvester Wheatsheaf.

Manow, Philip. 1998. "Welfare State Building and Coordinated Capitalism in Japan and Germany." Paper presented at the Conference on "Varieties of Capitalism," June 11–13, Cologne: Max Planck Institute.

Manow, Philip and Eric Seils. 1999. "Globalization and the Welfare State: Germany." Typescript, Cologne: Max Planck Institute.

2000. "The Employment Crisis of the German Welfare State." *West European Politics* 23 (2): 137–60.

Mares, Isabela, 1997. "Is Unemployment Insurable? Employers and the Introduction of Unemployment Insurance." *Journal of Public Policy* 17 (3): 299–327.

Marklund, Steffan. 1988. *Paradise Lost? The Nordic Welfare States in the Recession of 1975–1985*. Lund: Arkiv.

Marston, Richard C. 1995. *International Financial Integration: A Study of Interest Differentials between the Major Industrial Countries*. New York: Cambridge University Press.

Martin, Andrew. 1996. "What Does Globalization Have to Do With the Erosion of Welfare States? Sorting Out the Issues." Program for the Study of Germany and Europe Working Paper Series 7.5, Center for European Studies, Harvard University.

Martin, Cathie Jo. 1991. *Shifting the Burden: The Struggle over Growth and Corporate Taxation*. Chicago: University of Chicago Press.

1995. "Nature or Nurture? Sources of Firm Preference for National Health Care Reform." *American Political Science Review* 89 (4): 898–913.

2000. *Stuck in Neutral: Business and the Politics of Human Capital Investment Policy*. Princeton, NJ: Princeton University Press.

Matthews, Trevor. 1991. "Interest Group Politics: Corporatism Without Business?" In *Australia Compared: People, Policies, and Politics*, Francis Castles, ed., 191–218. Sydney: Allen and Unwin.

Matthewson, Donald J. 1996. "Welfare Reform and Comparative Models of Bureaucratic Behavior: Budget Maximizers and Bureau Shapers in the United States and France." *American Review of Public Administration* 26 (2): 135–58.

McFate, Katherine, Roger Lawson, and William Julius Wilson. 1995. *Poverty, Inequality, and the Future of Social Policy: Western States in the New World Order*. New York: Russell Sage Foundation.

McKenzie, Richard and Dwight Lee. 1991. *Quicksilver Capital: How the Rapid Movement of Wealth Has Changed the World*. New York: Free Press.

McNamara, Kathleen R. 1998. *The Currency of Ideas: Monetary Politics in the European Union*. Ithaca: Cornell University Press.

References

McQuaid, Kim. 1994. *Uneasy Partners: American Business in American Politics, 1945–1990.* Baltimore: Johns Hopkins University Press.

Mendoza, E. G., A. Razin, and L. L. Tesar. 1994. "Effective Tax Rates in Macroeconomics: Cross-country Estimates of Tax Rates in Factor Incomes and Consumption," *Journal of Monetary Economics* 34: 297–323.

Meyer, Traute. 1998. "Retrenchment, Reproduction, Modernization: Pension Politics and the Decline of the German Breadwinner Model." *European Journal of Social Policy* 8 (3): 195–211.

Milner, Henry. 1994. *Social Democracy and Rational Choice: The Scandinavian Experience and Beyond.* New York: Routledge.

Mishra, Ramesh. 1993. "Social Policy in the Post-Modern World." In *New Perspectives on the Welfare State in Europe*, Catherine Jones, ed., 18–40. New York: Routledge.

——— 1996. "The Welfare of Nations." In *States Against Markets: The Limits of Globalization*, Robert Boyer and Daniel Drache, eds., 316–33., New York: Routledge.

Mitchell, Deborah. 1991. *Income Transfers in Ten Welfare States.* Brookfield, VT: Avebury.

Mjøset, Lars. 1987. "Nordic Economic Policies in the 1970s and 1980s." *International Organization* 41 (3): 403–56.

——— 1996. "Nordic Economic Policies in the 1980s and 1990s." Paper presented at the Tenth International Conference of Europeanists, Chicago, IL.

Moene, Karl Ove and Michael Wallerstein. 1993. "What's Wrong with Social Democracy?" In *Market Socialism: the Current Debate*, Pranab K. Bardhan and John E. Roemer, eds. New York: Oxford University Press.

——— 1996. "Self-Interested Support for Welfare Spending." Paper presented at the Annual Meeting of the American Political Science Association, August 29–September 1 San Francisco, CA.

Mollenkopf, John. 1998. "Urban Policy at the Crossroads." In *The Social Divide: Political Parties and the Future of Activist Government*, Margaret Weir, ed., 464–504. Washington, DC and New York: Brookings Institution, Russell Sage.

Moses, Jonathon. 1994. "Abdication from National Policy Autonomy: What's Left to Leave?" *Politics and Society* 22 (2): 125–48.

——— 2000. "Floating Fortunes: Scandinavian Full Employment in the Tumultuous 1970s and 1980s." In *Globalization, Europeanization, and the End of Scandinavian Social Democracy?*, Robert Geyer, Christine Ingrebritsen, and Jonathon Moses, eds., 62–82. New York and London: St. Martin's Press, Macmillan.

Mosley, Layna. 1998. "Strong but Narrow: International Financial Market Pressures and Welfare State Policies." Paper presented at the Eleventh Annual Conference of Europeanists, February 26–28, Balitimore, MD.

Mushaben, Joyce Marie. 1997. "Restructuring the German *Sozialstaat*: Internal and External Forces for Change." Paper presented at the 1997 Annual Meeting of the American Political Science Association, August 28–31, Washington, DC.

Myles, John. 1989. *Old Age and the Welfare State: The Political Economy of Public Pensions*. Lawrence, KS: University of Kansas Press.

——— 1996. "When Markets Fail: Social Welfare in Canada and the United States." In *Welfare States in Transition: National Adaptations in Global Economies*, Gøsta Esping-Andersen, ed., 116–40. Thousand Oaks, CA: Sage.

Myles, John and Paul Pierson. 1997. "Friedman's Revenge: The Reform of the 'Liberal' Welfare States in Canada and the United States." *Politics and Society* 25 (4): 443–72.

Nannestad, Peter and Martin Paldam. 1994. "The V-P Function: A Survey of the Literature on Vote and Popularity Functions after 25 Years." *Public Choice* 79: 213–45.

Nickell, Stephen. 1997. "Unemployment and Labor Market Rigidities: Europe versus North America." *Journal of Economic Perspectives* 11 (3): 55–74.

Niero, Mauro. 1996. "Italy: Right Turn for the Welfare State?" In *European Welfare Policy: Squaring the Welfare Circle*, Vic George and Peter Talyor-Gooby, eds., 117–35. New York: St Martin's Press.

Noble, Charles. 1997. *Welfare as We Knew It: A Political History of the American Welfare State*. New York: Oxford University Press.

Noel, Alan. 1998. "Is Decentralization Conservative? Federalism and the Contemporary Debate on the Canadian Welfare State." Typescript, Department of Political Science, University of Montreal.

Notermans, Ton. 1993. "The Abdication of National Policy Autonomy: Why the Macroeconomic Policy Regime Has Become So Unfavorable to Labor." *Politics and Society* 21 (2): 133–67.

Obstfeld, Maurice. 1995. "International Capital Mobility in the 1990s." In *Understanding Interdependence: The Macroeconomics of the Open Economy*, Peter Kenen, ed., 201–61. Princeton, NJ: Princeton University Press.

Offe, Klaus. 1991. "Smooth Consolidation of the German Welfare State: Structural Change, Fiscal Problems, and Populist Politics." In *Labor Parties in Postindustrial Societies*, Frances Fox Piven, ed., New York: Oxford.

Ohmae, Keniche. 1991. *The Borderless World: Power and Strategy in the Interlinked Economy*. New York: Harper Perennial.

——— 1996. *The End of the Nation State: The Rise of Regional Economies*. New York: Free Press.

Organization for Economic Cooperation and Development. 1987. *Taxation in Developed Countries*. Paris: OECD.

——— 1989. *Economies in Transition*. Paris: OECD.

——— 1990. *Taxation and International Capital Flows*. Paris: OECD.

——— 1991. *Taxation in a Global Economy: Domestic and International Issues*. Paris: OECD.

——— 1992a. *International Direct Investment: Policies and Trends in the 1980s*. Paris: OECD.

——— 1992b. *Private Pensions and Public Policy* (OECD Social Policy Studies No. 9). Paris: OECD.

——— 1993a. *OECD Health Systems, Volumes I and II*. Paris: OECD.

References

1993b. *Taxation in OECD Countries*. Paris: OECD.

1994. *New Directions in Social Policy*. Paris: OECD.

1995a. *The Jobs Study: Taxation, Employment, and Unemployment*. Paris: OECD.

1995b. *Income Distribution in OECD Countries*. Paris: OECD.

1996. *International Capital Market Statistics: 1950–1995*. Paris: OECD.

1997. *Taxing International Business: Emerging Trends in APE and OECD Countries*. Paris: OECD.

Various numbers. *Financial Market Trends*. Paris: OECD.

Selected years, a. *Economic Outlook: France*. Paris: OECD.

Selected years, b. *Economic Outlook: Germany*. Paris: OECD.

Selected years, c. *Economic Outlook: Italy*. Paris: OECD.

Page, Benjamin. 1997. "Trouble for Workers and the Poor: Economic Globalization and the Reshaping of American Politics." Presented at the Annual Meeting of the Midwest Political Science Association, April 10–12, Chicago, IL.

Palier, Bruno. 1997. "A 'Liberal' Dynamic in the Transformation of the French Social Welfare System." In *Social Insurance in Europe*, Jochen Clasen, ed., 84–106. Bristol, UK: The Policy Press.

Palme, Joakim and Irene Wennemo. 1997. "Swedish Social Security in the 1990s: Reform and Retrenchment." CWR Working Paper No. 9/97, Center for Welfare State Research, Danish National Institute of Social Research.

Pampel, Fred C. and John B. Williamson. 1989. *Age, Class, Politics and the Welfare State*. New York: Cambridge University Press.

Pauly, Louis. 1995. "Capital Mobility, State Autonomy, and Political Legitimacy." *Journal of International Affairs* 48 (2): 369–88.

Pechman, Joseph A. 1988. *World Tax Reform: A Progress Report*. Washington, DC: Brookings Institution.

Perez, Sofia. 1998. "Yet the Century? The Return to National Social Bargaining in Italy and Spain, and its Possible Implications." Presented at the Annual Meeting of the American Political Science Association September 3–6, Boston, MA.

Perry, Richard. 1988. "United Kingdom." In *Growth to Limits: The Western European Welfare States Since World War II*. Volume 2. Peter Flora, ed., 155–240. New York: Walter de Gruyter.

Pettersen, Per Arnt. 1995. "The Welfare State: The Security Dimension." In *The Scope of Government*, Ole Borre and Elnor Scarbrough, eds., New York: Oxford University Press.

Pfaller, Alfred, Ian Gough, and Göran Therborn. 1991. *Can the Welfare State Compete?* London: Macmillan.

Phillips, Kevin. 1990. *The Politics of Rich and Poor: Wealth and American Electorate in the Reagan Aftermath*. New York: Random House.

Pierson, Christopher. 1991. *Beyond the Welfare State?* Cambridge: Polity Press.

Pierson, Paul. 1994. *Dismantling the Welfare State: Reagan, Thatcher and the Politics of Retrenchment in Britain and the United States*. New York: Cambridge University Press.

315

1995. "Fragmented Welfare Systems: Federal Institutions and the Development of Social Policy." *Governance: An International Journal of Policy and Administration* 8 (4): 449–78.

1996. "The New Politics of Welfare." *World Politics* 48 (2): 143–79.

1998. "The Deficit and the Politics of Domestic Reform." In *The Social Divide: Political Parties and the Future of Activist Government*, Margaret Weir, ed., 126–78. Washington, DC and New York: Brookings Institution, Russell Sage.

Pitruzzello, Salvatore. 1997. "Social Policy and the Implementation of the Maastricht Fiscal Convergence Criteria: The Italian and French Attempts at Welfare and Pension Reform." *Social Research* 64 (4): 1589–642.

Piven, Frances Fox. 1992. "Structural Constraints and Political Development: The Case of the American Democratic Party." In *Labor Parties in Postindustrial Societies*, Francis Fox Piven, ed., 235–64. New York: Oxford University Press.

Piven, Francis Fox and Richard Cloward. 1982. *The New Class War: Reagan's Attack on the Welfare State and Its Consequences*. New York: Pantheon.

Ploug, Niels. 1998. "Cuts and Reforms in Cash Benefit Systems." Typescript, The Danish National Institute of Social Research, Copenhagen.

Ploug, Niels and Jon Kvist, eds., 1994. *Recent Trends in Cash Benefits in Europe* (Social Security in Europe, 4). Copenhagen: The Danish National Institute of Social Research.

1996. *Social Security in Europe: Development or Dismantlement*. (Social Security in Europe, 1). Copenhagen: The Danish National Institute of Social Research.

Pontusson, Jonas. 1992a. *The Limits of Social Democracy: Investment Politics in Sweden*. Ithaca: Cornell University Press.

1992b. "At the End of the Third Road: Swedish Social Democracy in Crisis." *Politics and Society* 20 (3): 305–32.

Pontusson, Jonas and Peter Swenson. 1996. "Labor Markets, Production Strategies, and Wage Bargaining Institutions: The Swedish Employer Offensive in Comparative Perspective." *Comparative Political Studies* 29 (2): 223–50.

Przeworski, Adam and Michael Wallerstein. 1988. "Structural Dependence of the State on Capital." *American Political Science Review* 82 (1): 11–30.

Putnam, Robert. 1993. *Making Democracy Work: Civic Traditions in Modern Italy*. Princeton, NJ: Princeton University Press.

Quadagno, Jill. 1991. "Interest Group Politics and the Future of U.S. Social Security." In *States, Labor Markets, and the Future of Old-Age Policy*, John Myles and Jill Quadagno, eds., 36–58. Philadelphia: Temple University Press.

1994. *The Color of Welfare: How Racism Undermined the War on Poverty*. Cambridge: Cambridge University Press.

Quinn, Dennis. 1997. "The Correlates of Change in International Financial Regulation." *American Political Science Review* 91 (3): 531–52.

Quinn, Dennis and Carla Inclan. 1997. "The Origins of Financial Openness: A 21-Country Study of Its Determinants, 1950–1988." *American Journal of Political Science* 41 (3): 771–813.

Quinn, Dennis and Robert Shapiro. 1991. "Business Political Power: The Case of Taxation." *American Political Science Review* 85 (3): 851–74.

References

Radaelli, Claudio. 1997. *The Politics of Corporate Taxation in the European Union: Knowledge and International Policy Agendas.* New York: Routledge.

Ragin, Charles C. 1987. *The Comparative Method: Moving Beyond Qualitative and Quantitative Strategies.* Berkeley: University of California Press.

Razin, Assaf and Efraim Sadka. 1991. "International Tax Competition and Gains from Tax Harmonization." *Economic Letters* 37 (1): 69–76.

Reich, Robert. 1992. *The Work of Nations.* New York: Vintage Books.

Regini, Marino and Ida Regalia. 1997. "Employers, Unions and the State: The Resurgence of Concertation in Italy." *West European Politics* 20 (1): 210–30.

Rhodes, Martin. 1997a. "The Welfare State: Internal Challenges, External Constraints." In *Developments in West European Politics*, Martin Rhodes, Paul Heywood, and Vincent Wright, eds., London: Macmillan.

ed. 1997b. *Southern European Welfare States: Between Crisis and Reform.* London: Frank Cass.

2000. "Desperately Seeking a Solution: Social Democracy, Thatcherism, and the 'Third Way' in British Politics." *West European Politics* 23 (2): 161–86.

2001. "The Political Economy of Social Pacts: 'Competitive Corporatism' and European Welfare Reform." In *The New Politics of the Welfare State*, Paul Pierson, ed., 165–94. New York: Oxford University Press.

Riker, William. 1964. *Federalism: Origin, Operation, and Significance.* Boston: Little, Brown.

Robertson, David B. and Dennis R. Judd. 1989. *The Development of American Public Policy: The Structure of Policy Restraint.* Glenview, IL: Scott, Foresman and Company.

Rodrik, Dani. 1996. "Why Do More Open Economies have Bigger Governments?" NBER Working Paper # 5537.

1997. *Has Globalization Gone too Far?* Washington, DC: Institute for International Economics.

Rogowski, Ronald. 1987. "Trade and the Variety of Democratic Institutions." *International Organization* 41 (Spring): 203–23.

1998. "'Globalization' and Convergence: Getting the Theory and Evidence Right." Typscript, Department of Political Science, UCLA.

Ross, George, Stanley Hoffman and Sylvia Malzacher, eds. 1987. *The Mitterrand Experiment: Continuity and Change in Modern France.* New York: Oxford University Press.

Ross, Robert J. S. and Kent C. Trachte. 1990. *Global Capitalism: The New Leviathan.* Albany: State University of New York Press.

Rossi, Nicola and Gianni Toniolo. 1996. "Italy." In *Economic Growth in Europe Since 1945*, Nicholas Craft and Gianni Toniolo, eds., 427–54. New York: Cambridge University Press.

Rothstein, Bo. 1996. *The Social Democratic State: The Swedish Model and the Bureaucratic Problem of Social Reforms.* Pittsburgh: University of Pittsburgh Press.

1998. *Just Institutions Matter: the Moral and Political Logic of the Universal Welfare State.* New York: Cambridge University Press.

317

Ruggie, John Gerard. 1982. "International Regimes, Transactions, and Change: Embedded Liberalism in the Postwar Economic Order." *International Organization* 36 (2): 379–415.

1994. "Trade, Protectionism, and the Future of Welfare Capitalism." *Journal of International Affairs* 48 (1): 1–11.

Ryner, Magnus. 1997. "Nordic Welfare Capitalism in the Emerging Global Economy." In *Globalization, Democratization, and Multilateralism*, Stephen Gill, ed., 19–49. New York: St. Martin's Press.

Saraceno, Chiara and Nicola Negri. 1994. "The Changing Italian Welfare State." *European Journal of Social Policy* 4 (1): 19–34.

Sainsbury, Diane, ed. 1994. *Gendering the Welfare State*. Thousand Oaks, CA: Sage.

1996. *Gender, Equality, and Welfare States*. New York: Cambridge University Press.

Scharpf, Fritz. 1988. "The Joint Decision Trap: Lessons from German Federalism and European Integration." *Public Administration* 66: 39–78.

1991. *Crisis and Choice in European Social Democracy*. Ithaca: Cornell University Press.

1997. *Games Real Actors Play: Actor-Centered Institutionalism in Policy Research*. Boulder, CO: Westview.

2000. "The Viability of Advanced Welfare States in the International Economy: Vulnerabilities and Options." *Journal of European Public Policy* 7 (2): 190–228.

Schiltz, Christoph. 1998. "Pension Scheme of the Future: The Debate in Germany on the Problem of Provision for Old Age and the Search for New Systems," IN-Press Working Paper 14-1998 Social Policy. Bonn: Inter Nationes.

Schmähl, Winfried. 1993. "The '1992 Reform' of Public Pensions in Germany: Main Elements and Some Effects." *Journal of European Social Policy* 3 (1): 39–51.

Schmidt, Manfred. 1989. "Learning from Catastrophes: West Germany's Public Policy." In *The Comparative History of Public Policy*, Francis Castles, ed., 56–99. New York: Oxford University Press.

1994. "The Domestic Political Economy: Germany in the Post-1989 Period." Presented at the Annual Meeting of the International Political Science Association, March 25–7, Kyoto, Japan.

1996. "When Parties Matter: A Review of the Possibilities and Limits of Partisan Influence on Public Policy." *European Journal of Political Research* 30 (September): 155–83.

1998. "Sozialstaaliche Politik in der Ära Kohl." In *Bilanz der Ära Kohl: Christlich-lberale Politik in Deutschland 1982–1998*, Göttrik Wewer, ed., Opladen: Leske + Budrich.

Schmidt, Vivien A. 1995. "The New World Order, Incorporated: The Rise of Business and the Decline of the Nation State." *Daedalus* 124 (Spring): 75–106.

1999. "Convergent Pressures, Divergent Responses: France, Great Britain, and Germany between Globalization and Europeanization." In *States and Sovereignty in the Global Economy*, David A. Smith, Dorothy J. Solinger, and Steven C. Topik, eds., 172–92. New York: Routledge.

References

Schmitter, Philippe. 1981. "Interest Intermediation and Regime Governability in Contemporary Western Europe and North America." In *Organizing Interests in Western Europe: Pluralism, Corporatism, and the Transformation of Politics*, Suzanne Berger, ed., 287–327. Cambridge: Cambridge University Press.

Schwartz, Herman M. 1994a. *States versus Markets: History, Geography, and the Development of the International Political Economy*. New York: St. Martins, Press.

⸻ 1994b. "Small States in Big Trouble: State Reorganization in Australia, Denmark, New Zealand, and Sweden in the 1980s. *World Politics* 46 (July): 527–55.

⸻ 2000. "Internationalization and Two Liberal Welfare States: Australia and New Zealand." In *From Vulnerability to Competitiveness: Welfare and Work in the Open Economy*, Volume 2, Fritz Scharpf and Vivien A. Schmidt, eds., forthcoming. New York: Oxford University Press.

Scruggs, Lyle and Peter Lange. 1999. "Where Have All the Members Gone? Union Density in an Era of Globalization." Revised version of a paper presented at the 1997 Annual Meetings of the American Political Science Association, Typescript, Departments of Political Science, University of Connecticut and Duke University.

Shepherd, William F. 1994. *International Financial Integration: History, Theory, and Applications in OECD Countries*. Brookfield, VT: Ashgate.

Shepsle, Kenneth. 1989. "Studying Institutions: Some Lessons from the Rational Choice Approach." *Journal of Theoretical Politics* 1 (2): 131–47.

Siaroff, Alan. 1994. "Work, Welfare and Gender Equality: A New Typology." In *Gendering Welfare States*, Diane Sainsbury, ed., Thousand Oaks, CA: Sage.

Sicsic, Pierre and Charles Wyplosz. 1996. "France, 1945–92." In *Economic Growth in Europe Since 1945*, Nicholas Craft and Gianni Toniolo, eds., New York: Cambridge University Press.

Sihvo, Tuire and Hannu Uusitalo. 1995. "Economic Crises and Support for the Welfare State in Finland, 1975–1993." *Acta Sociologica* 38: 251–62.

Singh, Ajit. 1997. "Liberalization and Globalization: An Unhealthy Euphoria." In *Employment and Economic Performance: Jobs, Inflation, and Growth*, Jonathan Michie and John Grieve Smith, eds., 11–35. New York: Oxford University Press.

Skocpol, Theda. 1995. *Social Policy in the United States*. Princeton. NJ: Princeton University Press.

Slaughter, Matthew. 1996. "International Trade and Labor-Demand Elasticities." Paper presented at the Conference on Internationalization and Labor Markets, Workshop on Political Economy, September, UCLA, Los Angeles, CA.

Slemrod, Joel. 1990. "Tax Principles in an International Economy." In *World Tax Reform*, Michael Boskin and Charles McClure, Jr., eds., San Francisco: International Center for Economic Growth.

Smith, Adam. 1976 [1776]. *An Inquiry into the Nature and Causes of the Wealth of Nations*. Oxford: Clarendon Press.

Sobel, Andrew. 1994. *Domestic Choices, International Markets: Dismantling Barriers and Liberalizing Securities Markets*. Ann Arbor: University of Michigan Press.

Soskice, David. (1999). "Divergent Production Regimes: Coordinated and Unco-ordinated Market Economies in the 1980s and 1990s." In Hebert Kitschelt, Peter Lange, Gary Marks, and John Stephens, eds., *Continuity and Change in Contemporary Capitalism*, 101–34. New York: Cambridge University Press.

Spicker, Paul. 1997. "Exclusion and Citizenship in France." In *The Politics of Social Policy in Europe*, Maurice Mullard and Simon Lee, eds., 219–36. Lyme, NH: Edward Elgar.

Ståhlberg, Ann-Charlotte. 1997. "Sweden: On the Way from Standard to Basic Security?" In *Social Insurance in Europe*, Jochen Clasen, ed., 40–59. Bristol, UK: The Policy Press.

Steinmo, Sven. 1993. *Democracy and Taxation*. New Haven: Yale University Press.

——— 1994. "The End of Redistributive Taxation: Tax Reform in a Global World Economy." *Challenge* 37 (6 [Nov./Dec.]): 9–17.

——— 1998. "The New Political Economy of Taxation: International Pressures and Domestic Policy Choices." Typescript, University of Colorado at Boulder.

Stephens, John D. 1980. *The Transition from Capitalism to Socialism*. Atlantic High-lands, NJ: Humanities Press.

——— 1996. "The Scandinavian Welfare States: Achievements, Crises, and Prospects." In *Welfare States in Transition: National Adaptations in Global Economies*, Gøsta Esping-Ansersen, ed., 32–65. Thousand Oaks, CA: Sage.

Stephens, John D., Evelyne Huber, and Leonard Ray. 1999. "The Welfare State in Hard Times." In *Continuity and Change in Contemporary Capitalism*, Herbert Kitschelt, Peter Lange, Gary Marks, and John Stephens, eds., 164–93. New York: Cambridge University Press.

Stimson, James A. 1985. "Regression in Space and Time: A Statistical Essay." *American Journal of Political Science* 29 (4): 914–47.

Stoesz, David. 1996. *Small Change: Domestic Policy under the Clinton Presidency*. White Plains, NY: Longman.

Stoesz, David and Howard Karger. 1992. "The Decline of the American Welfare State." *Social Policy and Administration* 26 (1): 3–17.

Strange, Susan. 1996. *The Retreat of the State: The Diffusion of Power in the World Economy*. New York: Cambridge University Press.

Streeck, Wolfgang. 1993. "The Rise and Decline of Neocorporatism." In *Labor and an Integrated Europe*, Lloyd Ulman, Barry Eichengreen, and William T. Dickens, eds., 80–101. Washington, DC: Brookings Institution.

——— 1997. "German Capitalism: Does It Exist, Can It Survive?" In *Political Economy of Modern Capitalism*, Colin Crouch and Wolfgang Streeck, eds., 33–54. Thou-sand Oaks, CA: Sage.

Svallfors, Stefan. 1995. "The End of Class Politics: Structural Cleavages and Atti-tudes to Swedish Welfare Policies." *Acta Sociologica* 38: 53–74.

Swank, Duane. 1988. "The Political Economy of Government Domestic Expen-diture in the Affluent Democracies, 1960–80." *American Journal of Political Science* 32 (4 [November]): 1120–50.

——— 1992. "Politics and the Structural Dependence of the State in Democratic Capitalist Nations." *American Political Science Review* 86 (1): 38–54.

References

1998. "Funding the Welfare State: Globalization and the Taxation of Business in Advanced Market Economies. *Political Studies* 46 (4): 671–92.

2000. "Social Democratic Welfare States in a Global Economy: Scandinavia in Comparative Perspective." In *Globalization, Europeanization, and the End of Scandinavian Social Democracy?*, Robert Geyer, Christine Ingrebritsen, and Jonathon Moses, eds., 85–138. New York and London: St. Martin's Press, Macmillan.

2001. "Political Institutions and Welfare State Restructuring." In *The New Politics of the Welfare State*, Paul Pierson, ed., 197–237. New York: Oxford University Press.

Forthcoming. "Global Markets, National Institutions, and the Public Economy in Advanced Industrial Societies." *Journal of Comparative Policy Analysis*.

Swank, Duane and Cathie Jo Martin. Forthcoming. "Employers and the Welfare State: The Political Economic Organization of Firms and Social Policy in Contemporary Capitalist Democracies." *Comparative Political Studies*.

Swank, Duane and Sven Steinmo. 2000. "The New Political Economy of Taxation in Advanced Capitalist Democracies." Presented at the Annual Meeting of the Midwest Political Science Association, April, Chicago, IL.

Swenson, Peter. 1991. "Labor and the Limits of the Welfare State: The Politics of Intraclass Conflict and Cross-Class Alliances in Sweden and West Germany." *Comparative Politics* 23 (4): 379–99.

1998. "Efficiency Wages, Welfare Capitalists, and Welfare States: Employers and Welfare State Development in the United States and Sweden." Paper presented at the Annual Meeting of the American Political Science Association, September 3–6, Boston, MA.

Tanzi, Vito. 1995. *Taxation in an Integrating World*. Washington, DC: Brookings Institution.

Taylor-Gooby, Peter. 1996. "The United Kingdom: Radical Departures and Political Consensus." In *European Welfare Policy: Squaring the Welfare Circle*, Vic George and Peter Taylor-Gooby, eds., 95–116. New York: St Martin's Press.

1997. "In Defense of Second-best Theory: State, Class and Capital in Social Policy." *Journal of Social Policy* 26 (2): 171–92.

Thelen, Kathleen and Sven Steinmo. 1992. "Historical Institutionalism in Comparative Politics." In *Structuring Politics: Historical Institutionalism in Comparative Perspective*, Sven Steinmo, Kathleen Thelen, and Frank Longstreth, eds., 1–31. New York: Cambridge University Press.

Thomas, Kenneth. 1997. *Capital beyond Borders: States and Firms in the Auto Industry, 1960–94*. New York: St. Martins Press.

Thompson, Helen. 1997. "The Nation-State and International Capital in Historical Perspective." *Government and Opposition* 32 (1 [Winter]): 84–113.

Titmuss, Richard. 1974. *Social Policy*. London: Allen and Unwin.

Toft, Christian. 1997. "German Social Policy." In *The Politics of Social Policy in Europe*, Maurice Mullard and Simon Lee, eds., 144–69. Lyme, NH: Edward Elgar.

Torfing, Jacob. 1999. "Workfare with Welfare: Recent Reforms of the Danish Welfare State." *Journal of European Social Policy* 9 (1): 5–28.

Traxler, Frans. 1994. "Collective Bargaining Levels and Coverage." In *OECD Employment Outlook*, 167–94. Paris: OECD.

Treu, Tiziano. 1994. "Procedures and Institutions of Incomes Policy in Italy." In *The Return to Incomes Policy*, Ronald Dore, Robert Boyer, and Zoe Mars, eds., 161–74. New York: St Martin's Press.

Trifiletti, Rossana. 1999. "Southern European Welfare Regimes and The Worsening Position of Women." *European Journal of Social Policy* 9 (1): 49–64.

Tsai, Hui-Liang. 1989. *Energy Shocks and the World Economy: Adjustment Policies and Problems*. New York: Praeger.

Tsebelis, George. 1995. "Decision Making in Political Systems: Veto Players in Presidentialism, Parliamentarism, Multicameralism and Multipartyism." *British Journal of Political Science* 25 (3): 289–325.

   1999. "Veto Players and Law Production in Parliamentary Democracies: An Empirical Analysis." *American Political Science Review* 93 (3): 591–608.

Tsebelis, George and Jeanette Money. 1997. *Bicameralism*. New York: Cambridge University Press.

Tuppen, John. 1988. *France Under Recession, 1981–86*. London: Macmillan.

   1991. *Chirac's France, 1986–88: Contemporary Issues in French Society*. New York: St. Martin's Press.

United Nations Centre for Transnational Corporations. 1996. *World Investment Directory, 1995*. New York: United Nations.

van Kersbergen, Kees. 1994. "The Distinctiveness of Christian Democracy." In *Christian Democracy in Europe: A Comparative Perspective*, David Hanley, ed., 31–47. New York: Pinter.

   1995. *Social Capitalism: A Study of Christian Democracy and the Welfare State*. New York: Routledge.

   2000. "The Declining Resistance of National Welfare States to Change." In *Survival of the European Welfare State*, Stein Kuhnle, ed., 19–36. New York: Routledge.

van Kersbergen, Kees and Uwe Becker, 1988. "The Netherlands: A Passive Social Democratic Welfare State in a Christian Democratic Ruled Society." *Journal of Social Policy* 17 (4): 477–99.

van Wormer, K. 1994. "Privatization and the Social Welfare State: the Case of Norway." *Scandinavian Journal of Social Welfare* 3: 39–44.

Villadsen, Søren. 1996. "Local Welfare Systems in Denmark in a Period of Political Reconstruction: A Scandinavian Perspective." In *Comparative Welfare Systems: The Scandinavia Model in a Period of Change*, Brent Greve, ed., 133–64. New York: St. Martin's Press.

Visser, Jelle and Anton Hemerijck. 1997. *"A Dutch Miracle": Job Growth, Welfare Reform, and Corporatism in the Netherlands*. Amsterdam: Amsterdam University Press.

Vogel, David. 1989. *Fluctuating Fortunes: The Political Power of Business in America*. New York: Basic Books.

Waddam, Alex. 1997. *The Politics of Social Welfare: The Collapse of the Centre and the Rise of the Right*. Brookfield, VT: Edward Elgar.

References

Wade, Robert. 1996. "Globalization and Its Limits: Reports of the Death of the National Economy Are Greatly Exaggerated." In *National Diversity and Global Capitalism*, Suzanne Berger and Ronald Dore, eds., 60–88. Ithaca: Cornell University Press.

Wallerstein, Michael. 1989. "Union Organization in Advanced Industrial Democracies." *American Political Science Review* 83 (2): 481–501.

Wallerstein, Michael and Adam Przeworski. 1995. "Capital Taxation with Open Borders." *Review of International Political Economy* 2 (Summer): 425–45.

Wallerstein, Michael and Miriam Golden. 1997. "The Fragmentation of the Bargaining Society: Wage Setting in the Nordic Countries, 1950–92." *Comparative Political Studies* 30 (6): 699–731.

Wallerstein, Michael, Miriam Golden, and Peter Lange. 1997. "Unions, Employers' Associations, and Wage-Setting Institutions in Northern and Central Europe, 1950–1992." *Industrial and Labor Relations Review* 50 (3 [April]): 379–401.

Wanna, Jon. 1991. "Business." In *Intergovernmental Relations and Public Policy*. Brian Galligan, Owen Hughes, and Cliff Walsh, eds., 313–34. Sydney: Allen and Unwin.

Weaver, R. Kent. 1998. "Ending Welfare as We Know It." In *The Social Divide: Political Parties and the Future of Activist Government*, Margaret Weir, ed., 361–416. Washington, DC and New York: Brookings Institution, Russell Sage.

Webb, Michael. 1995. *The Political Economy of Policy Coordination: Economic Adjustment Since 1945*. Ithaca: Cornell University Press.

Weingast, Barry. 1995. "The Economic Role of Political Institutions: Market-Preserving Federalism." *Journal of Law, Economics and Organization* 11 (1): 1–31.

Weir, Margaret and Theda Skocpol. 1985. "State Structures and the Possibilities for 'Keynesian' Responses to the Great Depression in Sweden, Britain, and the United States." In *Bringing the State Back In*, Dietrich Rueschemeyer, ed., 107–63. New York: Cambridge University Press.

Weiss, Linda. 1998. *The Myth of the Powerless State: Governing in the Global Era*. Cambridge: The Polity Press.

Western, Bruce. 1997. *Between Class and Market: Postwar Unionization in the Capitalist Democracies*. Princeton, NJ: Princeton University Press.

Whiteford, Peter. 1995. "The Use of Replacement Rates in International Comparisons of Benefit Systems." *International Social Security Review* 48 (2): 3–30.

Wickham-Jones, Mark. 1995. "Anticipating Social Democracy, Preempting Anticipations: Economic Policy-Making in the British Labour Party, 1987–1992." *Politics and Society* 23 (4): 465–94.

1996. *Economic Strategy and the Labour Party: Politics and Policy-Making, 1970–83*. London and New York: Macmillan, St. Martin's Press.

Wilensky, Harold. 1975. *The Welfare State and Equality: Structural and Ideological Roots of Public Expenditures*. Berkeley: University of California Press.

1981. "Leftism, Catholicism, and Democratic Corporatism: The Role of Political Parties in Recent Welfare State Development." In *The Development of*

Welfare States in Europe and America, Peter Flora and Arnold Heidenheimer, eds., 345–82. New Brunswick, NJ: Transaction.

Willett, Thomas D. and Young Seok Ahn. 1998. "Upward Biases in Estimates of Capital Mobility for Developing Countries." Typescript, Department of Economics, Claremont Graduate University.

Williams, John and Brian Collins. 1993. "The Political Economy of Taxation." *American Journal of Political Science* 41 (1): 208–44.

Williams, Roger. 1993. "Technical Change: Political Options and Imperatives." *Government and Opposition* 28 (2): 152–73.

Williamson, John B. 2000. "Social Security Privatization: Lessons from the United Kingdom." Center for Retirement Research, Boston College, Working Paper 2000–10.

Williamson, John and Donald R. Lessard. 1987. *Capital Flight: The Problem and the Policy Response*. Washington, DC: Institute for International Economies.

Wilson, Michael. 1993. "The German Welfare State: A Conservative Regime in Crisis." In *Comparing Welfare States: Britain in International Context*, Allan Cochrane and John Clarke, eds., 141–71. Newbury Park, CA: Sage.

Wiseman, John. 1998. *Global Nation: Australia and the Politics of Globalization*. Cambridge: Cambridge University Press.

Wood, Adrian. 1994. *North-South Trade, Employment and Inequality*. Oxford: Oxford University Press.

Wood, Stewart. 2001. "Labour Market Regimes under Threat? Sources of Continuity in Germany, Britain, and Sweden." In *The New Politics of the Welfare State*, Paul Pierson, ed., New York: Oxford University Press.

Zevin, Robert. 1992. "Are World Financial Markets More Open? If So, Why and With What Effects?" In *Financial Openness and National Autonomy: Opportunities and Constraints*, Tariq Banuri and Juliet B. Schor, eds., 43–83. Oxford: Clarendon Press.

Zysman, John. 1996. "The Myth of a 'Global' Economy: Enduring National Foundations and Emerging Regional Realities." *New Political Economy* 1 (2): 157–84.

Index

Index

welfare state structure of, 53n
see also subject headings
disability insurance, 265
  in Britain, 231
  in Germany, 175, 178n1
  in Italy, 206
  in the Netherlands, 261, 289
  in Norway, 151
  in social democratic systems, 125
  in the United States, 219–21
dispersion of authority, 10, 35, 47–51,
  58, 62–3, 66, 103n2
  in Germany, 216–17
  social welfare spending and, 89, 95,
  97–8, 107, 111, 113, 116, 119–20
  in United States, 228–9
  see also decentralization of authority

Ebbinghaus, Bernhard, 212, 214
economic growth, 23, 81, 271, 273
  in Finland, 148
  in Germany, 172–3
  in Italy, 204–5
  social welfare spending and, 90, 121
  in Sweden, 135, 136, 137, 138
Edsall, Mary, 225
Edsall, Thomas Byrne, 225
elderly population, 72
  impacts on social spending, 81, 89,
  107, 121
  in Italy, 205
  in Sweden, 134
  in the United States, 222
  see also pensions
electoral systems, 44–6
  majoritarian systems, 5, 8, 11, 45,
  215, 236, 282
  see also inclusive electoral
  institutions, proportional
  representation
embedded liberalism, 28, 30–1, 32, 90,
  116–17, 120, 286
employers, 37, 38, 39, 41n, 42–3, 61,
  257–8
  in Australia, 242n
  in France, 193–5

in Germany, 184–5, 212, 214
in Italy, 202–3, 204
in Sweden, 135–6, 138, 158, 260,
  264
in the United States, 225–7
see also collective bargaining,
  corporatism
Esping-Andersen, Gøsta, 40, 46, 51,
  56, 63, 70n, 71n, 122, 123n, 162n
European Monetary System (EMS),
  203, 208
European Monetary Union, 29n, 205,
  209, 269
see also Maastricht Treaty
European Union (EU), 4n, 143, 185,
  186, 247n, 287
exchange rate policies, 13, 149, 153n1,
  243, 265n, 266–70, 273
  in Denmark, 143
  in France, 191, 198–9
  in Italy, 202, 205
  in Norway, 150, 152
  in Sweden, 134–5
exports, *see* trade

familialism, 163
family allowances, 68
  in France, 190, 196, 200
  in Germany, 172–3, 179, 188
  in Italy, 204
  in Japan, 70
  in social democratic systems, 152
family wage, 162
Fawcett, Helen, 231
federalism, 35–6, 47–51, 61–2, 98, 287
  in the United States, 228–9
  see also decentralization of authority
Feldt, Kjell-Olof, 135
Ferrera, Maurizio, 204n, 211, 215
Finland
  capital mobility in, 133, 149
  economic performance of, 129–30,
  147–50
  economic policies of, 148, 158,
  265–6
  political institutions in, 65, 159